GOING WITHIN TO GET OUT

A CREATIVE JOURNEY TO BUILD A NEW LIFE

WRITTEN BY AN ANONYMOUS GIRL

Balboa Press books may be ordered through booksellers or by contacting:

Balboa Press
A Division of Hay House
1663 Liberty Drive
Bloomington, IN 47403
www.balboapress.com.au
1-(877) 407-4847

ISBN: 978-1-4525-1200-6 (sc)
ISBN: 978-1-4525-1201-3 (e)

DEDICATION

To the Girls

CONTENTS

CONTENTS

THANKYOU

TO GLEN, MY DEAR FRIEND AND MENTOR, THANK YOU FOR JOINING ME ON THIS JOURNEY WITH *GOING WITHIN TO GET OUT*.

It was like Life, the universe, had it all planned way before I knew what my innocent writings in my journal - this book was going to be, do and achieve. I am deeply grateful your life's experiences, your knowledge, generous nature, hard work and big heart. It has been your understanding of the nature, the message and the vision for *Going Within To Get Out* that has helped it to grow to where it is at today. Your gentle guidance and commitment to the power of personal sharing and choice has not only protected the integrity of Going Within To Get Out it has strengthened it and catapulted it to another dimension way beyond my own imagination. It stands true, that together with others, so much more can be achieved through sharing.

THANKYOU

To the many wonderful people, friends, family, the girls who have experienced the program, professionals and in particular The Bridge Youth Service Shepparton, the staff for your support who have given so much to *Going Within To Get Out.* A special thank you to Graeme the CEO who went above and beyond for the program. As the result of your support you have enabled many young women and many others to embark on their own journeys to build new and happier lives for themselves. It's been a long and winding road since the first humble writings were written back in the 1990's and *Going Within To Get Out* has come this far because of your contribution, great and small.

To all of you, and you know who you are, Thank You from deep within my soul and spirit!

ABOUT THE AUTHOR

The author grew up in dysfunctional home who experienced sexual abuse, eating disorders and alcohol abuse. As the result of a moment of clarity, help of others and her own true grit determination eventually developed her own program from her experiences to create a happy, joyous new life free from the past.

AUTHOR'S NOTE

IT'S NOT ABOUT GOSSIP. IT'S NOT ABOUT FAME. IT'S CERTAINLY NOT ABOUT ME.

This is a story through my eyes only - so the presentation of the things I share with you may or may not be accurate due to my many limitations of being a human being. I know I don't see things how others see things. I know that how I see or understand things are always questionable due to my lack of knowledge, lack of professional qualification in various areas, lack of understanding on many matters, subjects, situations etc, so on and so forth. However at the time that I write both in my journal and twelve years later, I do believe to be true - only to me - at the time I have written these words.

Twelve years ago when I began writing in my journals I was very self focussed, not able to really understand others very well, as I was struggling to understand myself. In actual fact one of the main reasons I wrote in my journal was to understand myself better to create a happier, healthier and more fulfilling life. By no means that the way I perceive the characters in this book are a true statement about the characters themselves or what actually they may have or may not have said or done. The journaling is more of a true statement about where I was at with my thoughts, feelings and actions at the time; how I thought and felt about myself and what I was observing about myself in reaction to the people, places, things and situations I found myself in.

Writing was and still is a tool to help to know myself better rather than to use the writings as a source of gossip, criticism or assignation of others characters. I have found gossip and criticism of others a shear distraction from my own life. It has been a false way to create a bond with others or make me feel better about myself. Anonymity is a principle I practice both in my personal and professional life, and is a principle of the Going Within To Get Out program to create a sense of safety and trust in order to allow others, including myself to open up and be ourselves. Therefore I have changed all the names and identifying characteristics of all those I know and mentioned in this book to protect the anonymity and privacy of others. I have camouflaged, rearranged certain settings and events, including dates in service of my story and my personal shares in my journals.

Going Within To Get Out has been created and published for you to hopefully know yourself better, if you choose, to create more happiness, healthiness and fulfilment in your life or for you to know people in your life a little better if they have had experiences like me. I have chosen, at this stage, to be anonymous for many reasons. One would be to enable the readers to focus on themselves to have an experience with the book. The other, to protect the privacy of those I have met along the way on my journey.

I have to say I've always felt it was important to be anonymous if I had this book published to prevent the reader or myself to put me up on some different level. I see myself as an equal and I feel for my personal wellbeing I thought being an anonymous author would be one way I could achieve this. I know, having read a lot about and been to writer's workshops on how to successfully sell and market a book, that it's vitally important to have the author's name as the platform, the main marketing tool. However, I feel if I did that, put my name on this book and all the other marketing material in order to sell the book, I may leave one person behind who may be a bit like me who might think, 'Well, the author has been able to achieve all these things because they are, for a better word for it, "famous", so there's no way I'm going to be that, so there's no way I'll be able to do it.' The people who have read the draft of this book, before being sold to the public, said they really loved the fact the author was anonymous because they could imagine it was them who wrote this book or someone next door, or someone they know. This is the kind of intimacy I desire to have with you. For sure, it would be awesome, I imagine, to be famous or known for the work I have created - if the book really takes off - however it's not that awesome to be famous or receive that kind of recognition if I lose you or myself in the process. It was important from the beginning to lead by example that it is possible for an ordinary girl to create a book like this where she's designed the whole thing; the words, the illustrations, photographs and the layout. And another reason for this to be written by an anonymous girl is that she could be from anywhere or be anyone. The book, as I see it, isn't really about me anyway even though I've written all about myself and refrained from telling anyone what I think they should or should not do. I've chosen to write this book in this particular way in hope that the book will reveal more to you about yourself or someone you know - to have a real self recovery to build a new life.

GOING
WITHIN
TO GET
OUT

INTRODUCTION

A gorgeous friend wrote this for me when I shared my fears of not being good enough to write a book, and for feeling like a loser by ending up on unemployment benefits.

January 2002

For all the work you have done, are doing and will do, you will be highly recognised in the future. Patience is the key and to believe it will happen. The knowledge, wisdom and experience you have, the courage to share with others - if they are open - will assist others to heal their own lives.

Your knowledge, experience and openness to share are key issues. Remember to stay focused on the job at hand.

Do not feel guilty for believing you are not working, because you are. To write your own story will not be, and is not, easy. Try to distance yourself from the emotional pain and stay focused on the experience. If it becomes too much and something really hurts, think of me, call me any time day or night. Talking helps it go away.

I commend you Bella; you are a beautiful, gifted person, and it may only be your friends and family who are aware of this now, but the future will make other people, who don't even know you, recognise this.

Please keep this with you and don't lose it. Keep it for the future.

Love you with all my heart xo

Chloe"

Chloe's words felt right so I followed what I knew so I sticky-taped her letter onto my cupboard in my bedroom where I could see it to encourage me to keep going. That's what this letter did for me - it kept me going with the transition from typing out my journals - which I'd intended to keep private - into a book, which I was going share with many others - especially You.

BEFORE I BEGAN TO WRITE

I was living with my cousin and three others the same age. All of them had finished studying and were applying for jobs in their chosen careers. My cousin had graduated with honours. Their abilities were a bit overwhelming, as I was working at a local supermarket and I was taking food out of the back storeroom bins to eat - moments after it had been thrown away. I had an obsession with food. I couldn't stop thinking about it. I was always working out what I was going eat, when I was going to eat and how much I was going to eat. I loved food and yet I hated it. I wanted a skinny, perfect and beautiful body and I hated what my body looked like. The more I fought with food, trying to control how much I ate and what I ate, the more I thought about it and the more out of control I became with it. I was able to starve myself for long periods of time between the ages of 12 and 18 until I discovered I could stick my fingers down my throat when I ate. I thought I could get away with eating more knowing I could spew it up straight after. I felt relieved knowing I couldn't get fat if I didn't let the food digest through my body. I didn't know nor did I care about the damage I was doing to my body, or to myself, including the damage being done to my teeth. The obsession to eat drove me to steel food off the grocery shelves, the deli or bakery departments only to stick my fingers down my throat while I was trying to manage a large supermarket store. I felt bad about it. I knew it was the wrong thing to do. I knew what I was doing was dishonest. I couldn't tell higher management about it. I would lose my job. I was a hard worker. I knew that. I worked much of my overtime for no pay believing management would praise me for being such a dedicated hard worker and it helped me to justify stealing. 'Look at all the work I do for nothing, surely I deserve this food for free!' So I stole it. I was terrified of being caught, especially from taking food out of the storeroom bins but equally terrified about putting on weight.

I felt really yucky that I was allowing a guy at work, whom I wasn't attracted to, make sexual comments and advances toward me, so as I could keep him liking me. I stunk because I wasn't showering every day, perhaps every three to four days and wearing the same underwear inside out and back-to-front for days at a time. EW! I just couldn't be bothered, nor did I seem to care. I was depressed and had been for a long time. I knew I was different to those I was living with but I couldn't work out what it was. Not on my own anyway.

I looked forward to drinking. I felt excited about drinking. When I drank I could forget about my responsibilities, all the things that were stressing me out including what others thought of me. My body could relax and have a break from it all. Have a break from myself. I would drive home drunk after catching up with my work mates after work. I knew there was something terribly wrong with me. I was finding it really hard to get out of bed because I woke every morning with a sense of fast-approaching doom. My cousin would call me in the morning to encourage me to go for a run. A run was not going to happen. I did not have the energy or the inspiration to go for a run when I was feeling as low as I was. Plus a simple activity such as walking down the street felt excruciating because I was sure everyone knew what I was doing. Man, I was paranoid!

I had arrived at a point where I could see I was on a very slippery slide. I could see my drinking was controlling me. I could see I would surely die if I continued on this path and if I didn't do something about it, I would end up as a full-time drunk. I could see I didn't have to wait until my mid 30's - like my parents did - to sober up and make my life better for myself. I could see that I could stop drinking at twenty-two avoid my inevitable future as a hopeless and helpless drunk. I knew quitting drinking meant no more Sunday afternoons drinking with my mates, or going out and getting smashed, or drinking at my friends parties, or even having a drink at my own wedding. "ARGH". That was my way of life and I couldn't imagine another one. But I was in so much pain, that quitting drinking was the only way out for me.

I was not able to stop by myself. I couldn't trust myself with alcohol; I didn't have the will power. Even though I loved alcohol and what it did for me I felt like trash and I believed I was trash. I understood I needed something greater than myself to help me stay sober because I knew other people weren't enough to stop me. They had tried and failed.

My Dad had taken me to a twelve-step recovery meeting three years earlier. I was 19. I was still drinking at that time. I just wanted my boyfriend, Jarod back, whom I adored (even though he had been with other girls all throughout our relationship). He had had enough of me because I would flirt with other guys in front of him when I was drunk to make him realise what he was really missing out on. I remember sitting in the car out front of Dad's house and Jarod called me a slut and I felt so pathetic and desperate for his love back. So, I went to Dad and told him I thought I had a problem with drinking. I don't remember him saying very much however went to his bedroom and pulled out some flyers for me to read about alcoholism and invited me to go to a meeting with him. Dad had never done this before and I knew he had a sincere desire to help me. I didn't want to disappoint him so I went to the meeting. Everyone there was way older than I was and they were openly talking about their problems. Who does that? They didn't wear cool enough clothes for my liking. I judged all the alcoholics I saw as losers, certainly not able to get their lives together without a twelve-step program. I saw myself as different. I wasn't like them. I was still young with the world at my feet. I had plenty of time to get my shit together and get it together without the help of others. How on earth was I going to have fun without alcohol? Alcohol was awesome. It made me the life of the party. It was the one thing that made me happy. By the end of the meeting I told myself my drinking wasn't bad enough to stop entirely nor did I want to be a loser like them. So, I walked out believing I had over reacted to being dumped by Jarod and continued my drinking. Phew that was close!

I failed my first year of nursing in the big city and was really relieved I didn't have to do that anymore, however petrified about my future. What was I going to do? I returned to my hometown, moved in with my girlfriend and worked with Jarod at a bottleshop and returned working at the supermarket. My relationship with Jarod was an off again on again relationship. I was losing my friends because of it and I felt everyone in town knew what a dickhead I was for being with him as the rumours of his affairs with other girls continued. Also I felt increasingly ashamed and humiliated by my own drunken behaviour I displayed on the weekends whilst partying. I was finding it harder and harder to hide this ugly side of me from people. I had to get out of the hole of a town who I blamed for my struggles, 'If only people would mind their bloody business, I'd be ok'. I left for the big city once more but this time I would be the person I wanted to be. I could start afresh. So I thought.

I dumped Jarod - again - this time in my heart I knew this was the last time. I somehow worked out how to get into his computer and found emails he had written and received from girls in America where he was on holidays. I was managing the bottleshop while he was away. It was so kind of me to work for nothing. I never asked for money for the many hours I worked there. It was a family business and I thought I too would become family when we got married. Not that we ever talked about getting married! Anyway, I cracked the shits and took off to the city where my cousin lived and stayed with him for a week. His housemate Jo flawed me. Who was this person? The first time I met her she was cutting up pretty paper making cards. It was sprawled over her whole bed. It looked like a lot of fun but where did she find the energy to do that? I couldn't be fucked doing stuff like that. On the hot days she'd sun bake out the back with no top on! It didn't feel like a sexual thing she was doing. It felt more like, 'this is my body and my home and I'm going to sun bake now'. And I could not fathom the freedom she felt when she talked about going away on a 6 month trip without her boyfriend, who was totally cool with her going. I never knew people had relationships with such trust and caring encouragement toward one another. Whatever she had, I knew I didn't' have it. But boy I wanted it. Not that I would sun bake nude in my back yard even if I was the only person on the planet, but who would I be if I had freedoms like hers?

I was also reading a book called 'Super Joy', by Paul P Pearsall and it dawned on me. Here I was always looking for enough evidence of Jarod's sexual affairs with others to help me to leave him once and for all. Having enough evidence never stopped me from going back to him. He always had reasons, excuses, cover ups and said the right words to convince me he did love and need me. Even when I caught him going to a hotel room with another woman I eventually went back to him. In a still moment I asked myself. 'Are you happy?' And the answer was 'No I am not'. I was just not happy in the relationship and I just accepted and surrendered to this fact. I made the decision to leave Jarod and when I told him I could see in his eyes he was not able to know this time was the final time. I still remember driving away being present to the feeling of 'knowing' I felt at the time, it was the final time.

I applied for a work transfer to live in the city and it just so happened to be a transfer with a supermarket, which was only a 5 min drive from my cousins' place. He was kind enough to let me stay with him with the understanding it was a temporary arrangement. I ended up staying for 18 months. I'm not sure if he was too happy about that, but I surely was. My drinking escalated and he and his girlfriend were noticing how I was behaving. They started to make comments to me about it. "You change after you've had one drink". "It's dangerous going home with guys you don't know'. I hated them saying these things but I knew deep down that I agreed. I didn't tell them that though.

So when I hit my rock bottom with alcohol at 22 I asked a Higher Power, which was, at that time, the religious idea of 'God', to keep me away from a drink for that day. This time I was aware I needed to go back to a twelve-step program who could help drunks like me. It wasn't about finding the differences. It was about knowing I was the same. I was a young drunk and I knew I didn't look like an alcoholic - I wasn't living in a park wearing a long dark coat drinking from a brown paper bag. But I felt like one and I just couldn't keep up with the appearance of being okay anymore. I was full of fear and I knew management wanted to promote me, however I was not going to be able to do it and I didn't want them to find out what I was up to.

At the moment when I finally admitted I was an alcoholic, my Mum rang. She's uncanny like that! I told her I was an alcoholic and I needed to go to a meeting. She went silent.

"Mum, are you there?" I was dying inside petrified of what she must've been thinking. I never talked about my drinking with my parents. They too didn't know what I was up to and because they had been sober since I was 7 years old I thought they would be deeply disappointed and angry with me if they knew I was drinking. Mum did say to me when I was about 14 years of age that because both her and my dad were alcoholics that I too had a 60% chance of being alcoholic myself. It made sense at the time but there was no way I was going to be an alcoholic.

She finally said, "I don't know if I should feel sad for you or really excited for you." I was a bit confused as to what she was saying however I guessed she was sad that I had a disease called alcoholism, but excited that I was willing to do something about it. She didn't know how bad my drinking was. I don't think many of my friends knew how bad it was either. I was pretty good at hiding that kind of stuff. I didn't talk with others about my drinking or the effects it was having upon me, like the time when I shit my pants when driving drunk or when I wet my bed after a night of drinking or how I had to go out and drink by myself if I had to and walk home in the dark, or the remorse and humiliation I felt about my behaviour after a night of drinking.

I made the commitment to myself to go to every length to quit drinking and live a new life guided by a Higher Power of my own understanding. Wow, that was a new concept for me. I had been living life on my terms and I wasn't too pleased about surrendering my life over to something I couldn't trust or see. However I felt so desperate it was the only other choice I had other than to keep drinking.

I believed at the time if I didn't face my personal challenges, my days would become more painful and more difficult to face. I believed deep down I had a right to live a good life and I believed that great joy and great love was there for me. But I could also see that I needed to become willing to face what was really going on within me, and do something about it. I would need to open the doors I shut long ago if I were to enjoy a better way of living. I wanted to be who I was born to be, not what I had become. I was tired of being everyone else's puppet. I was tired of reacting to everything and everyone. I was tired of living in fear, disconnected from everyone, including myself and living a lonely life filled with despair. It was time to say enough!

Since writing the journals in this book I've been blessed with sobriety. I've been helping others to the best of my ability for the same amount of time. Being free from eating disorders for the same period of time is just a dream come true little own living a life free from long periods of depression and constant anxiety. Words cannot describe what it is like to live a life enjoying being free from the powerful and baffling effects of others sexual behaviour and disease. Thanks to Life, I am living a more happier, healthier and fulfilling life as my self-esteem and self-confidence continues to grow.

My life is not without situations that are either challenging or painful however I have developed a manner of living through using five main tools. These living tools keep me emotionally and mentally healthy, making decisions and taking actions, which feel, right and true to me. Together with my wonderful partner we create a home filled with love, care and attention for a gorgeous child and ourselves, which I can now do, having learnt the art of loving myself.

See Appendix: 'Do you have a problem with alcohol'

THE 'G' WORD

I write and talk about God, the 'G' word, a great deal in my journals. I grew up with parents who strongly believed in God and their personal understanding of God was different in some ways because my Mum went to different churches and Dad stuck to the same church throughout my childhood. However, they both introduced me to the Bible and I developed an understanding of a God from the Bible who was going to send me to hell for having sex before marriage, and for stealing, for lying and for being bad in general. I wasn't into the Catholic thing where I could repent, so I just told myself not to tell God what I was up to and then He wouldn't or couldn't get me. I felt great shame and disgust about my behaviour and it suited my habit of addictive self-loathing quite well and drove me further into self-hate and self-destruction. I really wanted to please God and wanted Him to approve of me and yet I could not match His intentions for me described in the religious material I was reading.

I did have a love for Something greater and bigger than myself.

When I walked into the rooms of the twelve-step meetings I heard a great deal about other people's understanding of their God or what they would refer to as a 'Higher Power'. I learned that I was responsible for my own experience in spiritual matters and it was left up to me to decide what I wanted to do and what I wanted to believe. A particular member who befriended me talked a lot about her understanding of her Higher Power and she explained it was like trying on clothes. She encouraged me to try on others' ideas about a Higher Power like trying on a jacket. I was to ask myself if it fitted, was it too big a concept or too small? This was new. Being made responsible for discovering my own spiritual beliefs and spiritual values was freeing, and so I could pace myself. If the twelve-step program was about anything it was about having a personal experience with a Power of my understanding, which could empower me to live the life I truly desired. I wanted to try on new ideas about what God or a Higher Power was because the one I had created for me was cruel, nitpicking, and out to punish me. I came to see that it wasn't a very loving concept so I started with the idea that the God of my own understanding was going to reveal 'Itself' to me. It had to be loving, kind, and nurturing. I was willing to grow toward wellness, sanity and happiness. I had tried to be perfect but I realised that my demand for perfection right NOW was also unloving and unrealistic. I had to learn about the gradual path, one day at time to the best of my ability. Fortunately, I am, after all, a perfectly imperfect human being designed to learn from experience to remember who I really am.

My concept of a Higher Power has changed dramatically since I first wrote these journals, however, I cherish the understanding I developed during this time because they brought me to the understanding I have today and the understanding I had was enough to get me where I am today. And it didn't really matter what my understanding was because it wasn't a requirement for my recovery from insanity, unhappiness and deep inner loneliness. I've simply enjoyed having an understanding which, when shared with others, is tremendous. When we are together, "something" just happens— like magic. I've found by connecting through the 5 main living tools, sharing, writing, creating, meditating and connecting with others and my community to be a great defence against the hopeless and helpless state of despair. And it is when I am doing these things that I am connected to that 'magic', to a power greater to myself.

It is this experience that I wish to pass onto you that it's not necessarily about a God as such but more about reconnecting with faith and hope in ourselves, in others and Life's flow that connects us all. And if you pass it on to someone you know then we are all connected through the enrichment of our own lives.

OTHER PROBLEMS

Quitting drinking, stopping my fingers going down my throat, being released from the obsession with food and my body wasn't the only thing I needed to do. I had other problems as well. I had tinea on my toes (from not looking after my hygiene), a stiff jaw, an unfed body, unwashed clothes and a messy room. I had a new car I could not afford. Rent and house bills I struggled to keep up with. There were piles of mail I hadn't opened. I ignored the phone when it rang. I felt constant guilt from the stealing my cousin's money and the lies I told. Grief and self-pity was a constant companion having lost friends and lovers. While the deep desperation to be gorgeous and liked drove me to unbearable self-centeredness and selfishness. It was hard to hide the yellow cigarette stains on my fingers or hard to ignore my aching teeth. The fear of having Aids or other sexually transmitted diseases popped up with the shame, which followed. I felt confusion about my relationships with others. My heart filled with terror and a head filled with a thousand voices. The inability to leave the bedroom or leave the house had left me. Depression, anxiety, paranoia had become my friend. Not knowing where I was going to live or where my next meal was going to come from when I had not managed my money well or made poor decisions. I was like an onion the size of a beach ball, and I had to peel away the layers to see who I really was.

I went within my heart and mind through sharing, writing, drawing, meditating and reaching out to my community asking others for help to get out the Old Thoughts which were no longer helping me to embrace New Thoughts to recover who I really was. I needed to heal my pain, release my frustrations, end the craziness and make new loving decisions. It took time, patience and endurance to know myself better and create a new life however by doing it I realised it was worth it - I was worth it. Like my good friend Gerry would say to me; "Anything is possible one day at a time - sober". As long as I'm willing there is hope.

HOW TO USE THIS BOOK TO KNOW YOURSELF BETTER

First I'd like to say there are no right ways to read or work with this book. Some people have read it through from start to finish. Others have done the same and re-read it and then did the creative exercises. And yet others have flipped to different parts of the book and read from there. I've heard many share about reading a certain amount and felt it necessary to put it down to digest what they have read until they felt ready to continue reading.

I imagine there is no time frame for when the book should be finished. It's up to you, as the reader, how slowly, or how quickly you would like to go. Some have had the intention to read it quickly or late at night before sleep and found that due to the emotional response to the journey the book took them on, steered them rather then they steer the book. Some found they couldn't read it at night, that is was rather a workbook that they would have to be emotionally and mentally ready for during the day. And then again I know one person who stayed up all night reading. Everyone is different, and everyone I imagine will respond differently to different things.

The book has shown me to lay it out in a sequential way to make it easy to follow and know what to expect. I have divided the chapters into twelve weeks, based on each time I shifted. Feel free to work on one chapter at a time, one week at a time.

The journals, Sacred Sharing, I wrote between the age of 23 and 27 which start each chapter and each chapter has a painting I created at that same time. I find pictures can say what my words cannot or enhance the understanding of my words. Two pages are provided for writing if you feel you would like to write about those things you relate to in the journals, whether you have felt, thought or done similar things to me or anything else you may feel like sharing. Sacred Sharing is about sharing whatever is in my heart and mind and the things that are going on for me without negative judgement. It was when I was willing to share all of me, seeing who I was, that started my journey to know myself better to then choose to create a happier and more fulfilling life for myself.

The topics Old Thought and New Thought arise from each Sacred Share where I reflect upon those journal writings 12 years later. I now have a greater understanding of myself; what was going on for me when I stopped drinking. I can see how the Old Thoughts lead me to feel, think and behave the way I did. It has been a healing process to look at myself through a loving, understanding and compassionate heart. I share the New Thoughts I embraced which played an important role in transforming me into who I really am and the happier and healthier life I am living.

I'm still a human being with many flaws and plenty of room for more growth. The difference between the person I was then to who I am today - I like and love who I am today and have been able to do this through the five main living tools I adopted to love and accept myself, right or wrong, good or bad, weak or strong. The five main tools, sharing, writing, creativity, meditation and community connection lead me to go within to be more self aware and accepting for a great change to occur to myself and my life.

The Sacred Creative Focus summarises the week's topic, which leads into the Sacred Creative Activity, and a visual example to assist you with ideas for your own creative expression on the two blank pages provided for you to do the activity. Whatever you create on the two blank pages will not be graded. I simply encourage you to give it a go, even if you believe you are not a creative being or if you don't like being creative. I've found using creativity as another way to be in touch with my feelings, intuition, subconsciousness and creative solutions to my daily challenges. I've seen things about myself, which I couldn't before through my creations. Some times a lot of time passes before I see what I could not at the time.

There are some materials you will need to do the Sacred Creative Activities such as throw out magazines, newspapers, picture books, pencils, texters, glue and scissors. However if you only have a pencil, fine liner or pen nearby they will be enough to work with. When you come across a Sacred Creative Activity, which suggests materials you don't have, it's okay just to use a pen to write or draw with. And it's okay to modify the creative activities to suit you, if you have an inspired idea. I say go for it! You might want to glue down some fabric, flowers or found items on the footpath, or sew on some cotton. There is no right or wrong way to express ourselves in the creative activities. It's more in the doing rather than anything else.

Sacred Meditation Activities are provided at the end of each chapter, which describe a particular task to assist with clearing the mind and relaxing the body. The idea of the meditation activities is to reflect on what is experienced after completing the activity provided. There are no right answers, however it is important to keep the focus on one task at a time.

Each chapter concludes with a Commitment Statement, which is similar to a positive affirmation to allow the mind and heart to be open for New Thoughts and new experiences. For me, it's been valuable to be willing to commit to myself to having an open mind - to feel sincere about knowing myself better. Am I sincere about creating a more happier, healthier and fulfilling life? Am I aware it is up to me to do this for myself? Have I been able to create a life, which I feel at peace with? Do I have room to grow? Could it be helpful to say a few words to myself which suggest I don't have all the answers or yet to know how to tap into those answers within? Sometimes my Old Thoughts are so ingrained I don't even realise that they are old and unhelpful. I've found putting aside everything I think I know allows my heart and mind to listen differently, feel differently and see differently to allow change within to happen.

OLD THOUGHTS V'S NEW THOUGHTS

Old Thoughts lead me to live an unfulfilled life. I could only change them if I became willing to face them, see what they were doing to me, and become willing to embrace New Thoughts about myself, about others and about the world in which I live to feel better about who I am and life I live. Embracing New Thoughts based on self-love, acceptance, and having faith in life changed my life and me.

The Old thought "I can get away with drinking" served its purpose. It covered up the truth. I had to have a drink whether I wanted to or not. I had a physical allergy to alcohol - when I had one drink I could not guarantee how many I would have. My experiences had shown me I couldn't get away with drinking anymore because it was exposing me to dangerous situations and actions. I was given a New Thought; "I'm an alcoholic and I need help". I grabbed it with both hands because in my heart, even when I didn't want to stop drinking, it was true. Something amazing happened from this New Thought. It changed my life!

Without understanding it fully at the time I accepted I had an illness, which affected me mentally, emotionally, physically and spiritually. This New Thought, 'I was an alcoholic and I need help' gave me the willingness to tell my Mum the truth about my drinking. She suggested I call a family friend who was a sober alcoholic to go to a meeting designed for those who had a desire to stop drinking. This sounded good to me because I definitely had a desire to stop drinking and I knew I couldn't do it alone. By the end of that meeting I felt I had found a place where I could call home; a place, which offered me real help and hope.

From one New Thought I made decisions and took actions toward taking better care of myself. I had begun creating a new life out of facing and abandoning harmful Old Thoughts and taking up loving new ones.

ABOUT SEXUALITY

I am aware there are many people who are same sex attracted to the opposite sex, or both sexes, same sex or not attracted to either sex or don't have sex or lots of sex or bits and pieces here and there and when it comes to sex where all shades of grey. I've written this book from my personal experiences and my attraction at the time. I have from time to time privately questioned myself whether I was attracted to the same sex and also whether I want to have sex and how much sex I was having too. I have had many very open conversations with people I trust to find out my own personal truth around sex and sexuality. So far I feel at peace with what I've discovered up until now. I'm aware that this too could change and if it did I would like to be included, valued and respected equally regardless of who I find sexually attractive or who I'm sexually involved with.

No doubt you may find things shared in this book you may not like or agree with. I encourage you to please take what you like and leave the rest. What I share in this book is what I have felt, thought and experienced, the things I've recovered and discovered about myself and when I look at some of these things I've written about I too have moved on from different understandings I had at the time when I wrote the words. I've left them there because the book will never see the light of day if I keep touching it up. I believe it's important to allow others to see what I have believed as those thoughts were stepping stones to what I believe today and who I am today. The earlier journals are shorter because I didn't know what to write, I was getting used to writing. I also wasn't convinced I could write or what I had to say on paper would have any value. So I kept on writing. I no longer desire perfection or the need to polish myself up to be liked or accepted. I like being a human being, warts and all and I feel those imperfections make me relatable and believable, at least to myself anyway.

None of what I have shared here is to be taken as gospel - it is my share about myself, holding nothing back in order that you might recover something about yourself or understand someone in your life a little bit more. I do try my best these days not to let others imperfections stop me from listening to what they might have to offer me. What others share with me, despite who they are attracted to, are one of the greatest gifts I receive in life.

WHO AM I?
WEEK ONE : WHERE AM I AT RIGHT NOW?

INTRODUCTION TO THE SACRED SHARING

I HAD DREAMED TO BE STANDING ON THE BEAUTIFUL SUNNY QUEENSLAND BEACHES FOR SOME TIME. WHEN I ASKED MARIKA (A VERY CLOSE FRIEND OF MINE I MET THROUGH MY MUM WHEN I WAS A CHILD) IF I SHOULD GO AND LIVE MY DREAM SHE SAID TO ME "IS FEAR THE ONLY REASON YOU WOULDN'T GO?" "YES" WAS MY IMMEDIATE ANSWER. "WELL THEN, ARE YOU GOING TO LET FEAR RUN THE REST OF YOUR LIFE OR ARE YOU GOING TO START LIVING LIFE?" I WAS 3 MONTHS SOBER AND I WAS SICK AND TIRED OF LIVING IN FEAR SO I CHOSE TO START LIVING MY DREAMS. I DROVE TO BRISBANE WITH TWO FRIENDS WHO DEPARTED SOON AFTER WE ARRIVED.

I STUMBLED ACROSS A FULL TIME JOB AS A LIVE-IN NANNY THROUGH A MEMBER I MET AT A 12 STEP MEETING. I WAS LOOKING AFTER FOUR CHILDREN; STEVEN (16 YEARS), THOMAS (12 YEARS), CINDY (6 YEARS) AND MIKEY (4 YEARS). THE MOTHER OF THOMAS, CINDY AND MIKEY DIED FROM A FATAL ILLNESS. THE MOTHER OF STEVEN LIVED IN ANOTHER STATE WITH HER ELDEST DAUGHTER WHILE THE FATHER, RICHARD, SPENT HIS WORKING LIFE AS A FILMMAKER MAINLY OVERSEAS. I USED WRITING AND PAINTING AS A WAY TO COMPENSATE FOR GORGING ON FOOD IN BETWEEN MEALS. I AM 23 YEARS OLD, JUST OVER A YEAR SOBER (WITHOUT AN ALCOHOLIC DRINK) AND MAREE WITH FLAMING LONG RED HAIR IS MY SPONSOR IN A TWELVE-STEP RECOVERY PROGRAM.

3/9/97 2:50 PM : Second day of my period. Heavy. A little uptight about how this afternoon is going to go. Steven has tennis at 5:15pm. Thomas' bus ticket needs to be picked up. Perhaps pictures with the kids. I'm a little agitated. Feel a little tired. Enjoying the sun and the breeze. I love the feeling of the warmer weather. I feel bloated and a bit overweight. I'm not beating up on myself today about it.

SAME DAY 4:45 PM : I'm pissed off. I've waited for Thomas for forty minutes and the kids are at home by themselves. I also need to take Steven and his mate to tennis. By the looks of it we won't make it. I want to yell and scream at him when he gets to the car. I want to eat the Ched biscuits that are sitting in front of me. Fuck this is hard. I feel full and fat all of a sudden. Half of me is trying to convince me its okay to eat, the other is trying to calm me down to accept there is nothing I can do.

4/9/97 : Third day of my period. I feel warm. I'm wearing a long dress. I feel feminine, beautiful and spiritually alive. I'm grateful for this moment of rest within myself. I'm uncertain what to do now. I'm afraid to ring the ladies (Richard had a few women I could call for help with the children or around the home) to relieve me for a break. Afraid to start eating for I may not stop and I may hurt myself really bad that way. I need to ring Maree, to tell her I can make it at 4 pm. I'm afraid of her; that I'm going to get into trouble. I feel tears in my heart. I don't know how to feel them and release them.

SAME DAY 3:45 PM : I'm itching to eat. I have lovely food inside my tummy. I went grocery shopping. I'm a little anxious to catch up with Maree. A little nervy about going to the sushi station where I gave the chef my telephone number to call me. He didn't call. So I'm afraid I look desperate.

I haven't called the ladies to help out this weekend yet. I keep putting it off and I feel bad about it.
6/9/97 SUNDAY 10:30 AM : I'm feeling annoyed. Trying not to lose my patience with the kids. We've

finished cleaning. I'm snappy and I'm not in the mood for love. I'm pissed off with my body. I exercise each day, cut out sugar in my diet and most fats and I'm bloating like a dead cow. It's yucky and horrible. I didn't enjoy my breakfast: watermelon, yoghurt and cereal, because I was feeling full. I drank lots of liquid last night and today, including orange juice, soda water, apple juice and decaff coffee. I'm angry because my period's finishing and I'm still bloated and fat. When am I going to lose this extra fat on my body? I need to ring one of the ladies for time off. I've procrastinated. I need to work out my debts so I can present them to Maree's husband for next week. I'm extremely impatient, waiting for my body to rid its waste. I haven't decided what to wear to the recovery BBQ. I'm afraid I'll get frustrated whilst trying to decide what to wear. I want to feel comfortable and look okay. It's torture on days like this.

SAME DAY 5:30 PM : I feel heavy. I feel annoyed and irritable. I need space. On Friday night I saw the sushi man. He appeared very keen. I don't understand why he hasn't called or why he won't call. Why don't the men I like, like me? I'm annoyed that dad hasn't been home to talk to me for Father's day. I feel horrible for being 70 kilos. I feel compulsive and uncontrollable. I'm angry with myself. I feel unattractive and unloveable today. I'm finding it hard feeling loving toward Cindy. I'm at burn out.

7/9/97 MONDAY 5:00 PM : Sixth day of my period. I've started to nibble on food without any control. It's fatty food for the kids. Today I'm feeling sorry for myself for not having a man in my life. I'm worried and annoyed that Mum hasn't called me back. It's her birthday today. I'm disappointed that I might miss going to the choir tonight. I'll have nothing to do on my night off. Today I wish I were 5 kilo lighter. I did go for a walk this morning. I have eaten a banana, cereal, toast, sugarless jam, yoghurt, pumpkin soup, rye bread, cottage cheese, and six biscuits. It's quite a lot really. I'm scared of being fat. I don't know what else to do. I hate compulsive eating. I'm tired today, more so than yesterday. I've been snappy and irritable towards the kids. Thomas and Steven stayed home from school because they are both ill. I'm starving for time away from them.

8/9/97 TUESDAY : I'm agitated. Woke up at 7:00 am instead of 6:00 am. Annoyed to hear I have to pick up my boss at 6:00 am Saturday morning on my day off. I'm angry and resentful today. I wish I were more loving and caring. But I'm not.

Things to do are: laundry, ring cleaners, go to a twelve-step meeting and ring Maree. I don't feel stressed. I've only had a decaff this morning. Last night I gorged on Vitari ice cream and popcorn at the movies. I didn't eat when I got home at 11:30 pm. I'm scared, like every other fucking day, about my eating. I'm afraid of gorging and over eating. I hate doing it.

SAME DAY 4:30 PM : I feel sad, lonely and isolated. I did all my things except go to a meeting. I felt distant from Maree today. She crashed (emotionally) and I feel alone. I feel scared that I might have memory. I'm not looking forward to it. I cooked myself a non-fat, sugarless cake today. I also allowed myself a two-hour sleep. I feel restless. I don't want to stop. I'm on the go. Today I ate fruit toast, yoghurt, nuts, bran, banana cake mix, and a salad cottage cheese pocket roll.

9/9/97 6:45 AM : I'm angry and resentful. I'm reading. I'm about to start my prayers. I'm angry towards this one guy who I know from Melbourne for liking me more than a friend, and expecting me to feel the same.

I'm pissed off with another guy for writing me an eleven page letter after I wrote to him and told him about how I no longer want to be friends because he tried to hug me and demanded to know why I didn't let him hug me. I felt uncomfortable because of it. I'm pissed off with the sushi guy for not calling me, especially when he sends me vibes of curiosity and intense interest. I'm pissed off with God because I'm still fucking single. No man loves me that I like or love. Aaarrhh! Do I deserve to be on my own? Am I ugly?

I'm finding it hard to be giving towards the children, whether sharing food, stuff, or my love. I feel smothered and trapped. I don't want to pick my boss up. I'm only going to because I feel obligated because he has gone out of his way to pick me up, twice. Cindy has school sports today. I said I would go. I didn't get the night off last night. I'm not travelling too well. I'd rather go to the women's twelve-step recovery meeting.

SAME DAY 12:40 PM : I'm tired. I'm afraid of eating. I don't know if I'm eating to shove my feelings down or because I'm hungry? I fear the night because I gorge after and during tea. I'm feeling so lonely and isolated within myself. I just don't know how to express it to anyone or whether or not I'm okay. Is it important? My stuff isn't high drama.

10/9/97 6:30 AM : I'm feeling physically full. I ate two lots of healthy cake with choc chip ice cream. I'm suffering today. I'm anxious about tonight, working out my finances with Maree's husband. I'm afraid that I will look stupid and unmanageable. I feel nothing special today. I feel bland. Looking forward to therapy and dinner with Maree and her family. I have a cleaner coming in to help. I'm not too fussed about the house today. Actually I'm scared about my birthday tomorrow. I don't know why. I pray my eating doesn't get out of control today. I'm losing weight and feeling better about myself. I'm afraid I'll fuck it up with gorging, afraid of mentally bashing myself up over it.

SAME DAY 1:20 PM : I'm feeling less congested. I've had a good cry with my psychiatrist. The thought of falling in love with my male friends sickens me. I am good enough. I'm worth every cent I work. I have a right and a desire to disagree and to say no. I'm a worthy person. I'm worthy of love.

11/9/97 7:00 AM : I'm feeling loved and happy. I'm not stressed about the day. Whatever happens - happens. Maree and her family spoiled me last night with a beautiful BBQ dinner, a gorgeous card and a priceless angel to keep me safe. I love my fat tummy. Maree made me a great fat reduced cake. Their love was shining and I could not deny it. Thank you God. I feel so relieved to have some guidance and support with my finances that Maree's husband helped me with. I'm very tired. I'm very fortunate to have such a beautiful family in my life.

Mum called me last night for my birthday. She told me about the day I was born at 6:05 am, about her one and a half-hour labour. She was in hospital for 15 minutes and out I popped. A member of the fellowship called me this morning to wish me a happy birthday. God loves me and I'll be gentle with myself today. I'm looking forward to a happy day. Happy Birthday me, you're 24 today!

13/9/97 SUNDAY 7:00 PM : I feel like I should be doing something. I've cleaned my room. Taping some music. I'm yet to talk to my boss about my wages. That can wait till Monday. I need to ring my cousin and ask him to help me organise the washing machine to Victoria. I'm a little uncomfortable about it. I'm worried the truckies' won't do it.

What I've eaten today: mandarin, banana, fruit bun, six mackerel sushi rolls, Vitari ice cream, nuts, and chocolate cake. I shouldn't have eaten the cake. Now I feel fat and ugly. I hate my body. I'm going into shock again. I've had two okay days accepting my body. I felt free to disclose some of the shit of my childhood at the twelve-step meeting. I cried a lot. I cried a lot at the Saturday morning twelve-step meeting. I hate the thought of others thinking that I'm unhappy and depressed. I don't know what to do with myself tonight. I feel uncomfortable with my fat gut and my fat legs. My hips don't seem so big anymore!

ANOTHER DAY : I'm uncomfortable about what I ended up eating last night: another bowl of ice cream and noodles. I painted what I was feeling, obsession and craziness. It has turned out exactly how I was feeling at the time. It makes sense to me. I feel I should be upstairs with my boss helping out. But this writing and my prayers are more important. He can manage. I feel the inadequate and people-pleasing side in me right now. It's not activated. It's just stirring. I do not want to listen to it. It's not healthy. I feel at this point I need just to get dressed and do what's in front of me and that may be tidying the kid's room. I don't have a desire to be with everyone this morning. I need to go to the bank and reorganise my banking system. I need to ring my cousin for that favour. I'm also happy to take Mikey to the water for a play and swim. I'm happy that I have a friend (the previous nanny) who is going to come along and learn the Saba dance with me Wednesday night. I've handed my obsession of food over to the care of God today. It's unmanageable for me. I pray for the courage to face my boss today about the work issues.

14/9/97 MONDAY 4:00 PM : Yeah! I want to eat! I've made myself sit down. I've turned on my music. I'm ready to paint my feelings onto paper. I don't know how to approach my boss about the things we need to discuss. I have to keep reminding myself I am not a second-class citizen. I'm a worthy person. I'm worthy of a pay rise. I feel I should be working right now. I've been out with Mikey from 9:00 am to 4:00 pm. I'm tired. I can't cook because there is no gas. I want a break. So I'm taking one. I felt more comfortable in my body during most of the day. I know I'm bigger but today I didn't feel fat. At the moment I hate my body, but at the same time I want to eat. Makes sense, not! About the wanting-a-man issue, I miss the drama, the specialness (that's selfishness) and the excitement and that's nothing honest or real. I'm afraid of loving or being with a well-balanced man because I'll feel like a retard. I won't feel special. I've needed to feel extra special to feel normal. If a well-balanced person treats me normal, I'll feel fat, dumb, and unimportant, like a six-year-old. Yuk!

15/9/97 TUESDAY : I'm resentful that Cindy is out of bed again before 6:00 am. The routine is she usually stays in bed until I wake her or put a teddy on her bed. I'm pissed off with myself because I haven't spoken to my boss about that stuff yet. He's extra quiet this time. There are not many spoken words between us. I can't afford to worry about what's going on inside him. I've got to tell him what's going on with me.

SAME DAY : Prayed. I confronted him. It has just worked itself out. He mentioned that I'd get two weeks off. Forty-five minutes later he wanted to know if he was up to date with my wages. I said: "Yes. Meaning that you pay me $250 p/w and pay for my two weeks off and we'll be square. I'd be happy with $350 per week while you're away on work trips regardless of if I work under or over my 65 hours for that week." He agreed and I feel much better. It wasn't that hard in the end. Now he wants me to talk to Thomas about his study because he's falling behind.

SAME DAY 3:45 PM : Yes, I want to eat. I got my hair cut off. It hasn't really bothered me. I knew I wanted it off. My long hair has been tied to the old Jarod days (ex boyfriend I was with between the ages of 18 and 21 years old) thinking that I'm only a woman as long as I have long beautiful hair. With my hair gone I do feel boyish, only when I'm not looking in the mirror. I quite like it. I feel I can't stop and sit still. The only way I can do that is by eating. I've eaten cereal, prunes, mandarin, crackers with cheese and tomato, biscuits and ice cream (after my hair cut). I haven't eaten much but I feel full. I hate feeling full, especially when I haven't eaten much. I hate not feeling hungry in the mornings or when it's eating time. Do I eat or not? I spent $70.85 on myself. I haven't spent over my budget but a part of me feels I've overdone it. But a larger part of me says I've worked hard and this is a lovely reward for not picking up a drink, a drug, a smoke, a coffee or sugar. Neither is right or wrong. I did it because I chose to.

16/9/97 WEDNESDAY 10:42 PM : I ate, at 4:00 pm, a bowl of Vitari ice cream, dried fruit and apple pie. Sugar is slipping into my diet. But the pain in the arse is, I don't understand all of this. All I know is, eating is a comfort for the feelings I don't want to feel. I can't get past it yet. My painting is helping. I had Helen (girlfriend I lived with prior being a nanny) over this afternoon. I was going to tell her not to because in the afternoons I write about how I'm feeling, and then I paint. It's become an important habit because I don't eat when I'm writing and painting and I feel more at ease with myself once I've done it. Today I hated myself for eating. Helen says I've become very negative, especially towards myself and she tells me that the weight will fall into place in time. Damn it! I don't want to wait any more.

Things to do; organise my bank account, call my cousin and go to the bank. At breakfast I ate watermelon and strawberries with a lemon honey drink. I question every piece of food I eat. I can't relax and just eat. I'm always afraid whether or not I'm eating because I'm hungry or because I'm shoving down my feelings. The moment of peace with my body doesn't last long enough. They're so hard to work for. When I bloat in the tummy I feel instantly disappointed in myself. That turns into: 'Why am I still fat when I exercise, eat low fat, no sugar foods etc?' Then I hate myself because I think that I'm stupid because I can't work it out. I feel blocked from the answer. I can't see what I'm doing wrong. I'm sick and tired of trying to deal with this 'food, fat, self hatred shit.' FED UP!! I've had eleven years of torture. I can't remember what I got told and explained to me by my psychiatrist last Thursday. I feel like I'm as thick as two bricks. I'm feeling angry with myself and with sick disgusting men with their thoughts and their wondering, raping eyes. I hate myself for being such an angry, perfection-driven, critical woman. I still feel disgusted in myself. I loathe myself. Frustrated. I want IT to be taken out of my body. I no longer want IT inside me. I want IT ripped out and shot. IT is murderous. IT'S poison. I'm dying with IT!

17/9/97 : Feel uncomfortable. Paranoid about having time off till 5:00 pm even though I'm entitled to it. For lunch I ate sushi and a banana. Yummy. I spoilt myself because it's hard to go to my psychiatrist to be honest. Eat three meals a day. Am I constipated? I'm going to see my doctor on Friday after the women's twelve-step meeting. I'm also to pay bills, etc. I asked my boss for monies owed and I'm upping my fluids.

18/9/97 FRIDAY 3:30 PM : Going to confront my boss about my boundaries in regard to Thomas. I am unwilling to be his mediator. I care too much for Thomas to break his trust. I'm scared, unsure and afraid that my boss will misunderstand me and become angry or resentful because I will refuse to do homework with his son. I will not sacrifice my truth for his approval. I feel fullish from lunch. I'm uncertain how to approach my boss.

19/9/97 SATURDAY 5:00 PM : While I was on the train travelling to Maree's, I felt a bit uncomfortable about not having a present or card for her (for her birthday). No bartering. I intend to do something instead of giving something in material form to express my love and gratefulness. My boss and I started talking last night about the 'issue'. Without any hesitation Richard totally disagreed with my intention to tell Thomas that I broke his confidence with his father regarding an illustration drawn by Thomas that suggested death. (I thought the drawing was suggesting Thomas had thoughts of suicide) I found it to be very concerning. I stood my ground even when he disapproved of my intention to tell Thomas. He says it's a big price to pay just to make me feel better about the fact that I had broken Thomas' confidence without considering Thomas' feelings. I'm going to see Maree about it before I speak to Thomas.

My eating. Well I'm thinking of going to Weight Watchers to try and find balance. Maybe going there will help me to better understand food and its true functions. I have so much jargon in my head about things to eat and things not to eat, etc. I'm so confused. I have no answer for my dysfunctional eating. It's becoming very tiring. I began to hate my body when it started to change. I felt embarrassed and ashamed of my boobs, pubic hair and periods. I was secretive, isolated and extremely fearful. This is when my food problem kicked off.

I've missed my stop. Now I'll be late to get to Maree's. I'm a bit nervy having to walk around at this time of night, 6:00 pm. Today I've eaten a banana, eggs on toast, chocolate cake, apple, mandarin and corn. I'm afraid to eat. I seem to have no control over eating. I'm afraid of money. I have an extra $100 this week. I'm afraid of telling anyone in case I spend it. Travelling is becoming costly.

20/9/97 SUNDAY : Dreamt of child abuse. I was speaking to a man laughing and talking as I befriend him.. Other things start to happen but I can't remember. I later saw him with two children, a boy and a girl. Something was said or something triggered the information that this man was sexually abusing these two children. I walked straight up to him very angrily and spoke directly and sternly to him. The children ran away. He was denying it. I said, "Children don't lie and make up this stuff." A part of me felt doubt but 97% of me knew of his doing wrong. I was not afraid of him.

I felt a sick feeling when the kids and I were sitting at the table and Cindy was in the bad books for taking $20.00 from my room. She finally admitted to taking it. I continued to talk and listen to the rest of the family. Cindy on the other hand started to grovel. She started by rubbing her head on my hand with her face. Then started to kiss my hand (whilst I was trying to eat). I didn't know what to do. So I did nothing. Cindy then romantically kissed my arm. This sickened me. I had to speak up. "Cindy there is no need to grovel. Please sit back in your chair and eat your food. You're very courageous for telling me the truth." I continued with what I was doing before. She started kissing me again after a couple of minutes. I repeated what I said to her previously with agitation in my voice this time.

21/9/97 MONDAY 8:00 AM : Walked with God. I really enjoyed it. I talked to Him all the way. Came back to Helen's with the milk. I did some sketching and exercised with ease. I'm sipping on water this morning. I've prayed to God about my fear about food and money.

I'm anxious about going to the police. (I had two very old fines I hadn't paid and I was required to go to the police station to sought it out) I'm holding it off till Thursday. I'll have more money at hand to prevent being locked up. Even though being locked up does make me curious.

I rang my cousin, Eugene, this morning. He wasn't home. He's partying at a huge celebration overseas. It sounds so exciting to travel and go off to different places. I chatted to his girlfriend for about 15 minutes. She's going to Italy for two weeks. I feel travelling coming on. I do need to be debt-free first. I'll hand it over to God. I enjoy others talking about it, those I care about and love. It tickles me pink. I'll send him some photos of me and a present in the mail. He'll like that.

There's so much to do in my holidays such as painting, meetings, swimming and being with the kids. I'm feeling extremely grateful to be alive and doing this thing called life. I feel sexually uncomfortable around my boss. It's a weird feeling. It feels like it's tied with his attraction to younger women. Hidden. Dirty. I question his relationship with his kids all the time in my head. I don't know if I'm wrong or right. I watch him. I question his eagerness to look after Helen's daughter, Camilla. I question the time he spends with Cindy in his bed at 5:00 am to 6:00 am. I question Cindy's innocent comment on her dad's penis, "... it felt yucky when I touched it."

I may be overreacting when my boss and I went out on the town with his oldest daughter, Sue. He commented on a girls' body, how sexy it was. "Too bad about the face." She was a size 6. His girlfriend is seven years younger and a size 8 and a very tall woman. It doesn't sit, or feel, right to me. I feel he'll never be attracted to me, which is a good thing, mainly because I'm too big and not girlie enough. I'm not a victim. My dad and I would play, laugh and joke around at 6:00 am when I stayed over at his house. He would be under his blankets and I was on top of his blankets beside him wrapped in my doona. I would wake up early because I was so excited to be with him. They were such lovely times. Cindy lies in bed with her dad under the blankets. It makes me feel sick.

SAME DAY 6:00 PM : Okay, I eat for comfort. It's lovely sitting on the balcony. Summer's coming. I've been remembering lots of my past between the ages of 12 and 22, triggered by the different smells that are around. Money is a worry for me. I'm doing "homework" in that area. I've spent over my budget by $10. I feel stress and consistent worry when I'm penniless. I know I'll be okay. I've been in more financial trouble than this. I need to practice my faith and compensate for my over-spending.

I've eaten popcorn, cereal, toast, chocolate bars, BBQ shapes and literally junk all day. Punishment is not part of my recovery. I've needed extra comfort. I find it hard to love and like me on these days. I hate living between 3:00 pm and 10:00 pm. It's hard work for me during those hours. Food becomes more difficult. I've been praying before eating.

22/9/97 TUESDAY 7:10 AM : I really need to speak to Maree about my boss and my emotions related to him. I question my feelings. Where do they start and stop? I've decided to wait to go to the police on Thursday, pay day, so that I have enough money to pay the fine.

I stayed at Helen's last night and I've decided to walk home from Highgate Hill to Taringa. I'm lookinforward to the walk. I'm planning to go to the women's two-hour meeting. The thought of painting afterwards excites me. I've prayed for the willingness to let go of my obsession with food and sugar. I've also prayed for the homework so I can bring it into balance. No wonder I received homework on food every fucking day. I feel like I'm hiding from Maree. I'm afraid of her disapproval or disappointment in me.

So I think I'd better call her and get that out of my system.

23/09/97 7:39 AM : I feel good. I have said my prayers. I rang dad to say hello. He makes me laugh. I love him so much. Thank you God for such a beautiful father. Today is the first day that dad's called me intelligent and I believed him. I soaked up his words like a sponge. I also felt good this morning because I didn't gorge last night. What a miracle! Especially when I was watching my favourite programs: Melrose and 90210. All I had was two biscuits and a Caro drink (decaff coffee).

Last night I spoke to Maree and we were able to sort out my stuff from Richard's stuff and from Helen's stuff. Basically I'm being territorial. Richards' relationship with my girlfriend has nothing to do with me. What Richard does is none of my business. I've got internal alarms going off because I've been abused. Helen's daughter is her responsibility and it's her responsibility to take care of her. If she asks for my opinion then I can tell her what I think about the situation. Till then it's in God's hands.

I plan today to walk into town, which will take one hour and fifteen minutes. There's the women's meeting on and I'm to baby sit Helen's daughter until 5:00 pm. I'd like to catch up with Clarke (my friend from my previous job) after babysitting. I feel free today. I'm not too concerned with the stuff in my head. I feel nervous about going to the police with my overdue fine. I'm afraid the fine will end up being an amount I can't afford. I panic when I don't have money. I feel under pressure because I'm to take my budget to Maree's husband for financial advice on the 22nd of October. I really don't want to disappoint her husband or myself. I don't want to feel the need to use excuses for my lack of responsibility for not keeping up with my finances. I pray that things will work out the way they are meant to, so I don't need to worry or panic: it's in God's care.

24/9/97 THURSDAY : I over-ate last night and yesterday afternoon on cereal, banana, nachos, a steak sandwich, and biscuits and low fat ice cream. I then continued to eat consuming three chocolate bars, honey yoghurt, noodles, a soybean drink, plus one and half litres of water and two cocoa drinks. At least my liquids are up. I did a three-hour walk today. Today I'm back to 69 kilos. I've gone up a kilo. I've increased my walking and fluid intake. Also my food intake is up and so is my sugar and fat. Tuesday was a good day, in regard to eating and feeling good with who I am, because I worked through my insanity. I painted, wrote, cried, went to a twelve-step meeting and spoke to my sponsor. Yesterday morning I felt good and spiritually replenished. I spent one-and-a-half-hours, by myself, in prayer and writing.

I have another forty minutes to get ready. Doing these kinds of things makes me feel good. I feel better just writing that down. Doing things for myself relieves the desire for eating and clears my mind and I feel happier and more content within myself. I have choices today. I was feeling that I had nothing to do today and that all I've done in my holidays is going to twelve-step meetings and psychotherapy. Boring. But that's not true. I've been walking and spending time with friends such as Helen and her boyfriend Marucio and Clarke, Maree and her family. It's good to remember that I'm a sick person getting well. Now I feel I'm keeping all of this information to myself. I'm not passing the message on to fellow friends in recovery. But first things first, I do what's in front of me.

All I have planned today is to go to the one o'clock women's group. I don't particularly want to go because my ego tells me I'm better than they are. So I'm going, to humble myself, to be with the other women and try to be there for them.

The good news is, I'm doing a poo in the mornings each day now. Some bowel movement is happening, progress is slow but it's bloody better than nothing. I can see that my body is changing shape. I may be still heavy, but my legs (thighs) are more toned, firmer and stronger than what they used to be. My hips are slimmer. It feels like the muscles are pulling them in. Also I'm more flexible. I've never been flexible in my life. But today I can see the difference.

It looks like Friday will be the day to see the police about my fine. Oh, how exciting!! It's a cloudy and rainy day. I really like these days. It gives me a gentle warm feeling that I can relax and go with the flow. I find it very soothing. I can relate this feeling back to being at high school. I can be soft and gentle with myself. I'm okay. Today's a new day. I don't want to allow myself breakfast because I know I over-ate yesterday evening. But my psychiatrist says that I'm to maintain three stable meals per day, including breakfast. Otherwise I place myself in a mode to starve myself, which will then, in turn, guarantee I'll gorge later. Damn! I'm enjoying the emptiness in my stomach. Danger!

25/9/97 FRIDAY : I ate four pieces of toast with jam and honey. I didn't over eat. I ate slowly. I watched T.V. with Helen. I'm now at Marucio's with Helen and I spent half an hour in the sauna. Great experience. Sweat dripping off my body. Breathing became deeper. We swam and did sit ups and ten push-ups. I've had a shower and I feel very refreshed and clean. I'm having doubts about my hair. It's hard to get used to. Sometimes I think I look like a boy and look unattractive. Today I have magnifying glasses on and my head is telling me that I am huge; a strong side of me is saying, 'Be gentle, slow down. Just for today we won't try and hurt you.'

I think it's about 1:00 pm. I haven't eaten since 9:00 pm. Helen and I are going to eat sushi. I'm to ring Victory Motors and the NRMA to organise my car to be fixed from the accident I had in December last year. Fear. I've been putting this off. Afraid that the insurance company won't cover the damage because I'm no longer insured. Afraid to see the police because they might be angry and talk jargon that I won't understand and they might lock me up. I wasn't comfortable about seeing my cousin, Luke tonight. Main problem is I don't have a car. I don't want to get a taxi. Also I'm afraid none of my girlfriends will come. I'll look bad. I chose to meet at a place full of grog. My cousins, Luke and Peter, and their friends drink heaps. So I had to make sure they were happy. I suppose mainly my fear is that they won't like me or make fun of me because I don't drink or smoke anymore. I'm afraid they'll feel uncomfortable around me, like lots of people do. During my prayers a thought came to my head: I don't need to wear masks. I can have fun with my cousins just the way I am.

I'm feeling paranoid about the fat on my legs and hips. I don't want to feel fat and unattractive. I need to remind myself today that I'm beautiful the way I am, especially on the inside. I'm bloating all over my body. Carrying lots of fluid.

SAME DAY 1:15PM : My stomach is in pain and gurgling because it's full of gas. I wonder if it's got something to do with the amount of decaff coffee I'm drinking. Today I've had three cups. Perhaps I can look at only having one in the morning and one during the day, the rest can be water, juice or milk.

I've been to the police station (very scary). The constable ended up being very helpful and caring. Went to the city council where he sent me. They rang up the court and I didn't have to pay anything at all. Apparently my two overdue fines have been paid for, by whom I don't know. Talk about little miracles. I felt a bit silly because the woman who had seen me there a week previously said out aloud, "I wouldn't have bothered with it if I were you." Like I was begging to be charged! I'm glad I did. God looked after me. Now I need to talk to the NRMA and Victory Motors and clear up with them about getting my car fixed. I couldn't have predicted the last outcome, how can I predict the next one?

26/9/97 SUNDAY 7:00AM : Okay, how do I feel? Not bad and not good. I haven't got my spiritual books to read today because I'm at Helen's. I'm here to mind Camilla, until three this afternoon. Yesterday I ended up walking to Marucio's. I had a wonderful time in the sauna and pool. Helen and I are encouraging Camilla to swim. She's a beautiful child. Then we had sushi in the city. I ate and thoroughly enjoyed a chocolate Sundae ice cream. 3:30 pm I walked back to Helen's on my own. I liked it. I did a lot of things that I enjoyed. I even enjoyed going home to lie down on the mattress to watch movies after giving myself a shower. I felt so comfortable and relaxed. About 6:00 pm I started to eat again. Ten biscuits dipped in milk, two slices of pizza, chicken and some watermelon. Full, too full. But I didn't punish myself. Mum pointed out to me that my self-will has taken over. True. Ten years of managing my eating and I'm nine kilos heavier. That says something. Relief is what I felt. So since then I've been handing my will over to God. I'm no longer going to try and manage my food. I will look after the important things and put the action in. For example drink plenty of water each day, exercise daily, eat three main meals a day, eat a variety of foods, keep away from alcohol, smoking cigarettes and pot, don't drink caffeine and hand the rest over. I'm not too concerned about sugar. I feel I'm pushing myself way too much. I have too high expectations of myself to rid all my addictions in such a small period of time. I feel at ease with that decision. Oh, also I'll continue my writing and my painting. I've noticed some emotional and mental changes since doing that. I have faith in my psychiatrist that he knows what he is doing. Memories of my grandfather; every time I saw him I can't remember speaking to him. I always cowered down to him. I had to be perfect and good. I only remember him when he was blind as a bat. But fuck I hated his hands. I hated holding him. It makes me feel sick. I have such an itchy vagina. I'm planning to see my doctor on Monday and to get it cleared up. It's pissing me off. The only reason why I'm writing this is because my head told me not to. So there! So just for today I hand my will over to the care of God. I give up trying to know the answer with my food problem and obsession. That's God's problem now.

I don't know if I like my haircut. I feel so ugly sometimes. I feel unattractive, like a boy. But I no longer desire a man that is only interested in my looks. I'm not interested in anyone. I just started to enjoy what it feels like to enjoy just being me. I have no plans today. Camilla and I ventured out to the pool and there was much controversy in my head. I didn't want people thinking I was Camilla's Mum, especially the men. So deep down I'm still looking.

28/9/97 MONDAY 7:20AM : I weighed myself and I'm 79 kilos. I instantly felt disappointed. But I remind myself I don't have the answers and to allow time for change. I miss my prayer routine. I feel I'm not doing it properly or thoroughly but that shall pass. I feel thick in the stomach. I'm drinking water at this moment. I stopped eating at 7:30 pm, record time for me, probably because I fell asleep early at 9:00 pm. I didn't over-eat. I feel out of place today. I don't know what to do on my holidays. I do have a house to clean when I get back. I have about nine people coming over for dinner tomorrow night. I hope it turns out okay. I'm looking forward to going home and doing Violet's painting for her twenty-first birthday. I'll see how that goes. So, I'll either go and do that, or go with Helen for a swim.

I'm starting to get a headache. I still feel funny around my boss. I don't know what he's trying to tell me at times, so I'll let it wash over me. He goes on about hours I work and that they shouldn't be counted. I feel he doesn't understand how hard my job is. So I just think to myself that he will never understand and I'm happy with the wage that he and I have agreed on. So when he goes on about the hours it's like he wants me to do more educational activities with the children, especially with Mikey. I can cope with that. I've started to do it anyway and I told him that. Okay, I feel lazy and I don't know why. I just feel out of place with the world, with friends and the things I do. I'm cold. I'm going inside.

SAME DAY 9:35AM : I'm hanging out with Helen again today.

I had a dream about diving into an uncovered ditch that felt smooth and perfect. I was trying to hide from the person with the bow and arrow. I protected the six-year-old child on my right. The arrow shot right into my belly button. It really hurt. Excruciating pain. This was a dangerous game. The man came closer with eight arrows all at once preparing to shoot at me again. But I saw and felt how much damage that the first arrow had done and I woke up crying. Then I dreamt about a mysterious man. He was tall, six feet and four inches, with dark hair. A new person, someone I don't know. He stood behind me, holding me. It felt warm and safe. Then there was distance.

SAME DAY 6:15PM : Maree says that perfectionism is another form of abuse. She also said that it sounded to her that my boss believes that I'm earning too much for the work I do. She believes that his way of thinking is not realistic and it supports my old thinking that I'm a second-class citizen. She says that it's Richard's problem, not mine. I'm happy with my wage. I'm not prepared to be taken advantage of.

I do feel fat today. I saw myself in the mirror and I looked really huge. So I reminded myself that I'm okay and it doesn't matter as long as I continue to write, drink water and exercise. I just wish I were skinny and attractive. I know I'd feel better. I'm totally obsessed with my weight. I long to feel comfortable in my skin. Well, today I've done nothing really, other than swim and sit in a sauna. It's hard just to sit back and relax. I'm full at the moment. Tossing over whether I should eat. Normal people wouldn't, but perhaps I'm just fucked up, a fat blob. That's a bit harsh. I'm going to watch TV. I'll relax and take it easy.

29/9/97 : I am bloated and full with clogged up wind. I'm very uncomfortable. I had too much bread yesterday. Stopped eating at 7:15 pm. I was full to the brim though. Drank four litres of water. From what I gather, having an itchy throat, I have thrush and no, I haven't been to the doctors yet.

Looking forward to the day alone. I'm planning to clean, cook and paint. If I can, I have a dinner on tonight for about nine people. I'm a little anxious. I'm going to need to spend money. This I'm not looking forward to doing. I hate spending money. It's not outside my budget. I'm only okay with the budget because I had no fines to pay so I'm $75 up, which I feel okay to spend on me because I'm on holidays. Great justification. So the question is how do I feel? I'm disappointed and angry that I'm a big bloated person. Angry and sad that this is the way I see myself instead of being free of self-hatred. I'm happy because I'm going to be doing things by myself, which I will enjoy. Free because it's a sunny day and I'm going to enjoy it. I feel like a retard because I'm nearly three years single. I'm lonely because I am single. I'm angry and scared that I'll always be single because no one good likes me. I'm angry with myself because I'm getting impatient and ungrateful about the man thing. Annoyed that I'm obsessed about food and singleness (men) because it means I have deep inside issues that I'm denying - still. Impatient that this is taking a long time to fix or mend. Annoyed that I can't remember, and then I could say it really happened. Worried that Linus (my other cousin) hasn't spoken to me in a long time...four weeks. I'm hesitant and scared about ringing the NRMA. Afraid that the NRMA will say that they won't pay to get my car fixed because I'm no longer insured with them. Silly really. I should just ring. I should stop predicting and face the music. Typical me, I'm procrastinating.

Thank God I'm doing a poo this morning. There is one thing I can see has changed. I'm guaranteed to do a poo every morning, whereas before it was a struggle to do a poo. Sometimes I'd have to wait two to three days.

30/09/97 : Stopped myself from eating my tea to write. I feel relieved that I spoke to my male friend Ben from Melbourne about how I feel. I'm not 100% attracted to him. I now feel responsible for his feelings. He's not really talking very much. I feel I've contributed to a boring, unadventurous weekend. I feel bad because I don't know how he feels.

I sat down with Richard before he left and spoke to him about having people relieve me for at least two days this week. He's to call me and let me know how he goes. I feel good that I've done this. It feels empowering although it was difficult. I spoke in a firm voice and I spoke honestly. We'll discuss a pay increase when he returns from his trip away. I've got to come up with a figure. I feel able to take care of the kids this time.

I feel uncomfortable that Ben isn't telling me what he's thinking or feeling. I ate a yucky salad, it didn't satisfy me. I found the dressing sickly.

Richard left the house and I felt relieved. I can get away with my sneaky hidden dysfunctional eating behaviour. I had a lamington with ice cream, chocolate syrup and four biscuits. Yummo! I haven't started to punish myself, yet. Why, because this is the first time I've stopped and observed myself regarding my eating behaviour. I've come to see that I always hid my eating even as kid. It's like lying or stealing, living in denial. I hid my gorging, my vomiting, my drinking, my starving, my feelings, my thoughts, my sexuality, my tears and my fears. I've hidden myself for all these years. I've hidden from others to avoid being abused or judged but behind closed doors I've abused and judged myself. The likely reason why I live quite comfortably without a man is because I know how to abuse myself without a man doing that to me. I've abused myself with or without food, over-working, people-pleasing and isolating myself from others.

ANOTHER DAY : The whole time I've been home from 12:30 pm until now, Richard has gone. I felt uncomfortable about not doing anything. An old feeling. I wanted to sleep, I was tired. Richard was painting inside the house and I felt guilty for not doing anything. I painted and that validated my nap; I needed validation despite being up this morning at 6:30 am, walking for one-and-a-half-hours and having a two-hour group therapy session. I woke up and could not continue to sleep because I didn't want Richard to catch me sleeping during the day with my fan on. I got up and made myself some salad while Richard was painting the walls, two metres away from where I was. I felt paranoid. Then I couldn't decide where to eat. I went down stairs to watch Oprah. I hated my salad because I couldn't get my fix. I went back up stairs and Richard had left by then, I planned it that way. I didn't want him to see that I ate all my salad by myself. I started doing the dishes, only because it was going to make me feel better, and it did. Richard said goodbye without looking at me in the eye. I get the feeling he's hiding stuff from me. I'm being paranoid. Inside I felt good because he saw me working and I no longer felt lazy. I also felt relieved because he had left and I could eat without him looking over my shoulder. I could eat crap—like lollies. Oh, I'm really functional! Okay I was in people -pleasing mode, then manipulating-mode, then abuse me-mode.

SAME DAY Why does it matter what Richard thinks of me? Damn, he's home again. I'm not going to leave my room just because he's home. I plan to stay in my room to continue reading and sleep if I choose. I then can get ready to be at the twelve-step recovery meeting at 6:00 pm and then be home around 8:00 pm to have a shower in time to watch my favourite sick shows - Melrose Place and 90210, goodie!

I'm okay to be me and to do what is good for me. Mind you I haven't been home since Saturday 6:30 am and today is Tuesday. Does Richard really give a shit what I do anyway?

What is the nature of my thoughts before my over-eating? I fear being seen as lazy, a person who has nothing to do, like a bum. A bum is useless, unworthy and bad. Richard is not speaking to me, which tells me indirectly that I'm not worthy enough to know. I'm to feel insecure and to doubt whether or not I'm a capable and worthy human being. Did I sabotage myself so that I didn't have to take some kind of action? I used to spend hours in my bedroom listening to music as a teenager. There I would cry, living out my life wallowing in self-pity, fear and resentment. I hid in my room because facing a problem or 'the' person that I was having difficulty with was too much for me. To get out of my bedroom I would go walking for hours with problems racing around inside of my head trying to find a resolve. I was free to be outside but I was locked and caged up on the inside. Nothing has really been mine. I had nowhere to go to be myself. Jarod used to spend a lot of time in my room to sleep, eat and watch videos. I hated this behaviour. I wanted to be with him, but I hated staying in my room locked away, detached from my family and friends and not being sociable. I stayed in the room with him all the same. Within me were feelings of guilt, anger and shame staying inside my room for all those hours with him.

1/10/97 THURSDAY 6:45AM : I have a head cold. I'm amazed about myself with regard to yesterday. I was running rough emotionally, mentally and spiritually. I was pre-menstrual and unwell. So I dragged myself to two twelve-step recovery meetings and at one meeting I sat and listened, and the other I chaired. I didn't over-eat and I ate well. I had a banana smoothie for breakfast, sushi for lunch, and four biscuits for afternoon tea. I stopped eating at 6:30 pm, the earliest for this week. Oh, I'm carrying lots of fluid and bloating like a dead cow. A day like yesterday kicks off my day well for today.

I told Maree about Victory Motors and the NRMA. I had to get that secret out, like Maree says: "…it disempowers the fear…" when I share my secrets.

I was agitated this morning. Camilla woke me up at 5:50 am today and cried until 6:30 am. So I got up, did the dishes and made hot cups of coffee for Helen and a hot Milo for myself. I feel better now. Thomas and his older sister who lives in Adelaide and her boyfriend arrived yesterday. I'm not looking forward to seeing his older sister because she asks too many questions and wants to know too much. I just don't get a good feeling about it. She's staying over for two weeks with her boyfriend. We get along but I feel, or felt, very much like a 'slave' or a 'second-class citizen' the last time she was here.

How do I feel? I feel ready for a slow, cruisy day. Today I plan to go to therapy, go for a swim and a sun bake and perhaps go home and go to the pictures with a friend.

Dinner on Tuesday with my mates went really well. They came over for a feast. We had fun. I had lots of fun preparing for the dinner during the day. I also cleaned mostly upstairs and started on a painting. Just spending productive time alone was enjoyable. Am I retarded for being unable to stay at home at nights by myself?

2/10/97 5:00PM : This morning I walked for half an hour, had a half hour sauna, ten-minute swim and a one-hour walk home. I ate four pieces of toast with jam and honey, five plates of sushi, and four cups of Caro and two to three bottles of water. I'm thinking maybe by eating between meals, foods that contain lots of sugar and fats, is a way of self-hatred. I'm sure you're saying: Der! My therapist says my eating may be a way of comforting my feelings. So my eating is a way for my disease to take away that feeling of happiness. If I have ceased fighting anything, including alcohol, where does that leave my disease in regard to my eating? My disease wins every time! Thomas rang when Richard wasn't home and he sounded different. I get a strong feeling he'll be returning back to Adelaide with his Mum. It's none of my business. I felt funny because at the back of my mind I was wondering whether or not he knew what I had said to Richard about his drawings.

3/10/97 : I'm angry with Richard for not telling me the real reason behind the car not being here at the house. I believe he's not leaving it here because he doesn't want me to drive it. I didn't say anything to him about it because he can do what he likes with his car and if he's lying then he is only lying to himself. He hides lots of his thoughts and feelings from me and it bugs me. I tell him up front what's going on with me. Acceptance here, on my behalf, would be good. I'm actually feeling now that I'm going to run late for my twelve-step recovery meeting. I do this very successfully—running late. I'm going to aim not to. I've got to see the police this morning.

4/10/97 : Oh, I feel yucky today and this is my attitude: 'Fuck men and fuck my body'. Who really gives a fucking shit how fat or skinny I am? Here I am trying to lose weight thinking I'll get a man. Guess what; no man that I like likes me. I find only half, good-looking nobodies or sleazy assholes like me. Fuck them. I am not stooping down that low, they can get fucked. I've come to realise that I've been trying to become this skinny person that I use to be when I was 16 years old (only 58 kilos) and after six years of my best thinking I've successfully ended up at 79 kilos and still single. I think I'm stupid. I'm really missing something here. That 'man around the corner' or 'Mr Right' is never going to come along because if he does I won't be good enough because I'm a non fucking drinker, a non smoker, non caffeine freak and I have bad and a fucked up eating disorder. Plus I'm sexually fucked up and can't have a relationship anyway. WHAT GAME AM I PLAYING?

Mind you, I'm coming off sugar. I gorged on sugar last night; consisting of five glasses of lemonade and raspberry soft drink, ten biscuits and two bowls of ice cream. So if I appear to be angry, discontent and irrational it's probably because of the copious amounts of sugar in my system. I know my body a little bit to know what's going on here. I still have a point about gaining weight, being single and who cares. I've been trying to lose weight (but gaining it) for the wrong reasons. Having the right motive would help. I just feel like I've ripped myself off for the past ten years of feeling good about myself. The thinking that I'm fat and ugly, torturing myself for every bit of food I eat because 'Mr. Right' might think I'm unattractive and unlovable is not a way of thinking that appeals to me. Like I want a guy to love the 'look' of me instead to love 'the' me that I am. I have a long way to go.

5/10/97 : I reached out to my sponsor, Maree last night when I thought 'it' wasn't important. Bloody good thing I did, I learnt that I had been shaming and abusing myself. I cried and released my tears. It was about my weight and my perceptions and beliefs about myself. I need acceptance around where I am at. There's only one of me and I am beautiful.

Today I am still afraid of food. I've prayed to God to give me some more homework on it because

I'm craving for emotional and mental balance. Just one moment at a time with God and I'll be okay. I'm questioning my thinking. It's negative and distorted most of the time. My therapist told me I need another outlet and suggested writing. Okay I'll do it, but for me I choose my outlet to be Maree, to share my angers, fears and secrets with. It's harder to tell another human being than it is to tell a piece of paper, which will be best for me that way. Sometimes it's too easy for me to write. I find comfort in expressing myself to another person for it is a release. I also hear another person's perspective, which is useful for me to hear. Also I love the honesty and support from others who care. It's good to hear I'm not crazy and that others have similar experiences as me and do similar things that I do and have done. Helen has let me stay over at her place for the past week and a half because I'm too afraid to stay at home by myself whilst I'm on holidays.

7/10/97 8:08AM : This morning I'm going through different thoughts and feelings and they seem to depend on what I did the day before. For example; yesterday was a good day for me because I had lots of fun with the children. We shopped, did the banking, went swimming and ate meals together. I tried to be honest, kept away from people-pleasing and focused on being me, on being true to myself and on not being controlling. I made amends to Helen because I spoke to her in a demeaning way. It wasn't easy because I seem to make amends on a regular basis to her. She disclosed with me her resentments towards me a couple days earlier. My little girl inside felt that Helen was going to try to be the big shot and that she would become bigger and better than me. I'm generally not afraid of Helen, probably because I see her as weak and an insecure person. At times I think I can take advantage of this. I do question the relationship I have with the women in my life. I see parts of me in them, emotionally damaged and screwed up. I identify with this, but I'm sure I feel empowered by the fact that I think I'm more developed than them, and I see myself as a leader in their eyes. My ego has me on a dysfunctional pedestal. I'm not better than they are. I do become a bit of a performer around these women. My male friends (there aren't many) are over forty years old, so this suggests to me that I'm afraid of younger men. Why? It sickens me with the thought of them falling in love with me. Its hard homework and I become extremely resentful. I have been put on the spot to be honest and then they get upset and blah, blah, blah.

Oh…I'm not happy with my hair, it sucks. I feel it makes me look ugly. I'm glad I got it cut off. I gave myself the permission to do something that I wanted to do.

I prayed today, that I might come to believe that God will change me. Hopefully he understands that the first thing I want to change is my eating obsession. Unfortunately I turned my will and my life over to him so he'll change what he knows is best, damn it!

12/10/97 : I feel good, quite okay. I haven't over-eaten since Saturday—what a blessing! The youngest, Mikey, slept in my bed last night with his gentle little hand on my face. He came to me for comfort and his older sister Cindy followed soon after. Later that day Steven held and fiddled with my elbow when I was driving the car. We were all talking and I let the children come to me, this way I know when they need me or when they want to be close.

SAME DAY 1:43PM : I can feel the change within me regarding food; it's a yummy feeling inside my tummy. It feels soft, warm and almost emotionally moving. This is the fourth day I've had without an obsession of food or my weight. I went to the Gold Coast yesterday and I felt safe and comfortable in my skin. I've experienced this a couple times before. I knew I looked chunky being eleven stone and I was okay with it and that was a beautiful feeling. I had acceptance and I allowed myself to be exactly the way that I am. I don't know how long this shall last. I know from the past that this will pass. Thinking this feeling will stay forever is another form of abuse because I will beat myself up for seeing myself as a failure thinking I must have let it slip through my fingers. I'm feeling like a woman. I've been feeling like a woman for four days on and off. Right now after seeing the movie, 'Something About Mary,' I feel whole, feminine, attractive and intelligent. I'm grateful for this moment of peace, thank you God.

14/10/97 6:48AM : I plan today to call my cousin Linus, take the kids to school, eat, have a shower and the rest is in God's hands. I don't know how I'm going to get the washing machine to Wacol. I'll have to see how it works out.

I'm feeling safe and my muscles and bones are sore. I've done some stretches and it's made me a bit reluctant to get on with my meditation and prayers. It is a peaceful morning. Mikey jumped into my bed at 4:00 am, he said he was scared. Cindy may be upset with me because I asked her to leave the room without explaining that playing at that time while Mikey and I are trying to sleep is not on.

I'm feeling good. I ate junk food last night and I didn't gorge or over-eat. It's a beautiful feeling. Today I feel light in my mind and body. I prayed for more homework on food. I really don't want to lose this good feeling that I'm experiencing. Today I'm planning to consider my goals and to write down what I think parenting responsibilities involve and what a nanny's responsibilities involve and take that to my therapist to see what he thinks.

15/10/97 6:48AM : Sent off the washing machine yesterday morning. God made it happen, all I did was put the action in and from there it was so easy. Today will be, or is, the sixth day without food obsession. Something has shifted and I do not know why or how. I'm excited at the moment. I've just finished my prayers, oh.... I forgot to meditate. I still have no idea about what my goals are. Perhaps art, areas to do with working with people, perhaps entertainment. They are my three big areas and there is nothing specific in any of them. Perhaps qualifying as a nanny would be a good idea. I've noticed I'm getting along with the children more. I have time out when I become critical, bossy or controlling with them and this has been helping me a lot. Taking time out for me to take deep breaths allows me to see what I'm upset about and I'm finding what I get upset about is not that important in the big scheme of things. It allows me to leave before I kill the joy and happiness in the moment with the children.

ANOTHER DAY 6:35AM : I've pictured myself as a public speaker for many years, even as a kid; something to do with motivation, inspiration, love and hope. Perhaps I'm already doing that in my sharing at the twelve-step recovery meetings. I want to give that which has been given to me so generously and freely. I have no doubt that there is a Power greater than myself. I call that Power, God, who is everything to me. The bastard hasn't, or won't, even tell me how on earth He has relieved me from food obsession in the past seven days. If He has taken that away along with the drink (alcohol), drugs, coffee and smoking, then what am I emotionally leaning on today? The closeness that I feel with my Higher Power is real, not that there are any big sparks or large bolts of lightning happening. I do recognise there has been a shift, only a slight shift, and I feel there is more room for love.

24/10/97 5:54AM
"God I open my heart to you,
Come and live in my heart,
Come and grant me love,
Come and grant me peace,
Come and grant me wisdom."

I heard this on Oprah today. I've been crying so much in the past week, especially since Thursday. A special person called Shaun has walked into my life and as Maree says: "It's antiseptic to a wound." The overwhelming joy and love that has been given to me hurts me like mad. This morning my tears fell as I spoke aloud the above prayer. When I ask God to come and grant me love, it hurts. When I thank God for the beautiful, special people in my life, I cry. I am so blessed just to be alive. I have been given so many beautiful things. Maree helped me yesterday by comforting me while I was cradled like a frightened, wounded bird. Her soft touch and soothing voice was what I needed in that moment. God knows what He is doing.

26/10/97 : I figure that thrush is not going to go away unless I go to see my doctor, so I'll go today. I can see that if I were someone else, I'd be rushing that person off to the doctor (when it started, not two months later). I've always left my medical needs to the last minute.

I haven't done my prayers as yet; hmm…I better do them once I've finished writing. Yesterday I cried my heart out as I shared at the twelve-step meeting; apparently no one could understand a word I was saying. I could see that one woman up in the front row understood some of the things I said. Every time I looked at her I cried more because her eyes were filled with tears. Yesterday, and the days previous, I found myself missing Shaun. I gather that would be obsession. Like anything, I'm going to have to learn about finding a balance and this time it's about love. At the moment I'm trying to tolerate the feeling of missing someone and I'm finding it difficult. I usually switch into feeling numb, like I don't care. I was grumpy with Helen last night because she was like acid on my wounds. I was feeling tender and very sensitive. I felt bombarded with her unhealed denial crap. I feel sluggish and tired today. I'd like Shaun to call me again. He's missed me every time that he has called this weekend because I haven't been home. I'm looking forward to receiving his letter.

27/10/97 : Richard told Steven that because I've organised tennis for him that I should drive my car. It's none of my business what people think or say about me but this has peeved me off. I'm planning to confront Richard about Steven's tennis practice. Also I need to make an amends with Richard for not letting him know where I had taken Mikey during the day, even though I want to blame Helen because she called me just as I was about to write a message for Richard and I forgot. She asked if I wanted to go tonight to the party to celebrate her partner's CD launch. I told her I didn't know, depending on whether Richard was going to be home or not. She asked for Richard's mobile number and I gather she's asked him if he wanted to go and so, yes, I'm pissed off that she's done that. Who does she think is going to look after the kids? Me, that's who! I'm not going because I'm in a bad frame of mind. I'm pissed off with myself because I don't feel anything toward Shaun. I wish I could feel something due to him proposing to me last week. He says so many beautiful things and I know he means it but where am I? I know I feel deeply for him but where are my emotions? Why aren't they operating? He said that because my emotions are running all over the place that he'll make sure that he's constant with being who he is and how he feels. I am not used to a man being so up front and real with me. I'm not used to it from someone I'm attracted to. My head tells me to be afraid because I'm a fraud and I make things up. He's going to move to Brisbane from New Zealand for me. What for? What if I don't feel anything towards him? What if I've lied? But this is what I've prayed for and what I've longed for, why isn't my heart in it?

Fuck it!

SATURDAY 3:21PM : I am so discontent. I'm frustrated and annoyed with myself. Why can't I be a normal human being? I feel that Pam can't help me and that she truly doesn't understand. I'm repeating myself to her about food, Shaun, Helen and me, me and more me. I want to have fun and be alive and so I don't feel any of this other shit. I feel like a pain, a nag, repetitive, low-key, and an unexcited, boring friend. I just want to have some real happiness. I get into people-pleasing mode because Pam has come from Western Australia to be here with me. I feel like a failure. Shaun's so excited to see me. I don't feel the same yet. I did feel excited about him coming over but it's vanished. All of my fucking emotions have gone. Now my angry emotions are here and I don't know why. FUCK IT! Why can't I be allowed to feel? Where's God and where is my gratefulness?

SAME DAY : Had a shower. Cried out some frustration and anger on the bottom of the shower in a foetal position. I don't feel any different. I feel a bit tired. Why does God hate me? I'm a big loser. I'm a liar, a dishonest freak. Love and God are stronger than my disease and my head.

SUNDAY : It's 10:00 am and I slept until 9:00 am. I didn't want to get up this morning. It's a cloudy day and I have no plans. I really don't know what to do with myself. I usually go to the early morning meeting at 8:00 but I've already been to five twelve-step meetings this week. I'm trying to allow myself a day where I don't need to pre-plan to fill my day in. It's hard to stay at home by myself and just relax. There's nothing wrong with it so I'm going to do it.

I'm agitated about my money. It's hard having a budget. I'd probably spend less not having one. I feel so toey about spending it because I'm afraid of running out. I spent $30.00 last night and feel like I have a hangover.

I went out with my cousins. I had a really good time with them. I did lots of laughing, mainly at them. I didn't need to stay out so late. I don't know what I was thinking. My anger this morning speared off from last night. My cousins and their friends had all these girls hanging around them and not one bloke approached me. I had this trendy guy bump into me and we boogied on down for a song before he was pulled away by another girl. Great for the self esteem—not! One of my cousins picked up and I felt like a real loser. This is why I can't be fucked anymore. Guys don't even notice me because of my fabulous boy looking hair cut. I know so many men like girls with long hair, oops! When am I going to start liking myself? Probably when I stop caring whether or not men like me and when I let go of wanting a man to fix me. Just for today I'm okay and this too shall pass. God loves me and I'm learning how to do it one day at a time.

19/12/97 : Things on my mind are: I told Mum I didn't want to hear what she had to say because it was too much for me to hear about "the spirits that are hanging around her." I explained to her that it feels like she "biffs me with her elbows" with the things she tells me. I've never told her that before because I just wanted her to love me, I was afraid to disappoint her in any way. She took it well by not speaking and getting off the phone straight after I said it. For the first time I could see that I have been emotionally enmeshed with my Mum. I felt/thought it was Maree's influence. I'm getting agitated. My writing is pissing me off. Fucking hell, I've never disagreed with her or said: "Hey Mum I'm not interested," at least not since my rebellious days at fourteen to sixteen years of age.

I tried to call Maree and her husband answered, blunt and cold as he sometimes is (doesn't talk much). Great, Richard's going away for about a month and a half for work. Shaun's arriving Saturday at 6:00 pm. I'm to pick him up. He'll be staying here for a while, I guess, if he's going to be looking for a flat to live in.

I feel pressure from Helen. I don't want to go to her dinner party; her cousin and boyfriend's friends will be there with their girlfriends. When I see them, I see sick. I see and remind myself that I was sick to attract them into my life. Yuck! I feel yucky about Shaun seeing what shit I liked. I don't want him to think it's a reflection of me. Now I'm paranoid fearing the possibility of him reading this. Fuck it I'm not going to hide my dysfunctional, yucky, angry, unloving feelings and thoughts anymore!

My car's pissing me off. What am I to do with it? To have it up and running I need it to be registered and that'll cost me $371.00 plus insurance $600.00, oh then $400.00 to have the bingle fixed. So that's only $1,371.00 and with new number plates that'll be another $200.00. Great, I don't think so. It can just sit there. I don't have that amount of cash to have it on the road, the best I have is $400.00. I'm tired.

22/12/97 : No I didn't organise anyone to relieve me. I feel like a failure and a dickhead and, fuck; I'm eating poorly and going quietly insane. I feel smothered by the kids. I can't be around them at the moment. Richard called and I thought it was Shaun. I got confused and I didn't express myself very clearly about the situation here and told him that everything was fine. Except, really, I'm losing the plot.

27/12/97 : I don't want to speak to Shaun. I don't know what my truth is because I have hurt feelings. Shaun's ex-girlfriend called. Shaun and I talked about it. Why the fuck am I explaining this to a piece of paper?

28/12/97 : I'm confused and tired. I tried to be intimate with Shaun this morning before having a shower with him. I was feeling aroused. I tried to take advantage of this. We don't kiss because his breath stinks. So after about 8 minutes I went cold. I stopped. I lay on top of my bed and as stiff as a board. He moved off about two minutes later. "You've shut down, haven't you, because there is no kissing?" "Yes," I said. I laid myself down in the shower in a foetal position. Fifteen minutes later I decided to pray while still in that position. I just want to know what God wants me to do. Do I leave or stay? I'm confused and I'm undecided. I just want out.

SAME DAY : Shaun's hurting. I didn't say anything to him. I'm always pulling away from him. Something has got to give. I can give myself permission to leave or stay. If fear is the only reason I'm with Shaun, then I need to say goodbye. If I love him and I want to give this a go, then I need to stay. Why is this a daily question and struggle? Am I acting on my old feelings or am I acting on how I actually feel?

SAME DAY : I feel like going to Shaun and saying soft, tender words because it's like I've ran over a bird. I feel like telling him it's too hard and it doesn't feel right anymore and put him out of his misery. I'm hurting and angry because I can't put myself first and work out how I feel. If I leave living with Richard and the kids, where would I live? What would I survive on? All wrong reasons to stay engaged to someone. If I leave, what would people think? What would Maree and Harold think? That I'm a loser…I'm a quitter…I'm mean…I'm selfish…I'm wrong. They won't like me as much anymore.

12/1/99 : I'm so exhausted and tired. I feel heavy, slow, and energy-less. I've been able to listen to my body today. I rested on the bed from 10:00 am to 2:30 pm. I laid out in the bath for 20 minutes. Sat in my towel in front of the TV for an hour and a half. Shaun's back from training. Today he smells like cow poo. I am aware this is all happening because change is about to occur. Tomorrow Shaun and I move into our apartment.

Monies are low for this month and for the next to come. I may need to put my studies aside until March. I need to speak to Maree about what to do, whether to work or not. I honestly don't see myself working for a month and a half. I haven't had the energy to do any exercise for the past six weeks. This changing and allowing love from a healthy man is very tiring. Shaun suggested he stay home and cook while I go and get Camilla. Not possible. Great suggestion—but I'm too tired to drive.

Twelve Years Later...
Going within to know where I am at and to walk
a path which was mine meant
taking action

OLD THOUGHT: I don't care about myself
NEW THOUGHT: I'm willing to start taking better care of myself

During different times of my life I didn't care about myself enough to shower and wash my clothes every day. I neglected my basic needs because I didn't love myself enough to care. Some days, weeks and months felt too hard that I just couldn't be bothered. I lived with the heaviness of depression in my heart, the weight of life's problems and the contempt I held toward myself for being who I was or who I wasn't. I was so far from who I wanted to be that my sense of being a failure held me down.

I tried to cover up how I really felt and thought by looking okay; plastering makeup on my face before stepping out of my bedroom door, wearing the 'right' clothes and hang out with the 'right' people. I bought the new car when I was 21, and made great efforts to buy material stuff and show everyone how happy and together I was (when I wasn't). I was trying to please others at the expense of my own sanity and peace of mind. However I never felt okay on the inside and the covering up didn't solve the self-hate problem—it made it worse.

Having rejected myself in this way I learnt that loving and liking myself was an inside job—not an outside one. Wearing the right clothes and looking okay and beautiful didn't stop me from telling myself how hopeless, disgusting and stupid I was every day. Buying a new car when I couldn't afford it didn't change my old thoughts, which constantly told me I wasn't good enough, pretty enough or smart enough to be loved and respected. "Things" were not able to change my harmful old thoughts about myself into the loving new thoughts, which I needed to adopt if I were to create real joy; freedom, energy and happiness because getting lots of "things" were not about taking care of myself. Trying to get the things, look like the "good" thing placed me in financial hardship and stress.

When I attended, I watched the people at the 12-Step meetings speak well of themselves; they faced themselves and made amends for the way they treated others and themselves. They cleaned up their lives, paid more attention and time to look after themselves in various ways. I could see they were able to become better people. They inspired me to do the same. I wanted to be a better person, a person I liked. These people knew who they were and were comfortable with themselves. I observed that they shared their experiences with others, including myself, some wrote out their thoughts and feelings on paper, others talked about expressing themselves through painting and meditating and all reached out for help from others in their community, which is how I met them.

I cleaned my bedroom. I stopped wearing unwashed undies. I bought new ones and threw out the ones with holes in them! I began reading a book about alcoholism to help heal my sick mind and body. I did this when I was on the bus to work, in my spare time, or while I was at a café spoiling myself with delicious cake. I stopped stealing food and deodorant from the shelves. I somehow stopped sticking my fingers down my throat. I began to spend time with people who I felt good around, and less time with those who wanted me back living a life of dishonesty and self sabotage. I also asked Maree's husband to help me with my financial budget and planning to get rid of my debts in order to be free from the anxiety and stress. I began to look after myself in many areas of my life that I had neglected and not being financially responsible was one of them.

At times I resented taking better care of myself because it took time, energy and money that I couldn't be bothered with. However, I noticed when I did it, and despite how bad I felt, I found that I did feel better within myself. A weight began to lift off my shoulders and I began to find a skip in my step. I certainly could stop worrying about if others could smell my stink, or if I died, my loved ones would find my previously used pads in my drawers. YUCK! Taking better care of myself only took one new thought, one new feeling, and one new action at a time. Little steps of change over time creates a big change in the long run.

OLD THOUGHT: I don't need professional help - I'm fine
NEW THOUGHT: Reaching out for professional guidance could be helpful

It hadn't occurred to me before the age of 23 to reach out for professional help. I thought 'Surely I'm not that screwed up that I would have to get help in this way. I don't need professional help, I'm fine." However, having met Maree and seeing how it had helped her I began to consider this possibility. I found myself strongly identifying with Maree's feelings when she shared her experiences about being sexually abused as a child even though I couldn't relate to her stories. She remembered so much detail; there was no denying that she was sexually abused. For me, I couldn't remember such detail or events in my childhood. I couldn't remember much at all. What I could remember never felt like it was bad enough for me to be really affected by it nor did I feel it was okay to say I was sexually abused. I was afraid to be a liar, someone to be looking for attention. I mean, how do I recover from something I had, at this stage, only fleeting memories about it happening? This lead me to feel very confused about it all, and I remained so for some time.

I couldn't work out if what I had experienced as a child with my grandfather had actually been sexual abuse. I did, however, work out I was definitely screwy when it come to relationships with the opposite sex. I felt this qualified me to find out why and I chose to see a psychiatrist. Maree was seeing one. I wanted what she had and so I did what she did - I got professional help. I came to believe that reaching out for professional guidance could be helpful.

It was extremely confronting seeing someone about my issues I had with the opposite sex. I would experience great panic and anxiety as I walked to see my psychiatrist. I found myself wanting to kill men looking at me as I passed them in the street on the way to my appointment. I would wait up to an hour or so in the waiting room and this did wonders for my nerves - NOT! I remember trying very hard not to talk about 'much' when I did go in. How funny is that? I've gone to get help and then I refused to talk. I didn't want to talk because each time I opened my mouth I would begin crying out of control. This just didn't feel right or sit with my image of who I was. I was supposedly all about 'looking fine' and it was really hard to look fine while blubbering uncontrollably. I found this experience to be baffling. No matter how fiercely I talked to myself about holding myself together, without fail, I'd collapse in a heap within moments after sitting down. I wanted my psychiatrist to think I was okay and I believed crying was a sign of being insane and not okay - even though I was insane and not okay. I didn't really want to know who I was - I was scared that what I would find would prove to others how crazy I was, and I'd also have a psychiatrist who could confirm it!

Today I don't have a problem identifying when I'm insane, as Salvador Dali (a Spanish man known for his surreal paintings from the early 20th century) says; "There is only one difference between a madman and me. The madman thinks he is sane. I know I am mad". Reaching out for professional guidance helped me to understand things about myself where others could not.

OLD THOUGHT: I can't write & it's a waste of my time
NEW THOUGHT: Writing helps to know myself better & opens my mind to new ideas

My first psychiatrist encouraged me to write and to ask myself if I was acting on my old feelings or how I really felt at the time? At first I didn't know what he meant and then I didn't know how to put words onto paper. I just didn't know what to say. I felt embarrassed and unsure about writing. I believed I couldn't write and that it was a waste of time. Plus I wasn't very good at English when I was at school. I remember in grade four for reading that I was put with two other students who had learning disabilities. I thought I must have had a learning disability too and developed the thought I was dumb and I gave up reading and writing altogether, unless I had to. I lost the excitement I once had for books. Reading and writing became a waste of my time. However this psychiatrist seemed convinced it would help me so I thought I would at least try as I had nothing to lose.

I was afraid of others finding my writings. I didn't want others to read my most inner private thoughts and feelings. I was a very private person even though in public I presented myself as being very confident and extraverted. I was very good at putting on a show. I didn't want others to know I was suffering. I wanted others to think well of me and I didn't think they would think well of me if they really knew what I was really thinking and feeling.

I found over a period of time writing really helped to relieve my fears, worries, and anger. Writing helped me to acknowledge the good in my life and the good things I was doing. I believe it assisted me to stay focused and determined to BE another way and live another way: a way of happiness, usefulness and purpose. I wrote to myself initially and somewhere along the way I began to write to my Higher Power, as I understood it at the time. The relationship between my Higher Power and I continues to change and grow. Hey, actually at one stage I abandoned it entirely, but that is another story. I like to call my Higher Power 'Life' from time to time and other times I feel giving it a name limits it in some way so I won't call it anything. And when I do this I feel It within and all around me without words or explanation. Without knowing it writing helped my relationship with myself, my Higher Power. It also helped me to become more conscious of my relationships with others, my actions and the decisions I was or was not making. I aimed to write every day. Of course this didn't always happen, sometimes days, weeks and even months would pass without putting pen to paper, however my intention to write every day helped me to start writing and even today I continue to so.

I came to enjoy writing and I find when I write something, which is extremely confronting for me to write I hide my journals in my clothes closet, in my drawers or among other books. Sometimes the fear of others reading my words still scares me and that's cool with me. But now you know where I hide my journals – now that's not too smart is it! LOL

OLD THOUGHT: I'm no good at art, so why bother
NEW THOUGHT: Creativity relaxes the body & inspires the heart & mind

I don't remember my art teacher at High School encouraging me to go onto further study in art. I do remember her criticising one of my favourite paintings (she didn't like the paint splats), which I spent hours staying back late at school to complete. I was really sensitive to criticism and believed there was no hope in hell I was going to be as good as Brett Whitely (the Australian artist who inspired me to paint and create) so why bother?

Soon after I began writing again in 1998 I come up with the idea that perhaps painting and drawing my thoughts and feelings on paper could help combat my craziness with food. It wasn't important whether my drawings or paintings were beautiful or well done. My drawings or paintings were not going to be marked by a teacher or critiqued by a critic. The main aim was to just be expressive through creativity, as I truly believed it would help me to feel my feelings, at least for the time I was being creative.

I made the decision to paint at around 4:00 pm, as it was the time when the compulsion to eat was very strong. I usually felt quite angry at this time, having to wait until I finished painting to go and eat. I'm so glad I did this. I have those paintings with me still today and I've included them in this book at the beginning of each chapter. They really depict exactly what was going on in my heart, mind and body. I had a freedom back then—just to paint. I lost that freedom between the end of these journals until now, twelve years later. I tried to make a business out of my art and I failed at it because I got caught up with trying to sell it and it distracted me from simply creating it, God love me.

I found over time being creative, expressing my thoughts and feelings through art showed me things about myself I wasn't able to see before. I have included at the end of each chapter some of these to give you some ideas for your creative work might look like. I also noticed I would have inspired new ideas and/or a clearer mind and more relaxed body to know what I needed to do for the day after being creative. The confusion in my mind would lift. I didn't know back then as I do now, that being creative is a wonderful way to meditate, as it keeps my mind focused on a single activity. It's very hard to create and still think and worry about all the things, which cause the confusion and stress in the first place. Being creative relaxes my body and inspires my heart and mind.

OLD THOUGHT: Meditation is so not for me
NEW THOUGHT: Pausing creates doorways to peace & problem solving

I had tried meditation a few times, by listening or reading about how others did it and it just didn't seem to work. I would try to clear my mind completely of any thoughts. When I attempted this way of meditation I failed at every attempt. My thoughts ended up giving me a commentary on what I was thinking about; 'ssssh', 'stop talking', 'oh you're still talking', 'shut up and will you stop talking', 'talking', 'talking' and 'I can hear you talking!' It was very frustrating and I would feel worse than when I started. So I gave up. I felt it just wasn't for me.

I don't know if you've done this; getting all your clothes out, trying each item on only to find you couldn't decide what to wear and not leave the house because of it? That was me. What to wear was a very stressful event and not knowing what to wear would stop me from leaving the house. This would infuriate me, and I felt hopeless because of it.

Maree suggested: stopping, sitting on my bed to ask myself some simple questions before reefing out my whole entire wardrobe. Was it a hot, mild or a cold day? What color do I feel like wearing? What material do I imagine on my skin? Believe it or not this was very helpful. In a more peaceful and less stressful and rushed state I was better able to make a decision about what I wanted to wear before moving toward the clothes cupboard. My decision-making can be blocked by stress, pressure, agitation or impatience. I rarely find myself unsure about what to wear nowadays and whenever I get stuck in any area of my life, I practice the same tactic: stop, sit and ask.

Little did I know this was a form of meditation? There are many ways of meditating and it doesn't always mean crossing my legs over the top of my head chanting "Um Pud a Moo Doo" I ran self-discovery workshops with a gorgeous girlfriend of mine, Stella who teaches meditation techniques and she has taught me a great deal about meditation. Before I met Stella I didn't really get into meditation nor did I care for it. I really couldn't understand the value of it. Stella and I first met at the beginning of 2009 at the suggestion of a mutual friend who believed we would work well together. However, we really didn't know how. We decided to take each other through what we teach others individually and see if we could join what we do together in some way. Stella invited me over to take me through Ego State Therapy, a process that involved a mix of meditation and visualisation. 'Cool', I thought, 'this will be a breeze; it'll only take about 10 minutes I reckon.'

In I went, the curtains were closed, I took my shoes off, sat down on a couch and closed my eyes and BAM within a very short period time I was taken right back to when I was sexually abused by my grandfather. Wow! I had not allowed anyone to take me back there like this before. I had one therapist who offered to take me back, but no, no, no, that was just silly stuff, which would leave me feeling uncomfortable being exposed like that in front of someone else. Stella is softly spoken and gentle, a real-life sweetie. I was like marshmallow in her hands. I felt really safe to go back to my childhood. Stella let me know I could always make the choice to stop if I wanted to. But I thought to myself, 'Bugger it, I came this far I may as well keep going and get it over and done with'.

I remembered what I felt at the time when I was at my grandfather's home. Dad and my two cousins were doing stuff, perhaps talking to Nanna, while Pop would grab my hand and put them where he shouldn't. I remembered wondering why Dad wasn't doing anything about it. I made up in my child's mind (I was about six) that I was making up what was happening; otherwise Dad would have said something. That was a breakthrough for me. It explained why I have struggled for so many years to believe what had happened between my grandfather and I. Up until that point from time to time I would tell myself I made up being sexually abused by him.

I had the opportunity in this meditation process to talk to my Dad, be my Dad and respond back to myself as him. I was able to call forth my adult self to look after my little girl who had taken up the role to look after me. It's a big job for a little person to live like an adult. I also realised in this process I came to believe I had no choice in my relationships with others. If others were abusive I would just have to cop it and tolerate it, just like I had to with my grandfather. Becoming aware of this thinking, which was no longer serving me well, gave me an opportunity to let go of the old thoughts and be willing to choose new thoughts and to have new thoughts, new experiences and new feelings.

This experience enabled me to take meditation more seriously. I've since learnt writing is a form of meditation. Drawing or being creative is a form of meditation. Going for a swim, weeding the garden, singing, cooking, dancing is a form of meditation. Focusing on one thing or one activity is regarded as meditation and that's the kind of meditation I can quite easily do. I was practicing many forms of meditation during the time I wrote these journals. I just didn't know it at the time, and the positive results have been endless.

I also hope after I have exposed myself to the world that at least one of you will go – "ME TOO!" – about something I've written! Otherwise I am seriously stuffed! LOL

SACRED CREATIVE FOCUS
WHERE AM I AT RIGHT NOW?

A very good friend of mine frequently mentions to me that it's about asking the right questions. I'm not sure what 'it' is however I do get "it's" about asking questions and surely I will get to the ones that will matter enough to create a positive change upon my life if I just start asking.

So, where am I at right now? I like to stop to have a moment to reflect upon my current situation. This way I can see what is or is not working in my life. I can tick off those areas in my life I am happy with and say to myself 'well done, keep up with what I'm doing there'. It's great for me to know what is feeling good in my life, to acknowledge this so I can consciously make a decision right now to continue to nurture what's bringing me happiness, inner health and peace. And then there's getting to know and discover those areas in my life which are not serving me well or bringing me some discomfort or pain. I've found bringing these things out into the light through self-questioning allows me to make new choices for new thoughts, renewed feelings and new wonderful experiences.

Some questions I might ask myself are; am I feeling good about who I am and what I do from day to day? Do I feel good about where I live, can I make the most of it? Am I comfortable in all of my relationships or are there a few which leave me feeling uneasy or upset. Am I nurturing relationships, which bring great joy and lift me up? Do I feel healthy; physically, mentally, emotionally and spiritually? Am I looking after my mind, my heart, my soul and myself? Do I find it easy to get involved with the community around me; finding work, enjoying study, joining sporting groups, visiting health professionals, engaging in social events or creative activities and knowing which services are available to me if I or others I know need help and support? Do I know what I really desire to experience in life? Do I feel I have purpose and meaning? Do I feel truly at peace with all that has happened, is happening and will possibly happen?

Do I want to know where I am at right now in order to know the things I'm willing to investigate about myself to create greater happiness within myself?

SACRED CREATIVE ACTIVITY

As I contemplate week one's topic: 'Where Am I At Right Now?' I cut out any words, pictures or shapes from a newspaper, magazine, and/or picture book, which might reflect some of the answers to this question. I cut around the objects in the pictures rather than the whole photograph. In other words, I cut away what I don't want. I choose the words, pictures or shapes, which jump out at me even if I think they are not relevant. I like to trust my subconscious, my intuition and cut them out anyway as they may make sense to me later on. When I feel I have cut out enough images or words I arrange them on the two pages provided. I try to let the images and words I've cut out tell me a story. A story about myself about where I am at right now.

I may want to add to the picture by drawing with pencil, pen, charcoal or paint if I feel this will further express what I am thinking or feeling about where I am at right now.

SACRED MEDITATIVE ACTIVITY

I am willing to put some time aside to stop, pause, and ask myself 'Where am I at right now?' by filling out the questionnaire 'Where am I at right now?' - see appendix. I choose two different coloured pens. With one color I answer the questionnaire reflecting where I see myself right now and with the other coloured pen I answer the questionnaire imagining where I would like to see myself in the future. This is a good way to see what is working well for me in different areas of my life and the areas of my life I may like to become willing to change to create more happiness and peace.

COMMITMENT STATEMENT

I .... am willing to put aside everything I think I know about myself, my life, my past, my future, in order to have an open mind and a new experience with where I am at right now. I am open to the possibility of knowing where I am at right now, receiving new thoughts, and living a new life.

WHO AM I?
WEEK TWO : DO I LIKE THE WAY I LOOK?

INTRODUCTION TO THE SACRED SHARING

SHAUN AND I MOVED INTO A TINY OLD FLAT SOME SUBURBS AWAY FROM WHERE I LIVED WITH THE CHILDREN AS A NANNY. IT WAS CLOSE TO THE INNER CITY OF BRISBANE. I WAS NO LONGER WORKING AS A NANNY FOR RICHARD. I HAD FOUND A NEW JOB BEING A NANNY FOR A FAMILY THAT LIVED AN HOUR AND A HALF AWAY FROM MY HOME AND I WOULD TRAVEL VIA THE BUS TO GET THERE. THIS WAS THE FIRST TIME IN MY LIFE THAT I FOUND MYSELF READING THE NEWSPAPER FROM THE FRONT ALL THE WAY TO THE BACK, WHAT ELSE DOES ONE DO WHILE SITTING ON A BUS FOR THAT LONG?

27/01/98: I'm annoyed that I'm full. I'm not hungry and my stomach isn't flat. I'm feeling restless and uncomfortable that Shaun has been exercising for two hours and he's fit and physically well built. I look at myself and I want to eat; yet I'm full of fluids and from eating earlier. I feel that Shaun is happy and I want to make him miserable like me. I made him feel bad for being on the phone, just by looking at him. Okay. I'm not hungry…solution…don't eat…food's not the issue. My feelings are. I'm ignoring things that need to get done and the list is already made. I know that this is stress and it is pulling me down. All of my feelings are built on fear. It's easier to look at food, my weight, and Shaun, than it is to look at the real source of the problem. These other things are not the source. They are the result of the festering fear of no action. Communication between Shaun and I is minimal. I need to up it a bit. I pray for the closeness and allow touch and intimacy to happen between us.

Shaun's now choked on my food. Be gentle on myself. It's okay to not eat because I'm not hungry. It's okay to feel fearful. Now I need prayer for the willingness to take the action I need to take in my life. I'm allowed to love and to be loved. Touching is safe and okay. Let's pray.

FRIDAY 8:30PM : Okay, I feel I've been using food as a comfort since Shaun left to go to Sunshine Coast at 2:00 pm. I'm not comfortable with eating because I see a chubby belly, fat arms and over sized knees. One side says, 'It's okay, in time my weight will balance out as I get well.' But the other side says while watching 90210 (one of my favourite shows) "I'm not a TV star with a size 8-10 body with beautiful hair (great hairdressers!), fabulous clothes and wealthy material things." I'm using weight to hurt myself. I have an old stinking feeling that if I'm not beautiful on the outside then Shaun will leave me.

I don't think that is the real threat. The real threat is other women. I feel so insecure and replaceable. I'd rather walk away from my relationship with Shaun than to find out what hell is going to feel like.

Fuck, Jarod gave me a good dose of all those feelings of not being good enough. I was hurting so much I had to use all of my survival mechanisms to cope, going out with him. I'd drink lots of Jim Beam, smoked cigarettes and flirted with as many men as possible to show him I didn't need him. I'd pretend I was not hurting. I thought I would pay men back by leading them on, then dumping them like dirt rags.

For the past week and a half I've actually been affectionate and instigating intimacy with Shaun and not shutting off. I've been trying other sexual positions, other than the missionary position. But I haven't gone overboard. I'm too embarrassed and ashamed to write the exact stuff down. I'm now thinking that I'm sick and dirty, and it's all because it's my way of keeping a man. My thinking is: let's get sexual and he'll stay and if he gets it at home he won't look anywhere else. Instigating sex makes me think he'll go because he'll get bored with me because there is no chase and he'll secretively find another woman. I think he's lying.

How can he like my body? He just feels sorry for me because I must have some genuine personality underneath the flab. It's been a nice special feeling being attracted to Shaun. He went to bed the other night without having a shower and he didn't stink. His skin was soft. I enjoyed his touch. He gives me hugs and kisses and touched me when I asked. He listens to me. He listens to my words. He apologises when he feels he needs to. He considers me. He tells me what's going on, on the inside, most of the time. I like it that way. He's funny and we love playing "Scrabble" together.

I do hit and squeeze his skin a lot—that's how I let out my frustrations. I clench my teeth because I'm angry. I get so angry, like a ten year old. I just wish I had a nice body that I felt comfortable with. Nice long legs to fit into any kind of clothes. Shaun's really working hard on building up his muscles. It's like I've had no eyes and I can now see. The thing is he continues to say that he's not attracted to skinny 'rakey' women; they make him feel turned off. My perceptions fucked and I wish I could just fucking bag myself all day but I can't because I can't afford to stay this way.

ANOTHER DAY : I haven't been writing. It has taken me four weeks to write and take up my therapist's suggestion to do so. Quick update. I find kissing Shaun so difficult, so difficult that I have only allowed him to peck me on the lips. Okay so I'm going to start allowing kisses, allowing myself to receive love and affection from him. I feel fear under it all.

I told Maree about my hidden secrets, such as taking a lollipop out of a bin at the house I'm working at. I was filled with an obsession to eat the lollipop in the bin. I couldn't let it go to waste. I felt gross fear and shame about what I had done. I've been punching Shaun because I'm filled with so much anger. My teeth nearly snap due to clenching them so tightly. I told Maree about how I yell at him and she suggested that I write when I'm feeling like this. I feel like a boiling pot with a lid and I'm the steam. I've avoided and put off intimacy with Shaun because I'm ashamed and disgusted about my fantasies that I have to have to reach orgasm. I fantasise about being degraded with old men and other women. I want to be able to have intimacy with Shaun without the fantasies. Why can't I do that? I reckon it's because it's a form of escaping from the reality of being with Shaun. I'm not actually there with him. I'm in the pictures in my mind. I feel no emotional attachment toward Shaun.

ANOTHER DAY : I have been extremely tired during the day over the past three months. I'm working from 8:00 am to 5:00 pm and I travel three hours to get to and from work. I'm eating breads (grain), fruit (x 4), rice, milk, cereal (porridge, 98% low fat corn flakes), vegetables, fish, raw-ish meat (not much meat) and some chicken. I am eating sugar on my cereal, lollies and ice creams on the weekends. Today I went for a walk/run at 5:30 pm to create some energy. Today I'm still a little tired. It's the best I've been in months. I assume the idea of moving to Townsville excites me because I can't wait to be with Shaun, it helps me through the day. My current job is tiring. I work as a cleaner, not a nanny. I do 95% of the household duties. My next job will be to work less hours, have more playing time and working with the children. By then Shaun will be bringing in a wage and that feels like a huge stress relief. I'm not looking forward to the weeks without Shaun. I believe I'll be here on my own for at least three weeks before I go to Townsville.

Olive, one of the girls I take care of before and after school and sometimes during the day, is six and her older sister, Wednesday, is eight. I've had difficulties with Olive since day one. She's rude, demanding, bossy and refuses to use her manners with me. My therapist told me I needed to remind myself that the little girl in me receives care, love and attention from me now and so I'm okay with what Olive has in her life. I'm also to bring in my adult self in moments of jealousy, resentment and hurt. Being an adult has been hard on numerous occasions. Sometimes I remove myself away from her to cope. She continually tells me to, "Shut up. Be quiet," and "Stop talking to me." So today when we were sitting at the craft table I asked her: "You don't like me, do you Olive?" I repeated the question because she ignores me whenever I talk to her. Apparently she behaves like this with her grandfather as well. He seems to force communication with her. He thinks about every word he says just like me. I've been trying to lighten things up a bit by singing, rhyming and dancing. I tell her things about me to see if that would help. Obviously not when she replied: "Yeah, I think that's what it is." My heart fell and I also felt very angry. I told her that she doesn't have to like me; it's impossible to like every one in the world.

ANOTHER DAY : Reading a magazine is much easier than stopping to write the truth. The truth is I want a day off tomorrow so that I can make sure all is organised before Shaun leaves for Townsville. I'm afraid to tell my employers. I'm afraid they'll bitch behind my back. Afraid they'll make me feel guilty or bad for letting them down.

I had a couple of hours off last week because I had a migraine. Today I have my period and that makes me feel shitty anyway. Well, all I can do is pray for the courage to let them know. This is important to me. Work does not run my life today. I no longer sacrifice my truth for other's approval. What the parents think of me is none of my business. All I need to do is take the action and follow God's lead and let him take care of the results...

I asked and it's okay that I don't go in tomorrow. The father was going to dock my pay by ten dollars and it felt good to be able to say to him that I had earned that ten dollars. He paid me the ten dollars.

ANOTHER DAY : Thursday, one week ago I had a migraine and ever since then I've been having consistent headaches. I have a bad knee that hurts when I bend it or sit with it crossed. I have a pain in my bum and the only relief I have from the pain is by pressing firmly on a spot (the nerve) near my bum hole. I've particularly noticed that after I've eaten dairy products, for example; milk, cheesecake and yoghurt, my stomach produces wind that makes me feel like vomiting. I either have to belch it out or it comes out the other end. It was so awful last night that I didn't eat anything until 10:00 am. Normally I have breakfast at 6:30 am. I was too afraid to eat because my stomach was so sore inside. My stomach is always very sore to touch. I've always had trouble with it. My neck and trapezius muscles are extremely tight, also very tight over my shoulder blades. I believe it has something to do with the stress of moving, not having Shaun around me, having to organise someone else to move into the flat in Brisbane and feeling the pressure of packing and cleaning the apartment. I also need to have my car prepared for the road such as the rego, number plate, road worthy and having the bingle fixed. My plan is to move to Townsville when I have everything ready. I know I need to put the action in and God will take care of the rest. But it's whether or not it'll run smoothly for me. I find staying home by myself frightening. I've told my neighbours to come running if I start hysterically screaming. I leave the TV on all night hoping it won't have a melt down in the process.

ANOTHER DAY : Since Shaun left for Townsville my eating has calmed down. I wasn't overeating before but I was eating for comfort when I wasn't hungry. I believe that my eating obsession has calmed down because Shaun isn't here. I used food to make me feel unattractive, bloated, ugly, powerless and fat to avoid being intimate or close to Shaun. I used it as an excuse and this makes sense to me. I will be more aware of myself when I'm with him again. I need a chiropractor because I put my back out about three weeks ago while I was on a morning walk. I feel so stiff. I'm afraid of being touched by another human being, especially by a male. I also need to see my doctor for my stomach problems and a pill update.

ANOTHER DAY : I'm proud of myself for doing the things that have been put in front of me. For example: ringing up the real estate to let them know my rent will be five days late. I'm proud of myself for following up my Group Certificate so that my accountant can do my tax.

There is one thing that I'm putting off and that is calling Richard to let him know that he's charging Shaun and myself for a phone bill that we have already paid. I need to ask for a reference from him and ask for my referdex (address book). I would also like to have the permission to speak with the children and to see them. I really miss Mikey. I feel like I've abandoned them. I'm also afraid that Richard didn't explain to them why I stopped looking after them. I feel they need to know that it simply was because Richard no longer wanted a full time nanny, which meant I couldn't afford to work there for the little hours he was offering.

I'm afraid of being on my own again now that Shaun's in Townsville. I feel a little lost and aware that I can't do everything by myself such as washing the dishes or making my own dinner. He did all of those things for me. I'm finding my own feet again. I haven't just sat back and not left the house because of fear.

Last Friday I got up on stage with some women I met that night and sang four songs in front of about 150 people. The amazing thing was that I wasn't afraid or nervous on stage.

Saturday I spent time with Graeme at the BBQ, and that night I went to my girlfriend's 20th birthday party and went out dancing. I was afraid that I would be unfaithful to Shaun. I did see a good-looking, non-toxic man. I knew I wasn't allowed to act out on the thought of kissing him but I had these doubts thinking that maybe I've made a mistake with Shaun. I found myself thinking I should be single and allowed to freelance, to try out some of these nice guys now that I'm attracted to them. I was able to see that it would be easier if I weren't with Shaun so that I could flirt with the men at the club instead. Reality is, for me, these potential men would also bring up issues within me just like all men do when I am with them. I'm with Shaun and I've made that commitment, I need to remind myself that my shit would stink even if I were with someone else. I felt bad for feeling attracted to other men. I'm afraid that Shaun would feel attracted to other females. I don't want him to. I don't want him to leave me for another woman or have him wishing he were with someone else other than me. I haven't said anything to him about it because I don't think he needs to know. I told a girlfriend who reassures me that it's quite normal and okay to find other people attractive. I don't like the idea of hiding it from Shaun, yet I don't want to hurt him.

Today I've eaten one nectarine, one banana, one plate of pesto pasta and some bread. I'm not repeating (belching) on any of these foods. I bet you if I had some dairy product within the hour my stomach would be getting upset with me.

ANOTHER DAY : I've given away half my wardrobe to a girlfriend. I've given her the clothes I hardly ever wear or that I don't fit into, and the items where the colours do absolutely nothing for me. I don't have many clothes left. I gave four to five large bin bags of clothes to her and I'm going to give Mum a bag too. A part of me feels a feeling of loss and I fear I've got nothing to wear. What if I need some of those items? Deep down I don't want them. I'm happier to welcome new clothes to my wardrobe more to my style and not dressing myself to be someone else. I want to wear colours I look great in. I want to feel comfortable. I want clothes to complement me. I'm hoping to buy contacts in the next two weeks and get rid of my glasses; I feel like I'm wearing a mask, that I'm hiding behind them. I want to allow others and myself to see my beautiful blue eyes because I've been told they are amazing. I've decided today to leave my hair colour the way it is. Blue eyes and brown hair are a wonderful mix and I'm looking forward to a fresh cut. I've disliked my hair for some time now. I'm aware that my new hairdresser will cut it ugly again. I want a cut that will complement my face, a cut that will continue to look good when it grows. I want my long hair back. I enjoyed playing with my hair when it was long. I can't do much with it at the moment because it's still too short. It wasn't cut the way I had imagined so I presume that down the track I'll be getting my hair cut again.

I have no idea what to do about our wedding. For example: Where are we going to hold it? It feels too much, yet I don't want to procrastinate and not do it. But to rush and not be financially, emotionally and mentally ready is not want I want either. I'm looking forward to finishing up with my current job. What I've learnt about babies is priceless to me but six to seven hours cleaning a house each day is not my cup of tea. I'm fortunate and grateful for the job and the money I have been given but I'm so relieved to have another working break, work can feel too much for me. I suppose the three hours of travelling to and from the job tires me out as well.

ANOTHER DAY : Eugene rang this morning. I ripped myself off $20.00 in my pay, I allowed myself to be a second-class citizen.

I have a fear about intimacy with Shaun. I'm eating food so that I get fat, so that I don't have to be intimate with him. I didn't enjoy the cinema because we were being too close. I think to myself that he's a dimwit. I need help with moving my things to Townsville. I need to find a new therapist and GP. I feel physically ill from the consistent headaches and upset stomach. I'm angry with Olive for being such a turd. I tell myself, 'She's only six years old, get over it!'

I got frightened when Shaun was becoming heated (horny) in such a short period of time, I felt sick. I hate my body and my hair repulses me. I dreamt last night of sex. I reached orgasm in my dream and when I woke up I felt sick and disgusted with myself. I don't like having sex with Shaun because I have to fantasise to enjoy it or reach orgasm. I shame myself because of this.

ANOTHER DAY : Today is my last day on this job. They would like me to be here tomorrow because the Mum's sick. I'm not going to. Stuff the money. I really dislike the amount of cleaning that I do and more importantly, I need to start to organise things for me to be able to go next week, God willing. I've been surprisingly good at returning phone calls and doing the things that are put in front of me. I've noticed that procrastination is painful.

I still haven't called Richard. I don't feel overjoyed about ringing him. I am fearful about confronting him about the misunderstanding about the phone bill. The man never rings me when he needs to talk or confront me; it's always left to me—spineless man. I miss the children and Shaun continues to remind me I haven't called them. Olive's been having a dig at me today and I can't be bothered with her shit today. I ignored her and told her in a bored voice that I don't care about her whinging today. Fuck being nice. She comes and goes with her niceness and it fucking makes me sick. Yesterday I let her paint my face and neck with dark red lipstick. I let her wash it off and make my face look pretty. She painted my nails and I enjoyed that time with her. I don't get too excited or interested because she backs off without warning. I don't give a fuck today because, thank God, this is my last day.

Twelve Years Later...
Going within to abandon my familiar past
was excruciating and terrifying yet it
enabled me to be who I am today

OLD THOUGHT: Compared to others I'm not enough
NEW THOUGHT: I'm unique there's no-one like me to compare myself to

I spent a lot of time watching TV shows wishing and dreaming I could look and be like someone else. I placed all importance on my appearance as being what made me worthy of love and acceptance. The shows with only gorgeous and skinny girls set me up for disappointment because I would compare myself to them and always fell very short in comparison. I wasn't able to love myself or like myself when watching such programs with gorgeous women on them. I wasn't capable of enjoying these programs for their intense mind-stimulating story lines. LOL!

It's a bit like having scales - I was always weighing myself to see how much I weighed. Did this practice help me lose weight, or did it only reinforce my negative thinking about my weight? I would beat up on myself if I gained weight. I thought beating myself up would also motivate me to lose weight. Do you think this helped me like and love myself? If you answered 'No', you're right. It didn't. And why would I want to like and love myself? Well, disliking, rejecting and hating myself was a miserable existence and I had no idea it wasn't about the food or the weight. My thinking wasn't quite right and it was hard to change the thinking. I gave away the scales because I recognised I wasn't using them for the right reason.

So, I made the decision not to look through magazines, watch shows including music videos, which were filled with women perfectly beautiful women while I found myself negatively comparing myself to them. I could listen to the music; I just wouldn't look at the screen. I knew if I did I would say to myself "You are fat, ugly, and stupid." While it sounds silly, I was very sensitive to these comparisons and I needed to get real about this. I gave myself some time to experience accepting my body and myself before I dived into the 'looking-good' stuff again.

The very skinny, gorgeous look can be deceiving. I was told in my starving and bulimia days that I was very attractive. Being attractive didn't stop me from hating myself, or being free from obsessing about my body. I was eating food as a weapon to hurt myself and to shut people out. Being skinny and attractive did not equate to being happy. The great thing for me is that I came to love and accept my body at the time it was at its biggest (Note: looking back I wasn't that big). The idea I had to be thin was no longer part of my evolving personal values.

These small and simple decisions became part of the solution to be free of the need to look like a super-model. The good news! Today, I love looking through art and design magazines. If I look through a fashion magazine, or watch a movie or TV show where all the actresses are supermodels and super perfect, I'm no longer threatened by these images. I no longer bug myself with comparing myself with others in this way. It's a glorious feeling to be free! Like I've said, I'm a legend. Oops, did I say that out loud? Hahaha!

OLD THOUGHT: I'm nobody without the right stuff
NEW THOUGHT: The right stuff is what is inside of me

I grew up in a commission home and I felt really ashamed that we didn't have the latest cars; the fabulous home, the beautiful furniture and just all the great stuff that other kids had whose parents had money. These kids got to wear cool clothes and play with all the new toys and games. They looked so happy. I just felt daggy, dirty and dumb. I just felt like I never had enough and the answer to my unhappiness was having the right stuff. Too bad my parents couldn't afford it. Some times when my friends lent me their clothes, I would keep them, hoping they would forget they gave them to me to borrow. Sometimes I would take what wasn't mine from shops. I felt bad, however the need to look okay was greater than the guilt I felt after I stole stuff. Taking stuff that wasn't mine didn't fill the void I felt in my heart; I just never had enough because I felt I wasn't enough. Along the way, I felt better by holding onto stuff I didn't need or want anymore. Just having it meant at least I had something and what if I actually wanted it for a rainy day. What then? Who am I without the stuff? A 'nobody' without the right stuff that's who!

Maree gave me a heap of clothes she said she no longer wanted. No one had done this for me before. I felt overwhelmed with her generosity and deeply grateful at the time. I was running out of clothes as I was putting on weight, out of control with binge eating, and stopping myself from sticking my fingers down my throat. She had planted a seed—give away what I don't need to someone else who was in need.

When Shaun and I moved to Townsville, I cleared away the clutter. I gave five large garbage bags of clothes I would no longer wear to a girlfriend of mine, practising I am enough just as I am. Boy she was over the moon! I didn't want to hold onto stuff out of fear of not being enough. I wanted to make room for clothes that I actually liked, not what I thought others would like to see me wear. I had come to see I had no faith in life to look after me. I believed I never had enough and therefore that's exactly how I felt. Letting go of these clothes did mean I had hardly anything to wear. But I learnt to be grateful for the little I did have and began to trust that more would come my way in time. It certainly made the decision what to wear for the day easier.

I come back to knowing and accepting who I really am and what I can be grateful for. I trust the universe will provide. I have friends who clothes swop with me; it's a bit like a treasure hunt. I give away my clothes and they give away theirs. And in the meantime I trust and look forward when the money begins to flow.

I began to experience liking who I was and to understand that knowing who I was came from the inside not the outside. I let go of relying upon material things to make me feel good. What mattered was whether or not I was being honest, kind, respectful, compassionate, patient and true to myself.

OLD THOUGHT: I'm only liked if I'm sexy and hot
NEW THOUGHT: I'm to be liked for who I am

I thought if I met the other person's sexual expectations it would: a) make me feel secure in the relationship b) ensure they would keep their eyes on me and prevent them from leaving me to be with someone else and c) put some brakes on them wanting to have sex with me all the time.

The con of all cons, 'I will only be loved if I'm sexy and hot'. I watched enough video clips and saw enough magazines, billboards, posters and girls around everywhere to tell me I have to be seen as gorgeous ALL the time to be worthy of attention and love. I pretended to myself and to the others, there was more to me than my body, however I didn't believe that myself. I competed with other women in my efforts to look the most gorgeous.

There was a time I would not leave my bedroom without makeup on in my own home. Well, you never know who might just show up on your doorstep right? It's incredible how I believed I had to plaster my face with makeup to be okay. The makeup companies have really worked on me; so much so, they convinced me that I am ugly if I have a face and a body without makeup on. I have a brain to use; I don't have to believe everything I see or hear. I can choose my own way of seeing things. I can choose my own values, principles and beliefs.

All this effort to 'pretti-er-ise' myself lead to emptiness and hollowness. Does it make sense that making myself pretty ALL the time stopped the people I was attracted to from looking at other women or from leaving me or getting with other girls while I was with them? No. Was it sound thinking for me to believe that being sexually 'hot' would give me the security I was looking for? Well, I thought it would and I tried this over and over and over again and the more I tried the more insecure and the more insane I felt and became. I didn't want to be so insecure. I wanted to be mature and well put together, but I came undone all the time and sometimes, even when I tried really hard to hide it, I just couldn't. The psycho, angry me took over and I would say and do things, which left me feeling full of despair, humiliation and isolated because I relied on being loved for my body and how I looked and not for who I was as a person.

I'd play games with others and myself by playing 'hard to get' to show I had self-respect and to demonstrate how good I was. I was petrified that I would be seen as a slut or a nobody, so I tried to combat this with being tough, apathetic and simply rude. I acted like I wouldn't just be with anyone because deep down I thought I was a slut because I was a sexual being. Plus I'd get with people I didn't really want to because when I drank I lost control of making good and healthy decisions.

Over time I have come to learn I was lovable just as I was. It's equally okay to enjoy my sexuality, the feeling of sexiness, however I didn't need to be hot to be loved or feel like a complete person. I didn't need to have a model's body to be loved. I didn't have to be super-tough, super-cool or even super-together (which I'd never been!) to be loved. I no longer desired the approval from others who thought my looks was more important than the person I was. It was a much better feeling knowing others loved me for me. My outsides were not matching my insides and I turned it around with love and acceptance of myself. I began to acknowledge the good things about me and those loving things I would do for others or myself. I began to believe that I am to be loved for who I am—I am perfectly imperfect and that's okay with me.

OLD THOUGHT: I'm fat and ugly
NEW THOUGHT: I'm a beautiful person

I tried every diet, every way to control my eating; every day was a new day and no two days were the same. There were many times when I didn't care about food and it didn't consume my every thought. Those times led me to believe I could get those experiences back. It was similar to sitting on a yo-yo, except the time came when the yo-yo didn't descend. It stayed up in the air and my efforts to force it down again were failing me. I wanted to be thin and yet I couldn't stop thinking about food and I couldn't stop myself eating once I started. I'd 'pay out' on myself every time I over ate. I found this very baffling, that I could not stop over eating. The more I ate the more out of control I felt, the fatter I would become. If I became fatter, I became more ugly and the more ugly I become the less likely to be attractive to anyone. So, I had to lose the weight and therefore I had to stop eating SO MUCH FOOD! And the more I tried to eat less food the more I ate! ARGH! This was soooooooo frustrating!

I ate so much food I had to exercise. I chugged my flabby body up and down Brisbane's suburban streets. For those who haven't lived in Brisbane some of the streets are as steep as Mount Everest—or at least it seemed that way to me. I was just as obsessed with exercise as I was with the food because I had been told exercise helps with losing weight and I was all about losing weight and looking right! The crazy thing was, it didn't matter what weight I was, I was never happy. When I was successfully starving myself for days and even weeks on end (with a few biscuits a day and some of the energy drink my Mum cleverly conned me into drinking) I still thought I was fat and ugly. I just didn't like myself. I didn't value my own intelligence, creativity, kindness or any of the things I had done or what I was doing. It's so sad how I overlooked the legend I really was! LOL. I over looked the beautiful person I was inside my body.

Little did I know that spending all my time thinking about food, my body and exercise, I missed out on living each moment fully and abundantly. My brain was driven by vain and self-centred motives all in the name of being beautiful on the outside in order to be loved. Well, I did not love myself therefore I was incapable of feeling love from others. Aah! Yes, getting my eating right would fix that—right?

I tried the following ways to find balance with my eating; only eating fruit in the morning and no eating after 8 pm, or no eating before 2 pm and no eating after dinner, or don't eat at all for a few days, don't eat carbohydrates, don't eat meat, or just eat vegetables, don't eat sugar, or only eat three meals a day, just don't over eat, or don't eat fatty foods, count my calories or eat healthily and plenty of exercise. I thought that continually finding some balance with my eating would help me. I thought if I just made a decision to start a diet would work, that I would be able to follow it through. I could follow through with diets for a little while, however in the end I could not sustain it. Sooner or later I'd think 'stuff it, I deserve to eat what I want' or 'now I can make up for the food I haven't ate' or 'who cares what I look like' or 'one slip won't hurt'. And the list goes on and on.

I was still focussing on food, how much food, what types of food and when to have food. I certainly wasn't focussing on loving and accepting myself the way I was. But I didn't want to love and accept myself the way I was because I didn't want to be the way that I was. I believed if I didn't love and accept the way I was I could then one day be some other way. This did not work for me because no matter how my body looked, I was never happy—because food wasn't really the problem, and my body really wasn't the problem either. I was just never happy because I didn't love, like or approve of myself at any time. I wasn't kind to myself at anytime. I paid out on myself and I was unaware I didn't need anyone to abuse me—I was doing a grand job all by myself! Beginning to love and accept myself the way I was as a vital key to my recovery from my eating 'stuff-up-edness'. My gorgeous girlfriend freely and generously gave this to me and I am forever grateful to her for that.

She suggested, "Why don't you just accept yourself the way you are?"

I said, "If I turn this over to my Higher Power, it will make me fat. If I let go of controlling how much food I eat I will turn into a whale!"

"How long have you been this way?"

I paused. "Um...I began binge eating when I was about 11 or maybe younger."

"If this is the way you are, then this is the way you are. Why don't you say to yourself when you start gorging on food, 'this is okay with me, I've been like this all of my life, this is okay with me."

I was so screwed up in my head and fighting the way I was with food, I thought I'd give this a try. I had nothing to lose. I could always go back to how I was if it didn't work, because that's what I did anyway with all my diets and fads and finding the bloody balance!

I hung up the phone and went straight to the fridge, reefed the pizza box out and snatched at the pizza and off I went shovelling it down, like a starved animal, only that I was stuffed like a pig. I freaked out, feeling out of control as I always did once I started eating. "Shit, I just got off the phone and here I am eating straight away, I'm doomed! What did she say to me...that's right...this is how I am, and I've been like this most of my life, so I may as well accept it...this is okay with me."

Something quite odd occurred. I stopped eating. I didn't feel like taking another bite of pizza. I threw the rest in the bin, put the pizza box back in the fridge and said to myself, "What am I meant to be doing now?" I just walked into what I was meant to be doing as a nanny, looking after the children. Voila`! I had no idea this was a beautiful beginning as I walked away a free woman. Something so simple, so kind and so loving that worked for me and as time went on, as I continued to practice love and acceptance toward myself, my state of body and mind, I discovered that I was a beautiful person, not the fat and ugly person I had convinced myself I was for so many years

OLD THOUGHT: I'll be happy once I have the perfect body
NEW THOUGHT: Happiness comes as I accept myself the way I am

Forcing myself to conform to how I wanted it to be instead of accepting it as it was, drove me insane, vain, unhappy and unsatisfied. I was forcing myself to look a certain way to feel loved. Once I started to feel loving toward myself, my outsides began to match my insides and the war on food and my body ended.

I learnt to eat when I was hungry, not when I thought I had to eat. I know it's a strange concept. Eat when I'm hungry. Odd! Who would have thought to encourage others to eat when they are hungry? Who started this 'eat at set times'? What if I'm just not hungry at those times? Food tastes so good when I'm hungry. How odd! After practicing loving and accepting myself during those times when I couldn't stop eating, or when I couldn't stop my thoughts from obsessing about food I discovered an important truth. I have a stomach, which tells me when I am hungry. My stomach physically lets me know when it needs food in it. I had forgotten to listen to my body I had relied upon a fixed time I was taught from my parents, diets, friends, teachers, bosses etc, etc. It was tough learning how to eat when I felt hungry because a) I resented waiting and would eat before I would get hungry as it would take too long and b) forgot what it was like to feel hungry. I became willing to eat when I was hungry. When I couldn't resist, I would eat and say to myself, "This is okay with me; I've been like this all of my life." As the result I realised when I obsess about eating food when I am not hungry I tend to lie to myself. I tell myself I will feel better when I eat the desired food I have in my mind. I tell myself I can fit it into my full stomach. I'd tell myself I didn't care when in actual fact I really did - a lot! I'd tell myself I will only have a little bit when I know I am going to have all of it. I'd tell myself I've worked really hard for it, or that I deserve it, I need it, I want it, I have to have it. Underneath all of these lies is one very simple truth I just do not want to hear, acknowledge or act on is 'I AM NOT HUNGRY!!!' And there's a very simple reason why I resist this truth. It gets in the way of my eating. It gets in the way of my gluttony. It gets in the way of my selfishness, self-centeredness.

The obsession to eat is all about me. Its what I'm going to get out of it. It doesn't matter if it's not my food, or if I need to consider if others want to eat the food I want to eat. I don't care about others full stop. All I am thinking about is me. And then when I eat all the food I then continue about thinking about me. How fat and ugly I am. How I won't be as skinny as the others. How uncomfortable I'm going to feel. How my clothes are not going to fit anymore. All of this is about me. It is not about caring about others or me. It's what I can get at any cost and then I resented that I couldn't have the body I wanted because I can't get away with gorging on food like most people on the planet. Like I should be treated so special. I thought I should be able to eat all the time when I'm not hungry and have the natural body shape I was born to have. So I accepted the need for the perfect body (thin arms, legs, flat stomach, light knees and right sized boobs) had won the war, and had done so the moment I began to reject the body I was born with. When I rejected my body, telling myself it wasn't the right shape or the right height or the right weight I began to starve and after starving I fell into binging and it turning into sticking my fingers down my throat. I was just in denial about that until I wasn't anymore.

I learnt I had an opportunity to understand and accept my selfish, self-centred, gluttonous, self-pitying thoughts. I began to say to myself 'I have been like this for most of my life and as much as I would like to be able to change these thoughts I cannot and this too is okay with me'. Having practiced accepting this side of who I am my selfish, self-centred, gluttonous, self pitying thoughts and the desire to binge left me. The fight for the perfect body left me. I embraced my flabby bits just as they were and I experienced happiness as the result. I began to experience a faith that my obsession with the perfect body would eventually pass. I learnt to listen to MY body and not someone else telling my body when to eat. I trusted my body because it knew exactly when I needed to eat. I practiced this over a long while as I developed a lifestyle where I have no set time for eating, no limits, no rules, and freedom came! HOW AWESOME!

I learnt to quit filling my body up with fluid before I ate or during the time I ate. I once believed this would stop me from eating so much. I came to recognise and admit it had a reverse affect upon me. I found when I did drink too much with my meal, a few moments when I stopped eating, I would become extra bloated and full...probably the food expanding mixing around with all the fluid I drank. I noticed this would set off the thinking "oh I can't eat now I'm going to explode." These were the perfect words to set off the rebellion within me, "I'll bloody eat if I want to I don't care how full I am." When this happened I would accept it and go with it and say to myself "This is okay with me, I've been like this all of my life. Why would I expect to be anything different?" I noticed that when I didn't drink soon before, during or soon after a meal, and if I did it was just a sip, my stomach come to learn when it had had enough. I practiced listening to my body. I learnt to listen to what my body wanted to eat. If it wanted pizza, a big bag of lollies, cream cheese on crackers, pasta, jelly slice, I would eat it and eat it if I felt like it at 6 am or 3 pm or, what the hey! Midnight! No more rules, just listening to my body. Over the years—yes, years—my body began to crave salads to pig out on. And now I rarely pig out and when I do I feel no fear about it. It's weird; it's wonderful and just simply unbelievable. I love good food; all food and I can enjoy it and get on with living—something diets and hating my body and myself never achieved. I'm a free person because when I thought I was being bad with food, or thought food was bad, or that my body was ugly and fat I would just say to myself 'I have been this way believing I have to have the perfect body to be happy all of my life and this is okay with me'. I loved myself as I was, exactly as I was—the greatest love I could ever give to myself, and it healed me. I didn't have to have the perfect body to be happy anymore.

The simple new thoughts, which healed my suffering from my eating disorders were:

It's okay to wait and eat when I am hungry. When I am hungry food tastes really great!

I can trust my stomach can indicate to me when I am hungry—not the clock.

It's okay to eat what I feel like eating, what is going to satisfy me, not what I think I should be eating.

All food is good and yummy - except for kidneys! Ew!

Letting go of diets to lose weight, to have the perfect body or to stop my unhealthy eating or thinking about food allows me to enjoy food, my body and my life.

Listening to myself and my body, loving and accepting myself creates a peaceful mind, a healthier body and happier life.

I love and accept my body and myself when I eat when I am not hungry or eat food I don't want to eat or eat when I am already full.

Happiness comes as I accept myself just the way I am.

See Appendix: Warning Signs of an Eating Disorder

SACRED CREATIVE FOCUS
DO I LIKE THE WAY I LOOK?

I am grateful for the body I have, it's not perfect and it doesn't have to be. I'm not like anyone else I know. There is only one of me. I embrace my changing body, whether I put on or lose weight, or my boobs loose their bounce having had a baby, or if one boob is bigger than the other, or when my skin collects more wrinkles, or how my thighs have darker and wider stretch marks, or whether my nose is more like a mushroom rather than slim and pointy. It is me.

The friends I choose do not have to look a certain way for me to like them. They are all different shapes and sizes and all have different taste in clothing just like me. I like who my friends are as people, they are more than just their bodies and so am I despite what the cosmetic or media industries or others (friends, family or partners) tell me. My friends don't have to measure up to some perfect physical standard to be liked or loved. I don't have to measure up to some perfect physical standard to be liked or loved either. I can embrace the body I have today even if it is not perfect. I imagine if I were standing with people who were starving of food, without money for clothes, safety or shelter would it be so important what my body looked like and what clothes I chose to wear? It's good to feel good and it's even better if I love my way there by accepting my body as it is right now.

It's a great feeling to take care of my body and to demonstrate that I am grateful for it. I mindfully and joyfully cut my nails, brush my teeth, clean my ears, scrub my feet, wash my hair, moisturise my body and sweeten it up a bit with some yummy fragrance. I can have fun with my body. I've had so much fun coloring and cutting my hair into all different styles. I loved doing that because I liked to explore different looks. It's about what I like. I now have brown hair instead of blonde hair, because I desired to accept the color of hair I was born with, rather than rejecting it. And now I really like it – for now. I really wanted long hair again, so I grew it long, and I really like it – for now. It feels great accepting the way I like to look. I choose clothes and shoes, I like, whether it's fashionable or not. I am my own person and its great to express who I really am with how I like to look and its equally wonderful to celebrate how others choose to look too, whether its something I would like for myself or not. I'm happy with and without, what a freedom this really is.

SACRED CREATIVE ACTIVITY

To have fun with how I see myself with scissors I cut out different body parts from a magazine, newspaper, or other printed material, perhaps including clothing, and other accessories I wish I could have. Once I've cut out what I think to be enough I arrange them on the page to create an image and when I feel they are in the right position on the page I glue them down.

SACRED MEDITATIVE ACTIVITY

When I have finished, I ask myself, 'do I believe I will only be happy once I have the perfect figure and when I have all the clothes and accessories to go with it?' To be happy now am I open to accept and love my body now as it is whether or not I have all the things I want?' Happiness is available to me now if I am open to it.

Before I eat, I ask myself, 'Am I really hungry?' I focus on my stomach and how it feels. If I feel that I am not hungry I imagine or even remember, how it feels when I am really hungry—when my tummy is rumbling. If I can, wait until I feel genuinely hungry so I can practice listening to my body. I'm letting go of knowing what time it is to know whether I should or shouldn't be eating. I'm going to let my body guide me. Or if I haven't eating in a long time because my thoughts are telling me if I eat I will get fat, this is a time to listen to my body rather than my old thoughts which are attached to looking a certain way to be accepted or perhaps a way to punish and hurt myself by starving myself. I'm going to find out what I feel like eating. This is about being connected to my body and letting my body connect with me. If I do eat when I am not hungry or after I've just finished eating I practice thinking loving and compassionate thoughts toward myself. If I pay out on myself for eating when I am hungry I do the same. Just for a few moments, I'm going to experience letting go of the old thoughts which slaughter me with words of hate, disgust and disappointment. I'm willing to know what it feels like to love eating food and accept my body and the way I look just how it is now.

COMMITMENT STATEMENT

I .... am willing to put aside everything I think I know about myself, my life, my past, my future, in order to have an open mind and a new experience with the way I look. I am open to the possibility to accepting the way I look, receiving new thoughts, and living a new life.

WHO AM I?
WEEK THREE : DO I LIKE WHO I AM?

INTRODUCTION TO THE SACRED SHARING

I MOVED TO TOWNSVILLE TO BE WITH SHAUN. WE WERE NOW LIVING WITH SHAUN'S COACH AND HIS WIFE AND THEIR CHILDREN. I AM WAITING FOR MY CAR TO ARRIVE FROM BRISBANE. I CHOSE TO HAVE TIME OFF FROM WORK DURING THE TIME SHAUN SEARCHES FOR WORK OTHER THAN RUGBY AS HE FAILED TO QUALIFY FOR PROFESSIONAL FOOTBALL.

ANOTHER DAY : I've been feeling yucky, snappy and really angry, and I've been a smartass to Shaun. Last Sunday Mum told me about Grandpa being a predator in the family. It's made me angry. I've been thinking about him a lot. I've been angry with the family members who knew of his behaviour who didn't do anything about it. I've been cold and nasty to Shaun since. I find intimacy extremely difficult. I feel too vulnerable and young. I don't like him touching my poonanny (vagina) any more. The spark and romance, the fun has gone. Shaun doesn't like being around me because I'm putting him down all the time. I see his weaknesses and I become angry.

I can't stand waiting for this fucking loan to come through. I need the money to pay off my car and the money I owe to the employment benefits. Shaun's been wonderful (even though I've yelled at him, gotten angry beyond measure, and lost my patience with the people organising the money.) I've blamed Shaun and his coach and it's probably not their fault. It's taken them fifteen days to work it out. I've taken my frustrations, feelings of anger, fear and impatience all out on Shaun. How do I stop myself? My food has been good. I've probably eaten too much sugar.

My period is due in four days, surprise, surprise! I'm only half bloated on the tenth day, amazing. I feel a bit of "pudge" on my body but nothing like I used to. I've been eating only when I'm hungry. I'm not eating so late and the evening meals have been lighter. I'm really aware of how I use food for my emotions. I do feel very stressed. I feel the fear of letting go. I'm afraid I may lose control, a fear felt by most survivors. I fear Shaun won't pull through. I have extremely high expectations of him and I know it is a reflection of me. I don't find him attractive today but my heart can feel his beauty. This has happened before where I couldn't feel feelings towards him. I know this will pass. I will start to allow myself to love him and him to love me. It's just soooo hard at the moment.

ANOTHER DAY : The wheels on my car were stolen last Saturday and the idea of organising new ones has added to my stress. The removal company may not replace them even though they were stolen on their premises. The owner said he might buy some new ones for me and I picture he'll get some very dodgy looking tyres.

Do you know what I'd like to do? I'd like to have a nice hair cut and buy some new clothes. I've been wearing the same clothes for the past seven days. Why? Because I've worn my other clothes so many times I'm turning myself off myself. Seeing them and wearing them makes me feel sick. I want new clothes because I deserve them. I need $1,000 to get my car on the road and $266 to give back to employment benefits. Looks like I won't be buying any new clothes for me. We spent $180.00 on Shaun today, (that was easy), and we got them all from Country Road. Shaun may be starting work with people who have special needs (maybe in the new millennium).

I feel like patronising Shaun. You see he hasn't sat down with me to work out our money situation. He doesn't think of doing that. This is one of the reasons why I can't relax because he doesn't take any responsibility regarding our financial situation. He just hopes and wishes it will all work out. He doesn't have a plan or any thoughts about it. It's up to me because I can't stand not knowing what we're doing.

ANOTHER DAY : I can't fucking relax in this house environment. I can't get to a fucking meeting. I have a fucking headache. Shaun being who he is, Mr Right Goodie Fucking Two Shoes – that's it, I'm fucking difficult, confusing, immature, out of control, Miss I'm-The-Problem-Always-Something-Wrong-With-Me-To-Fix. It's me, me, me it's my entire fault.

ANOTHER DAY : I'm sitting by the pool. The water is softly spurting out of the pump and making a humming noise. The children's laughter and squeals are coming from over the fence. There was a lot of talk about the effects of sexual, physical and emotional abuse from their fathers (mine from my grandfather), at the twelve-step meeting today. I felt the lack of support for these women—nowhere for us to go—only to each other. Another woman identified with what I said about feeling isolated and having fear of others. I related to a man who spoke of low self-esteem, being affected by the treatment from others and wanting to be a better human being.

An older woman found conflict with me. She asked how long I planned to stay here in Townsville. I told her one day at a time and that I really didn't know. She told me that I couldn't start a women's meeting and then not follow through by not staying to run it. What she said made sense to me, so I told her I could be here for ten years or I could leave tomorrow, I just can't make such promises. All I know is that I need a woman's meeting and I found the general consensus amongst the other women was the same. Whether it lasts or not is not up to me but entirely up to God. God governs our tomorrows, and all we need to do is put in the action where and when it is needed.

There's a reason why there are no young people around and so few women. I don't know what it is but something is amiss. My Mum says that its generally because there is nothing to keep them there. I don't want that woman crushing the idea of starting a woman's meeting due to the unknown tomorrow. She angered me because she wasn't understanding of me and didn't want to see the simplicity of it. I told her that I needed a women's meeting and that we have the foundations to start one.

I'm still having difficulty with myself, there is a tug of war going on within me. It has become extremely exhausting. I shared about it today at the meeting and I shed many tears. Yesterday I shed many tears after feeling the unwillingness to change. The quietness and niceness doesn't last long. My bitterness and anger has still got much control over my actions and words. Replacing the old with the new seems endless at this moment. My head is now telling me that I need a job to earn my keep. It's telling me that I'm lazy and I'd be more 'with it' and happier if I stopped running away. I'm to involve myself in this life. I feel too tired to do that. There's nowhere that I can imagine where I'd like to work. I do feel a little excitement when I think of a short course, although what would I study? Perhaps I could study childcare? I have a few clothes now, not too many but enough for me to feel comfortable. They are clothes of certain colours that enhance my beauty.

I'm not sitting with Shaun because he's sitting in front of the TV. I have a lot of built up anger and resentment about spending time in front of the TV or in the bedroom, and just being in the house during the day. It brings up feelings of laziness, hiding, worthlessness and nothingness towards myself and I project that upon Shaun when he does it too. A wonderful way to start the day is by going to the toilet and talking to God.

Today I came out and asked Shaun if he watches pornographic pictures on the internet? Of course he has seen them. So I then ask "Do you like them?" So he responds with "Hmm." I say: "That's a yes isn't it?" He says: "Well, yes." OUCH. Fucking dirty, disrespectful, unloving, perving, filthy fucker. You don't need to love me. Go fuck yourself over other women's naked breasts and hairy vaginas with their legs spread wide open. YUCK. The back of my fucking mind is saying: 'Well, that's okay for him because he's a man and men enjoy that fucking shitty stuff. It's just that I don't let myself enjoy men's naked bodies.' I'd only do it to get him back for being a hurtful, uncaring, sex, sick, motherfucker. That was the last straw with my relationship with Jarod. Once I found out he was enjoying himself and involving himself with the sex stuff over the internet, I ended the relationship. I fucking left him for good. My dad doesn't like porn material. He says there is no need for a man to read such things especially when you have someone you love in your life. So Shaun is sick and disgusting, a typical perverted man. I'm just a piece of meat. I'm the nice clean girl and he can still enjoy himself with other women because I don't give him what he desires. Oh, that's lovely. Fuck them in your head and smile your way with me and say to yourself: "It's okay darling I'll wait." Yeah, sure, while he gets off with merely looking at pictures of other women.

SAME DAY : How do I move from that yucky hurting area of my heart to understand that it's okay for him to look at other women sexually? Is that a reality I need to get real with? I don't want to. I'm not being kind to myself today. It seems like I just want to live in misery. I hate myself and say 'fuck you' to the world. I've been eating lots of fatty and sugary food in the past two days. I'm not over-eating or under-eating. I wonder if the sugar is affecting me today.

    I want to ring Maree but it's not my home here to call someone. The Mum here irritates me, the way she bullies and bosses her children around. The atmosphere here is horrible. I don't like her very much, yet I smile at her all the time like I care about what she is saying or doing. I'm being false, but telling her that I feel ill at ease in regards to the way she treats her children is probably not the done thing because its none of my business. Okay this is the go. Shaun and his rugby mate are off training. I asked his mate twice before they both left if he wants me to cook him tea and at both requests declined my offer. So off they go at 5:30 pm and I expected them home around 7:15 pm, but no, they arrive at 8:35 pm. By the time they arrive home I've eaten four bowls of custard waiting for Shaun so we could sit down and eat dinner together. But the fucked up thing is, I don't want too much tea, I wanted some but not a lot. So Shaun asks why I haven't cooked up all the steaks and I've asked him why would I cook up food for someone who said no to my invitation to my cooking? I've overeaten. I haven't done that in about six months and I've started a disagreement with Shaun. Why? Is it to do with not wanting to get close with Shaun? Intimacy?

Twelve Years Later…
Going within to like who I am to being
freed from my own limitations

OLD THOUGHT: I'm wrong if I think or feel differently to others
NEW THOUGHT: Wrong or right, I accept the way I think & feel

I made myself wrong for not liking pornography. My girlfriends would laugh in response to my horror to pornography. I would become so worked up because guys, including my own cousin, would tell me men love looking at porn and that it's a guy thing, it's what men do, or better yet I was told; 'You're frigid' or 'you'd like it if you watched it' or 'get over it'. Others would convince me women in pornography also love it and therefore I should get over feeling ill about porn. I didn't have confidence to trust how I felt simply because others thought and felt differently to me. I would think: 'well if they say it, it must be so!'

The simple fact is: I don't like pornography. I never have and I never will. I even tried to enjoy it once just to face it to see if I would like it and I was left to feel yucky for having done it. I felt alone and empty; feelings I did not like at all. It created emotional distance rather then emotional closeness with my boyfriend by doing something he thought was great. Just because something is great for one person doesn't mean it's going to be great for me.

As the result of thinking there was something wrong with me for feeling ill about pornography, my anger turned into a violent rage. I didn't feel I had any options: to love and accept my own thoughts and feelings about matters where others disagreed. My truth was that pornography was detrimental to my mental, emotional and spiritual health, and because I was hell bent on being in the relationship, I thought to be able to stay in it I would have to embrace ideas which went against my own.

Yet I hurt myself by abandoning how I felt about pornography. There's also something to be said about my old idea that whatever a guy says, goes. I have abandoned my own mind and heart to keep the peace and to keep someone loving me. It would have been very beneficial if I had expressed to Shaun how pornography made me feel without the expectation for him to do anything about it.

I now understand that I didn't know I deserved to be heard and understood, and not knowing this led me into arguments to defend my ideas or beliefs. When I get into arguing with someone about how I feel, I'm way off track and I've allowed the other person to get way off track also. Shaun defended himself when I asked him about pornography, instead of asking how it made me feel and why. I jumped down his throat because he defended himself, so instead of both of us engaging in how I was actually feeling we went into whether or not it was good or bad, who was wrong and right, all the while I missed a wonderful opportunity for both of us to know me better, to feel the pain and sadness I was feeling. We both skipped over that and it was never acknowledged, so I continued to feel wrong and sore.

Shaun couldn't watch the TV or read a magazine or walk down the street or even dare look at another woman. I was so insecure and jealous of every woman, and I couldn't cope with him seeing nudity. I never understood this crazy stuff I felt and thought. I wanted to get rid of it, I would have shot it if I had a gun. It's not very attractive hovering over my boyfriend's shoulders while he reads the newspaper to see who he was looking at.

I had no idea; it's really okay to trust my feelings. I no longer have to believe there is something truly fucked up with me if I think and feel differently to others. It's okay and I'm okay if I don't feel like being sexual with someone I love or anyone else for that matter. Wrong or right I accept how I think and feel.

OLD THOUGHT: I have to have sex to keep someone I like in my life
NEW THOUGHT: Who I am is enough

I have been sexual with others, like I did with Shaun, to try and create emotional 'closeness'. It's been my experience that creating closeness only through being sexual did not work. It made me very, very angry. And so it should, because I'm not listening to my feelings, instead I am forcing my feelings to happen. I also believed if I kept up with being sexual with him all the time it would stop him wanting to be with others. Having sex and being sexy didn't keep Shaun from wanting to be with his ex-girlfriend again. And when he didn't want his girlfriend again (if that were true?) it certainly didn't motivate him to want me to be with him any time soon.

Counsellors and friends have tried to convince me that men have to have sex to feel loved by their girlfriends. This concept had never sat right with me, I've been sexual with men to enable them to love me and it never made them love me any more deeply or at all. The men I loved didn't need to have sex with their parents, siblings or friends to feel loved. Why would loving me be any different?

I also feel if others only feel loved through having sex with me, they must be ignoring all the other loving things I do. They must miss the whole point of who I am if they only rely on being sexual with me to experience my love for them. They must be incapable of receiving my love when I'm communicating honestly to them, or sharing my heart with them, or when I'm laughing with them, or having fun with them or when I'm showing understanding or compassion to them. No, I have to have sex with them for them to feel my love! They can't feel it any other way! Today I understand I don't have to have sex to make them feel loved by me. In a relationship if they can't feel loved by me why on earth would they want to be sexual with me? And more importantly if I don't feel loved by them why would I feel like being sexual with them anyway?

Shaun was pressuring me to be sexual with him every day. It was really hard for me to let him know I didn't want to be sexual with him, and he persisted with being sexual with me anyway. I'd ask him to stop touching me and he would continue. What made matters worse, was that I believed Maree when she told me I wasn't allowing myself to be loved by him when I didn't let him touch me or let him be sexual with me. In hindsight, and a little more understanding, I felt disrespected by Shaun as he was not respecting my wishes to stop touching me. I could not create trust with him when he continued to ignore what I was telling him about what I needed and felt. I felt unimportant and I felt like a sexual object. I felt really angry when he would ignore my wishes, and this is how my resentment grew and led me to speak to him and myself very badly.

Through having a discussion with a friend of mine we discovered we thought we were afraid of leaving the guys we were so pissed off with because they weren't listening to us. We both came to see, there were many times we were not speaking up, and we were not communicating directly about what we actually felt. We thought that by not speaking up that would leave the other person confused; that we were okay with their sexual advances. We both discovered together that we pretending to be OK because we were afraid that if we communicated what we really thought and felt - they would leave us! So, the fear of losing the guy led us to accept sexual touch and sexual talk when we actually felt uncomfortable with it. The fear drove us to say yes instead of a strong and clear no. We prevented ourselves from finding out if we were loved and respected if we said no to sex.

Today I understand love is not about sex or being sexual - it may be a part of it, it's not all of it and it's not necessarily a sign of love. A sign of love is about listening to myself and being who I really am in the relationship, how I am getting along with others and myself. My love for myself or toward the other person is not measured by: whether we are having sex, whether I'm allowing myself to be touched sexually, or how often, or what type of sex, or what sexual position. To love or to be loved I need to know who I am is enough - I am enough to be loved for who I am.

OLD THOUGHT: My painful experiences will disappear if I wish them away
NEW THOUGHT: I accept the way I feel without judgement

I really struggled to be able to quiet my mind from criticising others and myself. At the time I felt so much, pain, hurt and anger and I really lacked the skills, knowledge and understanding to know how to work through these very strong emotions. What I have learnt since this time, what I began to do in my early recovery was to first acknowledge what I was thinking and feeling. The writing process gave me the opportunity to really get to know myself in this way. I have learnt the more I try to make these feelings go away, the fiercer they became. For example, the more I tried to make myself want to be sexual with Shaun and skip over how I really felt, the more anger I felt and the more I wanted to hurt him. The more I wanted to hurt him, the more confused and guilty I felt and then I turned against myself and hated myself more.

My experience is that when I accept how I feel, without judgment or wishing my feelings away, my feelings and thoughts calm down. By acknowledging and feeling my feelings I am respecting myself, respecting my thoughts, respecting my feelings. They are not good or bad; they are just what they are. Whether I think they are bad or not, do they go away by judging and rejecting them? Or, did it make matters worse?

It was a fact that I could not stop being a certain way or feeling a certain way or thinking a certain way, no matter how hard I tried. I had not considered simply accepting the way I was. I struggled with this concept because I believed if I embraced my thoughts, feelings and behaviours—which I judged as wrong, bad or unacceptable—they would get worse. If this is how I am and I'm trying to control it, imagine what I would be like if I stopped controlling the thing I was trying to control! ARGH!

In my experience the opposite has been true. What I resisted—persisted. When I want to resist something I know now I need to love and accept the very thing I'm resisting. If I am a certain way today, that's okay. This is how I am just for today. Trying to control, ignore, resist, deny or destroy my feelings hasn't worked; it led me to be fake, phoney and inauthentic. I accept that this is what I do. I try to control, ignore, resist, deny and destroy the things I don't like about myself such as what I think, what I feel or what I do. So when I do the very thing I'm trying to stop I remind myself this is the way I am and it's just for today, it may not be forever and my answers have not worked, so this is it for now.

When I try acknowledging, embracing and accepting myself just the way I am, good or bad, my fear of it growing out of control dissipates and soon I'm already thinking of something useful or loving. My freedom hasn't come from forcing myself to 'let go' or from trying to 'stop myself'. Freedom has come from loving and accepting myself at my worst—this is unconditional love in action, and it begins with me.

OLD THOUGHT: I have to put up with feeling uncomfortable
NEW THOUGHT: I acknowledge & trust my feelings

I didn't know I had a choice. I thought I had to stay with Shaun's coach and family. I was unaware of my options and so I continued to live in an environment, which was really unhealthy for my wellbeing. I felt sick, I felt frightened, and unwelcomed which left me feeling anxious and very uncomfortable. The coach's wife was very critical toward her children; she put them down, called them names and spoke to them disrespectfully. Her behaviour affected my emotional, spiritual and mental wellbeing and I expected myself to be able to be happy, joyous and free. I thought there was something wrong with me for feeling the way I was feeling.

Had I stopped to feel my feelings and know my thoughts, and took them seriously enough; I would have seen why this environment was affecting me. I may have realised that what I saw was the mistreatment toward children.

All I could see was that I was powerless over the situation. As my Dad says he has a hard enough time trying to change without trying to work out how to change others. Plus it's not my business to change others anyway, I feel when I do that or try to do that I'm interfering in other people's lives. However I now believe even though I am not able to change another I can still say or do something in response to behaviour with which I don't feel comfortable. I can take the right action for my own wellbeing once I acknowledge I am experiencing discomfort or distress. When I acknowledge my feelings I can trust that they need attention of some sought, something is going on that's causing them disturbance. Sharing with others, writing, creating, meditating or reaching out for help in my community (counsellors, health professionals, information on the net or the library etc) can guide me to what I need to do to take care of myself and/or the situations I find myself in. I can acknowledge and trust my feelings in order to do what is necessary to feel comfortable with others and myself.

It was fortunate Shaun found a new place for us to stay. Sometimes Life does for me what I cannot do for myself...thank goodness!

See Appendix: 'Are you affected by someone's sexual behaviour?'

SACRED CREATIVE FOCUS
DO I LIKE WHO I AM?

There were things I was doing that were also showing me who I really was. I had been writing from a very young age. I would write letters and notes to my Mum to let her know what I was thinking and feeling. I found it easier to write than to talk directly to her. I would write many letters to my friends, as I enjoyed writing. I was never a really good writer. I just liked doing it.

I enjoyed drawing and painting. I'd stay back at secondary school painting until 10 pm with Mozart playing in the background. I didn't think I was any good at art so I didn't go to Uni to learn how. I just painted paintings when I could. For example, when I was working at the bottleshop I set up a canvas and paint in the storeroom and painted in between customers.

I remember being a very shy kid. Although I was chosen from the school choir to sing the national anthem each week in front of 600 students - where did the confidence come from to do that!! I sang through the terror, that's how! I stuttered and stumbled when asked to read out aloud in class. I longed to be confident, loud, funny and out going. I didn't value my nature. I didn't know my talents, gifts or interests even when they were staring me in the face. The only way I found I could be myself was by drinking alcohol. But who was I without alcohol - really?

Is who I am about what I look like, or is it about how I think, speak, or act? Is it about how I go about my day, or how I handle a difficult situation? Is it about what I value or what I believe to be true? Is it about the people I care about and how I care about them? Are 'things' really important to me? What are the 'things' that matters to me? Is it about the food I like, or the activities I enjoy being involved with or the clothes that I wear, or the way I decorate my bedroom? What do I like doing? What would I like to do? Is it about my character and how honest I am with others or myself? Is being honest important? Do I enjoy gossiping and criticising others or do I find myself not repeating things said to me that I'm able to mind my own business? Am I a trustworthy and loyal person? Do I enjoy supporting and helping others? Am I courageous, kind, thoughtful, selfless, or forgiving? Do I do what is right for myself or do I tend to be a people pleaser and put others first? Do I have a positive outlook upon life? Do I stay true to what I know is right for me? There have been many questions I've been asked by others or myself to know who I really am. I began with a willingness to ask and answer some of these questions to get the journey started or at least continue the journey. I am really I just asked the questions because I began to make new decisions toward experiencing who I am which created new and wonderful experiences, feelings and thoughts toward myself and others.

SACRED CREATIVE ACTIVITY

I can either cut out a photograph and/or draw a sketch of myself on the right hand side of my page or on the creative space provided in this book. I write words and drew pictures that describe to me who I believed myself to be today around the image of myself. When I'm finished I then do the same on the other side of the page, draw or paste an image of myself and I write words or draw pictures around the image of myself. However, this time I imagine being free to be truly myself – the greatest vision of who I am. What would I thinking, feeling and be doing?

SACRED MEDITATIVE ACTIVITY

For this activity I try to go with my first answer and allow myself to have some fun. I simply answer the following questions either in my mind or write the answers down, depending upon how I feel at the time. I begin to imagine who I would be if I were someone in a past life. What clothes I loved to wear? What would I do for fun? What kind of people would I feel great around? What would have been my favourite food? Where would be my favourite place to clear my mind? What music would I like to listen to and if I played an instrument, what kind of instrument would I play? Would I have a hobby or special interest where I could lose myself for hours? If I had a secret love for something, what would it be? What would people say about me a - how would I like them to see me? I can get creative here by drawing or cutting out images of the answers that have come from these questions. Only when I've finished doing this I then read the following question.

Are there any clues in my answers about who I imagined myself to be in the past as to who I might be or like to be today? Perhaps I've lost touch with some of the things I like doing or perhaps it's a confirmation I am being who I really am which is also fantastic.

COMMITMENT STATEMENT

I ...., am willing to put aside everything I think I know about myself, my life, my past, and my future, in order to have an open mind and a new experience about who I am. I am open to the possibility of accepting who I am, receiving new thoughts, and living a new life.

CREATIVE SPACE

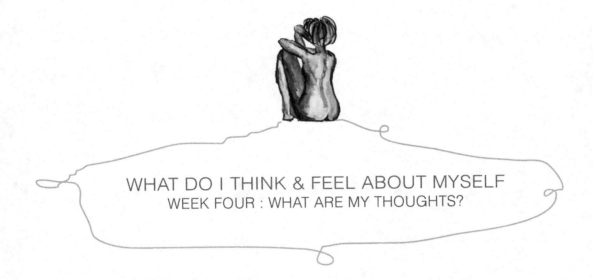

WHAT DO I THINK & FEEL ABOUT MYSELF
WEEK FOUR : WHAT ARE MY THOUGHTS?

STOP BEING OBSESSED WITH FUCKING FOOD. IF YOU JUST STOPPED IT, YOU WOULDN'T FEEL SO UGLY + BAD ABOUT YOUR LEGS, HIPS + STOMACH.
$70
DOES THE NECK LOOK FAT?
THIS IS HIDING + I LOOK OUT OF SHAPE
THE LEGS. IF ONLY THEY WEREN'T SO HEFTY

INTRODUCTION TO THE SACRED SHARING

I CONFRONTED SHAUN; I SENSED HE WAS WITHHOLDING SOMETHING FROM ME. I ASKED HIM TO TALK TO SOMEONE ABOUT WHATEVER IT WAS HE WAS NOT TELLING ME WHILE I ATTENDED A TWELVE-STEP RECOVERY MEETING. WHEN I RETURNED THAT EASTER SUNDAY NIGHT HE TOLD ME HE WAS STILL IN LOVE WITH HIS EX-GIRLFRIEND. I RAN AND HID IN THE WARDROBE, SCREAMING AND CRYING. WHEN I CALMED DOWN I CALLED MAREE. MAREE AND HER HUSBAND SPOKE TO THE BOTH OF US AND THEY ARRANGED A FLIGHT BACK TO BRISBANE FOR ME THE FOLLOWING MORNING AT 6:00 AM. SHAUN DROPPED ME OFF AT THE AIRPORT AND I WAVED HIM GOODBYE. A FEW DAYS LATER HE CONTACTED ME AND REGRETTED WHAT HE HAD SAID.

ANOTHER DAY : I can't pin point why I'm feeling the way I'm feeling. I believe that it has something to do with Shaun saying that he's still in love with his ex-girlfriend. I'm afraid he'll change his mind again having now gone back on saying he's in love with his ex-girlfriend. Afraid he'll find other women attractive and act on it. Afraid to decide for myself what I want, which may go against Maree's suggestions for me, and I'm fearful he'll leave me and sense my heightened insecurity. I feel sad, second best, fearful and continuously worried that these feelings won't go away. I'm hoping they will and I'm hoping Shaun won't leave me again. Prayer is what I need to do to reconnect with my Higher Power. I feel I'm talking myself into the logical learnt way of getting myself out of this pain. The strange thing here is I want to feel it and find out the exact nature of the pain so I can heal it, through feeling the full emotions and not just thinking it through with words.

I sounded out with a fellow member about how I was feeling lost, sad and afraid. She asked if there's any place I'd like to be and I pictured the sun and being settled in Townsville. Then I said it doesn't matter where I am because I've got to go through this anyway. She said: "Don't try and read my mind, it's not what I want—it's what you want." As I was driving to the meeting before I met my friend I was thinking to myself: "You're an adult, you made choices, choices that you made for yourself and no one else. I'm allowed to decide what's good for me."

My friend was helping me this morning to find out what I wanted. I'll tell you what feels right, although I couldn't have known this before because I was, and still am, afraid of going against Maree's suggestions and that is I don't want to be here in Brisbane. Brisbane is no longer the place I want to be settled in. I don't feel good about being in Brisbane for the next five months whilst Shaun is in Townsville. (Fear is reminding me what I'm writing is bad and not allowed). I don't want to be unemployed for too much longer. I don't want to be unable to complete a course due to travelling to and from Brisbane and Townsville. I don't want to be in both places. I don't want to not be able to be with my boyfriend and not have another go due to fear of not coping.

Staying here in Brisbane and the positives:
I have my sponsor nearby.
I have my close friends here.
I have a women's group here.
There are more employment and studying opportunities here.

My therapist is here.

There's more entertainment here.

There are more twelve-step meetings available to me here.

I can choose to visit Shaun.

It's easier for me to live in Brisbane.

The negatives of staying here are:

I'm physically away from my boyfriend.

I feel unsettled here.

It doesn't feel right to stay in Brisbane and visit Shaun in Townsville.

Brisbane is not where my heart wants to be.

I feel confused, lost, uncomfortable, sad and in the wrong place by continuing my life in Brisbane.

The swimming club I want to join is not here.

My home isn't here. I don't want to start anything permanent here because I just want to give it another go in Townsville.

SAME DAY : I need a home to go to. I need a phone I can readily contact my loved ones and my support people. My little girl is leaning on Shaun, missing him doing the things that I'm responsible for. I need to call those people who understand the 'abuse stuff' and what it is like to be an ex-problem drinker. I need the willingness to help others. I need to allow Shaun to be his own person. I need to pay closer attention to taking care of myself.

SAME DAY : I have a stronger willingness to adapt and accept my position in Townsville. I'm willing to make friends in and out of the meetings. I'm willing to participate in social activities, for example; going to the footy, swimming, dancing classes, courses and working. I'm willing to allow myself the time to gather myself so I can do all of this.

SAME DAY : I remember thirteen months ago returning to my Hometown (keep in mind I was using all possible addictions other than alcohol) I was fearful. I was doubtful about returning to Brisbane. I longed to be with my loved ones, the people I've known all of my life. I went to the twelve-step recovery meetings. I received support from my family (emotionally and financially). I sounded out my fears, my confusion at the time, my pain and my mistakes with them. A week later I felt a strong desire to return to Queensland and to give living there another go, knowing I could return to my Hometown at any time I wanted. The idea of returning to Queensland meant returning to the disaster of having no sponsor, no home, and no money to pay off the car. I had no money to pay the rent and food. It also meant returning to the telemarketing job that I absolutely hated, and having to face the guy I was dating at the time (I knew I had to let him go). I knew that my travelling girlfriend was not coming back to Queensland after visiting her family in Western Australia. The only thing I had and the only reason why I returned to Queensland was because I had met some people in the Fellowship there whom I sensed to be genuine. I remember their laughter, their honesty and their open conversations, the likes of Graeme and Maree. I wanted those experiences back in my life. So I returned to Brisbane.

My last drug use was on the trip back to Brisbane on the 4th of January 1998. I felt sad to leave my parents, yet excited about what was going to happen. It took me a while before I let go of my disastrous situation. God was my grounding and I knew He was with me every inch of the way. Maree came my way when I spoke to her about sponsorship and she asked if I wanted her to be my sponsor—and that is what she became to me. I truly practised Step Three—turning my will and life over to the care of a Power greater than myself, when Maree directed me back to my heart and I quit the low paying job in telemarketing. At the time I desperately needed that money and I needed somewhere else to live because I couldn't afford keeping the rental for a two-bedroom unit on my own. My car was in the repossession process and the only reason it didn't get taken away from me earlier, was due to the fact that I had to get it repaired. A week later after leaving my shitty job I had a full time job as a sales assistant in a clothing store and a part time waitressing position. I ended up paying $200 per week off my loan (which I did for another six months to catch up to my regular payments of $100 per week). As for the guy I was seeing, I dumped him and moved in with his sister, Helen and her twelve-month-old daughter for $25 per week. From there, my life continued to turn around and the faith grew from putting in the action first.

Things were happening beyond my imagination and were not in my control. I experienced blessings, tears, resting time, fun in the sun, and courageous moments of confronting my past to clean it up. I allowed myself to be myself at meetings, to be me with my Mum.

I went through a process of letting go the built up resentment I felt towards my oldest cousin, Eugene. I let go of the shame I carried by sharing my deepest darkest secrets with Maree, by doing the Fourth Step, by taking stock of my thoughts and actions. Step Five followed where I admitted my wrongs to someone. I felt the hope of recovering from my illness that corrupted my spiritual, mental and physical health. I gave up smoking after repeating out aloud the Sixth Step; ready to have my Higher Power remove those things I do that I shouldn't. I let go of drinking coffee and found within myself a 'quietness' that I described at the time as being 'dull' and 'boring'. It was a touch of peace and serenity. Peace and serenity washed over me by doing this work with Maree.

I continued to go to meetings, visited my therapist on a weekly basis, was able to be intimate with men and I found a balance with my eating. This way, I came to understand my feelings, take responsibility for my actions, and for myself. I'm to remove myself from the children when I have too high expectations either on them or myself. I had to learn my limitations, to ask for help, to be kind to myself and to do things that were fun for me.

I went to the AFL matches with Clarke (a friend), abseiling with my girlfriends, Latin dancing, swimming, fishing, kicking the footy, eating sushi and ice cream, going to the movies, kissing a gorgeous man, dancing to RMB music by myself, being swamped by the waves at the beach. I allowed myself to cry, to be cradled in Maree's arms shaking and moaning from intense emotional pain. Oh, it does sting when I let someone in my heart.

Don't forget the insanity prior to finding some kind of balance with my eating. I used to over-eat, binge and stick my fingers down my throat. I was crazy, I ate and ate non-stop for a whole week and I only had half an hour of relief from it. Wow, I don't have that today. Touching and kissing and being with Shaun, 'Is that what love feels like?'

Oh, but he stinks and he has a big nose and he wants to marry me. "Go away you bastard, Mr Nice Kind Supporting Caring Creature." If I walk away now I might regret it, yeah, but I know what my head is telling me and it's loud and clear. Oh, the fear and his penis!

I'm ugly but beautiful, a relief to be able to see that Shaun is handsome, loving and intelligent and I can't believe I came through that. I left the nanny job that was too demanding, working all week with four kids for only $500.00 without a break or rest. I lived with Shaun and then Shaun left. I left Brisbane to be with him, and then both of us came to a crash, and I'm back in Brisbane with things to look at within myself.

I'm on a couch, with Beethoven playing in the background, after coming home from a women's meeting. I'm allowed to feel what I feel today. I understand that God's got my future in His hands. I know what will be, will be. I know I am safe with Him. I know my God's a loving God. I can see the stuff I've come through and where I've come from. God is my God and no one else will replace Him. I want to go to Townsville as God will be there too. I can return for two monthly visits to Brisbane to be with the strong support I have here.

I have my heart set on swimming in Townsville and working with the children. I envision driving to meetings surrounding Townsville, as well as staying in touch with my support in Brisbane, my Hometown, England and Melbourne. I want to learn new things with my God and my boyfriend Shaun. Let's have another go, let's modify some things - yes - if that's what you want to do. Keeping in mind it's a day at a time, tomorrow will bring new challenges and I can sound out with others (Maree) and primarily with Shaun. If Shaun changes his mind or doesn't like the idea, then that will shift me another way. If the opportunity still stands in three to four weeks time then I'm willing to give myself the permission to go back home to Townsville. Within that time I will see my therapist and continue talking to Shaun and sounding out to Maree. I can ask Shaun's friend, who's in the employment industry, to keep her ears open for jobs relating to children and courses that might be available for me to inquire about. I can continue to go to meetings to help others and myself, understanding that things may change my course of direction. I'm to keep it simple, enjoy my time off, stay in constant contact with God and pray for God's will and not mine. I'm to allow myself to know myself and know what I want, and that's to let go of the idea that Maree and her husband and my therapist are my parental figures.

Am I to go to Melbourne and/or go to my Hometown for a week?

The positives are: I will get the time to spend with my parents and with my dear friends. I'll have a week off to do what I want to do. I'll get the opportunity to go to the AFL football matches.

The negatives are: it will cost me all the pennies I have saved to put towards moving back to Townsville. I'm aware I'm feeling fragile and I will not be around people that know and understand abuse if I go to Melbourne. I'll miss Maree and the possibility of seeing my therapist if an appointment arises while I'm gone. It feels too much to cope with. If I go to Townsville I must be able to attend regular meetings with my therapist and have a budget in place. Am I willing to travel from Townsville to Brisbane? Perhaps I could on a fortnightly basis. The train will cost me $120.00, which is only $60.00 a week. If I go by plane it will cost me $365.00 with two-hour travel, which is expensive. If I travel by car it will only cost me $100.00 and eleven-hours of travel, which is a lot of time and stress. Is it really worth it? Do I want to be with Shaun enough to travel so frequently to get therapy? Is therapy that important? Either I live in Townsville and have fortnightly appointments for an hour a week with my therapist or live in Brisbane and have regular visits to see Shaun in Townsville.

Twelve Years Later...
Going within revealed that in moments
which I didn't understand or accept
myself, I valued and understood in time

OLD THOUGHT: I have to please others to keep them in my life
NEW THOUGHT: Saying no says yes to freedom

I was afraid of people and of them telling me or governing what I do. I figured out I would work out how to stay sober by myself with the help of a few meetings and reading the text book from the fellowship which illustrated how to work the program. To my great disappointment, after six months of working out how to recover from alcoholism by myself, I was faced with having my car repossessed, unable to keep up with the rental costs or the utilities living alone in two bedroom flat, suffering from paranoia and agoraphobia which left me unable to leave the unit to go to the corner shop for milk. I had court orders from the State I escaped from chasing me for unpaid speeding tickets, parking fines and unpaid dental and hospital bills. I was simply unable to manage my life. I knew I had come to the end of that experiment when I thrust myself to and fro against the hallway walls, screaming inside my head, clenching the hair on my head. I was in agony from realising I could no longer live in isolation from others. I had come to the end of all my resources and had to admit I needed help. I thought this was the end of my life as I understood it, but in fact, it was the beginning of a life I had never even dreamed existed.

There was a woman I had observed for some time at the meetings. I felt she meant every word she said. I felt she was a person who actually walked the life she talked about and I really admired that quality about her. I needed to take action in my life, and make some tough decisions. I felt she would be able to show me how. I approached her at a meeting to catch up for coffee and I asked questions about sponsorship. She very kindly offered me her time to sponsor me, which saved me from actually asking. I was terrified of being rejected and humiliated had she said no. Phew!

Maree was absolutely wonderful to me. She took the time to share her own experiences, her newfound strength and her ongoing hope. She took the time to talk about her concept of God and to help me find my own concept of God. She took the time to talk about the difference between believing in a Higher Power and acting in faith in that there is a Higher Power. She fed me, gave me her clothes that she no longer wanted, she lent her car when I couldn't afford to put my own car on the road (the direct result of my drinking) and spent many hours with me to show me how she recovered from the disease of alcoholism. She lifted my soul when she spoke of us growing old together, that she would witness my future marriage and my future children. I felt loved and wanted. I felt I had found a true friend. I adored her and respected her deeply.

In quiet desperation to keep Maree in my life I agreed to something, which I felt somewhat uncomfortable about. It was early in our sponsor/sponsee relationship when she gave me an ultimatum. She would not sponsor me if my Mum were involved in helping me understand the disease of alcoholism and the program of recovery. My understanding of what a sponsor was at that time was that she was 'an ex-drunk helping out another ex-drunk.' My Mum was an ex-drunk wanting to help me out, and Maree didn't feel comfortable with that. She was entitled to feel and believe what she felt and believed at the time. I do not believe she is wrong for how it was for her. However, what did I believe and what did I do? I didn't want to lose Maree—I needed her support. I was afraid of losing her at a time when I felt most dependent.

I knew my Mum would always be my Mum; she wouldn't abandon me because I am her daughter. But had I followed what felt true to me at the time, I wouldn't have chosen her as my sponsor. I couldn't bear not having Maree as my sponsor and that such a loss would be absolutely disastrous. I didn't know then that, had I listened to my feelings, I would have realised that they were worthy of my trust, that they mattered, and that they were a great guiding force in my life.

Instead, I set the relationship up at that point to lean on her for everything. She wasn't comfortable with me going to others. I was to go to her because, without her, I was sure to get caught in the trap of only listening to what I wanted to hear and not what I needed to hear. That was perhaps something to be mindful of, however, it was not healthy for me to depend on one person to help me. I put her on a pedestal and I made her my little god and accepted her word as the only word. She alone had the right word and her words were greater than mine. I opened the door to being told what to think and how to act. I was to do what I was told to do and to believe that her words were the only truth.

It was a miracle that I was able to follow what felt right for me when I knew she wouldn't be happy with what I decided. It was the first time I knowingly and decisively made a decision against a person I had allowed to dominate me. It went against everything she believed I should be doing. And then, almost predictably my greatest nightmare was upon me! Wham! She dumped me. OUCH!

When I shared with her how I felt about Shaun pressuring me to be sexual with him when I didn't want to be, she encouraged me to be sexual with him and to allow myself to be loved. I took on what she said as the truth and believed I wasn't loving myself because I wasn't allowing myself to be sexual with a man I didn't want to be sexual with. I took her word for it and looking back, I now believe I was being guided to dismiss my own instincts and be sexually active regardless of how I felt. Today I believe this to be abusive toward myself by not respecting or accepting my feelings. I didn't feel comfortable being sexual with Shaun. Full Stop. I came to hate Shaun at the end of our relationship because of it. I lost all sense of self by trying to be sexual with him when I didn't feel comfortable about it. I now understand there was nothing unloving toward myself for not wanting to be sexual with someone whom I didn't feel comfortable being sexual with regardless if they are my boyfriend or not.

Shaun had told me he wasn't in love with me anymore: that he was in love with his ex-girlfriend. And when he changed his mind about that, he then encouraged me not to be with him for another couple of months during which time I had nowhere to live! Maree told me Shaun had jumped to the next level in the relationship and that I hadn't. I felt at the time this was not true for me.

I expressed to Maree I was feeling the need to go back home to be with my family, two states away, for a couple of weeks. Maree told me I was being a rebellious teenager or a little girl – telling me "You're running away". Maree told me I was not going to be safe anywhere else but Brisbane and that I would really struggle without my psychologist.

Had I not relied so heavily upon her, or placed so much importance on what she believed, these words would not have affected me so greatly. I accept full responsibility for this situation because I made a choice to only listen to Maree. By doing that I willingly entered into a relationship of dependence on one person and for that, I am responsible. If I had chosen to follow what I believed I would have begun creating relationships where I'm free to talk to whomever I choose. I would not have relied only on one source for my answers, nor would I have accepted being governed by another human being. It was a relationship where I was told what to do and was judged accordingly. Boy oh boy, some things take me a while to work out.

I also failed to share with Maree how I felt about what she was saying to me. I failed to share with her that I was not comfortable with being judged as a 'rebellious adolescent' or 'a little girl'. I failed to share with Maree how I felt disrespected and hurt by her comments, nor did I appreciate her telling me I was 'running away' from a situation. It wasn't up to her to make that judgment.

She didn't seem to believe that I had any capacity to know what I needed to do. I was silent about how devastated and distressed I felt that she dumped me the minute I chose to do something she didn't agree with. When Maree no longer wanted to sponsor me it was only natural that I would feel afraid, lost and vulnerable. I hadn't built any other open and honest relationships with others and all I was left with were her words, which were no longer serving me well. I had agreed to be dependent upon her for all my answers and when she didn't agree with how I felt and thought she abandoned me. However, by saying no to her I discovered new freedoms, the freedom to do what felt right for me.

OLD THOUGHT: It's weak & hurtful to tell others how I really feel
NEW THOUGHT: It's honest & real to share with others how I really feel

I have observed that in any relationship I have with others, I tend to avoid being open and honest should I feel hurt, threatened or harmed by them. This often turns out to be very unhelpful because not only does it help the other person know me a little more if I open up but it can also uncover mistaken ideas or thoughts I may have had.

I was too afraid to let Maree know how I really felt because I did believe at the time and for many years afterwards that to tell her about the times I felt hurt would make me look weak and what a bitch I would be if I hurt her feelings in this way. It didn't serve me very well by holding back the truth about this. I continued to stay resentful, feeling unimportant and inferior and worst of all when we did communicate from time to time I felt like a fake. Yuck!

With the help of reading 'Conversations with God', I realised it is okay to communicate with someone about any disturbances I may feel whether it is great or small or whether it happen yesterday or twelve years ago.

I wrote a letter to Maree sharing with her those things I felt grateful for, those things she did for me during a vulnerable time in my life. I explained to her that I had come to realise I had been unable to honest and open with her due to the fear of being weak and for hurting her however, understanding now I had only been hurting myself. I did mention at the start of the letter that what I was going to share with her was to be about my thoughts and feelings in hope that she might relate to them in some way to better understand me. I wrote about how I had harmed myself by agreeing for her to sponsor me with the understanding others could not. I explained how I made that decision to keep her in my life however it set me up to depend only upon her. She had become my authority the person with all the answers and the only person I would open up to. I explained that when she no longer wanted to sponsor me I found myself alone and afraid, as I had not created other relationships where I could turn to for love and support. Having put her onto a pedestal I had opened myself up to being judged and told what to do and if I didn't do what I was told I was criticised or viewed in a negative light. I shared with her how I came to understand my silence over the years was linked closely to the old need to gain emotional security through her approval. As the result I experienced feeling unimportant, dismissed and dominated. In the letter to her I took the opportunity to take full responsibility for all the decisions I made at the time and those I made along the way to stay silent in fear of being weak or hurtful. It was a freeing experience to be honest and real by letting her know how I really felt.

Guess how long it took me to share with Maree how I really felt! If you guessed 12 days, 12 weeks or 12 months, you guessed wrong. If you guess 12 YEARS later - you would be right! 12 YEARS! That's about 4,380 days later. Quick aren't I! I'm such a guru when it comes to relationships! LOL. I've learnt to accept that sometimes it just takes as long as it takes to work things out. My life is a lifelong process of deciding on how to live life! No wonder this book took what seemed forever to finish! You guessed it – it took 12 years and you know how many long and weary days that is! LOL! Maybe the book should be called 12 years to stuff up and make up!

Maree's reply was warm, understanding and compassionate. I realised it took me twelve years to build up enough courage to believe I could trust that I could handle a possible negative response from her and still believe I was okay. However I received a loving and respectful response and my heart went 'ahh...that feels better'. You could say I have found my Sacred Voice!

SACRED CREATIVE FOCUS
WHAT ARE MY THOUGHTS?

My thoughts can have the power to create how I feel. The question is; are my thoughts being checked or are they running a-muck around in my head causing emotional chaos in my heart? I had so many thoughts, some were quite fearful and self-hating and I wasn't at all happy with the way my thoughts were controlling how I felt about others or myself in my life.

My old thoughts can stop me from growing, doing new and wonderful things. These unchecked thoughts can hold me back from being my true and authentic self. I've noticed two things that can happen with my thoughts 1) I can't stop a thought from appearing in my head and 2) sometimes I can't seem to stop these kind of thoughts or pictures going around and around in my head. When I yell at these thoughts to stop or criticised these thoughts it seemed to give these old thoughts more fuel to really carry on and run a-muck. As the result of making a decision to be willing to check in with my thoughts I discovered a few ways in which I can work with them rather than against them to quiet them down a little.

Firstly I thank my old thoughts for sharing. I believe these old thoughts obviously think they are being very helpful, and I guess in the past they were. They stopped me from taking risks I wasn't ready to take. It's been helpful to acknowledge them, either through sharing them with others, writing them down or expressing them creatively through art to see what I'm dealing with. It's time to assess these thoughts. Are my thoughts like warning flags letting me know there's something going on with my life or within me, which needs attention or action? It's good to know if my thoughts are letting me know to put a pause in before I leap into something which might not bring about a great result.

Oh and then there are those magical thoughts that think of the best stuff - ideas! My thoughts have the power to create. I know this because as I look around me and see people's gardens, smell delicious hot bread at the bakers and notice every thing and object that isn't nature made has been created out of thought. My thoughts create too and the more I nurture those thoughts of creation; creating peace, love, happiness, joy in myself, in others, my relationships, the home I live in, the more my mind enjoys creating. Tapping into my creative mind, following it, trusting it and then living it creates happier living. There's a time to nurture my thoughts, challenge my thoughts or give some thoughts love to let them go to be able to pay attention to see where my creative mind desires me to be instead.

SACRED CREATIVE ACTIVITY

As I reflect upon the thoughts I've been thinking about throughout the day I cut out words and/or images (from children's books, magazines, newspapers etc) and paste them onto the paper. I might like to write words or draw images around the cut outs as well if I remember things I have or others have said or done which I've thought a lot about. Or perhaps I've played out past or imagined future scenarios or memories in my mind. I can do the same creative activity in a slightly different way by painting, sketching or drawing what I've been thinking about throughout the day. Once I've finished I ask myself, 'How has my thinking make me feel today?' Perhaps on the same piece or on a separate piece of paper I can write down how I felt at the time with the different thoughts I've had throughout the day.

SACRED MEDITATIVE ACTIVITY

I close my eyes and imagine there's an old typewriter on a table. I walk toward the chair in front of the typewriter and I sit down onto the chair. I take a few deep breaths and as I do I allow myself to become the typewriter. I remember the thoughts I've had over the week or throughout the day and I begin typing those words and let them flow naturally and easily onto the piece of paper. I imagine typing one word at a time. As I do this, I imagine I am now the piece of paper. I'm a piece of paper and I feel the words being typed on me being massaged by the words being typed on it. My new purpose, now that I am a piece of paper, is to stay very still and reserve any opinions or feelings about the words being typed onto me. I am now happy for the words to just be there. Can I allow the words to just be there without the need to judge or criticize or react to them, even if it is for only three seconds? Just right now I will not judge my thoughts that have been in my head. They are having no effect. They are just words, like an alphabet floating around in my mind flashing by for a visit. It is up to me to either let them move in as a permanent boarder, or let them leave after a short stay as a guest to my house would.

COMMITMENT STATEMENT

I .... am willing to put aside everything I think I know about myself, my life, my past, and my future, in order to have an open mind and a new experience with my thoughts. I am open to the possibility of becoming aware of my thoughts, receiving new thoughts, and living a new life.

CREATIVE SPACE

WHAT DO I THINK & FEEL ABOUT MYSELF?
WEEK FIVE : WHAT ARE MY FEELINGS?

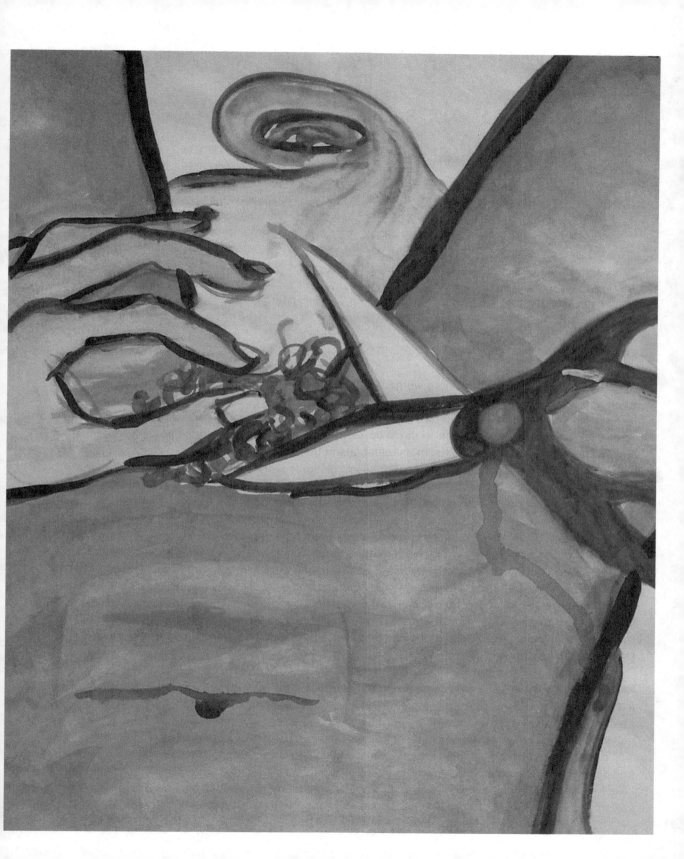

INTRODUCTION TO THE SACRED SHARING

I CALLED MAREE FROM GRAEME'S HOME TO TELL HER I WAS GOING BACK TO MY HOMETOWN BY TRUCK FOR A WEEK'S HOLIDAY. SHE DIDN'T LIKE THE IDEA AND INFORMED ME THERE WAS SOMETHING SHE WANTED ME TO TELL ME WHEN I RETURNED A WEEK LATER. OF COURSE I WOULD NOT BE ABLE TO WAIT THAT LONG, SO I INSISTED SHE TELL ME WHATEVER IT WAS SHE WANTED TO TELL ME. SHE SAID THAT SHE DIDN'T WANT TO SPONSOR ME ANYMORE. HER COMMITMENTS WITH HER FAMILY AND CAREER HAD BECOME A PRIORITY AND SHE HAD TO LET ME GO.
GRAEME DROVE ME TO THE TRAIN STATION, WHICH WOULD TAKE ME TO THE TRUCK I'D ARRANGED TO DELIVER ME HOME. I CRIED ON THE TRAIN. I DARED NOT CRY IN FRONT OF THE TRUCK DRIVER. WITH ALL THE OVERWHELMING GRIEF WITHIN ME I FORCED THE TEARS NOT TO RISE TO MY EYES. I DIDN'T WANT TO EXPLAIN MY SADNESS TO THE TRUCK DRIVER AS I DIDN'T WANT TO DUMP MY STUFF ON HIM—SO I WAITED TILL I GOT TO MY MOTHER'S. SHAUN RANG TO SAY HE WANTED TO GET BACK WITH ME.

ANOTHER DAY : Abandonment, here we go. I'm trying to trust Shaun again after him telling me only a week and a half ago; "I love my ex-girlfriend." He says it was because he was afraid and now I have Maree telling me she can no longer be my sponsor. How rejected do I feel? How do I keep strong through all of this? Shaun doesn't want me to move up to Townsville for another two months. Fuck them all. I feel (my head tells me) it's because I'm untreatable and that only my therapist in Brisbane can help. My head tells me I'm too much for everyone. Because I disagreed with Maree I feel it's my fault; I caused her to choose not to be my sponsor any more. She says it's me who didn't jump off to the next level and that Shaun did in our relationship. Only last week she said I jumped to the next level and Shaun didn't. She says I've been only talking therapy with her and not the program of recovery and I agreed she was not my therapist. I feel lost and totally unaware of who I am but everyone else can see it plainly. I didn't think I was doing that badly. I was going through a lot of stuff when I was living in Townsville. It wasn't my fault. Shaun said he loved another woman. Yes, everyone thinks I'm wrong, 'everyone' being Maree, her sponsor and my therapist. It feels like I'm using drugs and alcohol and everyone knows but me. I feel personal securities have been ripped out from underneath me. I fear things are going very bad. I fear losing it. I fear picking up a drink or abusing myself. I am very afraid. I feel wrong for going back to my Hometown and Melbourne. I'm picturing being at the train station and getting on a truck to travel home, taking 24 hours of travel to get there. Fuck you all.

ANOTHER DAY : Well, last week Maree dropped out of being my sponsor and, yeah, it's been hard. I've felt abandoned and angry that she left me when I was the first person she started to help one on one. So I believe there are unspoken reasons why she's chosen me to leave the coop. I reckon it's because she no longer had the answers for me (from her point of view) as I was disagreeing with her.

I don't regret returning to Victoria. Being with my Mum and Dad, being in Melbourne, I feel welcomed and comfortable. I've noticed that my rotten old stinking ideas are shifting. I can seek other's help here. I like having my choices back again, choices that feel right for me. I have her, Maree's, voice in my head saying: "You're in denial, you're the one who hasn't jumped to the next level, you're being a rebellious teenager or a little girl" or "You're on the run," etc. Since Sunday just gone I've been feeling internally free, relaxed, at ease and comfortable. I've let go of the idea that I know what to do and how to manage my life. Just for today I'm in Melbourne at a girlfriend's house and looking forward to catching up with other mates I haven't seen in eighteen months.

ANOTHER DAY : I haven't got anyone to talk to who is able to help direct me back to my heart and my truth. I used to have Maree and I haven't called her as yet. I'm too afraid. Afraid to tell her how it is for me and afraid of her saying that I'm going the wrong way. I didn't go back to Brisbane to see my therapist. Am I being a fool?

I feel nervous and anxious today. I feel alone and lost. I'm at Aimee's house and there are lots of people I could visit here in Melbourne. I could go back to my Hometown or Melbourne. I'm not feeling welcome in Townsville. I don't have a base, a home. The only secure thing in my life is God. He is with me always holding my hand. But where do I go? Today I'm going to a twelve-step recovery meeting. I've only been to one this week. If someone looked in on me they would say: 'You're not on safe ground.' I came to Victoria for a holiday and time away to see my family and friends, which I see as a good thing. I'm dealing with losing Maree as my sponsor and having mixed messages in my head about why. I think, 'Is it me? Is it because I'm fucked up and I can't do this on my own? Who do I turn to now? If something doesn't happen soon I'm going to die."

I'm afraid about the direction my relationship with Shaun is heading. I know he loves me. I know he is doing what he can to organise things in Townsville. What I don't understand is how he will not compromise with regard to his family. If there were a decision to be made between them and me he would choose them. He said that to me and it fucking scares me. It makes me feel second best. That means it feels dangerous being with him and therefore I cannot be with him. Is it too much to ask of a person? If a family member asked for something that involves me or would affect me, Shaun would not consider me in his decision making process because he feels obliged to do what he can for his family. It makes me feel insecure because I'm not a girlfriend to him where his family is involved.

Do I stay here in Melbourne for another couple of days feeling insecure, lost and frightened? Or do I go home where I can feel safe? I don't know. I don't know anything other than to pack up my stuff and get to the twelve-step recovery meeting in the city and see how I go from there. Another feeling I'm getting is that I'm coming to understand Shaun isn't enough. I mean, going to Townsville to be with Shaun is what people would do when they are in love. I'm someone who needs more than just one person to love. I need good twelve-step recovery meetings, a therapist, a sponsor, a support group, my friends and family.

Am I being realistic in my expectations? Is Shaun secure within himself to be with me? If he is unwilling to change, then what am I doing? If this man wants his family he can have them. Do I leave him because of this? Am I over-reacting? Something is wrong and I don't know what it is exactly or what to do about it. I feel I need to speak to someone who can help me find my answer and a solution. Shaun's on a fishing trip today so I can't talk to him. The girl he is staying with doesn't like me and makes it very clear over the phone with her grunts and moans. That puts me off giving him a call. I feel ill that Shaun chooses to stay with people like her. I hate not knowing what to do or what to think and where the hell this feeling is coming from.

ANOTHER DAY : Well, we just keep on moving. I could talk about Shaun but firstly I want to write about yesterday at the twelve-step recovery meeting. I was asked to share and I did my best. My uncle was there with his girlfriend. I spent the afternoon with them and it was great. My uncle has come a long way since the last time I saw him. He looks and sounds so well. I was overwhelmed with his insights and his ability to see things in a light I was blind to. He did not tell me what to do. There's been so much confusion in the past couple of weeks. He says I'm going well and that I'm just kicking off my shoes. He believes I'm coming to a change in my life and that I'm not resisting it. My heart has one answer and my head has many. I'm finding it difficult to go to my heart in relation to Shaun. This is so difficult. I feel like I'm in the waiting room while he organises things in Townsville. Things are falling by the wayside.

This morning he tells me his family comes first, oh how that hurts. Fucking hell, I can't afford to come second. He's willing to let me go because of his cultural ways and expectations of his family, regardless of the fact that his mother does married a priest who is unfaithful. She no longer speaks to her other sons. His cousin is married to a big drinker who runs riot in the family. His sister is in a physically, mentally, emotionally abusive relationship. I cannot see how they would be putting him first in their lives. The fact is I cannot feel second. I feel sad, lost, insecure, powerless, angry, sick and repulsed. Shaun is not willing to be any other way. He's fixated on how he sees things. How can I possibly find resolution? I'm willing to leave my home when he is not willing to leave his. I am not willing to be told by my boyfriend how things are going to be for me when his family are in need and my welfare, feelings and thoughts are to be ignored for the sake of being there for his family. Shaun said to me three weeks ago that he loved his ex girlfriend and now it's turned into 'I love my family.' So the man is not ready to move forward with me in our relationship. He's unable to move to the 'next level'. This is important because I need to organise and decide where I want my home and where I want to work. I feel I have to let him go. I cannot change him and he will not budge. He'll have to work it out for himself. He has God by his side just as I do.

I now have the willingness to call Maree's sponsor for help. There's no one else I can confide in or who could help me see and honour my truth. This is a big decision in my life, whether I chose to stay with Shaun and continue on that path or to leave him and do what I need to do on my path. I don't want to make any foolish decisions. Just for today I feel safe in confiding with Maree's sponsor. It feels too much at the moment living life on my own. I've been sounding out with many people and I'm becoming more confused and unstable. I have these tapes in my head. I have my therapist telling me to stay with Shaun because the idea of going to other men would be equal to running away from him. I hear my therapist reminding me to keep up the writing because food is my comfort and I need to write down my feelings. I hear him asking me: "Am I reacting to old feelings, or am I reacting to how I am feeling?"

ANOTHER DAY : I'm fucking feeling pissed off with Shaun. We're meant to be two people in a partnership. He asked me to marry him and now he's telling me I'm not enough to fight for. I'm doing all the work and he's doing nothing. His stubbornness makes me feel sick. I hate him for what he's putting me through and what he's telling me now. What a cunt! He's a selfish, inconsiderate fuck. He has no idea what he is doing to me. I want to fuck him off because of the shit he is putting me through. I left my home and now I'm wandering around bewildered and wounded. It's time I started to act on my life. He can do what he is doing but he can't have me because he is abusing me. He's not caring about me, only himself. Fuck him! I know that there are other men in the world that will put me first.

28/4/98 : I've just finished talking to Aimee and reading my morning daily meditations. It has come to my understanding that it is okay to let Shaun go. I do feel pain, sometimes it's less and sometimes it's more. I feel that Shaun is living in fear and living from his headspace. He's not ready to go to the next step; he said so himself. I need a man who knows he loves me and I need to know that I love him. I cry when I'm hurt. I laugh when I'm happy. I'm focusing on accepting the current situation and myself. I'm living one moment at a time getting on with my life.

I've spent the afternoon with friends of my cousins, sitting in front of the hot furnace. I jumped into the outdoor spa for two hours. It was great. I miss Shaun and sometimes wish things were different. Trusting in God is very important to me today. I say to myself often that this is happening for my highest good and God doesn't take away what He cannot replace. I believe when someone loves you (fair dinkum) they do not let you go or leave you.

I believe God knows what is best for me. I believe all the things that I want I still don't know how to get, so I ask God to remove my self will. I believe I did the best I could do at the time and thinking I was too hard or demanding is not how to love myself. I feel softer toward Maree today. I feel unwilling to ring my nemesis to make amends with her so I get that I need to do so. I love my hair today. I love my body today. I like what I'm wearing today. I want to be kind to myself today. This is all I have and it is this moment.

ANOTHER DAY : Yesterday was a good day. I was able to feel excited about life, my future and accepting Shaun's decision of not wanting to be with me. I felt freedom within and expressed joy in my heart. I spent the day helping a girlfriend with her work. I used it as a way to be an instrument for God, a way to pay back my debt to society for the things I had stolen. I noticed my girlfriend was very hard on herself due to her high expectations. She was asking impossibly high demands of herself and I can see that her self-esteem relies heavily upon her job. She was self-beating and self-punishing. I could see myself in her, so I gave her words of understanding and how I can be. I shared with her how I go about being gentle with myself to do what is right for me and at the end of the day it's none of my business what others may say or think of me.

I feel sad today though; I went to bed feeling this way. I had dreams about Shaun last night—not something I normally do. Most of the time I find Jarod in my dreams. Shaun and I were watching a pornographic movie with many women and to my surprise I wasn't disgusted or shocked. I felt aroused and nudged Shaun to come with me to the bedroom. My intention was to have sex but I noticed the bed was dirty, covered with cobwebs and hair. I didn't feel excited any more. In the other dream I had I was trying to get Shaun's attention from the other side of the grass field. He was with some others and he didn't notice me and I wanted to be intimate with him.

ANOTHER DAY : I want to see Lee (Shianne's younger cousin). I want to say hello and see if he would like to spend some time with me. I like the man. He's grown up somewhat. He's good-looking, easy to be with and I have a hunch he's attracted to me. I want to feel like a woman. I want to feel I can be with a man and I want to give myself the permission to be. I want to keep my heart open.
I'm afraid I'll have to tell Shaun. In one way I want him to be hurt and jealous so he'll realise he's made a mistake. I'm afraid he'll react badly if I am involved with another. He may make it difficult for me to have my car returned to me from Townsville along with my other possessions. I'm afraid I'll shame myself if I get involved with Lee. I'm afraid I'm being selfish regarding Lee because I just want to be with him and if the opportunity arose where he wanted to kiss me I hope I would allow myself to kiss him back. I'm afraid

if that situation did arise I would react badly and shut down like the other times I have done so with him. We did have sex a long time ago, I was drunk and I panicked (like I do with all men). He pulled out, as I was frozen, unable to move.

Shaun got sick of my crying in Townsville. He hated how I wouldn't be friendly with his new friends. I wasn't supportive enough of him because I was struggling so badly with adjusting to Townsville and my new surroundings. I also see that Shaun perhaps needed to have some solid support other than me to talk to—someone who had some understanding about my recovery and sexual abuse.

I'm finding it difficult today to find acceptance. Today I've had a shower and put some nice clothes, lippy and mascara on. I've done my hair and my clothes are in the washing machine. I've tidied the bathroom and the bedroom. I gave the dog a pat and now I'm going to read a book called, 'In the Meantime'. I'm understanding and applying what I'm learning from the book into my life. The book makes sense to me and helps me focus on my life and my relationship with my God. It's helping me to accept and is teaching me how to look after myself 'in the meantime'.

ANOTHER DAY : What I have learnt from the moment Shaun entered my life....
I could allow myself to kiss someone and feel like a woman.
I gave myself permission to approach him.
I learnt it was safe to feel and be intimate with a man, sober.
I came to believe I was lovable for being exactly who I am.
I learnt it was safe to be me with Shaun.
I learnt that my head could make me believe something that is totally the opposite of how I feel.
I learnt a lot about myself, my fears, my boundaries, my limitations, my courage, my pains, my happiness, my softness and my love.
I'm powerless over my ex-boyfriend.
God only gives me one day at a time and I can only do what is given to me and what feels right.
I've learned I did the best I could do.
I've learned I can love deeply.
I've learned to love Shaun, God and myself.
I learned I could be attracted to beautiful souls.
I've learned I deserve to be loved.
I've learned I am enough.
I have learned I need a man who loves me without doubt.
I have learned I respect a man who is honest at any given moment.
I have learned I am attracted to a man who is humble, who is spiritual, kind, sensitive, loving, patient, courageous, tolerant, and a man who has a good heart.
I have learned I am okay and that I am still okay to make mistakes.
I have learned at times I can be very hard on myself, on my boyfriend and on God.
I have learned I am not perfect and that shaming myself is not how to love myself.
I have learned I am courageous.
I have learned how to have faith in a boyfriend.
I have learned how to trust.
I have learned how to feel safe.

I have learned that God will remove my love toward another if and when He chooses, for my highest good.
I have learned it is safe to feel angry.
I have learned it is safe to feel my feelings.
I have learned that separation from Shaun in painful.
I am waiting and looking forward to seeing how God loves me by what is about to happen.
God does not take away something without replacing it with something greater, something I can never imagine.
I have learnt to trust God even only a little bit, when the pain is deep and very painful.
I know God loves me and loves Shaun and this is happening because there are some things we both need to learn.
I know we are both hurting, we will find little treasures and we are in God's care.
I have learnt that I love Shaun and its okay to let him go.

6/5/98 : I just had to write this morning. I had a wonderful conversation with Shaun last night. We spoke for about one and a half hours about how each of us is going. We were able to be honest and open with each other. He was proud of me for cutting my pubic hair (something I've battled with since discovering that my girlfriends have been doing this for as long as they can remember). He knows it took a lot of courage and willingness to do it. I told him I'd kissed two men. I wanted to know if he had kissed anyone and he hadn't, which led him to ask me and, yes, I had. He initially felt happy for me because he knows it's been a hard thing for me to do in the past. Although he could see my growth he shared that he still felt jealous. I couldn't quite understand because he doesn't love me and that's why we are no longer together plus I believe I'm a lot of work to be with. Towards the end of the conversation I heard sadness in his voice and it broke my heart that he was hurting. I didn't know that he wanted to see how we would go until the end of the year. In saying that, I have needs too and, I don't want to wait around for another seven to eight months just in case he will love me again. I will be hurt if he didn't love me again. I imagine that he will not be able to hold off being with someone else because he now knows I have been with other men. He doesn't want to call me too soon in case of sending me mixed messages.

I'm allowing myself to move to Melbourne. My dad and cousin are happy to hear that. I'm very excited about settling there. I look forward to buying furniture, clothes and other things for myself. It's a sad time for both Shaun and I but it's also an exciting time because out of this will come understanding, self-growth, self-love, strength and a stronger trust in my God. I know God is directing this play. I trust that what is happening is for our highest good.

I'm still afraid of calling Maree. I have good intentions of repaying the plane ticket she and her husband bought for me to get me out of Townsville to Brisbane. I know she loves me more than the money she's lent to me. I don't want to justify to her why I've chosen to live here in Victoria and move to Melbourne.

It's a beautiful day and I'm sitting out the front of my Mum's house in the sun with the breeze whispering through my hair. I have had about five weeks off work and I've needed it. I'm looking forward to working with children again, having my own home and developing new friendships. I look forward to seeing my old mates, going to the footy, saving money, going to the theatre, going out to dinner and lots of dancing. I totally love the book: 'In the Meantime'.

10 /5 /98 : Well what can I say? The past couple of weeks have been a blast! I'm amazed with how I feel,

how I've been loving toward myself and how I have been looking after myself.

I got myself in a muddle with a guy called River. There was a big misunderstanding because I failed to tell him how I felt towards him before we went out. When I saw him at the nightclub I acted out old behaviour by flirting with other guys and running around the disco with my head cut off because I was feeling insecure, unworthy, lost and confused. My cousin pulled me aside to talk to me and asked if I was okay. I wasn't okay. I was ratty. Unfortunately I was not able to listen and hear what my cousin was telling me. He was trying to reach out to me. He was telling me that I was his sister and that he was going through a lot emotionally due to coming to terms with the denial about our grandfather. I'm not being very receptive. Could be a couple of reasons and perhaps I don't want to deal with it or I'm not able to help him, I'm not a psychiatrist. My cousin and I have spent more time together lately and my other cousin, Eugene has been calling on a regular basis. It's been lovely. Eugene even spoke about the sexual tension he feels around girls and about his life in general. He never discusses work because I have no idea what he's talking about. Aerospace engineering and I don't mix. I realised that I wasn't being honest or being myself on Friday night and I couldn't listen to Linus. I think it had to do with the unfinished work that I needed to put into action with River.

I approached River and told him I felt uncomfortable, confused and afraid that he was jerking me around. Oh…the relief I was given after having the insight of 'try to be real and honest, remember your program!' I ended up playing pool and going home with him. We kissed and caressed and I was able to have intercourse. It felt nice but weird. My head was quiet and I was enjoying it. Something did feel weird, maybe because it was Shaun I had been intimate with last and that was over a couple of months ago, perhaps because I wasn't shutting down. We didn't reach orgasm because I didn't want to continue with it. I'm glad I didn't continue with it and I'm happier he was okay for us to let it go without any hassle. With River it felt like I was chasing him. It's like that at the moment because I'm on edge a bit. A lot has happened to me and I want things to happen the way I want them to—and instantly. We left it at that and fell asleep. He dropped me off in the morning and I got on with things.

I had a wonderful time with the girls and their boyfriends. Reminiscing with them is so much fun. I found a connection and love with Aimee today. I found it very easy and natural to be with her. I felt sad that I didn't have a boyfriend. My girlfriend will be getting married in six weeks time and it reminded me that I too was once engaged. At the moment I'm aware that I need to slow down. It's difficult because inside I feel I'm racing so fast. I'm extremely excited and fearful, free and close to my God all at once.

I walked right up to Jezza by accident at the bar last night. It was like he was a magnet. It looked as if I knew he was there and I was making a deliberate approach. We talked about many things. I reminded him of the way he treated me in the past after he had disclosed his feelings towards me. He shared that he felt like a fool the next day realising that he had blurted out how he felt towards me, all at once. I told him that it hurt my feelings the way he brushed me off the last time we caught up at the pictures; he didn't speak or bother to follow up with seeing me again after that. I felt he was jerking me around and to my surprise he apologised to me for not following his heart and letting fear take control. We laughed about the whole occasion and I expressed how I've been attracted to him for over seven years. He was shocked; "You never told me that."

He returned compliments and told me that he too has liked me for a long time. He has difficulty in expressing what he wants to say. I'm willing to go forward with Jezza. He has always been the most beautiful looking man that I know. Yum. I haven't yet been able to know him too deeply and, come to think of it, any other man. It's always been about me and my development, my growth and my presentation. I learnt a lot about Shaun but really I was in it for me. I am so consumed with, 'Oh my God! Jezza's in my life again, I must not fuck it up, or he might run away.'

In all honesty I have no control over Jezza, whether he stays or goes. I feel my little girl resorting to old survivor behaviour, wanting to control the situation. I'm not being relaxed. I'm afraid of being me. I'm afraid of showing my unmended stuff and scaring him. My perception is that he has a lot of growth to go through, especially expressing his emotions. I watch how he looks relaxed, at ease and doesn't chase or rush. I'm so full on, forward and quick to move. He was enjoying the moment saying it was lovely to be talking to me, while I'm trying to bring closure on how he feels and what he thinks of me. My hopes of him being my boyfriend is right at the door; all he has to do is knock like he says he will and walk right in. I'm holding off my full emotions because in the past he's let me down so many times before. I'm waiting for him to put in some action. I want to tell him all I know, everything I'm feeling and all the things I picture.

River and Lee and every other man are scrapped, no man can come and sweep me away while there is a possibility of Jezza becoming willing to give us a go, a long held dream come true. But in saying that I can't imagine Jezza staying for the long haul, mainly because there is much to fear, too many feelings to feel and it will be a confronting experience to go through. That includes me as well. It's in God's hands and I will be disappointed and hurt if he runs away again or if I react instead of acting to solve.

SAME DAY
What I want...
I want Jezza to love me.
I want him to chase me, to woo me.
I want us to have a relationship.
I want us to love each other forever.
I want to be myself.
I want to be able to relax.
I want to be able to slow down.
I want to take it easy so I can enjoy what we have today.
I want to marry him.
I want him to reveal himself to me.
I want him to trust me.
I want him to see me as me.
I want him not to see me as a scary person.
I want him to stay.
I want him to call me.
I want to know who he is on the inside.
I want to know if we're compatible.
I want to know if we can be intimate emotionally.
I want to know if he desires me as much as I desire him.
I want to know if he wants the best for each of us.
I want the dream stage to turn into our reality.
I want to believe his words.

I want to be able to trust him.
I want to know if he's reliable.

Do I know how to get what I want? NO! 'God please remove my self-will and the idea that I know how to get what I want, without even knowing whether or not it's good or bad for me. Jezza is afraid and so am I. I feel I need to accept that all I have is today and, that at any given moment, to enjoy what I do have. I'm also reminded not to panic. It's okay to be me. It's okay to let Jezza be Jezza. I have no control over Jezza's path. I have power given to me in the now and all I know is, I really enjoy being with Jezza. I felt so peaceful and content with him on Sunday. I was able to change my old behaviour. We had intimacy and it was beautiful. I allowed him to feel me, take my undies off and to feel my womaness. I reached orgasm. Then I thought to myself that it's okay to let him have intercourse with me because I wanted to return to him the pleasure he had given to me. I believe it only lasted for a minute. It was warm, exciting and safe. I didn't feel the need to talk! We were both dizzy like we were when we first kissed that night. We lost ourselves when we kissed for the first time. We rubbed and brushed our faces ever so gently.

I will never doubt my attraction to this man. I did with Shaun. I want to be able to experience that kind of closeness with Jezza again. It was beautiful. I love being in his arms. He doesn't have a built up body like Shaun's (he's a professional athlete) and his penis is not the same size. I love Jezza's imperfections and his humanness. I feel okay with him. With Shaun I felt fat, awkward and unattractive when I was naked with him because I compared my body to his athletic body. I know that bodies fade with age and it's the soul that we fall in love with. My body feels right with Jezza. I don't want him to be taken away. I know the chance of us not being girlfriends is 98% because that's how life is. This is what brings me back to living in the moment, not to fear what is not here yet. Let go…let go.

12/5/98 : I've been obsessing in the past week and a half. I haven't stopped long enough to realise it's my little girl trying to get my undivided attention. My little girl was sad – the abuse done to her by Pop. I haven't cried about it for a long time. I knew it had to come up sooner or later because of my cousin coming through his denial. I cried for my cousin and my own loss of self, seeing all I have been doing since the abuse is surviving. I cried for the fear I felt most of my life and for hurting myself, doing to myself what Pop did to me. Once he finished I carried on with the shame, the lies, the resentment, self-hatred and the self-abuse, I did to myself what he did to me. When I fantasise it's about old men and using their force upon me. That is what was done to me as a child when I didn't have a choice.

I remember when Shaun left to go back to Fiji (where he lived at the time). A couple of days later I became very emotional. I let Shaun in close intimately. He touched my soul and my womaness.

I kissed Lee a couple of weeks ago but I was stiff and I couldn't relax and my body couldn't move. I then kissed River and I was more relaxed and comfortable and allowed myself to feel like a woman, to be touched and caressed. On the second occasion I was with River we had intercourse and that's all it was, intercourse. I didn't shame myself and I'm surprised I didn't shut down or mentally abuse myself. I didn't want to continue to bring on an orgasm with him because I realised I could be intimate with another human being and I didn't want to shut down and do it all at once. It was sticky and a bit yucky, for whatever reason I do not know. I haven't told Jezza of my sexual activity before being with him; it didn't feel appropriate at the time to bring it up. I will explain and inform him when or if the conversation leads to me needing to disclose it. I don't know if he would understand and I'm afraid of him thinking I'm a tart.

Maybe I am? I certainly don't see myself as one. I'm so proud that I've been able to do what I've done.

17 /5/98 : I better keep this short. I'm going to run out of pages in this journal. I've taken serious notice at my craving for a cigarette fix. My head nearly had me sucking on a fag. I'd only have one! NOT – I'm an addictive natured person. So, as I've slowed down from my busy day helping my girlfriend, who smokes, I know there is something nagging me and it has nothing to do with sucking on a fag. One reason I've thought of is: I have unfinished stuff regarding Maree. I haven't contacted her for at least five weeks. It's based on fear; fear of her knowing what's going on inside my head, fear of being wrong and fear that I should be doing something better. I don't want to tell her anything because it feels like I have to justify myself to her. I don't want to hear her judgements about me like she has done in the past. She tells me that I'm a rebellious adolescent, or that I'm the one who didn't go to the next level with Shaun, or that I'm not going to be safe anywhere else but in Brisbane or that I'm going to struggle without having my therapist in Brisbane. With Shaun I felt like a disease, a cripple, it was always me and my problems and always something I had to look at because there was something wrong within me. I experienced the most beautiful feeling of intimacy in all my life and it wasn't with Shaun…it was with Jezza. Hey, guess who said they didn't love me enough to further the relationship? It was Shaun, not me! Fuck, thank-you God for that.

You know I don't even know how long Jezza and I will continue our affections towards each other but not being with Shaun to be with Jezza for the couple of days that I've been with him is worth it. I will never look back and say: "Damn! I should've persisted with Shaun."

I'm so angry with Maree and I know the anger starts within me. She is not a perfect human being. I'm the one who put her on a pedestal of perfection, righteousness and parental stature, not her. I need to forgive her for not being able to be my sponsor. I need to forgive myself for not being able to know how to respond and handle the situation. I was very hurt, I felt so abandoned and unlovable. I blamed it on myself because I didn't agree with her ideas of, or for, me. I don't know, but it feels like I've attached Maree's voice to my bad destructive self talk, like transference. I know she loves me but I really don't want to justify myself to her. I would really like to write her a letter, but my head tells me she'll think, "Oh, she hasn't gotten well. She's too afraid to talk to me over the phone."

I must remind myself that it's none of my business what Maree thinks of me or says about me. It's about my truth and I need to clear things up for me, for my wellbeing. I am truly grateful for her care, love, support and friendship. This is my truth and I need to express this so that forgiveness can take place.

ANOTHER DAY : I had such a lovely morning with Jezza and his friends. I enjoyed it because I felt relaxed and comfortable with myself. I sang (to the best of my ability at the time). I know if I were being totally me I would've sang my heart out. Intimacy with Jezza was delicious, yummy, and warm and soft like marsh mellows. We felt so right together, like we had been waiting for this moment all our lives. It felt instinctively natural and I felt that he felt what I felt – right now I'm thinking of why I need to leave him. Thinking I'm to stop fooling myself and that what I need is a man who can and will walk a path with me and who can be consistent and reassuring.

He never came to me once on Saturday night and that worries me. I certainly had to practice patience but I felt awkward and less than second best. I feel quiet inside when I think 'Let him go.' I don't want to do all of the work involved in letting him go. I know he doesn't need me and I'm sure that's a healthy thing and I can certainly get on with my life, which I'm doing today. Although, for me, I know I want to get to know Jezza, go out together if that's what we call it; but I'm not receiving such strong cues from him. I don't want to have to like someone so much. I became obsessed today, a natural thing for me to do. I know I have the ability to shut up shop when I want to. I need to make sure I let him go for healthy reasons and motives, not because it's going to be hard work or that I'm afraid of being hurt badly.

There's one thing I know, Shaun and I were only meant to be together for six months and for that I am grateful. I was able to go through some deep stuff and he was strong and brave enough to help for that time. Living in Townsville with him was a warning alarm because I couldn't be sexual with him. I realised with Jezza that I didn't need to have an orgasm to be intimate. I thoroughly enjoyed being close and, while being in that moment with Jezza, I didn't want to spoil it with the stress of having to force myself to orgasm as I felt I had to with Shaun. I had to force my wiring with Shaun. I'd get resentful if I didn't reach my peak as I felt ripped off and like an object. I'd say to Shaun that I love the simplicity of holding each other, to kiss and feel close and slowly become excited. It never happened. He was too interested in getting his penis inside of me. Normal I suppose, but with Jezza we were able to simply kiss, rub skin, touch and feel each other for a beautiful length of time exploring each other's bodies. We slowly removed pieces of clothing off each other and it was so fucking pleasurable.

Shaun has a beautiful heart and he was put into my life for many meaningful and important reasons and I'm so glad I'm not with him today.

ANOTHER DAY : I feel Jezza and I will not last. It's only been just over a week and I feel he doesn't want me enough and, in saying that, deep down I feel I don't deserve him. I have fear that he's going to treat me badly. I don't like either of those fears. You see I want all or nothing. He's patient and he takes things in his stride. I know he too is afraid, but I feel like an enormous freak of nature. I have a lot to learn. Jezza isn't going to give me what I need to heal – I can't say that. He won't heal everything, only certain areas within me. He's so adorable; I have always said he's the most attractive man I have ever known on this planet. Now that I have been given a chance to get to know this person I've become so afraid that I'm going to hurt this relationship, scare it, force it, manipulate it and fuck myself over like it's a big joke on me. "It's a trick! Look out! God's going to fuck with you this time, as if He's going to allow you to be with this man! Say goodbye to him soon sweetheart. You're not good enough. Never have been and never will be. Wake up and smell the roses and start looking elsewhere."

What a joke! I know better than to listen to my head. All I know is that it was a pleasure to be with him on Saturday night and Sunday morning. I've experienced something lovely. Seeing that I couldn't enjoy sex with Shaun, because we were not meant for each other, I forced myself to be with him. There are many more beautiful things to come my way. My God is a loving God and He doesn't treat me, or speak to me, like that. Only I do and I let others do the same. Today it's not allowed. I deserve love and I'm allowed to be loved. God is with me right now. He loves me the way that I am. He has faith in me. We have a lot of work to do together. I am safe because I am with the one thing (a God) that knows my path and confirms I am safe. I turn my heart and my life over to the care of my God. I also pray for Jezza to stay on his path and I pray for guidance because the truth is that I don't know what God has in store. I trust that whatever happens, it will happen for my highest good.

Twelve Years Later...
Going within to know my feelings gave
me the courage to face seemingly
insurmountable difficulties

OLD THOUGHT: I can rely on others to never fail me
NEW THOUGHT: I can rely upon a power of my own understanding

I felt let down by Maree when she didn't want to sponsor me any more, however it turned out to be an extremely valuable experience, even though it was very painful and frightening at the time. I relied way too heavily upon Maree. It was impossible for her to be or stay as my little God. Maree was only human and therefore limited to how much she knew for me or could do for me and therefore couldn't always be there for me. And I found that out when she ended her role in my life to sponsor me, it was then I employed a new Power of my own understanding. I needed a something, which would help me through my fears, my loneliness, my doubts and my moments of indecision. I needed to rely on a source, which was unlimited, supportive, loving and reliable and available 24 hours a day.

When Maree let me go as being my sponsor I felt so vulnerable and afraid that I felt I couldn't go to twelve-step meetings, or leave my Mums where I was staying. I felt so insecure I was afraid I would pick up a drink of alcohol because I wasn't getting to meetings and I felt unable to reach out to others. Mum was really good to me, making room in her home to let me stay while I worked myself out enough to make some big decisions.

It occurred to me the power greater than myself as I understood it at the time was the only way to stay sober. That relying upon either another human being, or myself or just on twelve-step meetings – was not enough to keep me away from alcohol - however a power greater than myself could. I came to see it was this power greater than myself who could do this for me when I felt I could not. I knew I couldn't, because I had enough experiences when I drank that I couldn't be trusted to keep away from alcohol because I had a mental obsession beyond my control which would lead me to drink. I turned to this Higher Power for guidance, instead of relying upon a human being, in this case Maree, to find my answers for me. I began to rely on this infinite source of power and strength and I was slowly guided to what I needed to do next one step at a time.

I once more could face my insurmountable difficulties with courage at this time with a new director; a new guide, a new found strength – my Higher Power who became always available to me when others were not. When I felt lost, alone and afraid I could talk to this power of my own understanding. I can rely upon power, it is always with me, and guiding me through each moment I live, so long as I am willing.

OLD THOUGHT: I'm to do what others think is right for me
NEW THOUGHT: It builds my esteem to trust what feels right for me

I followed my heart to go back to my Hometown as I had a very strong feeling to do so, even though my sponsor said they didn't think it was right for me to go. When I arrived to my Hometown I organised to go out with my cousin at a local pub. During our conversation I mentioned to them about a memory I had of us when we were children. I had tried to talk with this family member before about the feeling I had about been sexually abused by my Grandfather but they didn't think that was right and didn't believe me and nor did they want to have a bar of it. However on this day I described my memory to my cousin how he forced me to touch him inappropriately. I explained to him that my psychiatrist in Brisbane believed it could have been copycat behaviour—that he may have experienced sexual abuse himself. If there's a word to describe his facial expression it would have been 'mortified'. He didn't question my experience. He put his beer down and told me we had to leave. We went back to his place and he told me about a family event we were at also when we were children, remembering that we were all swimming in the pool. He remembered how he saw underwater that my grandfather was touching himself in an inappropriate manner when around children. Yuck! This was the validation I needed. I had memories of that day regarding my grandfather, that he was behind me in the pool feeling sick sensing he was doing something he shouldn't have been doing behind me and this verified my feeling—that I wasn't making it up just because my feelings didn't match what he had thought previously!

I felt really sad to see him so sad and so distressed, yet I felt very relieved for the both of us. I felt good about trusting the feeling within me to return to my Hometown as it lead me to meet with my cousin to have a conversation which was very important to me and my recovery from someone else's sexual behaviour. Going home and having this experience also showed me that my feeling of being affected by someone's sexual behaviour was true and accurate - that sometimes my or others thoughts or mind doesn't know everything and that it is important for me to listen to my feelings. I do know what is best for me when I listen to myself, when I trust what feels right for me. If I had listened to my sponsor I would not have left Brisbane and would not have had the experience I believe I was meant to have. And if I listened to my cousin believing that I had made up my feelings about being affected by my Grandfather's and his sexual behaviour I would have missed out building my own esteem to know myself, trust myself despite what others think or feel is best for me. Following and trusting my feelings, and knowing what was good for me took time to develop. I needed courage to have confidence in myself to make decisions based on what feels right for me. I was rewarded with a more loving view of myself.

OLD THOUGHT: I'm messed up if I make mistakes
NEW THOUGHT: Making mistakes makes me human

When I said, "Oh my God! Jezza's in my life again, I must not fuck it up, or he might run away." I thought I had the power to frighten people's love away. I thought it was because I was messed up that I pushed others away from me. I didn't believe I could be loved as I was. I felt I wasn't normal, that I was a bit screwy, which my cousin liked to remind me from time to time. I thought if my cousin thinks I'm screwed up he must be right. I found it really hard to be myself because I was trying to hide my imperfections, which would leave me hopeless and messy due to how I talked to myself. I tried so hard not to be the way I was, but I was the way I was and because of that I was very unkind to myself.

I was unable to relax and embrace myself while I was so attached to have certain people in my life. My emotional security depended upon others approval and this lead me to be agreeable when I did not agree, or smile when I was upset or pretend I was okay with something when I was not. It was exhausting trying to not upset others. EXHAUSTING I TELL YOU!

Aiming for perfection is like aiming to touch a mirage and yet others I liked and loved didn't have to be perfect. They could make all the mistakes in the world and that was okay and understandable however if I made a mistake there was hell to pay. I believed I had to get myself right and perfect for someone to love me.

I believed others would leave or stop loving me if I made mistakes. My drive for perfection was an expectation beyond my ability and I didn't know it wasn't possible to be perfect. I couldn't be myself knowing the risk could be losing someone's love.

Can I really stop someone from leaving me even if I don't make mistakes? Well, in my experience, time and time again, people walked away anyway for whatever reason, perfect or not. Maybe the question should be, will I love myself when others will not or cannot love me? Oh, that's a hard question! However, when I have let go of depending upon others to make me feel okay, to validate my worth as a human being, I've been able to risk showing others who I really am, how I really feel or think. I'm able with the help of my understanding of a Higher Power to ask questions to clarify things I don't understand, or share about how I feel upset about something someone has said or done, or able to express having a different point of view. If I'm not leaning so heavily on others to love me and if I ask Life to give me the strength and courage to speak up it's so much easier to express who I really am with others. And the beauty about this is, that I begin to like and love myself more as I've come to accept making mistakes makes me human.

OLD THOUGHT: I'm bad because I think about sick stuff
NEW THOUGHT: I am lovable and okay

This is never easy for me to talk about. I know I'm not the only one who is uncomfortable to acknowledge or talk about sexual fantasies or thoughts, which I find disturbing and disgusting. I'm going to talk about it because some of the women who have read my journals before having them published have shared with me how relieved they were to know they were not alone with experiencing screwed up sexual thoughts like me. I must say it's a bloody relief for me too!

I mean how often in conversation with others do I talk about having sex with animals in my dreams! Not many! The shame I felt around this has been intense to say the least. What would people think of me if they knew my brain dreams about having sex with rhinos, elephants, dogs and so on and so forth? How romantic! NOT! EW! After one of these dreams I wake up feeling dirty, grossed out and very confused as to why I would be having these dreams. Rarely did I ever have dreams about having sex with an actual person! So, I felt abnormal, sick, perverted, disgusting and very bad. The first person I ever told was my first psychiatrist who reassured me it wasn't anything to be alarmed about that it had something to do with being affected by my grandfather's sexual behaviour.

I'd find myself fantasying being sexual with perverted old men, dominating me in a sexual abusing situation when I masturbated. When I was finished I felt confused, afraid and extremely ashamed and alone. I can only talk about it here now as I have because I know I'm not alone with this experience either. Interestingly enough the women who have let me know that they have had the same fantasies have also experienced sexual abused as children. It has been, for me, very healing to talk about these extremely painful and uncomfortable truths about myself with people I trust. Knowing I'm not alone in this experience I've come to believe I am not bad, disgusting or perverted. I've been affected by another's sexual behaviour and this is how it shows itself to me.

As time has gone on, as I have learnt how to like and love myself more, and like and love others more, these dreams do not haunt me as often. Actually I cannot remember the last time I had sex with an animal in my dreams. And also in this time I have had some dreams of being intimate with my partner, which I feel is a real change and a sign of growth for me!

Let me also say, while I remember that I have also felt very ashamed to admit I have fantasised having sex with women. I was afraid it might have meant I was a woman who was meant to be sexually intimate with women and not men, even though that concept has never felt or sat right with my heart or mind, where as it does for some women. I do not identify with women who love women intimately and so this kind of fantasy frightened me, leaving me confused and yuck about my sexuality. Once again hearing some of my friends having had the same experiences relieved me of feeling alone and terribly afraid. I don't completely understand it, I do however love and accept myself for how I have been whether I understand or not. It's been a long time since I have experienced these fantasies either, especially since I've come to understand and accept I am not wrong or bad.

I remember when I was a teenager around 17 years old, I was really frightened about my thoughts when I saw little children, especially little girls because I imagined what sexual things might have been done to them or could be done to them. I was afraid I must have been a paedophile to have such thoughts because why on earth would I think this way? I would feel sick to my stomach knowing I thought this way and try to block these images out of my head, but every time I saw a little person, BAM, the disgusting thoughts would be just there like I had no choice. I never desired to act them out so why was this, what did this mean?

It was soon after these experiences, for some unknown reason, my Mum shared with me about how those who have been sexually abused as children can imagine awful sexual experiences being done to other children. I didn't tell her my experiences and I didn't tell her how relieved I felt to hear I wasn't a paedophile and that there was a good reason for the way I was. Interesting, as I write this I have just realised this was around the same time when I had my first experience of feeling sick to my stomach when I saw Dad's hands. Years later I come to understand through the help and guidance from Dr Wilmot that it was perhaps my Dad's hands were becoming more and more like my grandfathers, old and wrinkly. Hmm...looking back now I can see I was slowly beginning to awaken to being affected by my grandfather's unacceptable sexual behaviour toward me as a child. It would have been 4 years later I would be able to look at the real possibility for the first time of being sexually abused by him.

So I have felt sick by what I have thought and fantasised about and over time I have come to believe I'm still lovable and okay regardless of these things.

OLD THOUGHT: I'm childish if I don't want to talk face to face
NEW THOUGHT: It's ok to communicate in ways I'm comfortable with

I was worried about Maree judging me because I didn't feel comfortable or ready to talk to her on the phone. When I said: "Oh, she hasn't gotten well. She's too afraid to talk to me over the phone," no doubt communication has been extremely difficult for me and hey it still can be from time to time. Sometimes I need time to work out what a problem might be. Sometimes I might know what is upsetting me, yet I'm not too sure how to deal with it. When I do work out I have a problem with something and I know it's upsetting me and I've dealt with it and would like to talk about it, it doesn't mean I have the words to express it. But when I do work out the words it doesn't mean I have the courage to communicate those words either. See what an ordeal it can be for me. This is where time is really handy. If I give myself some time to work it through, there is no rush; it can take the pressure off to enable myself to think more clearly.

Talking about my upsets with others, especially those I'm upset by can be extremely confronting for me. It may not be confronting for the other person. The other person may be a really good listener who shows great understanding and compassion, this however doesn't mean I will be able to talk either face to face or even on the phone with them. My own fears of rejection, or lack of confidence to be able to express my feelings can get in the way of being able to talk face to face or on the phone with someone. It may be ideal for others to always communicate in this way, however this does not mean it is always ideal for me. I on the other hand, find it at times, easier to write. When I write, I have the time to think about what it is I would like the other person to know about my feelings, thoughts and experiences without being interrupted or distracted by what they say, don't say or how they look at me or don't look at me. Also if the person responds by writing it also can give me time to digest what it is the other person is saying. Slowing the communication dialog down can help me work through what is being said or not said.

I need not give myself a hard time if others do not understand if I don't always feel comfortable to communicate in ways they feel comfortable. It's not wise of me to express my private thoughts and feelings with someone on their Facebook, Twitter or blog etc where everyone else can read it. If it is personal to me, then it needs to stay personal and not to unnecessarily invite others into my private conversations. I don't need an audience. I may consider writing my words on paper rather than in an email or text if I'm not sure if the person I'm writing to is someone I can trust absolutely. Or if I'm dealing with a bully who doesn't respond to being told directly what their doing or saying is not okay then communicating is not necessary and I would be better to block them, keep a copy of what they might have written/text to me, report it and delete them from my internet connections and/or phone etc.

The main aim was for me is to find a way to communicate to the people who matter to me and in a way, which is comfortable and safe for me to do so. I do the best I can with what I have rather than not at all. As my confidence has grown from taking the smaller steps toward being open and honest with others it's become easier to communicate face to face or over the phone - when I feel comfortable or when it feels right to do so.

let go of the people
let go of what happened
it still affects me and I feel
responsible for the men
who don't want to be with
me - I feel deeply. I hide
little - I give my feelings,
thoughts and ideas.
sensitive yet strong.

SACRED CREATIVE FOCUS
WHAT ARE MY FEELINGS?

It's important for me today to stop and know what I am feeling and accept my feelings just as they are—the good, the bad and the ugly.

There are many ways to help know what my feelings are. Some ways include: creating art, writing, talking to an understanding person, reading books, listening to music, or punching the shit out of my pillow when I'm feeling really angry. Oh, and the best way for me to feel sadness is to cry. If my tears are stuck in my guts and won't come out, being patient is helpful, but so is watching a really sad movie. My Dad likes to gently tell me, "It's okay to be sad," when he sees that I am. I usually cry when he says that!

One day a friend and I were talking about feelings and he asked me, "What do you think is the most difficult thing for your brain to work out?" I thought about it for a little while and then I told him that feelings were really difficult for me to recognise at times. And he said, "Yes feelings are the most difficult thing for the brain to process". Phew! Nice to know there's a reason why I need time to get my head around how I feel!

I give myself time if I'm unable to work out how I'm feeling about a certain thing or situation. Sometimes understanding how I feel comes to me when I'm listening to someone talk about a situation in their own lives, or when I hear a song in a movie, or when I am folding my clothes. It may be the next day, the following week or even some months before a penny will drop about how I feel. In the meantime if someone wants to know how I feel about something I'm not sure about, I simply say, "I'm still working that one out" or "At the moment it's still a mystery to me". I no longer have to force answers or work things out immediately. It's okay to relax, take it easy and let life provide me an intuitive thought, a relisation or new understanding about my feelings in time.

SACRED CREATIVE ACTIVITY

I feel many of my feelings inside my heart so drawing a heart makes sense for me in relation to this activity. I stop and notice how I am feeling and how I have felt throughout the week and throughout the day. I write down all of those feelings inside the heart shape. I refer to the Appendix for the 'List of Feelings' if I need help to describe what it is I am feeling. When I feel I have finished writing my feelings down I think write about what has being going on throughout the past week and throughout my day. I look at what I've created and see if it makes sense why I feel the way I feel having experienced what I've experienced throughout the week and throughout the day. Have I rejected some feelings, as they are uncomfortable to feel them? Have I acknowledged and rejoiced feelings of happiness?

SACRED MEDITATIVE ACTIVITY

For this week I shall stop and be aware about I feel at any given moment. I will do this when I am in the shower, on the toilet, driving my car, sitting in a waiting room, washing the dishes, or going out for a walk. I will stop, listen, and to my feelings without judgement, criticism or analysis for a few moments. Just feel how you feel. I shall just feel my feelings.

COMMITMENT STATEMENT:

I .... am willing to put aside everything I think I know about myself, my life, my past, my future, in order to have an open mind and a new experience with my feelings. I am open to the possibility of knowing my feelings, receiving new thoughts, and living a new life.

WHAT DO I THINK & FEEL ABOUT MYSELF?
WEEK SIX : WHAT ARE MY ACTIONS?

138

INTRODUCTION TO THE SACRED SHARING

I MOVE IN WITH MY COUSIN LINUS AND WITH HIS GIRLFRIEND PETUNIA. I START SMOKING AGAIN AND HAD SEX WITH A FEW GUYS DRIVEN BY MY NEED FOR AFFECTION AND ROMANCE. I KNOW SOMETHING IS NOT RIGHT BUT WHO DO I TALK TO ABOUT IT NOW THAT I DON'T HAVE A SPONSOR OR A PSYCHIATRIST TO SPEAK TO?

23/5/98 : I never called Jezza and he has not called me. I don't honour dishonest men. Jezza has the inability to be honest and be open with me. I am open for an apology from him and I would've been open for a phone call to let me know that he no longer wanted anything further with me. He's thirty years of age and unable to take any responsibility. He sees other women. I'm glad my feelings were true. I felt something was wrong.

Moving forward...Mum and I are getting my resume completed. I'm job searching tomorrow in Melbourne. I'm very keen and excited about moving to Melbourne.

I told my cousins Peter and Ian about our grandfather and they had no idea. Peter was sceptical and not interested. Ian wanted to know more, it made sense to him, it explained to him why his father is the way he is. I had lots of fun dancing and mucking around with my cousins.

I went home with Lee (Shianne's cousin). He was horny. I kept shutting down. I felt cheap because I enjoyed intimacy with Jezza and felt sad to let him go. I'm jumping from man to man for a fix. My food has increased in the past four days and I've had two cigarettes in the past week.

Linus, Mum, Dad and I were talking and we all spoke about our past with one another including the marriage break up of Mum and dad. Linus walked out twice. I'm tired and hurting about Jezza. But it was an amazing experience talking to Dad about Pop and the secrets of the sexual abuse. More importantly, Mum walked up to Linus bawling her eyes out saying sorry for the pain she had caused him as a child. I thought Linus was going to push away with anger but he embraced her with tears. I felt so uncomfortable. Dad pulled me up to join them. First I pulled away and then Dad gave me a look I've never seen before and I knew I couldn't back down on this one. So, reluctantly, I went and joined in the group hug where we all cried in each other's arms for the break down of the family and the years of unspoken pain that we had all carried. I was aware that Eugene wasn't there and how I wish he were to receive the healing that we had.

Food, cigarettes and men are not going to fix this one. God works in mysterious ways. I need a therapist for the abuse issues. I can't do this on my own. I have much hope for Linus getting well. I'm very grateful for the grace of God helping me to stay sober. I'm afraid my eating is getting out of control. My little girl needs me more than anything right at this moment. It's time to go to bed; it's 6:20 pm. I want time alone to read Manhood, fall asleep and cry if I want to. 'God, protect me and hold me close. May I seek you in my troubles, as I am very vulnerable?'

ANOTHER DAY : I justify my smoking with thoughts like these: 'I'm being rebellious. This is my only high and I'm allowed to. It's my choice. I won't let fear stop me doing what I want to do.' It's only when I'm with Debbie that I want to smoke. I've been through a lot and of course I'm going to lapse one way or another. I have thought of many justifying reasons to smoke and it causes fear and disappointment within myself.

I feel disturbed and lost and I feel I'm living in denial.

ANOTHER DAY : I expressed myself to Linus about how he treats and talks to me in front of everyone. What he said, how he said it, was inappropriate. I don't regret talking to him about it. I don't mean to humiliate him in front of others. Linus told me that I was dumping on him. Yes, a part of what I was feeling was coming from unexpressed anger, shame, guilt, sadness and frustration that I feel towards Jezza. I felt that if I didn't say anything to Linus, it would mean I wasn't being honest with him. I am not shaming myself for making a mistake with Linus. I now know that when I would like to say something to another person, I need to do it privately, not publicly. I'm afraid of apologising to Linus. Come to think of it, he's out bike riding. I will not feel responsible for his choice to take off. He doesn't know how to handle it either. I feel uncomfortable if Linus… Perhaps I can write to him. The music is too loud and I can't read. I was joking with his girlfriend and I obviously hurt her feelings. She's sensitive. I feel guilt. I feel its unhealthy guilt. If I've crossed a boundary with Linus's girlfriend, then she'll need to let me know. I'm not responsible for how she feels and for the homework that she needs to do.

ANOTHER DAY : Jezza…well I say I'm over him, but a part of me isn't. I can see he's on a path that hasn't got me on it. I can't help but think that perhaps I've missed something or, more to the point, he's missing something. I have thoughts of him calling me, approaching me, taking me to the pictures, could he actually like me? I know it's too difficult. He doesn't express himself, especially his feelings, thoughts, hopes, blah, blah, blah. It makes it impossible to develop anything between us.

Fear. Deep-grounded fear. I can remember rejecting many men, until I was willing to see differently with the help of my therapist. I'd work everything out in my head, blame the other person and want them to chase me or fuck off. I was afraid of commitment. I had to find my rock bottom, follow my path to discover what I was doing to sabotage love. I was extremely shy. I needed alcohol to confront people, especially people I was attracted to. I'd forget things I said and did. I was ashamed of my drinking around people who didn't drink. To wonder what they thought of me was so frightening. I'd run and wouldn't call them back. I'd shrug it off as a drunken experience. I couldn't tell the people I liked, that I actually liked them. I hated the way I felt around the men I was attracted to. I was nervous, unsure, uncomfortable, inadequate, awkward, shy and speechless.

Fair enough, Jezza may not want to see me, for all of those reasons and probably more. I'd justify why I wouldn't let someone I liked know how I really felt about them so there wasn't any risk in hurting my heart. He may need someone to help pry open his heart a little to see love is worth it, to see what he needs to see to begin to heal. Perhaps I'm totally wrong and he'd be saying to me if he read this, "You think too much."

I feel sad we've parted again. Yes, I saw some growth. Yes, I was needy, demanding and I rushed everything. I couldn't slow down. It's something I can look at. Perhaps not. I trust in him and myself. I'd do it again if I had the chance and I would choose to go slower. I'd trust him again if he earned it. It's the action that he's missing. I need to remind myself that God may have someone else in store. I assume so. I can't save him, help him, or do anything. I do wonder what he felt about me describing his feelings, my feelings, thoughts, actions and experiences to him when I was lying beside him the other night. I described how being intimate with him felt for me. Oh, that was so nice. Oh, well, this too shall pass….

ANOTHER DAY : I enjoyed the day with Aimee and Ruby. We did some dressmaking, Shianne came by to visit and Debbie entertained us by playing the guitar and singing. Wow. I'm so looking forward to learning how to sing, dance, be stable and paint. I'm grateful for everything in my life. I'm grateful for the abuse, the alcoholism, my recovery, the people in my life, my family, my difficulties, my triumphs, my pain, my joys: simply everything. I'm tired.

ANOTHER DAY : I'm ready to call Rob (an ex-lover and dear friend) and give him the painting I promised to paint for him four years ago; I'm ready to release it and let it go, let go of that painted part of me. Some things are still open and not resolved.

I feel Lee's resistance towards me, which I can understand. I don't know if I need to apologise about anything. I assume he is hurt by my actions and my affection toward Jezza. He'll have his judgements. I will allow him to have those. I'm allowed to be sexually active with others. To my understanding Lee made no effort to follow through with anything other than the occasional fling. I had considered it to be more than just a fling with him, but I felt at the time he wasn't that interested in me. I've really tainted our friendship now. I pray for God's will and time for healing and closure. I pray the same for Jezza and myself. Perhaps there's dishonesty on my part that I need to be prepared to look at when participating in these activities. What are my motives? Where am I responsible when others are involved?

River also has stopped calling me, with good reason. I wasn't honest with him in the end. Perhaps I needed tell him that friendship is all I wanted. There are three men I have been involved with that I haven't found closure with. I recognise I certainly jump in quickly. I was in need of affection and romance. I've never been like this before because I was too busy shaming myself and hating men. It is wonderful I'm now free to explore. What concerns me is the hardness I feel towards myself. I leave unfinished and unspoken words with men. There must be a healthier and happier way. Yes! I don't know, but I pray for their souls and mine. All of us need healing. I am grateful that they were, and still are, in my life. I'm doing the best I can and I'm learning and growing. I pray for a sponsor and someone I can talk to one on one about all this stuff and more, so that I can see where I am responsible in these situations. I don't think I know where the boundaries are. I am not hurting souls deliberately. I just don't know where the boundaries are yet. I wish someone would tell me.

Twelve Years Later...
Going within to have a good laugh
comforts and nurtures my soul

OLD THOUGHT: I'm a psycho
NEW THOUGHT: I'm worthy of love & respect

I was greatly affected by Jarod when we went out together. He called me a slut on many occasions and he would talk about women with his mates calling and referring to most women as 'sluts'. As the result of being with a person like this, I came to believe that it was okay to refer to women as sluts. Jarod judged women who were sexual with others to be a 'slut' and this is how I came to think of myself as a slut because I was sexual with others and I desired to be with a man sexually. So, if others knew I liked someone or found out I asked someone out on a date I thought they would judge me as being a slut. Thinking like this lead me to feel dirty, disgusting and pathetic. Jarod never spoke of himself as being a slut even though he had many affairs (acted out sexually with others and desired women sexually) while he was with me. How convenient for him! I feel sad that I even considered women to be anything other than human beings. I feel sad I allowed myself to be manipulated into thinking I was less than worthy of love and respect just because I was a sexual being with normal sexual desires. I guess this is why it is really important to choose who I spend my time with.

Jarod wasn't like this at the very beginning of the relationship. He presented to me to be this really wonderful, caring, loving guy. I simply failed to accept the person he had become. I skipped over the real hurt when he began to speak to me disrespectfully by putting me down, calling me names such as 'slut', because I was determined to keep him as my boyfriend. This determination to have him in my life at any cost damaged my relationships with my family and friends. They became tired of hearing about my troubles with him and the 'on again and off again' relationship. They were tired hearing about and witnessing Jarod being with other women knowing I wasn't putting an end to the relationship for good. I lost my self-respect, self esteem and it validated my self-defeating belief that I was worthless, hopeless and useless, all because I wanted this man in my life. My own selfish desire to get what I wanted, whether it was good or bad for me, drove me to further self hate and self destruction. Little did I know I was grossly affected by his sexual behaviour and being affected by my grandfathers unacceptable sexual behaviour set me up to be with someone like Jarod.

It was a crazy circle of abuse, one that has been, for me, very difficult to break free from. I'd say being affected by someone else's sexual behaviour is more insidious than alcoholism, my eating disorders and surviving an alcoholic home put together. Looking back, and even now, it has affected every aspect of my life, one way or another.

Maree encouraged me to be sexual with Shaun, believing I wasn't allowing his love into my heart and life. This meant that when I didn't want to be sexual, I didn't want love in my life. Now I was desperate for love and I was desperate to feel love. I trusted Maree and I had no idea how to be in a loving relationship so I tried to be sexual with Shaun when I didn't want to. Later on I had one counsellor encourage me to do this as a way to desensitise myself. Just what I need! I was forced to be sexual with my grandfather when I didn't want to, so the solution to sexual healing is to force myself to be sexual when I don't want to again! What the? When I tried to be sexual with Shaun to allow love into my life, I wanted to kill him! I was being sexual before I truly trusted the person. I didn't understand when I was sexual with someone before I trusted them, I would freak out by freezing, not talking, going cold, running into the toilet, curling up in the shower to cry or even yell. I looked like a psycho so it must mean I am a psycho and the only way I thought to stop being this way was to practice being more sexual.

Why on earth is it not okay to be sexual with someone, even if it is my boyfriend, when I don't want to be? Why does it mean if I don't want to be sexual it must mean there is something wrong with me? And if I have problems with being intimate why is the solution to force myself to be intimate or point the finger at me to change? If I say no to being sexual and if the other person sulks because I'm not sexual with them is there something wrong with them? If someone doesn't talk to me, or calls me names, or puts me down, or threatens to leave or finds someone else or stops being affectionate, or loving, or kind, or stops spending time with me because I don't want to be sexual with them – Is there something wrong with them rather than wrong with me?

Let me think about this. Do I have rights to my own body or not? If I do have rights then I have the right to say no, is it a loving act to be persecuted for it? When I allow others to criticise, reject, humiliate or threaten me because I choose to listen and respect my feelings, is that love? When someone makes a sexual demand upon me, is that love? If the other person is not happy with being with me because I want to listen and respect my feelings, is that love? If I feel someone is manipulating me into being sexual, do I feel I'm being loved? Are any of these things demonstrating to me that the other person is showing me they love me or are they showing me they are only concerned with all they can get out of me sexually?

It only became my problem when I believed I was the problem. While I believed I was the problem, the person with the actual problem could avoid, skip over and deny the problem starting with them. So oddly enough I always attracted to people who made out that I was the problem if I wanted to say no to being sexual and say yes to being actually loved and respected. I would always end up being a mental and emotional mess, while they always appeared to be normal and okay. I was the 'psycho chick'. It's a bit like, when I wanted to get at my cousin Linus back when we were kids, I would kick him under the table when Dad wasn't looking and Linus would retaliate by hitting me back with this fist. Dad would turn around and witness Linus hitting me and so Linus appeared to be problematic, while I looked innocent shaking my head indicating to Dad, 'Gee what's the matter with him?"

So I ask myself today, did I need to have more sexual experiences to feel like a complete, whole and beautiful person? No I didn't, however I did, and I found out it did not produce my desired result – to be whole, complete or feel like a beautiful person. If anything it took me further away from who I really was, an experience, which I now believe, was necessary so I could make another choice – not to do anything I'm not comfortable with and know I am a beautiful person whether others like it or not. I am worthy of love and respect.

See Appendix: 'Are you affected by someone's sexual behaviour?'

OLD THOUGHT: Saying loving thoughts to myself is stupid
NEW THOUGHT: Talking to myself with kindness & respect heals my self-hate

Throughout my journals I repeated positive affirmations. I constantly said to myself over and over again loving and kind words. I am deeply grateful for being so determined to turn my destructive thinking, old thoughts, around by repeating words of acceptance, acknowledgment and love. My persistence played an important role to love myself.

I spoke to myself very badly for years and years. I rejected anything I did that was worth acknowledging, I allowed myself to compare myself to others in a negative way, and I developed old ideas and values which drove me to insanity and misery. To think badly about myself day in and day out for years was not and did not change over night. It was going to take time and it did take time to change how I spoke to myself and how I treated myself. Writing words of kindness and love toward myself was one of the many ways of loving myself again so as I could live a more peaceful and joyful life. I wanted to feel connected with others, and myself to no longer feeling alone. I wanted to enjoy living. I wanted to be free from the pain in my heart and the madness in my head. I wanted to be doing things, which brought me joy. I wanted to feel proud. I wanted to feel free of shame, guilt and humiliation. I wanted to know who I was.

When I hated myself I made decisions in all areas of my life based on downbeat thinking. I didn't feel good enough, smart enough, capable enough, or worthy enough to do those things, which would have brought me great joy, self love and respect. I accepted less and less and less in my relationships with others, with myself, in my working life, and simply with everything in between. I didn't have many hobbies; I didn't have many things to look forward to, because I wasn't good enough to do anything. My life felt empty because I was empty of self.

I realised during the painful breakup with Shaun, I needed to be 'there' for myself. I had learnt to rely on others to make me feel better, especially guys, however others were not responsible to meet my own needs. My Dad says to me time to time "it's easy to love those who are easy to love and hard to love those who are hard to love" and I guess that means me too. I made a decision to love myself the most while I was grieving, in the most pain. I wore my favourite clothes every day. I wore my favourite perfume, listened to happy and uplifting music and chose not to listen to sad, 'I can't live without you' music. I would eat my favourite foods and spoil myself by going to the pictures. I treated myself as I would treat someone I adored and I discovered it made me feel better. In my changed actions I was showing myself I am loveable, I will be okay and I can still be open to experiencing joy even when I am feeling sad.

Talking and treating myself with great respect was vital to creating a life of happiness, peace and wonderment. Perhaps in many ways I repeated loving, kind words to myself for as long as I did until I did believed them enough to show it in my actions. It was hard work. I now wake up with joy in my heart - the impossible became the possible. A must experience! The power of letting it begin with me is something I have learnt from the twelve-step programs of which I am a member.

SACRED CREATIVE FOCUS
WHAT ARE MY ACTIONS?

What am I doing which is working, creating happiness and what am I doing, which is not working, not creating happiness?

Now this can cover a lot of areas in my life such as, what am I doing about my health; my physical health, mental health and spiritual health? If I want my physical health to in good shape am I walking, getting involved in sport, performing, dancing, gardening, and cleaning the house so on and so forth? Am I eating a range of foods, which are good for my body? Am I drinking enough water, drinking too much coffee or alcohol, popping pills, taking drugs or mis-using medications? Am I visiting my doctor and dentist on a regular basis?

Many years ago I knew my there was something not right with my thinking, especially when it came to relationships, so I made a commitment to see my psychiatrist on a regular basis. I knew there were things my friends and family were beyond their abilities and things I didn't feel comfortable sharing with them. I went to 12 step recovery meetings, read self help books and spoke and listened to others. I began to improve my mental health by being creative, writing, gardening, bike riding, going to social events and meditation (pausing and being still when I become confused or overwhelmed or just in need of being present rather just thinking about my thoughts).

At different times I went to church when I was younger however as I got older I found my spirituality by embracing the beauty of nature; a bright rainbow or the rain drops on leaves or the incredible beauty of flowers or the sunset setting across the paddock or ocean. I read about and listened to others share about their spiritual journeys. I'd ask them what was it they did to experience a connection with something larger than themselves, to feel all would be well regardless of what Life can throw my way. I adopted my sponsor's daily practice of reading spiritual recovery books whilst sitting on the toilet. It was one place I'd visit every day for a few minutes so why not read while I'm sitting there? And this helped readjust my thinking to remember to ask my LIfe to guide me, show me what it needed me to do for the day rather than what I could just get out of life for myself. This daily practice allowed me to spot check, what am I doing? Writing was also very good for that – what am I doing? Why am I doing what I am doing? Do I like what I am doing? Will I continue what I'm doing? Do I need help to do something I desire to do or do I need help to stop what I'm doing if what I'm doing is not working for me? Am I doing things, which bring me joy, peace and serenity or do I have room for doing things a little bit more differently?

SACRED CREATIVE ACTIVITY

What am I doing? Well I'm going to draw up 10 boxes, just like a comic strip, side by side one another. In each box I consider each question below carefully and draw a picture and write words to answer each questions. This sometimes helps me to see what I DID, why I DID what I DID and to know if what I DID is what I really wanted to DO. If I discover I didn't really DO what I would have liked to DO then I can perhaps work towards DOING what feels right for me.

Q 1)   Who am I upset with?
Q 2)   What happened?
Q 3)   How did it affect me or why did it upset me?
Q 4)   What did I think was going to happen?
Q 5)   What did I DO in response to what happened?
Q 6)   What was the outcome of what I DID?
Q 7)   Did my actions make things better or worse for me? Why?
Q 8)   What do I think now about what I did?
Q 9)   Did I get real help or support or did I deal with it by myself?
Q10)   If there were a next time, could I do something differently?

SACRED MEDITATIVE ACTIVITY

In quite moments I can reflect upon whether my actions, what it is I am doing, is serving me well or not. What are the things I'm choosing to do that make me feel bad or good about myself? Can I do less of those things that make me feel unhappy? Can I do more of those things, which make me feel happy? I can make small steps toward doing things that I feel good about? I can investigate how others go about doing what it is they love to do. I can ask for help or support to help me to DO the things that I feel would bring me more joy, peace and happiness.

COMMITMENT STATEMENT

I .... am willing to put aside everything I think I know about myself, my life, my past, my future, in order to have an open mind and a new experience with my actions. I am open to the possibility to be becoming aware of my actions, receiving new thoughts, and living a new life.

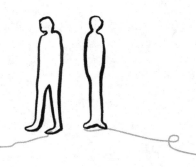

HEALTHY RELATIONSHIPS WITH OURSELVES & OTHERS?
WEEK SEVEN : RESPECTING MYSELF & LETTING GO OF OTHERS APPROVAL

INTRODUCTION TO THE SACRED SHARING

I APPLIED FOR A NANNY POSITION IN MELBOURNE AND MET THE MOTHER ON FRIDAY MORNING. I TRAVELLED VIA THE TRAIN, AS SHAUN HAD NOT RETURNED MY CAR FROM TOWNSVILLE. WE GOT ALONG FAMOUSLY AND WE AGREED I WOULD START WORK ON THE MONDAY MORNING. STILL LIVING IN MY HOMETOWN MEANT I WOULD HAVE TO FIND ACCOMMODATION IMMEDIATELY, WHICH I DID. THE SATURDAY NIGHT WAS MICHELLE'S WEDDING SO I ATTENDED THAT WITHOUT KNOWING WHERE THE GOODNESS I WAS GOING TO LAY MY HEAD THE FOLLOWING SUNDAY NIGHT. I CALLED MY UNCLES' GIRLFRIEND, WHO I MET THREE MONTHS EARLIER, TO ASK IF I COULD STAY WITH HER. SHE LIVED FIVE MINUTES FROM WHERE I WAS TO WORK AS A NANNY. SHE MADE HER DECISION ONLY HALF AN HOUR BEFORE THE TRAIN WAS TO LEAVE MY HOMETOWN ON THE SUNDAY TO GET ME TO MELBOURNE BY 8:30 PM. WASN'T THAT GOOD TIMING!

ANOTHER DAY : I quickly want to write about my feelings in regards to Lee. I feel yucky, bad, guilty, ashamed, and crazy. It's coming from what I perceive he is thinking and saying about me. Lee really backed off and now he's hardly speaking to me. He will talk, but I know something is wrong. I feel bad because I've done something to upset him but I don't know what it is. Okay I'm carrying unhealthy guilt. Yes, it was inappropriate to touch his face on Saturday night when I was saying hello. I learnt he is annoyed with me and that kind of behaviour doesn't fix anything. I'm not responsible for his inability to speak his truth or tell me his boundaries or what he expects of me. I do not need to shame myself for having sex with Jezza. I've been shamed enough. No more. I am a woman who has needs and desires and I am allowed to make choices that feel right for me. I left my number for him to call. He didn't and that's okay. I've gotten on with living my life. I am not going to fall apart for being expected to know how I've upset him.

I'm getting the feeling I'm discovering how Jezza might feel. Hmm! I'm ready to let go. It's a bit meshed up. I'm not responsible for what Lee says to anyone. I know who I am. I need more experience with having sexual relations. I was off balance and I still am. It's okay. I don't have to be perfect today. I have been to a twelve-step recovery meeting this week. I have been well looked after, loved, cared for and supported. I am sober and I'm beautiful on the inside and out. I am blessed in hundreds of ways. I deserve it. I don't need to meet others' expectations of me. I pray for Lee, his heart, and God's will in his life. I pray for forgiveness for myself for shaming me and giving my energy to Lee. I pray for resolution. Thy will be done.

ANOTHER DAY : Goodness I felt pain when I heard the song 'Angel'. It's a beautiful song. Jezza played it to me six weeks ago. I felt hurt when I was listening to it. I tried not to feel by telling myself, 'It's okay, Jezza is on his path. Be happy for him and pray.' The song had nearly finished before I thought, 'I'm not allowing myself to feel.' So I then said: 'Okay pain! Let me feel you.' I want to know its okay to just ride through this feeling. A feeling I have felt years ago, an old feeling—a very sad, longing, missing and hurtful feeling. 'Why?', 'How come…?', 'Was it me…?', 'If only…?', 'Why didn't I…?', 'Why didn't he…?', 'Can we go back…?', 'I'm so fucked'; all the unwell times flashed through my mind. I don't know how to do the sexual relationship thing yet. I'm getting the feeling of needing a therapist. To me my smoking at the moment is a sure sign of survival. It's a decoy. I'm lacking the support I need. I'm safe and I'm okay.

I just didn't like the pain that I felt. I didn't cry.

Jezza's off and away overseas today and I can feel it. I wonder what I'm healing. I do trust in my Higher Power. I do trust there are more healing men to walk my way. I believe they will have beautiful souls. I don't know who they are.

I'm tired. I really feel comfortable in my job and where I have shelter. I reassure myself that I'm here for a reason. 'Lord please stay close to me. I know you love me. Please help me love me. Please help me get through this. We're doing this together, with love. How I am so blessed.'

1998 : After the twelve-step recovery meeting I asked Carl if he wanted to spend some time together over the weekend. He said yes to Friday night. Someone came up and interrupted us so I waited out the front for him. I spoke to the girls out the front about what happened and they congratulated me for being so brave. I felt stupid for waiting out the front, all needy looking and everything. When Carl came outside I told him I had felt uncomfortable for asking him if he wanted to catch up. He reassured me it's all about fun, blah, blah, blah, and we left on a good note. He rang me tonight at 9:40 pm to say he can't make it, without an explanation and I didn't ask for one. We left it at that. Part of me is relieved knowing it's for my highest good. Another part of me thinks, 'Why? Was it me? Was I rushing into things?' I'm allowed to ask someone out. I'm allowed to acknowledge that I'm attracted to him and its good practice for me to make the first move. I don't feel comfortable sharing this with other members. He didn't hide, lie, cover up or pretend. I respond to honesty. I am not confused.

ANOTHER DAY : I feel rat shit today, physically. I've had a bath, dressed myself, drank orange tea, read my readings in the sun and my body is saying 'ouch.' All of my muscles and limbs are aching, my head hurts, my throat feels like I've smoked ten packets of cigarettes and I'm tired. I believe it's because of a couple of things: my huge fear of attending a particular twelve-step recovery meeting full of young people, and the meeting is set up in such a way that those who want to share volunteer to speak in a room with about fifty people in it. During the week I'm continuously catching myself trying to figure out what I'm going to say. It's tiring. I'm trying to protect myself and I find that I have obsessive thoughts. I believe it's because there are deep feelings and thoughts running through my body that are not true. I don't want the members to dislike me, hate me, judge me, misunderstand me, talk behind my back, be false to me or tell me off.

I don't want to get into trouble for asking Carl to catch up with me, or for wanting to get to know him to see if I am truly attracted to him or not. Carl saying 'no' has brought up feelings of shame, confusion, fear, doubt and desperation. I am still trying to figure out what to say on Tuesday night at the twelve-step recovery meeting. It's so annoying. I'm afraid of fucking up on my own because I don't have a sponsor or therapist to talk to. I don't trust my adult self because I feel she's not fully grown up or developed yet. She's still wired and hasn't got a firm grip on life to look after 'all of us.' Who are 'all of us?' I think there's: my little girl, my psycho, my protector, my survivor and my hyperactive side. They are all in there representing themselves when they are triggered at different times. My defects of character (those things I shouldn't be doing) and fearful survivor coping techniques are not who I am. If I am judged by my behaviour either by others or by myself, then we are not getting the full picture. We are witnessing a human being acting on old habits - it's not who I am. Who I am on the inside is hidden and kept quiet. My soul is a powerful instrument of God. It is not afraid of rejection or humiliation. I am a beautiful woman.

156

I'm afraid of people rejecting and hurting that priceless part of me. I've been vulnerable before and I've been hurt, especially by my grandfather and in my sexual relationships with men. I can't remember what my grandfather did. I feel the feeling of much disgust and yuckiness when I think of being around my grandfather and the men who I've been attracted to. So revealing my vulnerable side and womanly side to Carl was an extremely brave and refreshing thing to do. Unfortunately because it's new and the last time in my childhood when I did that, I was shamed, made wrong, became unimportant, made useless and powerless, unlovable and I was unprotected. I haven't developed healthy responses and so I fall into old coping thoughts—obsession, fear of getting into lots of trouble, and shame if I get found out.

ANOTHER DAY : It's safe today to be me. It's safe today to express my truth. It's safe today to trust my adult within. It's safe today to feel my womanliness. It's safe to feel my feelings and sensations. It's safe today to let others know how I feel and what I think. It's safe today to slow down and stop. It's safe today to do the best I can at any given moment. It's okay to make mistakes. It's safe today to have feelings of fear, panic, doubt, happiness, sadness, and feelings of grief. It's safe to express myself and to be heard. It's safe to tell how it is for me. It's safe to be disliked, to be bitched about, to be doubted, not trusted, misunderstood, different, similar, unwell, well, clear, and unclear. It's safe to smile, to flirt, to be acknowledged, to be noticed, to be loved, to be touched, to be breathed on, to be looked at, to be warm, to be cold, and to be comfortable and uncomfortable. All of this is a part of who I am but it is not who I am. Perhaps there's more to be revealed. I'm okay to be who I am. I don't need to rely on old habits and behaviours. I can start trusting new loving ways. I can begin to trust God and myself. That process has already started.

Write about the ways I'm still affected by the abuse.
I'm afraid of getting into trouble. I'm paranoid. I'm highly sensitive to people's expressions, voice tone, body language, bodily movements, what their interests are and their status. Deep down I feel ugly. I can't follow through with what I want. I get mixed messages from people and I don't know how to respond or how to deal with the situation at hand. I have great difficulty with men who like me and with men whom I like. I'm very shy around the men I'm attracted to. Intimacy is very difficult. Two months ago when my relationship with Shaun ended I found that intimacy with the men I got involved with after him was easier. Now it seems impossible. I don't have safe sex either. I doubt myself. I have difficulty with food. I have used drugs, cigarettes, alcohol, work and relationships to avoid looking at myself. I'm still dealing with the second-class citizen stuff. To show affection toward the children whom I work with is where I find the struggle. To play one on one with them is hard. I'm learning how to live my life as a sober 24 year old.

Where are you at regarding your feelings of self worth, your work, your relationships and your sexuality?
I have a job in which I feel safe. I'm treated with respect and trust and honesty, and this makes me feel like I'm an equal. I feel trusted, reliable, responsible, happy, challenged and refreshed by the growing changes that are the result of the hard work I have done on myself. I am still a perfectionist. In regards to relationships I still feel like I'm the 'crazy one', the 'idiot', the 'over-bearing-mad-woman', the 'sicko'. I find it difficult to allow myself to be who I am. Thinking that I'm a bad person and disliking parts of me is what I find difficult to shake. Sexuality is fucked. End of story. I can masturbate but only now and then. It's becoming less frequent. The craving for a man 'out of the movies' is growing. The longer I wait, the

more desperate I feel, the uglier I feel on the inside because I know I'm a beautiful looking woman. People say to me, "You're gorgeous! I can't believe you're single!" or "Why did Shaun let you go when you're so beautiful?" or, the one I love the most "What's wrong with you?" It's probably because I'm not a good lover in bed.

How is your life limited?
Every day I remind myself I'm allergic to alcohol and that I'm a survivor of sexual abuse. I struggle with relationships particularly with the men I like. It is awful the way I treat myself when I take the risk of letting someone know that I like them. I find it hard to allow new people into my life. I find it hard to reach out to others most of the time.

Write about the strengths you've developed because of the abuse. Think of what it's taken for you to survive.
It's taken determination, courage, willingness, faith, self-belief, patience, deep love of self, a relationship with my Higher Power and learning to trust others. It's taken a great deal of understanding the effects of sexual abuse. I'm good at organising and cleaning. I'm creative, artistic and humorous. I'm accepting of others. I'm playful and I relate to children well. I have an ability to speak on their level. I've developed a deeper knowledge of human behaviour so that I've become helpful to others. I'm reliable, trusting, lovable, fun loving, daring, and funny. I can dance. I love to kick the footy, sing and paint. I can manage and get through a crisis. I've learnt how to relax, breathe, heal, learn and change.

What are the qualities that helped you make it so far?
I used to pray to God to kill me in my sleep. I used to hold my breath hoping I would die. I just didn't want to face another day. School was, most of the time, a petrifying experience. It was a time of instinct and survival. Michelle was suicidal. I didn't admire her wedding. I don't admire Miohelle. Only that she has survived. I know nothing about her. I enjoyed my time at the wedding because I felt beautiful and allowed myself to be me and allowed myself to have fun. But it was sad—the emptiness, the family she's getting herself into, the false dream. Yuk. The pretence. My girlfriends saw beauty and I saw loneliness and denial. I have done the religion thing by going to church to find relief from my pain, fear, powerlessness, anxiety, shame and guilt. I did the secret planning of suicide in 1993. I did the bulimia, anorexia thing. Start the day for a new start to the 'diet' and end up overeating by 3pm. I did the stealing thing and that began at the age of 5 from Mum's purse. Stealing back what was stolen from me. Starving was a way I thought I could stop developing into a physically mature women. It was my way of saying 'no.' The only thing I can't relate to is gambling and popping pills, thank God for that.

ANOTHER DAY : Shaun rarely stimulated me. I had to stimulate myself by fantasising. My fantasies are still abnormal by imagining being with older men and degrading myself. I'm feeling yucky right now. It's time to write down the things that are wearing on me. I don't want Travis as a friend. I don't mind his friend but I don't know him that well. I wonder about the spare room in his apartment. Joe, I like him but his friendship is not going to go anywhere with me. I'm not keen on keeping up with his friendship. Adrian, I feel for him but he isn't my type of friend. He has many insecurities and issues and I don't want to be the rescuer any more of other people who are not well liked or loved. That used to me but I'm not responsible

158

for them and their unhappy lives.

ANOTHER DAY : I don't like the sound of someone eating, sipping and making those disgusting wet mouthy noises. I have yucky feelings attached to Maree, Jezza and River. Having sex with River was nice at the start but it became dry and sticky and I had to stop. Shaun—remembering having sex with him was disgusting. He'd start talking about the day while we were making love. I was trying really hard to orgasm with my fantasies. The thought of Shaun makes me feel sick. He had a bubble, an air pocket on his penis! Yuck, I found it so hard to have sex with him. He'd try all the time. If only he'd stop and let me initiate first. It makes me angry. After all that, all my money, effort, and letting him touch me, and he leaves me for his ex-girlfriend. He told me that he loved her when I was most vulnerable. I don't honour that in a man. I don't honour his inability to set boundaries and stand up for himself. Fuck that, if that's what I have to experience next time round.

ANOTHER DAY : I feel bad about Lee. Hey, he's 20, only young. I couldn't have sex with him because he really liked me. I felt he couldn't commit anyway and he was way too young in his mind and now he just sees me as a bitch. My sexual relations are pretty fucked. I've got stupid memories of what Maree had taught me about relationships and what I've associated with her. She's a beautiful woman, but I hate thinking of her because it's like I'm going to get into trouble by her or she's going to see that I'm fucked up. I'm tired of thinking and feeling that I'm a sick person. I want to see some worth, some self-acknowledgment for wellness and growth within me.

ANOTHER DAY : I must write down these two things. Did it ever cross my mind to ask, 'Why did he (my grandfather) do it to me? Did my little girl just put it down to believe it was because I was dirty and ugly?' Maybe he chose me because I was beautiful and precious and he wanted that for himself. He wanted my innocence. I'm a beautiful looking woman. I have always been an attractive girl. Lots of people throughout my life have told me so, even my cousin Linus. I can now say and acknowledge that I am not only beautiful on the inside; I am beautiful on the outside. I am no longer dirty and ugly or unattractive. Did it ever occur to me that the reason why people are not approaching me in the twelve-step recovery meetings is because I am a confident person who is okay? Did it not occur to me that I no longer attract sick people as much because I know who I am and that I am well? I see myself as being 'well' because I can now say 'no', because I am enough. Maybe I have a huge amount to offer to others. I have a great source of love, truth, energy, joy, happiness and God-given gifts. Even Aimee told me yesterday that she sees me as an incredibly strong person, stronger than herself. Big words coming from Aimee. Though the strength she speaks is not mine but my God working through me, I tried to tell her that and accept her compliment at the same time and found it hard to do. I feel good talking to my housemate. She's a really beautiful person. I'm looking at my food cravings and I've discovered that it's a distraction from living in the moment. I need to focus on the 'doing'. I need to create a life for me so that I'm not requiring another person to fill me. So I've asked Linus to make two canvases for me to paint. Yes, I have two paintings in mind. I am planning to paint. I walked today and I made a commitment that I will exercise daily. Tuesday morning I'm walking with Aimee. Today I walked and ran down St Kilda beach. My body enjoys exercise, it truly does. My mind is clearer after exercise so that tells me that my brain needs it too.

ANOTHER DAY : I haven't done some writing in a while. I hate it when I allow someone and myself to upset me. I enjoy my resentment, fear and shame-free days. I parked in this spot where I knew this lady would get upset. I did it to stick it up her arse. To tell her that she can't tell me what to do. Unfortunately I couldn't argue with her when she asked me to move. She doesn't have a drive way and fuckin' hell 'Miss fucking bully, you'll do as I say because everyone else does.' Fuck her and fuck I'm angry. The thought of her thinking she's got one over me infuriates me. I didn't want to give in, except she had a car full of groceries and she had nowhere else to park and I knew it. There was no way I wanted to make amends to her, so to avoid that I chose not to say anything other than a measly, "Okay, sure." God, I was shaking on the inside. I wished she didn't have a valid reason for me to move. Now I want to park there when I get my car so I can have another chance to tell her what to do. I'm angry because I looked like a dickhead. I was unable to stand my ground. I felt weak, intimidated, speechless and powerless. I hate her for making me feel this way. This happened about eight hours ago. I want to work through this so I can be free from it. I also know that I have sadness under the anger.

SAME NIGHT : I've surrendered to God, to my anger, to not knowing how to change it. I've surrendered to feeling powerless and for not expressing my anger. I've accepted that I put myself in a position to be hurt. I've accepted that I do not have the answers. I've finished crying. Last night I dreamt I had a newborn baby in my arms. The feeling was incredible when I realised it was mine. It was amazing that this new life was feeding off my breasts. Mum was standing in front of me. The baby turned grey because I wasn't feeding it long enough or when I was supposed to. I believe the baby was dead in my arms and I was overwhelmed with the disbelief that I forgot to feed my newborn due to feeling so overjoyed. I tried to feed the dead baby. I only remembered this, this afternoon. I was carrying the feeling of the dream with me all day. Now I'm crying because my grandfather sexually abused me when I was this young, six months old. The dying baby looks like me when Pop interfered with me. How could I forget I was sexually abused, that those things happened? I dreamt three to four weeks ago that Mikey, who is four years old, was in my arms swimming in the ocean with his sister Cindy, aged 6. The kids were hit by a person on a boogie board who was riding a wave. I ended up on the beach relieved to find Cindy to be in my arms and alive, but where the fuck was Mikey? I ran towards the water where I found him very upset and crying. The relief and sadness was overwhelming. I felt such a strong love for these children, especially Mikey. I felt so sorry that he got hurt. I believe that this dream was a flash back, symbolising the effects of abuse made by my grandfather. As soon as I started writing and picturing the grey baby, it flashed through my mind that the grey baby was me. That's what I looked like when he got to me. It's a memory. I'm crying. I cry for a reason today. I've gotten very tired very quickly. I got to see how beautiful I was before he fucked with me. Before he stole my innocence and wounded parts of me. I was gorgeous. I was innocent. I was fragile. I wanted love. I was soft and I was warm.

ANOTHER DAY : I've been hard on myself today about my weight, about my performance at my job, about my looks. My food is hard work. I'm not over-eating but I am aware I'm eating on feelings most of the time. I can see I'm in love with the idea of being with Jezza. The truth is he's not a person that I could see myself hanging out with. I can see he is a valuable person, although generally it's been a struggle for us to communicate. Simple communication breakdown occurs between us and because he is so reserved it makes it more difficult. If he weren't so attractive to me would I still be attracted to him? I guess

160

not. Perhaps it would be easier to get along with him if he weren't so damn good looking. All I know is this, that when I remove my little girl fantasy of 'the one for me' crap, there's not much left. It's easier for me to really like someone who is unavailable and I am going to change that. I feel awkward, insecure, fearful and confused when I'm around him and that reminds me of the years I spent with Jarod, my ex boyfriend. I do not need to treat myself like that any more.

I desire to be around people that I can be totally myself with. I need self-acceptance and love. It's amazing how my feelings are attracted to this person (Jezza). I'm also aware that if there were another person in my life I was strongly attracted to, I know the focus would be off Jezza. So I'm also recognising that sad feelings, feeling incomplete, feeling of loss, feeling of regret, the 'if only…', the 'what if?' is the core of this. This is a part of being a victim. There is no drama in my life. There is nothing terrible happening, so of course my head has to find something and it's attached itself to Jezza, where it can take me to yesterday, tomorrow and fantasy land. So, it's a distraction from living in the moment. I've been hurting myself by doing that. I try to compensate for treating myself this way by looking for comfort somewhere because I feel unhappy and suffer from low self-esteem stuff. I comfort myself with food. I then have a vicious cycle on my hands once more. Another man or Jezza is not going to take this hurting stuff away. My little survivor within me wishes this to be true, but it's not. The fairy tale of 'happily ever after' with 'the one' is only a fairy-tale. I do deserve love. I am loving and lovable. The false expectations, demands and responsibilities I put on someone are unrealistic, unhealthy and unloving. The only way for this to be healed is daily love toward myself—to be able to receive love from others, to give love to others, and not specifically in an intimate relationship with a man. I can't make 'love' walk into my life. Being single is not a message of 'I'm unlovable' or 'I'm not good enough.' I'm single for God's reasons. Also, because I have a beautiful deep soul, I feel that there is going to be only a certain few that will hold such quality, strength and love for me. God will specifically place them in my path. There is no 'one' man for me. I am loved by many. I'm to heal in many areas and I can be healed.

Pop,
I don't feel anything right now but I'm writing to you to put closure on our relationship. Can you tell me exactly what you did to Linus and I (and Eugene?) You see, I can't really remember. I remember you sitting in the middle of the back seat, (Don't adults usually sit by the window in the car?) and remembering something in regards to your private parts. You held my hand and put it somewhere you shouldn't and I felt sick. I always felt sick coming near you to hold your hand.

From the age of 5 for some reason I wasn't aware of my dad's private parts but I knew where yours were. In the pool you were behind me, Linus says that Eugene and he used to duck their heads under the water to see what you were doing. Good on you! You were deaf and blind, unhappy, cranky and never had anything to say. Yeah, I've had a pretty hard time, especially in relation to male relationships. I'm actually pretty fucked there. I assume that what you did to Linus, my cousins, and I (God knows who else) that you were treated the same way as a child.

At the moment I have no anger. I have sadness that we didn't establish a loving Pop-granddaughter relationship. I didn't have that with you. So I didn't miss it. You hurt me. You make me cry. You make me do insane things. I react insanely and like a petrified animal when

I'm intimate with a man. You see, my feelings only fuck with me when I like someone. That's when I get pissed off with you. When I can't explain myself, when I have to push people aside, push people away because they care and they like me. I know the Divine lived in you. I know you were unwell spiritually, emotionally and mentally. I know you were a sick man. I know you're now in the heavens loved unconditionally.

My life is so much more beautiful than yours ever was. You gave me the most beautiful father a daughter could ever ask for. He didn't want to be like you. If it weren't for you I wouldn't be here. I thank you for bringing my Dad into this life, so that I could have the beautiful family that I have today. Thank you for your secrets for they helped me to be open and honest. Thank you for the abuse - I am a highly sensitive, compassionate, understanding, creative, courageous, loving, attractive woman who is whole today. I continue to develop a closer relationship with the Higher Power that you are with today in heaven. You deserve to know what Love is too. We are both loved equally. I forgive you for your inappropriate, incestuous acts towards me. Please leave room for me to write another letter when I'm hating you.

Your grandchild.

26/1/99 : I have come to see through an upset with Marco, that I experienced feelings and thoughts about not feeling good enough. When Dad was no longer living with Mum, my brothers and I, what sticks out for me is the feeling of not being enough. I sat in the car out the front of the express supermarket at 12:30am grieving for the break up of my Mum and Dad. I believed when my Mum and dad divorced that I was replaceable. I told everyone I was happy about the divorce when I was actually hurting deep inside. I can also see how I compensated for failing to be enough. I took up being perfect, fulfilling everyone else's needs and not my own. I can see how this has affected all of my male relationships. As a kid I saw my Dad leave me, even though it was us kids who left with Mum to move into town from the farm. I didn't know why Mum and Dad broke up when I knew that Dad had stopped drinking. I'm open to the possibility of sharing this with Dad. I have no idea how the outcome will go. I'm open to a miracle.

Tonight has been a breakthrough because before this insight I wanted to tell Marco to get lost because I felt he was making me feel this way and thought he was manipulating me. I felt replaceable because Marco commented on the young actresses in the movie we saw tonight. I've felt with all my boyfriends that I'm replaceable and this time I wanted to see where it was coming from. It took me about 15 minutes to gather myself and express to Marco my feelings of insecurity and vulnerability. I felt the need to pick a fight because I wanted to blame Marco for my feelings of jealousy, anger and hurt. I've felt for a long time that my boyfriends could make me feel good enough. Tonight I'm reminded that that's not possible. A human cannot do that for me. I am responsible for how I feel, not another human being. I also became aware of the thought of, 'I must lose weight', 'I must look better than I am', or 'be better than I already am'. I was in trouble, stuck in the old and the new and there was only one way to go and that was to the core of the upset. I let Marco continue food shopping while I sat in the car and looked at what was really upsetting me.

See Appendix: 'Are you affected by someone's sexual behaviour?'

Twelve Years Later…
Going within to find the beautiful gifts
which dwell in my memories of when I
didn't know how to love myself

OLD THOUGHT: No one will stay with me unless I'm great at sex
NEW THOUGHT: Great, shocking, or no sex I'm loved for who I am

"I need more experience with having sexual relations. I don't know how to do the sexual relationship thing yet." I feel sad I thought I had to be better at sex to be a whole person, someone who would finally achieve the right standard to be loved. I assumed there was something wrong with me if I couldn't perform like a porn star or be a beautiful elegant lover like in the movies. I had to satisfy the other person's sexual need, desire and wishes because that's just what I thought great women had to do. I believed the other person had the right to expect this - to meet their sexual needs.

I would shut down or freeze at times during sex. Did I really want to be sexual with them? In my journals I do say I want to be sexual however, most of the time my motive was to be loved, to have someone want to be with me and I thought I had to get the practise to be great at sex. I didn't understand why I was shutting down and freezing. I felt humiliation and great mental confusion about this. I believed it was because I was screwed up, stuffed up by the sexual abuse as a child and thus why I had to try to be better at sex. I was screwed up in a way but not in the way I had thought. My thinking was distorted by being affected by other people's sexual behaviour toward me.

My Mum said some of her boyfriends desired me—I was a teenager! I remember answering the phone, Mum wasn't home, and her ex began talking to me about my breasts. I would've only been about 11-ish at the time and I didn't think I had much boob to talk about. I don't know if I was even wearing bras yet! I froze, my body stiffened and I couldn't move. I felt I had to listen to this person because they were an adult, 'I have to listen to what adults tell me and plus they had been kind to me.' There was a little mouse walking on top of the stove, I was petrified of mice! On this day this mouse became my saviour. A thought in my head instructed me to just focus on the mouse and watch every little move he made and I did just that. I cannot remember the rest of that conversation this person was having with me.

Mum also told me that one of her boyfriends wrote me a love letter when I was sixteen. I do not remember this letter. My mind has blocked out a lot of my memories and from what I've read the brain can block out or forget painful memories. I feel my mind has been very kind to me to block some of this stuff out, even though at times I have felt it would have been easier if I had remembered what had happened to prove I was sexually assaulted. However, I can stop wondering why I think I have to meet men's sexual desires and needs. I was exposed to others' inappropriate sexual behaviour throughout my life. Why would I think anything different if it has been my experience that others have ignored my rights as a human being to satisfy their lust?

I've come to learn and understand I was shutting down and freezing up while being sexually intimate because: a) I didn't want to be sexual b) I didn't know I could stop at any time and that it was okay to respond to my thoughts and feelings. Just because I started to be sexual I thought I was bad, dirty and wrong for saying yes to being sexual and then saying no during it. I was damned either way!

It's only natural and normal for me to desire someone sexually and be sexual with someone if their feelings are mutual - but it is also natural and normal for my feelings not to desire someone sexually, or to stop being sexual after experiencing sexual desire. The idea I was wrong and bad if I said no at any point before, during, or after lead me to shut down, freeze up and continue to hate myself. I am lovable if I feel sexual desire toward someone. I am lovable if I don't have sexual desire toward someone. I am loveable the way I make love to someone or the way I have sex with someone. I am lovable if I say no to someone I love who sexually desires me. I am lovable even if I say no to sex for eternity. It's my body, it's my right to say yes or no, as long as I know it, accept it and understand it, I will make better choices for myself when it comes to sex. I now know another truth; I'm to be loved for who I am whether I'm great, shocking or choose not to have sex at all.

OLD THOUGHT: Who cares if I don't practice safe sex
NEW THOUGHT: I'm working toward caring about myself one step at a time

Okay, what was going on for me not to have safe sex - sex with a condom - I knew the risk involved in having sex without a condom, and catching sexually transmitted infections (STI's) such as Aids? Was it because I was uneducated, stupid, lazy or scared? I think I fooled myself to believe nothing bad would happen to me and if something bad did happen I convinced myself I didn't care anyway.

The first person I had sex with was with Max. I was 16 at the time and we practised safe sex at the beginning of our relationship. It was around the time I had been exposed to watching the TV advertisement showing a black-cloaked deathly figure holding a long shaft with a curved machete at the top end. It was a TV advert informing everyone that unsafe sex was deadly. My interpretation was that the devil was going to get me for being very bad if I had sex. I didn't like going to doctors. I didn't feel comfortable making the phone call, or waiting in the waiting room, or the worst bit, talking to someone I don't know about my most private details about myself. I also hated putting myself into a position where I would be asked to take off my clothes or have something jabbed up my arse or in my vagina or expose my boobs. YUCK! I didn't talk to my Mum about this stuff or anyone else.

Max began to pressure me to go on the pill because he didn't want to wear condoms anymore. I didn't want to let him down or leave me so I went to the doctors to get the pill. It made me feel sick and fat. I couldn't afford to be fat when my worth was based on how I looked. How could I expect Max to be with me if was fat?

I tried different scripts and the results were the same. I had heard about diaphragms and couldn't imagine anyone sticking something up my bum just so I could have sex. Why I thought it would go up my bum I will never know! It was definitely a sign I needed more education about the different options for contraception. Diaphragms go up your nose! LOL Okay they don't, they go into the vagina, but I wasn't going to find out what other options there were. I imagined them to be invasive, uncomfortable and embarrassing. I kept clear of those experiences as much as possible.

The other problem I had with the pill, I'd forget to take them on a daily basis. I would just take the extra two or three together depending on how many days I would forget, not realising the danger of pregnancy I had placed myself. I was afraid of asking questions, afraid of looking stupid, so I went on my merry way with my technique of damage control.

I hadn't told Max I went off the pill and he didn't 'pull out' in time when he was coming...I had to tell him I wasn't on the pill. I don't remember how he reacted to this other than deeply worried. I remember he went with me to the doctors to ask for the Day-after pill—now called 'an emergency contraception.' I am really glad he supported me by going with me to see the doctor. It was less frightening having him there. It felt like a shared responsibility.

Today the emergency contraception can be bought over the counter at any pharmacy, and there are some pharmacies that give them to young women under the age of 16.

When I was with Marco, I knew I didn't want to have children to him. I trusted my friend Marika with all of my heart and knew she only wanted what was best for me. She told me many stories about herself over the years—the trouble she would find herself in and out of. I knew I could ask her, if I fell pregnant, to come with me to have the child aborted. I also knew I would not be judged or condemned by her. When I did ask her she was understanding and did not hesitate to tell me she would definitely go with me. I wasn't able to leave Marco or practice safe sex, however I was able to make a plan for the worst possible scenario if I fell pregnant. I know that is back-to-front, however, I was working with what I was capable of at the time until I was capable to turn that around. My self-esteem and ability to take care for myself has taken years to develop and is still an ongoing process. There was a time I didn't care what happened to my body or myself because I hated myself so much that I knew I wasn't going to change overnight. The 'I-don't-care' factor affected all my decisions in all my relationships and it included my attitudes and beliefs around my sexual conduct. I can't change what I have done; however, I can change what I can do now and in the future—one step at a time.

OLD THOUGHT: I'm a slut if I have condoms
NEW THOUGHT: It's my body & I have the right to protect it

My relationship with Marco didn't last and I remember at times trying to fumble around with condoms but this stuff made me feel really uncomfortable. I had screwed up ideas about it. I felt I couldn't have a stash of condoms because I thought others would think I was a slut to have condoms. I thought others were sluts for having condoms. I didn't want to be responsible for ruining another's good time or upsetting them by talking about condoms. Anything like that was just too awkward and confrontational. I hated feeling awkward and talking about these types of things.

I placed myself in serious danger because of my fears, insecurities and impaired self-esteem. I would rather keep the other person happy by not causing a fuss than to protect myself from catching STI's or falling pregnant. I didn't have the confidence or self-assurance to talk about it to the people I was sexually involved with. I felt ashamed for not protecting others or myself by not practicing safe sex, however, I didn't have the know-how to stop myself from being this way. The whole subject was too overwhelming for me, especially when I didn't talk to others or read about it. I felt cut off from the world with this stuff.

After being diagnosed with having crabs, a doctor talked to me about how people catch them. I vaguely remember her telling me my boyfriend could have given it to me by being with other people. I had been with him for some time and I felt offended that she dared to accuse him of such a thing! She obviously didn't know what she was talking about. I also didn't really understand what she was talking about but I wasn't going to ask questions and embarrass myself by letting her know I didn't know about STI's. So I took one of the other options I could comprehend and understand at the time. I convinced myself I must have caught it from a public toilet seat. When I told Jarod about it, he confessed he had them too. I loved him, he was my one and only—my life—I couldn't get angry with him. How could I when I was the one feeling dirty for having crabs! I blamed myself and apologised to him for the STI's, even though I hadn't been with anyone during the time we had been together.

Friends and family, even teachers, were constantly telling me that he was seeing other girls. I found it really hard to get him to admit it, and anyway, I couldn't believe what I was hearing unless I saw it with my own eyes. The crazy thing was I did see it! I saw him kissing a girl on the dance floor the night of his 21st birthday party IN FRONT OF EVERYONE! I still got back with him and believed he only did this once—until I did it myself. I kissed someone else to see if it was easy to get away with 'picking up' behind his back—and it was. Then for some unknown reason, the penny dropped – FINALLY! He had been with a large number of girls while he was with me and we didn't wear condoms. So this meant I was exposed to catching STI's the whole time I was with him. I just felt dirty and ashamed and hid this from others.

I lived in la-la-land believing good guys don't have STI's or Aids so I didn't have to worry about condoms. Good guys or good gals are not immune to getting STI's if they practice unsafe sex and that included the people I really liked. It was just a way of thinking to cope with not having the inner resources to take care of others and myself.

It was in my first two years of being sober, aged 24, that I bravely visited a very friendly and caring female doctor who took swabs from my vagina to check for any abnormalities and sent me off for blood checks. Her warm nature relaxed me enough not to freak out and encouraged me to see doctors more often. I got the all clear from the swabs and I was too afraid to find out what the blood test results were. I couldn't cope with the idea I could have Aids. I knew I needed to take responsibility for my sexual health and others, but I just couldn't make myself do it even though I really wanted to. I didn't tell anyone about it, and I didn't have any support with this. The best I could do at the time was to go through the process of having blood tests without checking the results.

I've asked myself what motivated me to go to see the doctor for STI tests in the first place. It was around the time I was introduced to an older beautiful looking woman from one of the 12 step women groups I attended in Melbourne. She appeared and sounded like a good person, full of life, love and passion. She was a mother, married and successful woman and she spoke openly about having Hepatitis C. I was shocked that she did so with ease. The old idea that beautiful and good people don't get STI's was smashed, and the new idea that anyone can catch STI's, including myself, replaced it. The way she spoke about having STI's left me feeling I had nothing to feel ashamed about if I had caught any STI's. She wasn't ashamed or embarrassed—so why should I? She had survived the tests, faced having an infection, found a way to live with it and still be happy and free. I remember thinking that if she can, then so can I.

It's because of this experience and many others that I choose to tell it the way it is about all the different aspects of my life to hopefully create a pathway for others who have been too afraid to speak up. If you identify with some of the things I've said, done, and felt, I hope it tells you you're not alone, or that someone you know is not alone.

It's really important I take care of my own body and health. I need to rely upon myself to protect myself from STI's. I'm the one who is responsible for carrying condoms or using contraception pills if I am sexually active despite what the other person thinks. It's my body—it's my life.

I continued to work at building my self-esteem and self-worth, which enabled me to go through the process of having blood tests and facing the truth about my health. I made a joint decision with someone I desired to be intimate with, to have our sexual health checked out before being sexually intimate together. I was 32 and this was the first time I would find out that I didn't have any STI's. What an absolute miracle! A life's blessing for me.

I was willing to deal with consequences of my decisions in the past to not practice safe sex. By this time I had many caring, reliable and loving friends whom I could depend on if it were to be the case that I had been infected with an STI. Having someone to walk with me through this difficult, fearful, and confronting experience made it that little bit easier to go through with it. I come to believe I deserved to look after myself and to be free of living in fear—free of the fear of the unknown.

See Appendix: 'Are you affected by someone's sexual behaviour'

SUGGESTED CREATIVE FOCUS
RESPECTING MYSELF AND LETTING GO OF OTHERS APPROVAL

Being sexual with someone or considering being sexual with someone, is to be a mutual decision between myself and the other person. I've needed a lot of support and understanding regarding mutual intimacy, love, attraction, and what is okay or not okay for me. It's an ongoing journey really—a bit like life.

Over time I have learnt the importance of letting go of another person's approval and whether or not they agree or disagree with me; whether they like or dislike my decisions about my sexuality, or whether I am comfortable or not comfortable about being sexual. I can try to seek approval from others in all sorts of areas of my life. For example, what I study, what work I choose to do, what clothes I wear, what my hair looks like, what decisions I make in relationships, what I say, what I do, how I act and how I should feel or think. I've found when I'm seeking others approval to make sure I'm okay I'm really seeking disappointment and unhappiness. It's in seeking what feels right for me, what I want and need to do, which creates happiness for me. I'm to seek self-approval, as I will feel respected by my ME. When I respect myself I feel good, my mind thinks clearly and my body relaxes. The truth is others will not always give me approval - it's simply not possible for others to always agree with me nor I with them. And when I surrender what is right for me to keep another happy I then lose myself and that's not a good feeling either.

I sometimes have to go out on my own without the support from those I'm seeking support and approval from. This, at times, takes great courage and faith because my choices may not bring about the desired outcome I'm seeking. Perhaps proving "others" right as some people call these experiences "mistakes". I call them valuable experiences because it is through experiencing that I am given another opportunity to make another choice and I can be a stronger and wiser person for it. Plus I've found more often than not when I have respected what I want and need to do things usually work out pretty well. Very well actually.

When I respect and accept my true self; my body, my looks, my gifts, my talents, my natural character, my interests, my dreams, my choices, my thoughts, my feelings and what I want to do I begin to let go of others approval and experienced the joy that comes from self respect. Respecting myself is another great way to love and accept myself. And when I'm loving and accepting myself I am creating real happiness.

SACRED CREATIVE ACTIVITY

I imagine drawing a picture of myself holding a tool kit. Not any kind of tool kit, a sexual health tool kit or perhaps I'll call it a making love tool kit. It may contain the things I believe I need if I am going to look after my body, such as protecting it from STI's, or from falling pregnant or getting someone pregnant before I or the other person is ready. Abstinence from sexual intercourse is the 100% way too to prevent pregnancy. Having condoms also prevents pregnancy and many STI's. It might be about decisions, like being tested for STI's either alone or with the person I would like to be intimate with. Perhaps my sexual health or making love took kit contains reminders to look after my emotions and mind such as listening, trusting and respecting my feelings and thoughts before, during or after being sexual or making love. Things like, 'It's okay to say 'no', 'It's okay to change my mind', 'It's okay to wait until I feel comfortable whether its simple touching or making love', 'It's okay for the other person to change their mind'. I draw, sketch, paint or cut out image/s and/or words from a magazine, book or newspaper, about what I believe is involved with looking after my body, my mind, my spirit, and my feelings when it comes to sexual intimacy.

SACRED MEDITATIVE ACTIVITY

I sit with my eyes closed and take a few moments to focus on my breathing. I take a few deep breaths into my stomach. If I find it hard to do that, I lay on my back as it that can be helpful to breath deeply. I begin to imagine driving along a road and when I look up I see a big billboard with the words 'I respect my body and my life' written on it in large white letters. I keep driving as I allow myself to feel what it is like to go to a place where I respect my body, my life and my decisions. As I keep driving I pass another billboard. It is blank and I imagine a picture that shows what respecting my body and my life looks like.

COMMITMENT STATEMENT:

I .... am willing to put aside everything I think I know about myself, my life, my past, my future, in order to have an open mind and a new experience with respecting myself and letting go of others approval. I am open to the possibility of respecting myself and letting go of others' approval, receiving new thoughts, and living a new life.

HEALTHY RELATIONSHIPS WITH OTHERS AND MYSELF
WEEK EIGHT : BOUNDARIES WITH OTHERS AND MYSELF

INTRODUCTION TO THE SACRED SHARING

I HAD A MONTH TO FIND A NEW HOME. THE RENTAL HAD COME TO AN END AND I HAD NOT FOUND ANYWHERE TO LIVE. I HAD MY CAR PACKED WITH ALL MY BELONGINGS; I WAS HOMELESS. THERE WAS ONLY ONE PERSON I FELT I COULD RING TO HELP ME OUT. I CALLED MY UNCLE'S GIRLFRIEND AND HOPED THAT SHE WOULD BE OPEN TO THE POSSIBILITY OF HAVING ME STAY AGAIN FOR ANOTHER SHORT PERIOD OF TIME. MY UNCLE ANSWERED THE PHONE, HIS GIRLFRIEND WAS NOT HOME, AND I TOLD HIM OF MY SITUATION. HE ASKED IF I WOULD WAIT UNTIL HE CALLED ME BACK, SO I WAITED. HE CALLED BACK NOT TOO LONG AFTER AND OFFERED HIS FLAT FOR ME TO STAY IN, AND TOLD ME THAT HE WOULD MOVE IN WITH HIS GIRLFRIEND IN THE MEANTIME. UNBELIEVABLE! THAT DAY I MET HIM AT HIS FLAT, HE GAVE ME HIS KEY, HE HAD COLLECTED HIS THINGS AND I HAD A HOME. LIFE WORKS MIRACLES! DURING THIS TIME I ATTENDED A SELF-IMPROVEMENT COURSE, WHICH A FRIEND OF MINE PAID FOR AND SOON PICKED UP A NANNYING JOB IN BRIGHTON

28/1/99 : 11:40 am. Moved into my uncle's flat last night in Prahan. This morning I didn't want to get out of bed. I'm not looking forward to child minding. I've decided to follow my gut feeling and not take up the full time position. I've worked out that I'd prefer not to have the parents' home while I'm looking after the children. My paranoia and feeling uncomfortable becomes too stressful. The other thing on my mind is that the lady from the nanny agency hasn't called me since my interview on Tuesday. I'm concerned and feeling as though I'm being avoided. I'm ringing her tonight after my 5:30 pm appointment with the Will family. I'm excited to meet with them.

I have two speeding fines and three parking fines that I don't know how I'm going to pay for. I'm $402 in arrears with my car loan. I'm feeling lethargic, unmotivated, uninspired, doubtful and fearful. Keeping in mind I fell down a hard wooden flight of stairs on Wednesday morning. My knee is not co-operating. My knee aches, it's hard to walk and it hurts when I bend it. Doesn't look good for interviews hobbling around everywhere. I need a physio but to find money for that would be a miracle. So this doesn't help, does it? I'm grateful for the flat. My uncle has given me his flat for me to live in. I'm so grateful for the haircut Aimee gave me Wednesday. I'm grateful for my housemate for doing most of the cleaning of the house we've just moved out of.

I approached Antonio (the guy from the twelve-step recovery meetings) tonight. I spoke to him about my fear being the reason behind not speaking to him for the past two and half years. He commented about how many people take him as being scary. Perhaps now that I think about it, it's his anger I have sensed in him that puts me off talking to him. Also I sense his fear of closeness. He probably doesn't realise I find him attractive and that I have pondered about the possibility of us being together. What comes up for me is that he would take me as being promiscuous. I've already made up my mind that he thinks I'm a slut. I've always thought he's seen me that way which is another reason why I've kept my distance. I think if I show him any sign of affection he'll certainly conclude I'm a tart. Strangely enough I've never dated anyone in the fellowship and I've been around for two years. So what does that mean? Is that how I saw my Mum? No, that's what other people said about her and how they saw her. Maybe it's because Mum has only had relationships inside of the fellowship and all the men were sick and mistreated her and I'm afraid of that happening to me. I'm carrying a story that if I date someone in the fellowship then I'm a slut and that I'm only in the fellowship to pick up men. That is far from the truth. By being this way I get to be insecure, emotionally closed and intimidated. What I get out of it is that if I ask anyone out I get to prove to others that it's true. Also, by not dating I get to prove it's not true. I feel wrong for being attracted to someone in the fellowship and I make the men wrong by thinking that they think I'm a slut.

I get to dominate others by avoiding them like I'm avoiding Antonio. I get to dominate by being single, silent and skimpy with my sharing. I feel untouchable. The feeling of 'I'm too good for you' comes over me. How I justify the reason for not asking Antonio on a date is my thinking, 'He's too angry, he thinks I'm cheap, he hates me, as if he'll like me, and he'll see right through me, and humiliate me'. I invalidate him by saying I had no idea what he was talking about when I had a pretty good idea. I invalidate him by assuming and judging him so harshly. I love feeling better than him. I love rubbing it in his face that I'm happy, attractive, fun loving, and free. What's present to me right now is the cost of thinking this way. I'm ripping myself off from the possibility of knowing him, of looking into his eyes, of relating, of understanding him, of experiencing fun, love, affection, joy, satisfaction, and fulfillment. Giving up my ego actually frightens me.

6/2/99 : It's time to write. I feel ill at ease. I feel guilty about something I've done. I worked last night and earned $100, which is fantastic and today I spent $60-$70 and I feel bad. Keep in mind I always feel like this when I buy myself something and it's not often that I do. So what is it? Now I feel tired. I slept from 12:30 pm to 2:15 pm and 4:00 pm to 8:00 pm. I don't feel I have enough money. Like I'm going to either die or get into trouble. I feel answerable to someone but I don't know who. I don't feel I'm worthwhile enough to buy new shoes, tops, skirts, undies or socks and that these things are not my priorities. That's what my head tells me. What is left is only bills and food. Why is it not okay for me to have nice things? By the way, there are great bargains at the moment and the clothes I want are for work.

I've had a sleep and I just don't feel good. I feel lonely and feel like I'm missing out on something. I feel a little anxious about tomorrow being my first working day. What to do? There's washing, cleaning the kitchen, calling the kids. So let's do that. I can catch a twelve-step meeting tonight at 7:00 pm in Prahran.

7/2/99 : 11:45 am. Goodness, I'm experiencing an emotional roller coaster. My loneliness vanished when I received a surprise phone call from Dianne (a girlfriend in Melbourne), whilst I was walking down Bridge Rd to Richmond. I felt touched that she rang my mobile. She shared with me how she's 'really' been going for the past three days. She trusts me and values my input and my listening. I value her friendship. I also shared openly with her. There's no communication problem between us. She suggested I look at psychology. It keeps coming up, either that or my art. Listening to others, I hear that they see me differently to how I see myself.

I did feel comfortable at work today, my first day. Liz and David's money doesn't bother me—which is great. I do see them as the same as me. I do still have the thoughts running through my head telling me that I'm not good enough. I finished at 11 pm. Between 8:30 and 11 pm I watched TV as I didn't know what else to do. My new bosses Liz and David went out shopping. I experienced the feeling that I'm to be busy doing something all the time and to be perfect. It reminds me that I failed to be 'something', which creates yucky feelings where I want to get out or run away. It's not the people I work with. I like them very much. It's the stuff I make up in my head that hurts me and I've hurt myself in this way for years. I've come a long way and there's more to come.

14/2/99 : I feel full of fear. I can't rid myself of it. I wish it wasn't there. It sits in my heart. It hurts and it's annoying. I want to enjoy the moment. I've talked about it to others. I've gone to twelve-step meetings that help me to look at myself and be responsible for my happiness and meetings that help me to recover from being ill when I abused myself with alcohol. I called and received coaching from the self-improvement organisation and still it persists. What I resist persists. I've sat here and searched my mind—and found nothing. I've been praying—and heard nothing. I walked for two hours this morning—and worked out nothing. I've eaten a balanced and wholesome diet and—still nothing has come up. I've called the people back who have left messages on my answering service and, fucking hell, it's still inside me. I want it to piss off. I'm making the feeling wrong for being there. I feel that I choose it because I'm threatened. I'm threatened by my new job. I have a fear of making a mistake and being judged because of it. I'm afraid of being spoken about behind my back and, more importantly, getting into trouble. I have a big fear of getting into trouble.

I feel tired at the moment. I want a breakthrough from this anxiety like I did last week. I felt relief for two days. Wow! It felt wonderful. How or why it happened I don't really know. I felt excited about my job. I wasn't tired. I could hardly sleep because I was that happy. Perhaps the fear crept in when David mentioned projects he wanted me to do with the kids for this week. It made me think: "Oh, shit! Can I do them?"

The fear of the unknown scares the hell out of me. I feel uncertain about my ability to do my job. I'm in a new environment and I have nothing to go by. I have no routine. I'm out of my comfort zone. I really am. I'm powerless over this situation and my fear. I believe that God has an answer and that there's another way. I'm willing to take the necessary steps.

My want list is: I want the fear to go away; I want Joshua to do what I say so I can look like I have some control over the situation and some ability to do my job; I want Liz and David only to be kind and think nice, great things about me; I want my vitality back; I want someone to help me; I want someone/something to take this anxiety away.

Do I know how to get what I want? No way. Am I willing to abandon my self-reliance? Yes, I'm willing to abandon my self-reliance. 'God, please remove my self-will and my self-reliance which is failing me right now; for it hasn't given me what I want and I don't know if what I want is even good or bad for me. Please God, remind me you're the one who is running the show.' I realise it's not my job to do or be everything, or to know everything, or to be perfect and superhuman. I am willing to be considerate of myself, to be gentle and understanding of myself; I allow myself to be human. I'm living in the moment. I'm ready to go to work and let God go before me and to do what is required. I will seek God in all things I do today. I accept God's assignments for me today. I will do what is for my highest good and for my own growth. 'Thank-you God, I now feel relief from the pain I was feeling.' Let's go baby. I'm open to the possibility of passion and fun.

28/2/99 : Today is a hard day. The reason for writing is that I got up at 5:45 am to go walking and I didn't want to go. I saw Marika at 6:00 am and I was feeling low, guilty, ashamed, and worthless and had a strong wanting to get out of the feeling. We walked until 8:00 am and I talked to Marika about my insane night with Marco. I was obsessed about having to eat liquorice allsorts, clinkers, and choc tops at the Jam Factory. I cried. I got stuck. I couldn't make a decision. If I made a decision I was afraid I couldn't change it once I made it or get to go where I wanted to go. Marco was with me. He listened. He held me. He gave me space. He gave me a massage. He related. He came along. He just wanted me to rest and have some quiet time. I didn't. I couldn't keep still. I wrecked the night. I yelled at him for not understanding. He got frustrated with me and saw me in my drama. I couldn't get out of it. I'm tired as I write in bed. I ended up driving away in a desperate state of confusion, anger, fear and loneliness. My behaviour reminded me of the 'Jarod' days. Maybe Marco got tough with me because I said Shaun was weak and that I found he never stood his ground either, with others or myself. He let me walk all over him. Who knows?

I am home. I've had a shower. I let the tears flow. I feel pain because of the way I treated Marco and especially of the way I treated myself. I called a girlfriend and shared with her about my night and she understood me. I laughed with her relating to what she was saying to me. I felt good, clean and cleansed.

ANOTHER DAY : Today I'm afraid of being lazy. It's 9:00 am. My body, emotions and mind are exhausted. I pray for acceptance, kindness, consideration and compassion towards myself. I rang and left a message for Marco apologising for the way I treated him and for making him feel bad. I informed him of what I did when I left him. I would like him to ring but, then again, it would be good never to see him again because then there would be no work to do on myself and I could run away. I don't really want it, but it's my old way of coping. You know: 'Just let him go. I'd be better off and he'd be better off without me.'

SAME DAY 2:10PM: Called Marco again. Left a message. My self worth is attached to his forgiveness of me. I can't shake off the guilt yet. I called Mum and I cried. I told her I was sorry for making her wrong. It brought up old feelings. She explained what was happening to her at the time and it was around the thinking that she doesn't have to be everything to everybody all the time any more. I want that one. She suggested I get to a twelve-step recovery meeting. I went to the Gallery twelve-step recovery meeting at 12:30 pm. I was asked to share. I spoke about the 'Ecstasy' Linus took and the effect it had on him and about my upset with Marco. I felt better for going.

I'm going to work now. I'm feeling fearful of not being good enough for the people I work for. I'm afraid of making a mistake. I'm afraid of my food obsession. God, I hand my fears and inadequacies over to you.

ANOTHER DAY : I feel full. It's my emotions and thoughts. I feel like there are ten different people inside of me. Note: I'm with Marco today! At times I have feelings of pleasantness and happiness wash through me, but more often I'm defensive, argumentative, and insecure about my body size, my intellect, and my emotional stability.

10/3/99 : I'm sitting on the toilet and I haven't done a poo all day. When I don't give myself the time in the morning to flush out 'what's up there' I become jammed. Food is plentiful.

I'm away with the family I am a nanny for. I'm getting over my need to look really good. I'm letting go of comparing myself to Liz and not feeling good enough. The idea that I must look good to be a good worker is not doing me any good. I don't feel over-worked even though I've worked from 6:30 am when Joshua woke up until now. That's a total of 15 hours. Only about three hours is the most I've been on my own with the children. I'm surprised how balanced I feel.

I know I've eaten a lot of food, not overly. I know I'll put the kilo's on, but I don't really care. I feel spoiled. The food is divine. The Hotel we are staying at is absolutely fabulous and I don't feel responsible for Liz and David's feelings and thoughts today. I'm aware that there are a few things that I must miss the mark on, but I'm human and I allow that. I've noticed I'm not entertaining the children much. I'm actually entertaining and playful when the parents aren't around. Why? Who knows? I feel relaxed and at ease when Liz and David are not there. More and more I feel that way with them there. I'm just not as playful or joyful.

I spoke to Dr Wilmot my psychiatrist yesterday. I spoke to Carl, the guy I asked for a catch up and he rang me back and told me he changed his mind about our arrangements and I felt ashamed that had I asked a male member in the fellowship out on a date. I'm very glad I spoke to him. Back then I felt so slutty and paranoid about it. I've never felt comfortable around Carl since. On Thursday I approached him after the meeting that we were both at. I told him I felt incomplete about that particular night. I shared with him my feelings of guilt and shame and the fact I feel uncomfortable around him. I told him how I carry on pretending to be 'cool' and together and that I'm fine. I told him I was tired of pretending. He acknowledged me for saying what I had said and that he wouldn't have had the courage to do so. Also he let me know the reason for calling me back and cancelling that night, after we had arranged to catch up outside of the fellowship, was because he has a girlfriend who he is still currently seeing. He said he was the selfish one for not letting me know that was the case and leaving me uninformed. Very interesting! He said it was something he thought he could get away with (catching up with me) to boost his ego, but then realised he was playing a game and so he pulled the plug on our catch up. He apologised for not being honest with me. Then we talked about other things and that felt great.

I shared my anxiety of late and the suggestion from my therapist, my Mum, and Marco, was to take anti-anxiety pills. He related to my feelings and reminded me it is being a person with this particular disease that I'm prone to feel the way I feel because I'm highly sensitive and insecure. What a relief! I could see us becoming better friends and I'd like that very much.

It took 15 minutes for my bum to let go of some poo, I'm grateful for the 'some'. I've been nibbling on little 'nasties' today such as bread and lollies. I won't give myself a hard time but I need to be careful. Inside I feel calmer probably because of a combination of things. I want a break from the self-improvement organisation I've been involved with. I went off track with my program when I first started going. My meditation, prayer and healthy way of eating went down the tubes since going there. Something doesn't feel right about being a part of that organisation. I want to give myself the permission not to go there any more.

I have, for the fourth time, told Marco that friendship is all I can handle. Through the help of talking to my housemate I've become aware I was pretending to myself (and to Marco) that he was enough for me—and he's not. I shared with Marco that all I want is for us to be with people who we really want to be involved with, and not just having sex with each other just because there isn't anyone else at the present moment. Since then the anxiety has been lifted. Talking to Mum has also helped. Can't quite remember why. Oh, yes. Choosing joy now. I've been focusing on anxiety so much that I felt that's all I've been feeling. Not the case, I've been experiencing joy and different kinds of joy more often. So, let's focus on that shall we! Change direction of the sails of my thinking to create joy in my life. I've been sitting on this toilet for half an hour and my bum is numb! And now my feet are tingly. I feel so normal and not up or down. How bizarre! I'm not in a crazed space of mind.

I asked for an hour break. God, the guilt and feeling of laziness and the thoughts of 'I'm demanding and ungrateful' have come up. I feel like I'm a worthy person and that I'm not a robot. I have given myself a hard time justifying why I need a break. Good for me for asking for time out. Congratulations for minding the children for long periods of time without a break. Most parents would be losing their minds. I'm an employee. I need to remember me. It's great that I asked and that they gave. I didn't sacrifice my truth for their approval. If Liz speaks about me behind my back, so be it. It doesn't mean anything. She's entitled to. It's none of my business. I talk behind others' backs on the odd occasion. It's called being human. I feel better for having the break, to be able to relax and to write. I'm glad I brought the notebook along. They're back and my break is over. 'God, please direct me from here. Show me the way. May I see love and feel love. May I be an example for others. I hear them outside. I wonder why they aren't coming in. Oh, well.

I'd like to talk to someone, but my phone is expensive to use. I'd like to talk to Dad. I'll see how I go.

ANOTHER DAY : I had a great afternoon yesterday. I got off the idea that I was bad for having a break. I've done very well so far. I have no resentments.

Marco rang today and I called him back. He was concerned about my sanity. I'm well. I'm okay. I have lots of energy left. Only thing is the food. It's so yummy and lots of it. I'm eating more than usual. So I feel I've put on about two kilos. That's okay. I don't want to get any bigger. I'm starting to feel uncomfortable. It's not a bad thing that I'm eating more. My sanity is intact. My morning reading and prayers are helping me a lot.

I let go of some poo last night and more this morning. I'm on the toilet now and it's a struggle. My body is holding on. Normal I think.

Marco's well, he told me I looked beautiful on Thursday. He said I was glowing and that I looked like a beautiful woman. Space has been created since we agreed to have a platonic relationship with each other and I've noticed that there is much more caring, understanding and fun going on. Sex complicates things. It truly does.

ANOTHER DAY : I can't bend my knee. Something is certainly up with it. I need to see a physio.
I skipped lunch today. It felt great. I didn't need lunch. I've eaten so much lately. I'll make up for it tonight. For dinner I had...I'm obsessing about food. It's not the problem. I ate lollies tonight. Let's not obsess. I know I've put on a couple of kilos. I love food, especially food I'm not allowed to eat. Liz and David put the kids to bed tonight so that I could have an evening to myself. I'm afraid that I will stay like this (obsessed about food and my body) and as I write I know it's got nothing to do with food. The problem is within me. If I had a man I wouldn't eat. I would fantasise about the guy and stop eating. This feeling I know well. I'd like to take myself to the movies tomorrow night. I'd like to learn French. I believe I could learn fast and well. I'd really like that. I'd like to buy some paints and do a portrait of Marco. That would be fun.

ANOTHER DAY : I've kept my cool all day. I haven't pretended to be someone that I'm not. I haven't entertained today...okay, perhaps a little. But it's because I wanted to. I haven't taken on any guilt or responsibility of Liz or David's feelings or thoughts. I've been loving, caring, generous, understanding, patient, tolerant, imaginative, clever, thorough, responsible, trustworthy, honest, capable, energetic, fun loving, affectionate, friendly, thoughtful, attentive, alert, active, spontaneous, skilful, encouraging, positive, sincere, sporty, peaceful, gentle, comforting, serene and open.
I stole...well...I ate the jellybeans in secrecy. I'm allowed to eat them. I just felt bad for eating them. The movie is over. I don't have much general knowledge, yet I'm intelligent. How does that work? I also want

to play piano. I trust that these things are part of the bigger plan. I sang in a choir as a kid. I sang in front of 600 students alone with one other girl my age in grade five. For a shy and reserved kid like I was, that's not a bad effort. I don't remember being acknowledged for that by my parents but today I acknowledge me. I taught myself how to play the organ. I drew because that's what I wanted to do. It was something I truly enjoyed. I love dancing. There are so many things for me to do. The promises out of the twelve-step book are happening and growing. One day at a time - anything is possible. 'Thank you God, for my sobriety.' Too bad that I'm full. That's what happens when I eat too much. Weight can be lost. I'm okay. I'm sober. I will get over it. I am over it. 10:45 pm it's time for bed.

14/3/99 : While I'm sitting here in bed doing my reading and enjoying my quiet time, I'm remembering Liz's reaction to a couple of things that happened today. When I had soymilk brought to the table for my cereal I noticed that she would make these glancing looks at David and I felt like I was a joke to her. I'm being paranoid, thinking she's spoken behind my back, and at those moments I've felt like a hypocrite. I see myself in her. I've done that to people. Instead of speaking up and being authentic or minding my own business, I've made a face at the person who knows what I've said behind their back. There's nothing wrong with it. There is nothing wrong with me. I need not justify my choices or make her wrong. It was a short moment. I'm doing the best I can with food. I'm rather fucked up in that area of my life so it's fantastic I'm not starving myself or purging. She doesn't know me and I accept her imperfections and defects and I'll accept mine.

I'm going to ring Dad now. I spoke to Joyce (Dad's partner) because he was out. She lost Scrabble to both Linus and his girlfriend. Linus would be overjoyed about that. I returned Liz's call; she couldn't find the kid's stickers and throughout most of the conversation we laughed. It was refreshing and we talked about the movie, Magnolia, which I saw last night. I thought about mentioning what I wrote earlier, but I backed out. Now as I write I will be open in sharing with her about what I feel and think. Why not? It may lead to interesting insights. I'm feeling good, light and happy. I'm still in bed and I told Liz that. I'm doing my own thing and I've missed this time to myself that I spend in the mornings and at night. It sits well with me.

I have my therapy today with Dr Wilmot. I'm concerned about my feelings I have about him suggesting drugs to me to help deal with the anxiety that I've been going through. Instead of wanting to work through my upsets his answer was to use drugs.

23/3/99 : Finished work at 10:00 pm. I rang Marco and went over some things and I shared with him about some of the stuff that came up for me on the weekend in Bendigo with my Dad. It feels like weeks ago and it was only three days ago. I find it hard to say, write, explain, or to whom to express it. I don't want to even think about it or feel it. I don't want myself to think Dad sexually abused me. I don't want anyone else to think that. I don't want anybody, including myself, to think Dad and I have a sick or perverted relationship. Where the fuck is this shit coming from? I cried when Marco asked: "Does your dad look like your grandfather?"

At first only his hands resembled my grandfather's and then I thought: "He's getting old, looking old, has a lot more wrinkles and looks more fragile."

Tears flowed out of my eyes and my chin quivered. Marco touched on something. I'm aware of my inability to be close with my Dad. It's hurting me that I can't - I CAN'T! Men who like me more than a friend

I feel sick to be with. The feeling is the same with my Dad. What is it? What does it mean and how do I fuck it off? My Dad has not touched me. I couldn't tell him I was feeling sick and uncomfortable around him. I don't want him to be hurt by telling him I feel uncomfortable around him. He probably sensed something. When we were booking at the hotels I was aware the people behind the reception might've thought we were a couple. I was aware that perhaps this was not a done thing, father and daughter sleeping in the same hotel room. Doesn't matter, we sleep in separate beds. I felt paranoid, insecure and fearful.

It all started when I sat at the table with Dad at the Chinese restaurant. I was about 17 years old. I looked at my Dad's hands and I was riddled with sickness in my gut. I felt mixed up with guilt and shame inside. That's what I'm feeling now. I feel like I've done something wrong and there's something wrong with me. I need to talk to someone. To talk with someone who isn't going to think my father has sexually abused me. To talk with someone who knows my Dad. Hmm. I don't know. I'm handing this over to God. I'm willing to work on this.

26/3/99 : Carl (the guy from the meetings, who rejected me on a date, because he had a girlfriend and didn't tell me that was the reason why at the time) asked me to have sex with him tonight. Just sex. No commitment! A one-night stand! He has a girlfriend! They have a monogamous relationship. It's 12:41 am Monday morning, it's actually the 27th. I've been talking with Carl for about two and half hours. Great conversation. It was in depth and there was lots of sharing between both of us. We were relating and laughing a great deal. I can't believe I just said no. Before I told him about the part of my mind that wondered about the possibility of him and I having a relationship later on down the track, he said: "There's no way I'd be in a relationship with you." Talk about being to the point and being honest! I didn't take it too harshly. I felt a little foolish and like 'Little Miss Rush.' When he asked me to go home with him to have sex I laughed and said: "God must be playing a joke on you because I can't even have sex with a boyfriend, let alone have sex with someone whom I hardly even know. Imagine me having sex just for the night and just for the sake of having sex! I think you need to tell your girlfriend that you've asked me to have sex with you and see how she feels about that!" Meanwhile, I'm thinking the whole time he was talking to me he was thinking about getting a root out of me. Oh, well it's his loss for not being able to really enjoy the conversation as it really was, as I did.

27/3/99 : I just told Marco I can no longer be a friend to him. I thanked him for being a part of my journey. He said that it's been coming for a long time. I wasn't going to say it until he brought it up by asking, "Why do we fight so much?"

My reply was, "It doesn't help when you say I'm wrong, and you're right, and telling me that I'm fucked."

Then he went on about how I make him wrong. It was at that point I had enough. I feel like I'm talking to a sick and unwell person. When I leave him I feel physically unwell, even when I talk to him on the phone. He said he feels the same with me. I don't have an answer. So I threw the towel in and realised that my recovery is the most important thing to me. If it means ending a friendship to have my serenity and peace, then so be it. We're only hurting each other and so we're having a break. I'm feeling quiet inside. I'm waiting for pain or guilt or some yucky emotion to come over me. Yet all I feel is quietness. A part of me wonders whether it was necessary. It doesn't feel like I'm letting go of so much. He rang me after five days of not talking and asked me around. I said I'd call him later. He called me again at home at 9:00 in the morning. Carl said it last night, men just think about sex. That's what Marco wants. No commitment. I don't want that with him. It's passed and gone. I do feel there's something unsaid between us. I'll speak to Dr Wilmot and someone I know in the fellowship. I'm looking forward to speaking with Dr Wilmot about my uncomfortable time I had with Dad the other weekend. I'd like to know what it's about.

I didn't eat the bowl of cornflakes and fruit tonight. I decided to get changed into my pajamas, brush my teeth and write. I've had a rest day with the food. It's from sharing with others, looking after myself, asking someone to be my sponsor and saying 'no' to Carl. I know things about me today that I never knew. Helen told me today that I'm a strong woman and that I stand by what I believe and say. I'm not needy because I don't need a man to survive and that tells me that I've come a long way.

I bought Linus a shovel from the market. I rang him at work to tell him. I also found a Billabong jumper that Marika has soaked and washed for him. I realise there's not much giving going around in my family other than birthdays. I'm now breaking out of that and I'm going to give. It feels great. I feel lovely in my skin tonight, what a relief and a God-given blessing! I have some beautiful things coming my way because I am willing to receive them. I enjoyed my time with Liz and her children tonight. I shared with her what happened last night. It felt good to share intimate things with her and she responds with great care. She has so many gems to pass on. We were all so happy.

28/3/99 11:30PM : I saw Dr Wilmot today and I cried lots. It was difficult for me to talk about my Dad and very difficult to speak about what happened with my grandfather as a child. I was acutely aware of my body language. I was looking away, scratching my neck and staring into space. Dad's getting older and appearing more like my grandfather everyday. I'm to distinguish the difference between Dad and Pop and not to let them be confused into being the same person. It's not Dad's fault for looking physically similar to Pop. In regard to feeling yucky with Dad when we were finding a hotel room together, it brought feelings of something being hidden, disgusting, secretive and out of the public eye. The way my Pop sexually abused me was when my family were around. To everyone else Pop was being affectionate but he was making me touch him inappropriately. There's a relationship between that and my difficulty with others seeing my Dad and I together, because in the public eye we can be perceived as boyfriends or close friends. I have feelings of shame and guilt, that I'm bad or that I'm going to get into trouble. All of this is not true of course, but it feels real for me. Dr Wilmot tells me that I'm a controller and a perfectionist (he said this gently of course). Wow, I am. It causes me stress and anxiety being this way.

I explained to Dr Wilmot that I didn't get sober to take more drugs to band-aid my problems. I told him that I do not want pills and I asked him not to offer pills to me as a solution to my problems. I told him the first thought I had when he offered the anxiety pill to me as a way of managing my anxiety was, 'Ooh, I can take those pills instead of eating.' That's not the correct way to approach the possibility of taking medication. The way I choose to deal with my levels of anxiety is to continue talking with him and others whom I trust. If that doesn't work I will consider it then, but only then. He acknowledged my request and understood what I wanted for myself in my therapy with him. That was that. He said it's certainly okay for me to let go of my friendship with Marco for the meantime. He says Marco is being 'prickly' because he wants to take control of the relationship. When Marco says, 'You're fucked', Dr Wilmot says that's where 'Marco's fucked' (I don't think he used those words exactly) but it's reassuring that there's nothing wrong with what I've done.

29/3/99 11:38PM : Today Dad rang at 9:00 am. I told him about the Bendigo weekend and how I felt and how I couldn't tell him because I was afraid of hurting his feelings. I told him how I spoke to Dr Wilmot and shared with Dad what it was all about and what it meant. Dad said he thought I might've been thinking those things and that he didn't want to say anything in case of bringing up something I didn't want to unearth. He also said he never had much to do with his father (that's probably a good thing) and that Pop got sicker (talking mentally, emotionally, and spiritually) as he got older. I told Dad I don't like this stuff (feelings of yuckiness with him) coming up because I can't be close with him and I find I have to push him away. I cried once I got off the phone, driving in my car and delivering neighbourhood watch pamphlets. They were deep and moving tears. Not sad ones. I felt overwhelmed with the healing.

I spent time with Dianne. I really enjoy our friendship. She is a beautiful person. I saw Marika briefly. She also said in relation to the Bendigo trip with Dad that she already knew I would have been thinking that stuff. She said that she knows me very well and knows how I think. Wow. She reminds me I can tell her anything. I'm beginning to really trust her with things like that.

I rang my sponsor and she wasn't home. I called another woman I've met in the fellowship and she's absolutely delightful. I related to what she had to say. It's taken me two and half years to feel comfortable enough to ring someone and to be me. It's a breakthrough. We're developing a friendship and it makes me smile.

Tamika rang, an old friend, how sweet. I look forward to speaking to her soon. I felt touched that she called.

I'm going to my Hometown this Sunday. That excites me. I'll go there Saturday night after baby-sitting. Liz and David really wanted me to care for their children this weekend. How could I say 'no?' So I said 'yes.' I spoke to Fiona (the morning nanny) about my childish and self-centred behaviour today. I've been jealous of her earning more money than me for less hours of work. I attached my self-worth to the money, thinking to myself, "She must be better than me because she earns more than I do, which means I don't matter and that I'm less than her" along with the rest of the bullshit that goes on in my head. It felt so good to air it.

ANOTHER DAY : I made an error in my calculations with my pay for the third time. I left a message for David's secretary and apologised for not taking the time to count my hours correctly. That took courage. I was in fear, but I needed to do it. I feel so dumb. I'm afraid she'll be thinking I can't count. I don't think I can count. It doesn't mean I'm dumb, it just means I need to take the time to do it correctly.

I will let Nick know (Liz and David's gardener), that I have my suspicions about him having extra feelings for me. I'm probably off track but I'm going to voice it anyway.

God's done much work through me today. He's a miracle worker. 'Thank you God for all the things in my life today, I'm very spoilt. Thank you for giving me courage and willingness. I feel good in my body. Food hasn't been a huge focus and I didn't hurt myself with food by over-eating today. Thank you for the break!'

5/4/99 : Helen just rang from Queensland; she's upset and crying, not knowing what to do with Mauricio, her boyfriend. I listened to her, took her through the steps and suggested she get help and perhaps find a support group - a women's group of some kind. I suggested she buy the beautiful book, 'In The Meantime'. Goodness that's a lot. I also said I'd call her tomorrow night to see how she's going. It's great that she can call me while she's upset late at night. It's not easy picking up the phone. It would've been a good stepping-stone for her.

I caught up with my sponsor today after the twelve-step recovery meeting. I'm feeling a good feeling about her and a good feeling about me. Something about her attracts me—maybe it's her sobriety, her use of words, the way she used to drink, her openness, strength and her efforts in service within the fellowship. I enjoyed being with her and getting to know her.

I had a great time with Linus, Dad and Mum on Sunday in my Hometown. It was also fabulous catching up with Tamika, Debbie and Simone. I may see Ruby this weekend. It felt so good to be back at home. I felt no awkwardness with Dad. I told him I loved him while we were in the car going back to Linus's after being at the pictures. It's so good to be able to give back. It's a wonderful feeling. I bought pizza and chocolate for the girls. Linus loved his shovel and jumper.

Today, listening to what was being read out at the meeting, a penny dropped. I could see my demands and expectations upon Eugene, my cousin. My demands upon Eugene leave me feeling angry, resentful, upset, unsatisfied and unfulfilled. What I can do is let it begin with me. Let me give to Eugene—to be generous, thoughtful, delighted, self-expressed, open, loving, affectionate, interested and compassionate. What I can give to Eugene is more important than what he can give to me. Yes, I have had another breakthrough. Things are happening. I'm receiving so many memories of my past. I'm remembering beautiful moments that remind me of different times in my life that were happy and full of love. The temperature triggers these memories, the smells in the air from different plants and even the cosiness of my clothes. It's great. I have a feeling of belonging, oneness, love, wholeness, togetherness and godliness. It's 12:50 am. I must stop writing and sleep. I'm having some beautiful days. As I spend more time with God, doing service, giving back, changing my eating habits (less sugar and dairy products etc), walking 3-4 times a week, reaching out to others, ringing others, asking another person to be my sponsor, going to more meetings and making a commitment in the women's group—there has been a difference occurring in the quality of life that I live.

ANOTHER DAY : I took Marika along to meet Dianne's friend today up at Romsey. She's an artist. Her works are amazing and she has lots of them. She shows great dedication. I don't know how she found the energy and inner devotion to complete so many art pieces. I could do works of that standard and even better, but I don't. I'm not doing, or following, my passion. WHY NOT? I know I'd feel fucking fantastic if I did. I'd be in my element. Fear is in the way. Bugger. Anything is possible one day and one moment at a time. In the moment there is no yesterday, tomorrow, fantasy, fear, anger or regret. God and His/It's creation is present and that's what I'm part of. All I need is to look at my collection of paints to see what I need to buy and also buy something to paint on and then do a painting by next week. Easy peesy lemon squeezy.

I'd love to do Marco's portrait, especially now that we're not talking. I wonder what might come of it. I want to see if I can do it. If he criticises me, then he does. It's what I think that matters. It's my desire followed through with an attempt. There may be some people-pleasing involved but mainly because I've committed to do it. I'm aware that Marco believes he knows art. I believe he's full of himself. But my fear is being criticised and disliked. Being seen as a joke as an artist scares me because it's rejection. It's something I really enjoy and it moves, touches and inspires me. I'm lazy, stubborn, ignorant, arrogant, self-centred, self-abusive, full of pride, insecure, insufficient, inconsiderate, invalidating of others, dishonest, close-minded, self-loathing, self-pitying, self-defiant, self-reliant, demanding and ungrateful. I stand in the way of my happiness, my love of art and my learning. Today I learnt that every gun is unique due to the making of the barrel and the individual imprint it makes on the bullet. The Coliseum is in Rome. Romsey is next door to Sunbury, just past the Tullamarine Freeway. Italy is somewhere I'd like to travel to. I'd like to begin painting on small boards and have them framed. Small pictures in still life, of anything, and I'm tired and good night.

6/4/99 : Gratitude List time. I'm feeling greedy and paranoid about Fiona, the other nanny because she is earning more than I do with fewer hours and with extra days of work up her sleeve.

It's time to look at what I have. I also need to remind myself that God knows what He's doing. He knows my tomorrow and my days to come. If I needed extra cash I would already have it. I'm taking this weekend off and not signing up for more work. I'm going to relax and have some fun. I'm grateful for God in my life and my special relationship with Him. I'm grateful to be alive, I have clothes, I'm fed at work, I stand by my friends and by my family, I can buy gifts and buy things for them too, I can see and I can see beauty, I can walk, talk, laugh and cry. I have a bed to sleep in, a fan to calm me at night, a unit to live in and the money to pay for my rent and my other bills. I have a great therapist and fabulous friends inside and outside of the fellowship. I have a job and the kids to teach me lessons in life and love. I have my freedom, freedom to choose. I have my personal gifts and talents to celebrate. It's a sunny day and I have a car that's mine, socks on my feet and a bed with sheets that I lie between. I'm excited that my cousin Eugene is coming home for Easter. I have a twelve-step recovery program to help me live a serene, peaceful and purposeful life. I'm involved with the Neighbourhood Watch program to keep me safe in my home. I have white towels to dry myself with. I'm grateful for the generosity of others, their time, money and care. I have my sobriety. I'm no longer a smoker. I'm not over-weight. I have my health, my intelligence and willingness to allow God's will in my life and I have love in my heart.

15/4/99 9PM : I'm staying over at Liz and David's house at the moment. The TV and Foxtel are not co-operating so I'm left to sit here and write. My knee popped out of place so I went out and bought myself a brace. No mucking around this time. I'm booking myself in for therapy on Monday. Strange how I've done this on the day that Marika's gone into hospital for an operation. I'm buying her a Liz George book for some good reading; she's one of her favourite authors.

I asked Courtney to be my sponsor and she said she'd love to. Oh, I'll ring Dianne like I said I was going to, I nearly forgot. God works in mysterious ways: she's not home so I rang Wayne. That was easy. He's going to go out to have some fun with his workmates tonight. I'm looking forward to 12:30 pm tomorrow. A break from work. Yippee! I like Wayne. I feel excited and nervous—a yummy buzzy feeling inside. I so like his nature. I feel safe and warm around him. I don't know if he likes me any more than a friend. I would hate to make him feel uncomfortable and ill at ease like I felt around Bob. I mentioned my sensitivity about men in the fellowship and how I don't usually date them. I do hope he realises he's an exception to the rule. I'm enjoying it for what it is. I must be gentle with myself and not rush ahead. I'm also aware of the tape in my mind that tells me I'm not worthy of such a lovely, gentle man. The mental tape tells me he's too nice for me and I'm not good enough. Along with, "Why bother following the journey to find out whether he feels the same because once he sees what I can be like at times, with my fucked up stuff, he'll be put off like the rest of them." Although Marco was never frightened by my breakdowns or by my nasties, he was a strong soul and very nurturing. I felt it to be that way with him. He rang tonight having a realisation that he really cares for me and wanted to know if I wanted to give a relationship with him a go. This time he wants to make a commitment, I don't. I'm emotionally unattached to him. So I said no. I don't have those feelings towards him. I do wonder what it would be like to be with someone in the fellowship, having a program and a Higher Power in their life. I've never had that before. How I wanted to say to Wayne when he asked me "What is it that you want that you do not have?" I replied that I want to be with a guy that I really liked - to have a boyfriend. Slowly, slowly, there's plenty of time for things to unfold and it's in God's hands. Courtney reminds me that I'm not that powerful to scare and push someone away and there's nothing I can do if it's meant to be or not meant to be. And now I feel like Shakespeare. I'm dribbling. I'm tired and bored, oh great.

17/4/99 : Had a wonderful time with Wayne tonight. The nachos with cheese, salsa and guacamole we ate were great. The picture we watched was 'Erin Brockavich' and I found it truly inspiring and moving. Wayne's just lovely. Boy I jumped out of the car in a hurry when he arrived at my home. The thought of him kissing my cheek was too much for me to handle. No rush. What will be will be. I liked how he agreed that I'm not a freak and that he's figured that out. I'm just extremely frightened of being liked by someone whom I like.

Marika spoke about a woman who shared the same hospital room - how she had survived being tortured and raped by several men and I thought to myself that the abuse of my grandfather was not to that extent, not that I can remember, and for that I'm very grateful. Why does the abuse of my grandfather still have its effects? I mentioned to Marika that the effects of any abuse could be lessened by the support given to the person who has been abused at the time of the abuse. That's when I shared with Marika that my mother would walk by me as I sat on the lounge room couch, not saying anything to me as I rocked backwards and forwards for three to fours hours at a time. Wow. Marika said it sounded like some kind of autism. I kept everything locked up. How could my Mum have done that? I became present to the abuse of my Mum. I feel, at the moment, the damage by her was greater than the abuse of my grandfather. The fact I've avoided speaking of her and dealing with the real issues regarding her and not feeling angry has concerned me. I don't remember much. I say I do but there are a lot of gaps in my childhood memory. Lots. Getting to know someone is not an easy task for me. God, I kept everything that mattered to myself and I felt so alone and afraid. It just wasn't possible for me to learn because I hated living, except being with my Dad and the dogs. I lived for my Dad. My love for him kept me alive and I have no doubt about that.

ANOTHER DAY : What's up with me today? I'm pissed off that I got another parking fine when I went shopping to buy clothes to look good for Wayne. I'd rather save my pennies for going out and other odd bods until next payday.

I got jealous and hurt that Matilda, Dads ex-wife, picked up my cousin Eugene from the airport. I feel replaceable. I do not want to ring anyone yet. I was angry, and then the tears fell as I walked into my flat. I know I'm in addictive mode by the way I'm shopping, not eating enough and over-working. Eugene is here and the last time I saw him I broke out in addictions such as; of smoking cigarettes, cigars, food, sugar, and mood swings. I stripped off my clothes. I frantically washed my car. (I stripped when I walked into my flat, not when I was washing the car!). Am I building myself up for a huge self-abuse binge? Note a pattern here. When I meet new man, Eugene comes home from overseas. This is the third time this has happened. I've started to introduce my family to the men in my life but I hate reintroducing them to the new ones. I think to myself that I'm too difficult. We all know why the men won't want to be with me because she fucks it up, she scares them off, and that's just the way she is. Hmm, whenever I hear from the men I've been with that there's something wrong with me, it might be more of an indication that I've hit a spot or two in them that they are unable to deal with. It's not necessarily all me. I'm not closed. I'm not vindictive. I'm not nasty nor bad or hurtful. I'm going to hand Eugene over to God. I've had enough of carrying him on my shoulders. It's been my choice of course. I don't have to get involved. I don't have to impress Wayne. I don't have to work Sunday. I don't have to give away too much to Eugene when I can't afford it. I don't have to do anything at this moment other than breathe. If Eugene wants to talk to me, he'll ring. I'm really looking forward to seeing Wayne tonight. I'm looking forward to not working tomorrow and getting through tonight's work.

24/4/99 : I'm going to my Hometown tonight at about 10:30 pm. I'm anxious. Something is not right. Wayne's coming with me. Am I pushing it? Time? Money? Hmm!

THE NEXT DAY : I'm sad. I can't write what's happened. It's too long. I've been through the sexual abuse stuff and it's been an emotional roller coaster with Wayne. He sees me as too problematic. He says I'm too much and that his head is scrambled. He said it's basically over between us. Mum won't agree with the conclusions I've come up with. She's not supporting my self-destructive thoughts about myself. When I'm in my stuff I have a choice. I am always worthwhile. I am not afraid of myself and I am not afraid of God. I am not afraid of my feelings. I am not afraid of being weepy, sad, wrong or insane. I reveal the fear in the other person and that doesn't mean that I'm fucked. There's a part of me that knows the truth. He's not only afraid but also hurting. I can feel my emotions and I can describe them. I can identify them and express them clearly. I was confronted with a person with fear. Men can't handle my stuff. Men's support is showed in a different way. Love all of me not parts of me. Wayne revealed my weirdo side. These are my feelings and I've got to love that part of me that I want to get rid of. I need acceptance of myself. Keep looking at the weirdo stuff—the crying and the thinking. The thinking in my head is that I'm not lovable, I'm fucked and they are stupid, sad, silly things—lots of snot and crazy thoughts. I can be complete when I love myself. Mum hopes that I can find what I really think and feel and stand up for 'her' (that would be me and that includes the weirdo and fucked side). Wisdom is within me. I feel I have a great capacity to love. I have a great trust in my God. I have faith. I have a great level of acceptance, tolerance and compassion. I understand I can't see the whole picture and I know my God can. I am beautiful and magnificent. I speak the truth. I express my truth. I'm supportive and nurturing to others and myself. I am not to judge.

ANOTHER DAY : I was getting angry with God for being a bastard. Telling Him I wanted to be with this one, meaning Wayne. I've been through this before. Wayne said, "You're a beautiful person, I really love you, but you're still blaming me for what your grandfather did to you and I can't be around that." I told God he was nice and I stopped. My perception of the person became clearer. Here I am setting on my bed crying because this person doesn't accept or want to be around me because I'm trying to heal from the pains of my childhood and I've got this perfect picture of him! God removed Wayne for a darn good reason, not because I'm not worthy or because God wants to hurt me, but for my highest good. I now know when I'm upset I can ask for a hug off my Mum. Mum saw me upset yesterday, and she apologised because she forgot that when I was with her, and I cried this way, it was because I was being abused in some shape or form by someone else. All I probably needed was a cuddle and some reassurance that what I was going through was okay. I was in the process of being healed with my Mum. Wayne may just be a distraction of what's really going on here. All I ever wanted was my Mum's support, comfort, cuddles and compassion. She had the ability to see me upset, acknowledge and tell me I'm okay and that I will be okay. She sees it that way too. I have an abundance of healing going on within my family.

What about Eugene? I haven't demanded anything from him. I haven't picked up cigarettes, cigars or overdosed on chocolate to cope and I've been emotionally stable around him.

I must let Wayne follow his path. 'God I ask for the strength to forgive myself for not saying anything more to Wayne than: "Okay, thank-you for ringing and getting it clear. That's it, goodbye."

I pray that's all I needed to say. I trust he is in God's hands and that I am also. Yes, I'd love him to turn around and say: "Sorry, I've made a mistake, can we have another go."

'God, please remove my self-will and my self-reliance. Remove from me the idea that I think he's the only 'one' and the best 'one' to be with. It's obvious he's not right now and that's okay with me.'

ANOTHER DAY : I'm physically tired at the moment. I have no energy. I ate Tim Tams and chocolate biscuits last night. I'm aware of what chocolate does to me. How about a pat on the back, for not picking up smokes or cigars and for not totally bingeing out on coffee, Red Bulls (high caffeine soft drink) and sugar? I'm going through an emotional roller coaster at the moment. I'm blank in the head and I feel distant. I'm finding it hard to pray because my mind is elsewhere. I feel I need time out with God.
I have Debbie coming tonight; this is new for her to visit me and I'm excited about it.

Wayne isn't sitting well with us just being friends. He asked me if I were vindictive. Look out here I come! I have some pretty nasty thoughts running through my cranium. Fear is what stands in the way and faith is the only way through this one. Now that I know he's hurting and that he's changing his mind, I'm now reconsidering what I want. He prays for me to find relief from my past so that it no longer moulds me. I like the emotional effects. Wow. Through my upsets it brings me closer to the people around me. My upset with my mother brought about a new closeness. Mum's realisation that at times all I need is reassurance and affection is a real breakthrough. I starve for my Mum's love. I crave it and I've been seeking it through my boyfriends. I have a need to be told that I'm okay, I'm enough, I'm wonderful, I'm intelligent and I'm lovable by my mother. I didn't feel lovable to my Mum. She deliberately chose to ignore my emotional, mental and physical needs when I was child. She called while I was living in Queensland and told me that she would deliberately ignore me when she knew I needed a hug or comfort. She apologised for treating me this way. I need healing around that. For me it's not time for a mental psychoanalysis, it's time for love and compassion.

I fear something in Wayne. I know something and by not acknowledging it I may put myself in a position to be hurt. It's a recurring feeling in me. It's not a gentle feeling. I feel my little girl is not safe. Words of ignorance and arrogance will swiftly crush my gentle spirit. This is why I have a calling to go and be with God. To walk in the botanical gardens with God, with myself, and with the world, is what I need right now.

Let's go.

ANOTHER DAY : Acceptance is what I want from my boyfriend; also some patience, tolerance and compassion. I need that. I'm okay to be where I'm at today. Whether Wayne likes me or not, is with me or not, I need to like me and be with me always. It is my right to be around people who accept me. To be around people who are not afraid of me. It's my right to choose not to be around people who attack me by pulling my curtains down and leaving me naked. I do not need to explain myself. God knows my needs. He knows me better than I do. 'God, I ask you to put a man in my life that is supportive, gentle and not damaging.' I believe if I ask, I shall receive. It's important for me to recognise this, so that this is what I know I can handle. Anything I cannot handle I can walk away from to look after myself. I'm important enough to me to do what is required for my wellbeing. I've been though a lot of self-doubt, self put-down and unhealthy guilt because I'm not able to love myself particularly when men are involved. Wayne is not everything to me. To him he is, to me he is not. He's another fellow human being with his ideas and coping mechanisms just like me. He is about wanting to be happy, safe and content, just like me. He's not wrong and neither am I. He reminds me of the way I was. Thinking that I must go to as many meetings as possible, that I must do exactly what is suggested by my sponsor, believing the sponsor is always right and believing that I must follow the logical mind for it will keep me safe. Aaarrh! Yuk! For me, being that way wasn't loving toward myself; it was keeping others happy and living in fear. God keeps me away from the first drink and directs my life from my heart and no one knows what is good for me other than my Higher Power. That's why at that time I needed more. I needed a total breakdown.

I'm still in denial about my relationship with Maree. My mind tells me she can't be wrong. She was so beautiful, magnificent, knowing and helpful; how could she be wrong?

My good friend, Graeme, who has been around for many, many years sees things much differently about the way I was treated by Maree, along with my Mum and other people. I tell them the things I think they won't judge her by and still they see otherwise. I feel guilty because I know she gave me so much of her heart, time and effort, how could she be possibly damaging? Despite the fact I was an emotional, mental and spiritual mess when I finally stepped foot back in my Hometown where I felt the safest place for me to be. 'God, I ask to see the truth in all things. I pray for the strength not to sacrifice my truth for others' approval.'

ANOTHER DAY : Have I been lying to myself? Yes. I am fully self-expressed. I laugh when I am happy and joyous. I cry when I am grateful, wounded, sad, and when I sing and when I love people and animals. I stop to observe the little things. I'm generous, caring and thoughtful; I believe what is God's is mine. My words are caring, loving and gentle and I have a great capacity of acceptance, tolerance and compassion for others. I'm fully alive. I do not need to hide this from others. I do not need to feel shamed about whom I am or the way I am. When I shame myself I walk away from who I am. Let Wayne criticise me, judge me, be hard with me. Go ahead. I will not fall off my rock for God will hold me still and safe. Let my wisdom, knowledge and love shine through. Treat him as a fellow member, as a fellow human being. He is not my enemy. He is an instrument to bring out in me that, which is not love. Time to cross the road and be supportive, strong and loving. May God be my strength and my guide to show me how to love this man exactly the way he is without criticism, judgement, impatience and resentment. Wayne is just as afraid as I am when it comes to closeness. He is going to attack me because he likes me. He is going to be what I was like a while ago, in early recovery. Am I committed to this person or am I just pretending? Am I waffling? I have just been waffling. I am committed to loving Wayne. I am committed to loving myself and loving my God. If it's not right, God shall remove Wayne. I am powerless over what will and what will not happen. I take a stand in being loving. Wayne takes a stand for me to be who I am and not what my grandfather or my mother has shaped me to be. "A condition is something that we believe will make something better than it already is". My condition on Wayne is for him being compassionate, gentle and accepting at all times.

1/5/99 8:30 AM : I'm playing my South African music. I've had a shower and I'm in bed writing. I spent the weekend with my family. What a wonderful feeling to have spent time with the two beautiful women who are my cousins' girlfriends. How wonderful it is to have two sisters.

Wayne brought up children last night. I felt he already had a pre-judgement of me thinking I wanted kids and that I wanted them now. If I fell pregnant to Wayne I would go through with the pregnancy. Wayne wants to have kids in three years time and with someone he loves. He trusts that he'll know who that will be, when that will be, and the right time for him. I trust it will happen (having children) in God's time, regardless. It's warming to know that a part of Wayne's dreams and desires is to be a father and be a part of a family. It is what I want as well. There is something very beautiful about this man. I could fall into his skin. The woman in me is so taken by him. His skin and the shape of his face, his cheeks and hands I find incredibly attractive. I feel so safe and warm in his arms. It's so good to feel that this feels perfect for me right now. In his words he says we made love. He felt embarrassed saying that to me.

5/5/99 12:58 AM : I'm feeling peaceful, safe, protected, warm and comfortable. Wayne is in Gods hands. I'm powerless over everything. I'm human and I'm okay. I've hit another bump with Wayne today. My mind was racy and I was feeling insecure. I wanted intimacy probably because I wanted reassurance. We talked through this one instead of it becoming 'too much' (Wayne's favourite words). I watched and listened to him babbling on, listening to his brain talk. "Wayne you're afraid too," I said.
His response was: "Well look at you, you wanted intimacy and acted quite the opposite, you're the one who's afraid and insecure."

Wait for it, my response to that was: "You're right Wayne, I am afraid and at times I feel very insecure and it all boils down to your fear of getting hurt and being fucked up. Guess what, that's my fear too. Neither of us wants to end up like our Mums."

Over the phone tonight I shared bits of my childhood and my upbringing by my mother. I think he's becoming more compassionate about where I'm coming from. If he's not, I certainly am. I've accomplished so much and it feels wonderful. He said that I'm still wanting affection and to hear that I'm okay from my Mum. My response to that was: "Yes, you're absolutely right and I'm working on it."

I became aware that what Dr Wilmot has said to me about my responses being different, and I'm owning my stuff, and I'm beginning to feel okay, is because I'm accepting that I'm only human. Yippee! I'm so happy to be home by myself. I love my own space and company. Good night.

ANOTHER DAY : My goodness, I've slept in until 11:45 am. Wow. I'm so cosy and warm. I have a couple of things to do today and that is: pay my rent of $435 and my car insurance of $200. Hopefully I've got enough left over until next Thursday, being payday. I want to ring Marco and perhaps write a letter to Louise. I dreamt about Jarod's (my ex-boyfriend) younger sister this morning. I dreamt that she was getting married and I missed the ceremony. I made it to the reception and it was amazing. There was a huge house and each room had a different theatrical theme and each had a set of musicians. I felt a little jealous. I ended up running after a capsized floating tube. She saw me and wanted to talk to me privately. I was in a rush, she was crying and I was aware that I needed to make amends to her. She didn't know where I had to go. I didn't say goodbye. I really wanted to know what she'd been up to for the past three years. I find her, in real life, to be manipulative and cunning, but also giving, caring and very self-orientated. She's a survivor. Maybe I'm sad and feeling jealous about being left out and left behind. I felt sorry for her and she was aware that I had grown as a human being and that I was well. Then I ran into John. He was offering his home for me to stay over for the weekend because he was going away with his family. I got really excited because I could invite Wayne to stay with me. It would feel like a holiday.

7/5/99 : I'm hurting and aware it's because I'm not feeling lovable or 'enough' and I'm thinking that there's something wrong with me. Wayne is distant and not being affectionate so I've taken the blame. I asked him if it was only I who was feeling uneasy and he said: "Yes." I've had difficulty with anxiety, feeling uncomfortable, fear of rejection and I am fearful of his personality changes. I'm fully aware that he's looking at me, all fingers pointing my way, thinking it's me that's got the problem. Well yes, my emotions were uncomfortable and I didn't enjoy most of my time with him at dinner or the movies, particularly the way he said to me: "It's time to drop you off home because it's late and I'm tired." My intuition tells me he's not being authentic, open and honest and when he denies it I immediately go into thinking I'm wrong and I must be making this up in my head. I'm not wrong. I can feel it. Something was up and I've told myself not to wear it. He has an inability to deal with his stuff and that doesn't mean it's because I'm fucked or insecure. I deserve love. It reminds me of the time when both my Pop and my uncle died. Jarod, my ex-boyfriend, didn't give a rat's arse.

I've had an upset with Nana having her leg amputated and the least Wayne could do is show some kind of affection or concern. I can now trust that because he's a man of the logical mind and not of the heart, that my relationship with him will be a continuous battle. Well, I will surrender. I'm not playing these games with him. The head's too quick, it has too many laws and reasons and it's not my way of living. He can have it. I'm perfectly beautiful in and out in my eyes and in God's. Am I like Wayne? My God, I have a hard time liking myself when I'm self-centred, distant, and not wanting to be affectionate. It doesn't matter that he won't think twice about tonight when I've come home and I've cried, listened to music, had a hot shower, put the fan on, put the heater on, put on my 'jamas and started the oil burner to deal with my emotions of upset. My goodness I look after myself. He overeats, smokes, and he's cold. He doesn't talk at depth, and I've been thinking that there's something wrong with me, because my mind tells me he doesn't like me, and that he's trying to like me but I've been 'too much.' Blah, blah, blah! It's not that important. What's important to me is that I woke up this morning happy and loving God, the world, and myself. Wow. I told Dad he's one in a million and that he's done a fantastic job as a father and that I'm very grateful for him being in my life.

ANOTHER DAY : I'm still feeling sore in my heart about Wayne. It's 1:30 am. I'm still in fear. So what if he does go! They all do, why would he be any different? How can I convince myself that I'm okay? That's the goal of my therapy with Dr Wilmot; to know that when I feel that all is against me, or when I feel that my world is falling apart, that at the end of the day I still know that I'm going to be okay. I've had some challenging homework tonight. It's time to sleep. I'm going to shut out the light. I only need to close my eyes and talk with my loving God. I am everything and nothing and bloody beautiful. I was a lady in red tonight at the meeting, how striking. I felt wonderful.

ANOTHER DAY : Guilt and fear cause me anxiety. Where's my magic wand to wish it away? I went out walking with Marika and I caught up with Scott, my friend from the self-improvement organisation. I rang Louise to see how she is. I laughed. I'm thinking a lot in an attempt to work out my shit. It's not about Wayne is it? It's about me. I've carried yesterday into my today and Wayne's probably over it and here I am still in the shit. It's about my Mum. It's the fear of rejection, abandonment, the feeling that I'm in trouble and that I'm not lovable and not enough. How do I shift through this? I'm in bed at 12:15 pm. I'm tired. The fan is on. I know I'll feel worse by trying to have a nap while I'm filled with anxiety. I had a late night last night. I only had six hours of sleep. 'God, I pray for some compassion, gentleness and love toward myself. I don't have the power to be these things so I ask it from you to instill it in me. God, please remove those things that stand in the way of my recovery.'

ANOTHER DAY : Thank God I brought this book along with me. I feel bad, sad and angry with myself. I feel I can't be forgiven. I'm angry that Wayne can't trust me and that hurts. I repeated something I heard that another person said about me. How come I'm the bad guy here when the topic is about me? It's about what I apparently said in a meeting, that being: "I love going out to get a fuck?" This is not what I said or meant. I feel guilty for breaking Wayne's trust. I did not repeat who informed me of what this someone said about me. I only shared the words that were spoken by others about me.

I'm paralysed in the car. I couldn't be in his presence knowing he won't tell me anything any more. Am I not worthy of trust, even though I broke it and admitted what I had done along with an apology, knowing that my motive wasn't a bad one? The reason why I repeated what Wayne had told me, was for my healing, because I was affected by what he had shared with me. I want to know what's a healthy response to this mess. I'm feeling messed up and I don't want to feel this way when I go to work in the next 15 minutes. Wayne's learnt the lesson not to repeat anything to me because I can't be trusted in his eyes. Well, he's known me for a month. I need to allow him to say what he needs to say, as much as I say what I need to say. I said to him there are many things I don't say to him because I don't trust him. He feels bad that he repeated something to me that he was to keep confidential and said that he's to blame as well, as he can't share stuff in the fellowship with me and that's probably healthy but it still hurts. I don't feel worthy when he talks like that, so I then feel angry that he makes me not feel worthy of trust and he's the one who told me to drop it and not to let it become anything more. But how do I do that? I feel guilt, sadness, the need to be trusted again, and to be forgiven. Feeling this way is demanding upon my emotions. I don't want to rely on his forgiveness to feel okay. Inside tells me I can't be with someone who doesn't trust me. Is that a condition or is it me just having double standards?

'God grant me the serenity to accept the things I cannot change, courage to change the things I can and the wisdom to know the difference.'

Truth: I'm a trustworthy person. I'm worthy of forgiveness of myself, God and of others. I'm not a bad person. I'm allowed to make mistakes. I'm allowed to be human. I'm allowed to be loved. I'm allowed chances. I owe it to myself to forgive myself. I'm okay. I'm loved. I'm caring. I'm open. I'm honest. I'm not malicious. I'm not vindictive. I'm entitled to forgiveness as much as anyone else. If the kids had done this I would forgive them and trust them again. 'God, I trust and pray that what's been said and done is for the best. I will receive those things that come my way.' My lesson at the moment is to allow myself to be human. I'm not bad or untrustworthy or unforgivable. 'God, I'm open to the other lessons. I trust that you know what you are doing'. I'm courageous for saying something. I'm entitled to ask that what I say in a meeting is to be kept confidential and I'm not afraid of knowing the truth.

I'm at my job, child minding and the little one is asleep. It's 7:00 pm and my goodness I really scrolled out a lot of stuff here but I feel better for it. I'm not so heavily burdened. I wish that it wasn't this way. I don't regret saying what I said. I need to ring Courtney over this one. I will call her now… so I rang Courtney while she was racing out the door. I told her the tale and she affirmed that I have not mentioned his name so therefore I had not broken his trust; he's a big boy so he can handle it and get over it. My guilt is just co-dependency on my behalf. I've let that go. At the end of the day, am I right with God? Yes, I am. Wayne may need something to pull him away from me and that I can understand. If he likes me and wants to be with me he can forgive me and accept what I've done.

Funnily enough, before I finished talking to Courtney she suggested for me to speak to the person who made the comment about me to clear it up. She would have done the same as I. I love how she openly expressed she was running late due to having sex for two and half hours. Wow. How womanly, I admire her generosity in her sharing with me. I love that. It's not something to be ashamed about. Thank you God for Courtney in my life.

ANOTHER DAY : I have to write. I honoured myself today. Wayne needs me to abort if I fall pregnant to him, for him to feel safe and secure being with me. My truth is that I cannot, at this point, guarantee abortion if I fall pregnant. Not that I want children. Life has its own way of doing things, and if it's a possibility, then I can only see that sex is out of the question. So I told Wayne that and the result is that we are both going to have a couple of days to think about it. Wayne's not interested in being with me if there is no sex or intimacy. I do not want to be with someone who does not want to be with me because I'm not wanting to have sex. It's in God's hands now. That's okay with me. I want to be with someone who doesn't see me as someone who is in 'their' way of 'their' career. He may not like me enough. They generally don't. Well done, it's created a space of love, strength, compassion, passion, trust and safety. I do matter to me. Wayne matters to him. We don't see eye to eye on this subject. I do like him enough to give it a go, to stay with him and work through the obstacles, the force behind me is much more powerful than the obstacle in front of me.

I was more like me at work today. I could tell by my voice tones, how I interacted with the children and how I responded to Liz and David. I voiced my opinion about meal times and Liz agreed. She said David will support me and he too stands by me. I did a bit of pampering of myself today but not as much as I would have liked. Liz bought me another bracelet to replace the bracelet I lost. We all went out for Chinese at the casino. It was very elegant. I'm treated with respect and general care. I was relaxed and comfortable because I am accepting who I am and believing I am okay. I didn't need to make a scene about what I need. It happened over dinner—God tapped me on the shoulder. Throughout the night I've been responding the way I would respond. Fantastic. These guys (Liz and David) spoil me. How different from the days when I worked at the supermarket or for Richard in Queensland. Wow.

I will pray for Wayne. I did request something of him and that was for him to be open to the possibility to see me as 'me' and not as a woman who's going to trash his sobriety or his name in the fellowship. I'm also not a woman that has a desire to 'trap' a man by having a baby. I'm neither of those 'kinds' of women. He asked me not to treat him as if he is my grandfather who sexually abused me. Fair call. Note: I had nothing to say about that one. He matters enough for me to give up my story that's attaching him to be my grandfather. Perhaps I may be enough for him to give up his story about me. Maybe. In saying that, if

God doesn't want him in my life as my boyfriend then neither do I! I'm going to pray now, for the both of us and for my other loved ones. 'Thank you God, for another day.'

I also let Wayne know that if he needs to know anything more about me or if he makes up any assumptions, to ring and ask me first before making them concrete facts. I told him that I'd wait for him to call me if or when he decides whether he wants to stay or go in our relationship. I told him that ending or continuing the relationship is okay with me. I meant it. Every word today over lunch with Wayne was real and loving. Thank you God for treasures like the author of book 'In The Meantime', what a great teacher of love for me and for others she is. Thanks.

we are all
single

yet together

in one

Twelve Years Later...
Going within to remember that healing and
new love is available to me during times of
anguish and deep sorrow

OLD THOUGHT: Everything sucks & life's against me
NEW THOUGHT: Thank you life for all I have right now

My Mum would say to me; "If you're not happy with what you have, how can you be happy with more?" I didn't have much in the first place to be grateful for; surely I need to have the stuff and great experiences that I want to possibly be thankful and grateful? What are you talking about Mum? I don't have enough money. I don't have enough good clothes because I can't afford them. Not having nice clothes to wear stops me from going anywhere, down the street, out with friends, going on a date. I can't travel anywhere because I don't have any savings and if it weren't for my girlfriend cutting my hair on the cheap, I'd have re-growth down to my knees! I felt at the time that everything sucked and life was against me. I found it hard to make ends meet when I was drinking because I had my priorities around the wrong way; spending what I had on alcohol, cigarettes, too much food, clothing I couldn't afford, buying a new car I couldn't afford etc. And when I sobered up I still found it hard to make ends meet because I started to only work where I felt useful and purposeful, and not just for money, which meant I had less money.

Well, there's something about what my Mum said which felt true. I knew there were a lot of other people in much worse conditions than myself who would have cut off their right arm to have a little bit of what I had. I had a bed to sleep in. I had a bed with sheets, a doona and a pillow. I had a roof over my head. I had legs to walk on. I had eyes to see with, hair to brush, ears to hear with and lots, lots more. I had enough food, I surely wasn't going to starve, as thousands of kids live on the streets in Australia do. I didn't feel worthy to have more while I was ungrateful for what I already had. There was a tiny incy-wincy part of me which also believed I deserved more, and this was enough to think maybe good things will come my way.

Good things came my way as soon as I began to recognize what good things were. If I saw someone smile at me down the street, I felt acknowledged, I was thankful. If someone gave way to me, when I was in my car or as a pedestrian, I felt considered and I was thankful. If someone called me up to see how I was going, I felt cared about and I felt thankful. Recognising the impact upon me that those small acts of kindness from others had upon me, I felt inspired me to do the same for others. The good feeling was contagious and something I wanted more of, rather than trying to get good feelings out of objects, clothing, partying, drugs, alcohol, cigarettes and food—and this way was harmless and for free! It seemed to attract more and more good stuff into my life. Funny that!

OLD THOUGHT: I'm feeling bad & down and that's all I feel
NEW THOUGHT: Joy is available to me if only I'm willing to feel it

It's interesting how I focused at times only on my suffering. I was mentioning the things I was grateful for which was great, however I easily skipped over experiences where there had been joy or even laughter because of the constant feeling of anxiety, fear or worry. When I feel bad, down and out it's easy for me to think this is how it is going to be forever! I then fall more deeply into the feeling of doom and then continue to fight the reality that I actually do feel doomed. Whether it's real or not does not matter. I feel what I feel and when I fight against what I feel, it grabs me more fiercely.

So, it's a bit of a balancing act. I encourage myself to feel my feelings of badness, downness, sadness, anxiousness or other 'nesses.' Quit the fight and accept how it is for the moment, for it is only for the moment I am feeling this. I am willing, during these times, to remind myself that joy exists and available to me. It really helps if I am open to it. It's much more difficult to experience joy if I don't invite it in to my life, or fail to be aware of its presence.

Then there is patience. This is where trust in life, and believing I deserve to feel goodness, comes into it. When I fail to bring about joy into my life and heart I accept it, I am willing to be willing to wait until it passes for however long it takes, and get on with what I need to do for that moment, to the best of my ability.

Joy is available to me when I believe and trust it is waiting for me to invite it in and to welcome it into my life. If all else fails, smiling when I don't want to, can be an invitation to feeling joy. Doing something wacky, funny or silly is another fabulous tool to get the joy juices going. Or, what my mates and I have done on the odd occasion, we'd laugh the loudest, silliest laugh we could conjure up together, and before we knew it, we were laughing hysterically at, and with, each another. I find looking for the humour important to my emotional and mental health. Like my Mum says, "Life is too serious to be taken too seriously".

Okay here's one for you. After having my baby, my body is just not the same. My boobs have lost their bounce; they're flat and point to the ground. My bum will never be the same because when my baby was born the surgeon cut it to high heaven, and someone else sewed it up. It seemed like hours and the fact is my vagina flaps in the wind—so I'm screwed! Mind you, I still like my body regardless of all its imperfections. I don't need to be a Barbie doll to be loved. I love myself just the way I am – 99%! I do have my moments.

So here I am getting back on top of things, I'm standing in the hallway thinking I had enough time to change clothes before going to the toilet. Off come the pants, out squirts my wiss, as I trip and slip on it, crashing into the wall toward the toilet. My flappy flange just couldn't hold it together and without it slipping me up with the urine leakage I would have missed out on the huge laugh I had at myself imagining what I would have looked like if someone were watching. I was watching and I caught the humour. Joy is forever available to me if only I am willing to feel it.

OLD THOUGHT: I'm lazy if I'm not working or doing something all the time
NEW THOUGHT: Resting & looking after myself is healthy & enjoyable

Learning to listen to my body and myself. That was hard to do when I had a mind which told me I was bad and wrong for resting, or not doing something productive, like working ALL the time. I believed I was lazy if I wasn't seen to be working or doing something all the time. I felt worthy if I was doing something and unworthy if I didn't.

Things I began doing to look after myself: I read uplifting literature and books I enjoyed, went for walks with either my Higher Power or my dear friend Marika in the botanical gardens, down the street, in the bush. I wore my pj's as long as I liked during the day or when I get home from work. I slept when I was tired, that was a strange concept! Or I rested my body when I was weary. I wore my favourite perfume for the hell of it and used the crystal glasses to believe everyday is a day to celebrate. I bought food and cooked food I loved. I wore clothes I felt really comfortable wearing and chose colors, which lifted my soul. Sometimes I'd do something wild and throw on a caftan, or a big silly hat! I rang friends I felt really accepted and loved by. I chose to do random spontaneous things for others for the sake of it. I wrote when I felt like writing or lost myself in watching a good film—or two! I picked flowers, collected stones, studied and appreciated street art, graffiti, or a brilliant building. Or, I could imagine what happened over the years to a shaggy washed-up house or shed.

All of these things were healthy for my soul, heart and mind. These are the many ways I began looking after myself and I found these things very enjoyable after a while. I didn't believe I deserved to be happy or to experience nice things so this is why it took a while to receive the joy and happiness, which comes from looking after, and being kind, to myself. It was foreign at the start and now it is a way of happy living.

SACRED CREATIVE FOCUS
BOUNDARIES WITH OTHERS AND MYSELF

Recognising what my limits are creates healthier relationships with others and myself. For me it's about knowing what I can or can't do for others, what I am or am not comfortable with or what I like or don't like. If I don't know answers to some of these questions I end up thinking, saying and doing things, which take me, away from who I really am, who I really want to be. I am ultimately taken away from feeling happy, healthy and fulfilled. I've found knowing my limits is an integral part of taking care of myself. When I take good care of myself I feel good inside.

Saying "no" when I need to say "no" increases my sense of self-esteem and self-confidence. It also creates a feeling of inner happiness, healthiness and fulfilment. It's when I'm not able to recognise when to say "no" to others or to myself I create unhealthy relationships because I'm letting others and myself do or say things which makes me feel uncomfortable. I don't know about you, but I hate feeling uncomfortable. The discomfort can feel like sadness, anger, anxiety, fear, restlessness and discontent. I can feel pissed off and/or disrespected, offended, unimportant and invisible when I let others do or say things to me I don't like.

I can say "yes" when I need to say "no" to please the other person. It's an old way to keep people happy with me, too afraid to deal with being disliked, or not being the favourite, or being criticised. I also can say "yes" to something when I need to say "no" because I want to procrastinate, avoid or deny the truth about something or someone.

Knowing myself, my thoughts, my feelings and what I'm doing helps me to know whether or not I have appropriate limits that are good for me. I now practice distinguishing between what is right for myself and what is right for others. When I lovingly let others take responsibility for themselves, even take responsibility for their own disappointment, pain and life's situations they are faced with - I feel healthier for it. It's a freeing feeling walking beside someone and taking care of myself in all aspects of my life.

In moments when I feel like forgetting I have limits as to what I can or can't do, I pause and ask Life to give me a new thought, a new awareness, or a new truth. The anxiety lifts from me and happiness rises up within me once again. I am able to do things freely, which brings me joy—such as learning how to weld metal or to make a pavlova! I need to be brave and spend time with those I feel great around. Now is the time to create relationships with others who respect "no". Now is the time to create a life where I am doing the things, which bring me joy.

SACRED CREATIVE ACTIVITY

I think of someone I feel good around and someone I don't feel good around. I draw a simple line drawing or stick figure of the two people I have in mind. I draw the person I don't feel good around on the left-hand side and the person I feel good around on the right-hand side of the page. I cut and paste words from a magazine, a newspaper or write words (see the 'List of Feelings' in the Appendix) in and around both of the people I know, which describe how I feel when I am in their company. I can include the things they say to me when I feel upset, or how they are with me when you tell them about something I'm excited about. I write down what they are like when I want to explore something new, or when I share how I feel, or about the things I do or not like. I sit and contemplate any differences between the two people and perhaps see why I feel the way I do in their company.

SACRED MEDITATIVE ACTIVITY

Having done the Sacred Creative Activity I begin to observe how I feel with the people I choose to spend time with and I do this without negative judgement or criticism toward myself or the other person. It's a time for me to simply pay attention, to observe my feelings and how I am with the people in my life. I ask myself, are there people in my life I feel good to be around and if so, am I nurturing those relationships? Do I let others know how good I feel in their company? Do I show my thankfulness in some way for the qualities they possess as a person, which allows me to feel good about myself when I am with them? Do I make others feel good about who they are when they are in my company?

COMMITMENT STATEMENT

I .... am willing to put aside everything I think I know about myself, my life, my past, my future, in order to have an open mind and a new experience with boundaries with others and myself. I am open to the possibility of creating healthy boundaries with others' and with myself, receiving new thoughts, and living a new life.

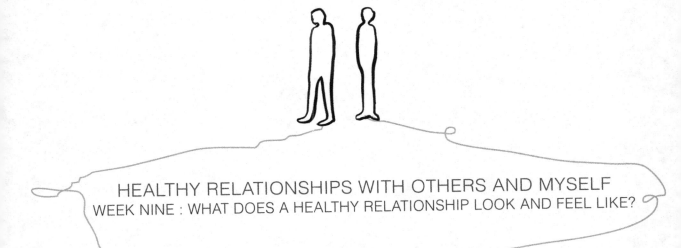

HEALTHY RELATIONSHIPS WITH OTHERS AND MYSELF
WEEK NINE : WHAT DOES A HEALTHY RELATIONSHIP LOOK AND FEEL LIKE?

INTRODUCTION TO THE SACRED SHARING

MY UNCLE ASKED ME TO MOVE OUT OF HIS FLAT WHEN I WAS TO RETURN FROM THE HOLIDAY IN QLD WITH WAYNE. WAYNE OFFERED FOR ME TO STAY WITH HIM DURING THE TIME IT WOULD TAKE TO FIND A PLACE TO LIVE. IT TOOK AROUND FIVE WEEKS AND AT THE END OF THE FIVE WEEKS I WAS VERY EAGER TO LEAVE. I LONGED FOR MY OWN SPACE, MY OWN HOME TO CHILL OUT, RELAX OR TO REFLECT.

ANOTHER DAY : My stomach is fucked, clogged. It's annoying. I'm putting on weight. I know I am. I had five coffees yesterday. God, that's a lot. Jezza (I have liked this guy since I was 16) hasn't called. I was hoping he would have. Who would hope a guy would call them at strange hours during the night? Look at me, a looser. Hmm, my tummy feels somewhat hungry. A good sign. It's 9:10am. I'm waiting for Courtney to call. I'll call her. I can't wait until I go to a meeting today. I didn't ring Kevin (landscape gardener for Liz and David) back last night. I couldn't find his phone number. He'll be wondering why I haven't called. I'm afraid he might be keen on me. My fault. I asked him out to the pictures for something to do when I was feeling lonely. When yesterday came, I found I wasn't lonely and I didn't want to catch up with him any more. He invited me to see him this Sunday and I said yes, to people please, I didn't want to hurt his feelings. I feel like a nasty person and this is what I fear with Jezza - that he only likes me as a friend and I must make him feel awfully uncomfortable because my feelings are deeper than that. Really, I wish he would just tell me he only likes me as a friend and put me out of my misery. If I definitely knew that, I would accept it and move on. But because he hasn't told me he interested in me I always have hope that maybe he likes me too. So I must tell Kevin that we're only friends and nothing more. Knowing my luck he probably sees it that way anyway and I'll make a fool out of myself. At least it will be out of the way.

Now I'm suppose to write three pages because that's what Julie Cameron suggests for my morning pages out of the book, 'The Artists Way.' I'm curious how this book will affect me. How incredible the woman who wrote that book is. It's the perfect book for me to read. I want to keep it simple and focus on daily efforts, not committing myself to do the twelve-week course. I pray for a miracle, a breakthrough. My life would be so much fun if it included all the creative things in it that I like for example: painting, drawing, framing, dancing, singing, and writing. It's me to the tee. Seeing that I don't start work until 2:30pm each day I can fit some of these things that I love into my life.

How embarrassing telling Jezza that I wanted to write a book, especially on the steps to bringing oneself back to living in the moment. I'm sure he's thinking I'm a dreamer: "she doesn't know how to paint and she's no good anyway, she hasn't travelled the world and she has no desire to. She's so ignorant."

ANOTHER DAY : Okay lets write. I feel somewhat off. To begin with, I feel clogged up in the stomach because I ate too much last night. I hurt myself doing that. I haven't done that in a long time. I ate at Marika's (I met Marika through my mother when I was nine and she is my dear friend today). She asked me if I'd stay for tea with her and the love of her life, Gerry. I was delighted to fill in the time with them over yummy food knowing that Troy (Lana's' friend) was cooking back at my place planning to dish it up in a couple of hours time. I thought I could get away with eating two meals, but three hours later I was not hungry. I missed sitting down with Troy and Lana, instead I went out and got a video with another friend.

When I came back I ate some meat out of the fridge with mayonnaise. Lana yelled out from the lounge room that it would have been nice of me to have eaten the meat from a plate. She was hurt and angry that I had already eaten and chose not to be part of the dinner when she spent her money and time with her friend, Troy, and cooked for three hours to create a beautiful meal for me. For me! I thought I was just joining them for dinner! I didn't realise the importance of me being there. So I felt bad and sat down and ate a plate of food. The mushrooms and meat had been soaked in red wine prior to being cooked. I didn't care, I ate it anyway so they would feel better and I felt like shit. Still they asked why I was eating when I was not hungry, which angered me because I was eating the food to make them happy and they took the piss out of me anyway.

I dreamt of Wayne wanting another woman and I felt jealous.

ANOTHER DAY : Great it's Cup Day and I'm so tired. I'm in bed and it's 9:30am. God, Wayne's on my mind. I wish it would go away. God, I pray for him and his sobriety. I pray for your will in his life. I pray for another love in his life. I pray for the release of the negative words he said to me. He's allowed to say what he likes and it doesn't mean that what he does say about me is true.

I'll be earning $21 an hour today and I may only work eight hours, so that's $168 for a day's work. Great, because I need my teeth fixed, a new seat belt, a car service, hand brake fixed and new glasses.

Yes I want to see Wayne to see what he's doing and what he looks like. I want to go to the BBQ and be amongst the members and have some fun in the sun. Staying at home by myself does not appeal to me. Wayne may not be there. If he is and it's too much, I can leave. All I know is, I'd like to go. At the back of my mind I'm wondering if Jezza will ring because I know he's in town.

8/11/99 : Oh my, I'm suffering from period pain. I'm very sore and my belly is aching. It's just after 9:00 am and I'm feeling a little guilty for being in bed. This writing helps a great deal. A couple of months ago I was getting up at 6:30 am and walking, helping Marika, going to meetings, going to work and finishing very late at night. Wayne would fall asleep around 12:00 midnight and he would wake me throughout the night. I had many sleepless nights with him. No wonder I became so fatigued. I was on the go the whole time. Now at least I can come home from work to unwind and not be pressured to have sex. I can go to bed and sleep the whole night through. I've noticed I've been waking up around 8:15 am. Dr Wilmot says that resting for the time being will do me the world of good.

ANOTHER DAY : What Wayne did was very hurtful, telling me to get over my sexual abuse and to stop blaming everything wrong in my life because of it. He wanted me to prove and demonstrate to him that I love him by working hard to get him back and then told me that I'm no longer the beautiful person he thought I was. He called me a manipulative, game playing person. He told me never to call him again or go to the same meetings as he. I can see now that's very vindictive of him to say these things. I understand it's because he's hurting. I ask to be freed of the burden of the guilt I have felt because of this. He was being nasty. I'm happy you took him out of my life. Thank-you, I needed my happiness back.

ANOTHER DAY : I have to write. I feel hyperactive, I'm thinking and feeling too much. I'm afraid of getting into trouble by Wayne.

I'm taking Lana's friend along to the lunchtime meeting tomorrow. I can't get him sober or keep him sober, but somehow I feel responsible. I am responsible to carry the message and to hold my hand out to help another if they need help. I'm still hurting about not being with Wayne. I accept that our relationship is over; I just miss him. I'm not to blame him for the relationship breaking down. It's simply not meant to be for me right now. He probably still thinks I suck. Good for him. Let him think what he likes.

10/11/99 : My eyes feel crusty. I have the dentist appointment this morning. Just a check up, thank God. Thank-you God for giving me a job that pays me enough to go to the dentist.

Now I didn't fall asleep until after 2:30 am and I'm up at 8 am. Well that's life. I'm probably missing Wayne 'cos I can't have him. Bullshit, you're allowed to miss him. I can't believe he still pulls his pants up to his chest and then fills his pockets up with bulky items that hang down to his knees. So, God, tell him to pull his pants down a little, okay, just take care of him.

I pray for Troy. He is nervous about receiving his pay tomorrow, afraid of what he'll do with it. May I be a useful instrument for you, God. May I keep the wrong words in and let the right words out.

I need to continue reading 'The Artist's Way'. It would be good for me to start the morning writings. First things first. I'm thinking it might help to unblock my creativity and it will, if I choose to put action to it. God, I pray for the willingness to continue with the book.

11/11/99 : Keeping Troy busy is probably a good thing. At least I'll be getting to more meetings. If he picks up a drink, good luck to him, the chances are that he will. God, I pray I don't take on feeling responsible for that. It is his choice.

12/11/99 : When mum moved us kids to town without Dad, I went through a great amount of pain. I remember standing in the bathroom brushing my teeth without any energy thinking to myself that 'this is too hard, I don't want to go to school.' There were 600 kids at the 'new' school, compared to the one we left behind that only had 19 kids attending. My heart was broken and I don't think I knew what it was at the time but it hurt like mad and I just didn't want to be there, I wanted to die. I remember waking up at Dad's house (the old farmhouse) lying in the bed in the lounge room and the room was spinning. It reminds me of being drunk. I wonder, was I? I don't remember feeling sick in the stomach though. So I most likely wasn't. I was sad to go back to Shepparton to my new home with Mum and my cousins. It felt weird. I don't know why I was the only one who went to Dads. Maybe I wasn't and us kids took it in turns.

My girlfriend Shianne is going through the 'I'm ugly and my body is horrible and I'm never going to get any love that I want' stage. I use to ask my God are there any men out there for me? I didn't notice when I stopped being that way. Today I'm sad and missing Wayne and I trust I'm meant to be single and that love will show up. I do fear the panic and nervousness I will feel when and if I see him. What will he look like? What will I think and what will happen? I went to the Saturday meeting last night and I experienced a mild panic attack because Wayne goes there sometimes.

I would like to ring Kevin and make my amends for not calling as soon as I could to explain to him I didn't ring him because I lost his number. I feel uncomfortable with him, feeling that he likes me more than a friend.

Jezza contacted me Thursday around 5:00 pm, Melbourne Cup day. I rang him back at 9:00 pm and he was drunk, as I expected. We didn't catch up because I decided not to. I wanted to preserve my energy and go home and say 'hi' to my girlfriend Ruby as she was down from our Hometown. I felt happy that I did. I based my decision on, "I don't have to work it all out right now with Jezza. Jezza can wait until I do know what I want."

13/11/99 : I'd really like to follow up with Megan's offer to teach me how to play the guitar, sing and write songs. I also want to learn how to dance a particular dance and master it, that would be great. I love dancing. I've created two paintings, one where I'm cutting my pubic hair. How revealing, but my friends saw it and they weren't disgusted. It's like standing nude in front of my friends.

I'm missing Wayne so I need to remind myself he's here in spirit. His love is in my heart. He's being looked after by God. The fact he hasn't contacted me suggests to me that he thinks he is right about what he said. A part of me is holding onto the thought that maybe he and I will get together again soon. The truth is I don't know what will happen between us in the future. He may have already met someone or fallen out of love with me. The fact is he is not here. He is not talking to me and I miss him. That's okay with me. Jezza only rings me when he's had a few beers.

14/11/99 : I see Dr Wilmot today, he'll be so wrapped to hear about my art.

In my dream I was flying over Brisbane's ocean waters and I remember thinking: "it's not as far as I thought." I was carrying this guy on my back who turned out to be my boyfriend. I was so happy to see the city of Brisbane. Joy rushed through my body. I was lying down with this hairy-faced man being intimate (it's great to dream about being with a man instead of animals such as elephants, dogs, rhino's etc). I dreamt I was masturbating and accepting myself.

Dad asked me if I was manipulating and playing games with Wayne's heart. Hmm, when I got back with Wayne I said I wasn't passionately in love with him. I said my love will either grow or die. I was a little confused. I told him my truth. He was very insecure and so was I. It didn't work out and I'm not responsible for all of it. I think I did play with his heart. My intention was not to hurt his feelings. I really wanted to be in the relationship. I wanted so much to be with him but I discovered the second time around that something didn't feel right. I was so unhappy and exhausted. It's up to me to take care of myself and it's not up to my boyfriend. I need to make sure I get enough sleep. Dad thinks it's great that I'm doing lots of things that make me happy because that keeps my mind off the boy stuff. He says the boy stuff will work itself out if I continue to focus on what I'm meant to be doing. There's a lot more to life than stressing and worrying about boys. Courtney suggested that I read, 'Love Addiction.'

I'm rather afraid of reading it. I don't want to be more obsessed than I already am.

15/11/99 : I couldn't sleep last night. My brain was repeating what happened yesterday. It wasn't a good feeling seeing Wayne with another woman last night. My insides died and my body fell to pieces. I looked at him and held my look until he eventually looked away. I didn't assassinate the girl in my mind by having to put her down to make me feel more superior to avoid feeling rejected. She did look like the girl from his office that he would talk to me about describing her as a bag and put her down for being dumb. The thought crossed my mind that Wayne will be happy with her if she doesn't challenge him in any way by not having any boundaries around what she will or won't tolerate. It's none of my business. I had my cry last night. I can hardly see through my crusty eyes this morning. To love means to want the highest good for someone. God, I pray for your will in his life, for his happiness, love and joy. Please forgive me for finding that hard to do last night. I was being very selfish. He doesn't want to talk to me and that's okay with me.

If that is what God wants, than that is what I want. It is over.

I had a great session with Dr Wilmot. I was very happy and funny. He said that going back in my mind over what has happened in the past only hurts me. He said I can now give up going over the past. I need my self most during these harder times. Fuck feeling bad and speaking nastily to myself. I need to go to the toilet, brush my teeth, get dressed, read my daily beginnings, say some prayers and thank my God for the acceptance of being me, for feeing alive and loved.

16/11/99 : I've missed my dentist appointment by mistake. I've realised something. I have not accepted my relationship with Wayne is over. I am not having a relationship with him. He is not here. He is not talking to me. I have been waiting for him to do something. No wonder, when he told me not to contact him - it leaves me waiting for him. I don't want to wait any more. I don't have to. It is finished. There's nothing to do or say. Subject closed. Caput! God, I pray for the willingness to let go and to accept. God, I admit I am powerless over Wayne. I do believe you have an answer. I am willing to follow the steps to be open to what you may have in store for me. What I want is for him to ring me, talk to me, say sorry for saying the things he said. I want him to say: "I don't think you're manipulative or playing mind games and I know you care for me deeply." I want him to say: "Sorry for demanding so much from you. Sorry for not giving you the space that you asked for. Sorry for making you wrong when you didn't want to have sex with me. Sorry for blaming the sexual abuse for your reason for not wanting to have sex with me. Sorry for telling you that I've never had problems with girls not wanting to have sex with me in an attempt to make you think there was something wrong with you. Sorry for not allowing you time to find your own way. Sorry for blaming you for blaming the sexual abuse for the sadness in your heart. Sorry I made you wrong for being sexually abused. Sorry for abusing you now by punishing you with my silent scorn." I want to feel free from wanting Wayne and for wanting reconciliation. Free me from this bad feeling, the pain and my internal torment. I want to let him go. I want to be free within me to let him be loved. I want to be free to love. I want to be free to let me love and to be loved. I want to accept and move on. I want to be free from all of this today, right now. I want to tell him how hurt I've been. How much sleep I've lost and it's his fucking fault. I want him to stop torturing me, to stop this nonsense. Where's my friend? He said he would support my healing of sexual abuse. He said he loved me and he's not even talking to me. I want freedom from my internal war, for feeling like a bad person, to stop thinking he's going to call. I want to love myself. I don't want to need his love to feel okay. I don't need his approval to feel okay.

Do I know how to get what I want? NO I DON'T. Do I honestly know what is good or bad for me? No I don't. I do not know how to achieve these things, to get what I want without knowing whether they are good or bad for me. Am I willing to hand it all over to God who might have another answer I have not thought of? Yes, God. I am willing to hand over to you my powerlessness over Wayne. Am I willing to forgive myself for being self-reliant which has failed me; otherwise I would have what I wanted? God, I ask that you please remove my self-reliance; thinking that I should know how to get what I want. I pray for the forgiveness of myself for expecting myself to know it all. Where am I? I am lying on my bed, writing. Am I willing to stay in the moment for just three seconds, because that's where God is and all the power is in the here and now? Yes, I am willing. Done. Am I willing to do God's assignments that he gives me today? Yes I am.

17/11/99 : I'm back from getting my tooth pulled out. I have cotton gauze placed where the wisdom tooth once was. I do love Wayne. He's a beautiful person. I'll love him from here. I accept he's not with me. I love him all the same. Wayne isn't talking to me and because I saw him with another woman doesn't mean I'm nothing, bad or horrible or that he even hates me.

I love my body at the moment. The figure I've always wanted has arrived and it's mine. I'm happy. I am comfortable. I am satisfied. Wow! Of course my mind says, 'yeah, but you'd look better with a six pack on your stomach and skinnier thighs and have the knees like the models do.' Thanks for sharing.

It's very cold outside and the workers outside my window are sawing, cutting and hammering. I'd love a rest. Yet it is so noisy. Keep on writing to the end of the page. Barry was great to talk to. He's about 44 years of age. I'm aware he could fall for me. It's not hard to do, fall in love if your heart is open to it. Wayne used to say I was far more intelligent than him. I don't really see that. Marco was attracted to me because of who I was and he ended up hurting me for being me, just like I did to Wayne. Sorry God I will do better next time.

19/11/99 : 10:00 am I've just woken up. I remember waking during the night talking to Jezza in my sleep. What I remember is being in a pub with his friends and feeling uncomfortable, thinking that I shouldn't be there. He was listening to a questionnaire being broadcast over the radio. He was answering all the questions and writing them down. He was doing that so he could win a date with a gorgeous woman. I felt disappointed, but thought fair enough because he is a single man and he can do as he pleases. I was wanting to get changed out of my shorts and into my jeans thinking I'd look dressed up and sexy. I listened to my answering service later on when I got home and Jezza had left a message telling me he couldn't catch up with me. He sincerely told me why and what was happening and how he felt. I was touched by his honesty. It no longer mattered that he was no longer coming over to visit me. His friend asked me why I wasn't pissed off about what had happened and my reply was: "I have my mum and my cousin to visit this weekend in my Hometown and I chose to go for it'll be fun and I know it's okay for him not to turn up." It felt good that I was detached from my expectations upon him. I also dreamt that his father was a verbally abusive man. This is the third time I've dreamt this. I asked him about his dad in my dream and Jezza said: "He's okay." I continued to ask: "He's abusive, isn't he?" I can't remember any more. There are reasons for his behaviour. I need to be, or would like to be when I'm talking with him. I called him last night and left a message on his answering service. I didn't feel sad or stupid that he didn't return my call. It won't stop me from calling again if it feels right at the time.

I dreamt of Marco last night and I was telling him never to call me again. I haven't spoken to Marco for about five months now. I stopped talking to him because I felt uncomfortable being with him. The last time I visited him he touched my boob and I certainly didn't feel good about that. He hadn't accepted that it's my body and he has no right to touch my boobs under any circumstances. I do like the guy despite his inappropriate actions at times.

I feel bad for washing my clothes at work. I'm open to talking to Liz and telling her what I did and how I feel about it. I was joking around with David yesterday saying I'd hate to cross his bitchy side and his response was, "that would never happen because you're too straight and honest." Being called 'honest' is one complement I receive from others and it's from people who have known me for long and short periods of time. It conflicts with Wayne's last words: "You're a manipulative and game playing person and you're no longer the beautiful person I thought you were." He would not know the impact those words have had on me. Six weeks later I can still hear those words he said to me loud and clear every day, all day. I'm not a manipulative and game playing person. It's not all of me. It is a part of my defects of character. I wouldn't be human if I didn't have those defects of character to some degree. I'm not bad or wrong or unlovable because of it. To heal doesn't mean I need his words of approval and words of forgiveness. I won't need them. If I am right with God, then I'm okay.

I think I'd love to go walking with Barry and his dogs today.

Dear Wayne

I've got 10 mins before I go to work. I've found the willingness to write to you. Yes, I'm nervous and scared. I also have a lot to say. I'm so affected by what you said to me; that I'm a manipulative and game playing person. I feel, and have felt, like a bad person ever since. I have not been able to let it go. I've been praying, talking to members, my parents, my friends and my therapist and still the guilt and shame persists. I was and I am hurt by it. I feel like you're punishing me. I have not called, text or gone to the meetings you attend, except for Saturday night live, to respect you boundaries. More so, if I did do those things, it would convince you more that I was playing games and fucking with your head. It's come to a time where I need to have a say. I need to give myself permission to respond. I've been a victim. I've been fearful, sad and deeply hurt. I wish, no I, yes I wish I could just talk with you, person to person. I miss my friend and companion. I have in my mind that you hate me that you're very angry with me, but I also know Wayne to be gentle, loving, caring and open. Not just an angry, hurt person. I'm sorry for hurting your feelings. At the time I was very tired and confused. My motive was not to hurt you. I broke it off between us to save you from being hurt any further. Now I'm only hurting myself. I want you to know you matter to me very much. I love you and care for you very much. I have to go to work. I trust and pray that you and I are in God's hands.

21/11/99 : I've got pains in my tummy. It's early, 8:20 am. The bloody bins are so loud.. It's gorgeous outside with grey clouds scattering the sky. It makes me feel relaxed. Obviously I'm not sending that letter to Wayne. I found talking to Simone last night comforting to understand that Wayne took my inventory and lashed out and perhaps enjoyed every bit of it. Good on him. I can accept that. I can accept that I am not responsible for how he reacts and deals with emotions. If he wants to talk to me he will. I feel relieved that I'm not carrying that burden anymore. If it creeps up again I'll write another letter and let him have it. Drinking coffee is giving me anxiety. It's time to stop drinking it, bugger! It's been good while it's lasted, but I can let it go now. I've thought about painting again this morning. It's been a couple of days now since I last picked up a brush. I need to remember to continue to read 'The Artists Way', reading it might help. I'm afraid of starting. Of course it's about 'I might fail'.

ANOTHER DAY : I've got pains in my tummy. It's nearly time for a poo. Simone stayed over last night. I'll invite her along to a twelve-step recovery meeting this morning. It will do us both good. I'm plugging into the twelve-step recovery program for I grew up with alcoholic parents, drinking friends, cousins and my ex-boyfriend is a sober alcoholic. I certainly belong in those rooms. Barry will probably give me a call this week for lunch. Bob will take me swimming in the ocean this week when I'm ready, perhaps Thursday or Friday. I need to pay for my phone bills, mobile and home, pay the rent and electricity. I have the money and that feels good. I need to put my car in for a service for my hand brake and seat belt. Barry has offered me to help walk his dogs. I'm going to have to write faster. No I'm going to have to take time out for a poo. Aarh, that feels good.

God, I turn my life and will over to your hands today. I thank-you for blessing me with sobriety. Thank-you for a job that is honest, loving and manageable for me. Thank-you for Lana, she's fantastic and a most beautiful housemate. Thank-you for my bed, the covers on my bed, my clothes and how I feel good in them, the money to play with, to pay my bills with and the fantastic dentist I've met who ripped out my tooth. Thank-you for him. Thank-you for my fabulous therapist. Thank-you for the twelve-step recovery program and the fellowship. Thank-you for getting both of my parents sober. Thank-you for my beautiful cousins and their beautiful girlfriends. Thank-you for the fan, what would I do without a fan in my bedroom I do not know. I've had a fan in my room since the age of five and I love it through winter, spring, autumn and summer, thank-you God for that invention. Thank-you for my flat and it's great location in Prahan. Thank-you for my physical health. Thank-you for getting me back into painting and drawing again. Thank-you for all of my beautiful friends. Thank-you for the love and challenges in my life and for being with me all the way up until this very moment.

23/11/99 : It's 5:50 am and I've been awake since 5:00 am. I can't go back to sleep. My mind is torturing me. My right leg is aching, according to Louise Hay it symbolises paralysis; not moving forward, unstable in the male area of my life. Wayne rang me yesterday once he read my letter (I did decide to drop it off in his mailbox). He told me to move on. He told me we weren't compatible and we are to now find our soul mates. He sounded like me; open, free and accepting. I was stuck. I haven't found acceptance at all. I told him I still had hope and I will need more time to heal. I'm angry that he's okay with how things are between us. I told him he was lucky. He asked me why and I said because he's over it and over me. My mind is torturing me telling me he sounded as if he had met someone else. I feel worthless and stupid for not moving on. I'm annoyed with myself for being affected by this. Let's remember some things. I broke off the relationship. I didn't want to have sex with him any more. I was being sexually, emotionally and mentally turned off by the things he would say to me. I wasn't connecting with him. I couldn't look deeply into his eyes. I didn't feel the closeness he felt when we made love. I found myself being turned off by his looks, fuzzy hair, thin lips and light eyelashes. I couldn't connect with him on a spiritual level. I found myself always holding stuff in because I felt he wouldn't understand. I kept a lot of information to myself in case he would misinterpret what I was saying and overreact and not relate. He'd call me 'Buba', what's up with guys calling me 'Buba'? I hate that word, I'm not a baby. I was continuously over tired when I was going out with him. I physically looked like shit. I had a virus in my eyes and rashes on my face telling me I wasn't willing to get honest and take a good look at myself. I had hives on my face when I was talking to him on the phone yesterday, which is caused by great stress. It didn't, and rarely did we, feel 100% right for each other. I felt I had to stoop lower to be at his level. He wasn't mature. He only saw things in black and white. He only saw the logical side of everything and forgot about the matters of the heart. Most of the time he wouldn't go with the flow because he was so demanding on my time and energy. I was exhausted and worn out. It's taken me until now to recover my spark for life and now that he's been on my mind I haven't had a good sleep in a while.

Fuck, my legs are hurting. I hate the aching and I hate the aching in my heart. I'm envious of his acceptance and the clarity he has. I can have that too if I choose. What's the truth? Let's not drag it on.

I ended the relationship because I wasn't happy. It was too much and too full on. He couldn't give me a break. I found myself having to practice great patience and tolerance of him and the fucked up things he would say. He certainly was a challenge. He isn't my boyfriend today and if God wanted him to be, he would be. There is something great in store for me. I bet my eyes are puffy from crying. Hey, my leg feels a bit better. How amazing. I feel more relaxed. I'm powerless over Wayne and what he does. I want him to be happy and to have abundance in all areas of his life. I have been an important part of his life, there's no doubt about that. I too am irreplaceable, special and unique. It's okay with me where we are at. Thank-you God for his phone call, it's alright, I don't have to be in fear of him any more. I just wished he had said something ages ago to let me know that he wasn't so angry with me any more. He gave me the impression to keep out of his way or else. So I was battling with the fear of his anger for the past six weeks. Now I no longer need to. I was very courageous to put my letter into his mailbox to free myself of being confronted by those words. Nothing is what it seems. I should not compare my insides with his outsides. I should not compare my healing with his joy and happiness for that moment on the phone. I trust God knows what he is doing.

23/11/99 : I'm picking Troy (Lana's friend) up today to take him to the midday meeting. I'm temporarily sponsoring him and Simone (fellow friend in recovery). This Saturday I'm going to show Leanne (fellow friend in recovery) through the steps. God has me busy. Charlotte (fellow friend in recovery) rang me yesterday. It was a great step for her, a big step for her. I enjoyed listening and sharing with her. I'm finding that sponsoring and helping newcomers is just like a friendship, getting to know each other and sharing stories and personal experiences.

Perhaps tomorrow morning I'll go swimming with Bob. Lana said she would come with me because I don't feel 100% comfortable going on my own.

Mum pointed out that the 'game player' comment by Wayne is how Wayne sees himself otherwise he wouldn't have seen it so strongly within me. I feel that it wasn't nice being told that I'm a manipulator and game player and then six weeks later after I made the first contact it's: "Oh no, I got over that ages ago, you should have too." What! I'm sorry but why didn't he call me to let me know this? Why did he let me hang. I see too, that I was in the middle of his game. I didn't know how he's going to react. His happy-go-lucky attitude on the phone surprised me. So my racket, as Mum pointed out, is I've lost the best man in the world for me and I'm a loser. This kind of thinking continually makes me feel bad. Mum said I've had it for years. It's going to take a while for me to be gentle to myself. To make him wrong I go into my winning formula, which is, I'm bloody wonderful, don't you realise who I am? This makes me feel better about myself temporarily. So when I recognise I'm doing this I can acknowledge it, thank it for sharing and move on with what ever is at hand. A lovely thing my Mum said last night was: "I love you deeply." It appeared that it was Wayne who loved me deeply, well so did I, just differently. He was extremely insecure and that explains why he was so emotionally demanding and I was so focused on my boundaries. I was taking it in my stride and he was so in my face. He isn't wrong for that and I can get off the wheel of, 'I'm the one who fucked it up.' Courtney congratulated me on waiting until I was ready to be clear before I made any contact with Wayne. She said it was wonderful to see how I gave myself the time and patience to work through my stuff. I've attending meetings, seen Dr Wilmot, sponsored new members, continued painting, continued writing and resting has helped me through this painful time. Many changes have been occurring and I'm sure I'm not even aware of them yet. I know I'm more settled. I'm not over eating or obsessing over food and that in it self is a miracle. I'm open to the possibility of incredible unconditional love.

26/11/99 : I've had a break through with my feelings with Wayne. It occurred to me at the meeting yesterday morning that making Wayne wrong for what he said and how he reacted and so forth (blaming him for how I feel) meant I was making myself wrong. I have been like Wayne in my past and then I thought, I'm human and I'm not going to make myself wrong for being that way. Wayne did what he could with what he had at the time as much as I do what I can with what I have. The pain I've been carrying all this time has healed.

Bob just rang and I feel he's becoming too affectionate again and I need to remind him that nothing is going to happen between us.

I felt jealous when the girls said that Wayne's really good looking; it cut like a knife. Something that relieves me of that pain when I ask myself, do I really want to be with Wayne? NO. I suppose I also get that feeling of I've missed out on someone great and so I now feel rejected. I wonder if I'll ever talk too him again.

Friday night Shianne, Lana and I caught up with Len and his friends. Shianne and Len's friend Gavin bailed out early and the rest of us moved on from the Point to the Sane Bar. We ended up having a great time. Len and I danced for a long time. It was a lot of fun. We're all going dancing tonight at the Bullring: Latin American dancing. Oh, Lana won't be able to because of her foot.

I have no idea what to do today. Perhaps I'll do some painting. I'm not going to a meeting today I've had enough of those for now. I need to let Courtney know that Mum's more than happy to talk about her experience of depression and so forth. Keep writing, I must have more than relationships to talk about. I'm certainly writing much differently compared to how I was writing one and half years ago, about awkward, hateful feelings, obsessions with food. I was very stressed and manic, full of fear, full of doubt, full of insecurities; I was smoking and it was like I had mad cow disease.

27/11/99 : Barry is intense. Lana, Barry, Len and I went out for dinner and pool last night. At the beginning of the evening I was uncomfortable and nervous so I handled it with uncontrollable laughter. Lana knew why I was laughing. I'm becoming attracted to Len. It's growing and I can't stop it. I tell myself it shouldn't be there. He's not six foot and three inches and doesn't look like a movie star. I'm sure love is suppose to look like that. There is chemistry and it feels really pleasurable. Barry spoke of taking photographs of my face with Lana. I felt so humiliated. I put my hands on both sides of my face and looked down. I wanted to cry. My first thought was a picture of a porno like shot. I don't think Barry was meaning that kind of photo. Len was there and I thought he would be thinking I have loads of guys hanging off me giving me heaps of attention and complements. I felt embarrassed and disgusting at the same time. I felt like running to the toilet. Moments before I was in the toilet I became aware of feeling dirty and guilty for being attractive. I felt wrong and bad for looking beautiful. I felt very vulnerable at the table. At Barry's house Barry went on about how he feels very protective of me, which brought up a lot of emotion for him. He also said that I needed something from him. I'm not sure what? He reminds me of my Mum. He's analytical and very deep. That's okay. He won't be complementing on my looks any more after tonight. I told him not to and I'm glad I did.

Len's very easygoing. He's not abrupt or dominating and that really attracts me. I feel physically comfortable with him. I haven't told him about my sexual abuse history yet. He'll find that out later. I'm afraid my attraction to him is growing. I'm afraid of being close to him. My mind tells me I'm rebounding and I'm making him more than what he is. But I have many men in my life as friends and my feelings towards these men have only been platonic and that hasn't changed. I think also, "come on, you only left Wayne seven weeks ago, so you can't possibly like Len." I think because he's not drop dead gorgeous my mind tells me that the only reason I'm becoming attracted and having fuzzy feelings is because I'm desperate and needing reassurance. My heart has another story and that frightens me. He's so nice. I really like nice. He's relaxed and I like relaxed. He's comfortable with himself. I'm going to go with the flow and make it up as I go. We'll call each other this week. I do look forward to that. I'm very curious about my attraction to him.

Last night I couldn't stop thinking about kissing him and I wanted to tell him I was feeling that way but I didn't because there's no rush. I don't want to pressure myself. I want to ease into this and also I'd really like him to ask me to kiss me or make the first move. I sense the desire and that's what I want. It's romantic. Wayne said to me on our second or third date, "What is your motive?" I should've said: "To stalk and kill you with my long white fangs and draw every red drop of blood out of your body so you can look like a weak little fool sucked in by dangerous blood sucking vampire." I can't picture Len being like that. Wayne was very demanding and insensitive to the pain I felt around my sexual abuse. He was indeed in many ways inconsiderate and selfish. I'm sure I was to. Wayne was very 'Wayne' orientated and narrow minded. I wasn't safe to share my inner self with him. I can see why I didn't want to have sex with him any more. We weren't connecting on a deeper emotional level. It just felt like a physical thing for Wayne. I don't know how I stayed with him for so long under those conditions. But I did. Thank God for the red socks. It was the red socks he wore on the day I introduced him to my girlfriend Ruby (whom I've known since my school days) that pushed me over the edge. We picked him up at 8:30 am and we went down to Ackland St in St Kilda for something to eat for breakfast. The man hadn't done his blonde fluffed up hair and he wore daggy dumpy clothes (as always) and I took deep breaths to cope with that, but did he have to wear those bright bulky red socks that stood out like a beacon? That was it! I knew there and then that man was not for me because I could not cope with my feelings of disgust towards him any longer. After saying goodbye to my girlfriend as she departed down the stairs I turned and looked at Wayne and asked God to give me the right words to say what I knew had to be said. I sat down beside him with my heart pulsating out of my chest and said these simple six words: "I don't love you enough." Okay, it was five and it felt painful and glorious all at the same time.

28/11/99 : It's going to be 35 degrees today, hot. I'm going swimming with Len today. I'm excited about it. I'm afraid of being judgemental of his body and of mine. I'm afraid I'm going to be frumpy and he's going to be too skinny. I can't be attracted to that. I don't feel feminine. So, God, I pray for acceptance and non-judgement. I pray for more love. I pray for my heart to dance today and let my mind rest. My little girl inside of me is going to have some fun.

Okay, I did another little painting last night of my legs and feet. What I thought was painting me from my reflection in the mirror. That would be good, it's non-threatening and it'll be good practise.

30/11/99 : I had this dream that my Uncle Percy left his marriage with my Aunty Lilly and went up bush in the North of Australia and he was flirting with other women. I arrived and he was having a merry old time with my Mum's Dad, another uncle and three more of my male cousins aged between 15 and 16. Mum was organising something with her mother. I sat and watched for some time until I couldn't take it any more, it became too much. I stood up and blurted out very loudly what I could see was going on and that I was very concerned what the teenage boys were witnessing. "You can choose to deal with your fear through alcohol and run away from your responsibilities and hide in bush but it won't make things better. You need to know there's another way and that is to deal with it what you're running away from and ride it through the hard time. The bush holds great strength, but it won't carry you through. It will fade and die and so will you if you continue with this false belief." I went on and walked straight up to their faces and spoke to their hearts and I saw myself in another light. I saw how amazing I was. I felt the love and the impact of my words. I could see myself speaking life's truth in front of crowds of people. My Nana came up and held my hand, together we sat at the table and we said some prayers.

2/12/99 : Len's a really lovely guy and I'm afraid of failing already. Afraid we're not suited; afraid of being something I'm not. Right now I do not want a relationship, I do not want to kiss or have sex with anyone. The desire is there but I do not want to follow it. I've rushed the last two relationships and I found, in both of them, I fell out of love and lost my attraction towards them. I discovered that I no longer wanted what I first wanted. I also found that in both relationships I felt enormous sexual pressure and stress. I do not want that in my life again. What if I don't end up liking him? What if I do have a problem with his body size? His knees are smaller than mine. He's heaps shorter than I can cope with. Physically I feel we don't match. I feel bad for being judgemental but that's how I see it. Can I like the facts? Hey, I have a right to say what I need to say. I don't have to like someone just because they like me and just because they are there. I feel pressure and I find it hard to communicate. I pull away and lose my ability to speak. I don't want to just go along with him to make him happy. I need to tell this person where I'm coming from. I need to tell him my fears, my wants and my needs. I need to know from him that he won't pressure me to do anything that I don't feel comfortable doing, for example; kissing him. I want to know for myself what it is I want. I want him to know that I'm afraid of rushing into a relationship when I'm not ready, when I'm unsure how I feel towards him. I want to get to know him. I will talk to him and see what he has to say. I cannot afford to keep silent for the other person involved to save them from hurt feelings or to keep them around. It's not worth it. Len will appreciate my honesty and openness and, if not, I will. It's in God's hands once I say what I need to say. I have nothing to lose, only to gain. Yes I'm freaking out.

3/12/99 : Mmm…Kissed Len yesterday at the botanical gardens. I couldn't help myself. I couldn't hold myself back any more and I made myself fly so high in the kisses that I went giddy and had to lie down. I wanted to, so I did. Last night we were kissing in the bed and I had my top off.

6/12/99 :I really like Len but I'm already noticing that I'm thinking something is not right. Damn it. I'll see how it goes. I'm not going to have sex with him unless I know for sure what I want. Our bodies don't match. I still think I'm too big. My hips are so much wider than his. I enjoyed kissing him last night. I need a break from him, some time out for myself. Slow things down a bit. Before you know it we'll be in a relationship and probably one I don't want. I don't want to get tired. Not like last time.

   Yes I got down on myself for not having a career like my good girlfriends Aimee and Sally and they have such beautiful boyfriends. I don't have a career or a long term wonderful, movie star partner. I

222

dreamt that Courtney was taller than her man and another couple were of the same. In the dream it was okay to be the same height, or even taller than your boyfriend. I've had tall men around me all of my life. Let's take my Dad and my cousins for example, they are tall. I like tall boyfriends, I feel feminine.

You know the kiss with Len on Sunday was like a hit, because it's like a fantastic feeling for the first time and then chasing it again and again trying to have that same experience that will never be. I know I made myself feel that way. I don't know who or if I will ever have a soul mate. Yes I'm a little scattered. Yes I'm aware I haven't stared the 'Artist's Way' book. I'm afraid of doing the work.

8/12/99 : Yesterday I was bombed out. I've been resting to regain my strength. I'm enjoying space from Len. I wonder if what I'm experiencing is normal. Spoke to him on the phone for 1 hour and 45 minutes last night. I really enjoy talking to him. My, if I stopped criticising him and stopped getting into the fear of 'he's not the one' I'd be better for it. I'm so afraid he's not the 'one'. I trust that you, God, know what you are doing. I will pull away if necessary.

I'm going to pull away from Barry. I don't feel comfortable around him and he makes me cry a lot. Mum always points out to me that some people who make me cry are some how abusing me. I want to talk to Courtney about that. Troy is on my mind, but he has to want to stay sober for himself, I can't do it for him.

ANOTHER DAY : Simone came over yesterday very upset. We started questions in the workbook, which goes through the Big Book for our recovery from alcoholism. When my aunty did the questions in the workbook, she went a bit weird and I don't want that. We'll make it up as we go. Getting sober is such a fucking hard thing to do. Helping Simone shows me how courageous I've been to get and stay sober.

Barry asked me the other day if I had an untreated mental illness such as bipolar disorder so I spoke to my Dr Wilmot about it yesterday, informing him Mum has the bipolar disorder and asked him if I did. He said, and I agreed after answering his list of questions, that I don't have it. I'm not mad! I'm not crazy for thinking I didn't have it! I'm pulling away from those people, Barry for example, who have a negative effect on me where I begin to doubt myself by thinking I'm 'nuts'. These kinds of people only make things harder for me. My Mum has been so right for so long. She's always said if I become deeply upset by someone it's because someone is abusing me in some way. I believe her now. I have many people in my life who don't have that kind of effect on me and those are the people I want to be around.

Len wants me to be his girlfriend, how beautiful. I would enjoy it very much to be his girlfriend, however, I'm still enjoying dating him. So the girlfriend thing can wait just a little longer. Thank God he's not like Carl, the 'I want to have sex with you but not a relationship guy'. Len said he'll wait to have sex until I feel ready. I feel like I'm falling for him.

21/12/99 : I got a little scared yesterday about feeling that my legs look fat. My goshness I haven't worried about my weight for such a long time, I feel rather silly for writing it. I can remember when all I did was worry about how fat and ugly I looked. Haven't I changed!

3/1/00 : For goodness sakes I really like Len but I'm confused why I don't want anything more than friendship. I'm such a moron for sending Jezza a text message. I don't care what anyone says, it wasn't right. I'm all over the place. This is old behaviour. I'm living in a fantasy world again thinking he's the man for me. I believe I can't be with Len because he isn't tall, dark and handsome like Jezza. I am mad. I need to focus on my creativity instead.

4/1/00 : Eugene, my cousin, called and I had a new experience with him where I was able to be myself and I believe it's because I have changed. He travelled to France through Paris over Christmas and New Year. I'm not jealous because I know he deserves it. He has worked very to get to where he is today and it's a miracle considering the home he was brought up in. I am proud of him. My journey has just begun and I wonder where it will take me.

I told Len I only want friendship between us. It was so hard to tell him. Jezza didn't respond to my sms. I always put him on the spot. I'm sad about leaving us as friends. I think having been sexually abuse makes my relationship with Len confusing. I just want time for my soul to heal.

9/1/00 : On Sunday I exposed my feelings to Jezza. I read to him something I wrote two years ago, telling him I believe he was my soul mate and told him of my fear of being with him. I shared my dreams and hopes with him and he said he feels the same way! What an incredible moment for both of us however, after discovering he didn't ring to let me know he wasn't coming to see me on Monday as promised I have begun to think he doesn't really care. I started to think, am I being a pest? I don't think I'm really committed to being with Jezza. It's easier to think, 'oh, it's still not the right time'. But you know I'm looking for the easier way out. I want to follow him. I'm expecting him to change over night. I have a choice. I can let this slip by or I can allow God to show me the way to allow Jezza to know me. I can relate this situation with Lana. It's been up to me to let her know that I'm there for her and I'm not leaving her. If she doesn't want me as her sponsor then it's up to her to say something. Lana has needed to know that even though she's busted, I am still here encouraging her. I understand how it felt to be vulnerable, scared, insecure, worthless, sceptical, hopeless and desperate. I know all I wanted was someone who I could trust. I really liked Maree and I didn't believe she'd want me to be apart of her life. I didn't feel worthy. I needed her to ask me to sponsor me and I was so delighted. I became scared of failing her and as I knew I was unreliable, dishonest and irresponsible. I thought to myself that she'd soon discover it and reject me. I began to learn and understand myself through her stories of her own experiences. It took a very long time to trust her. Courtney, my sponsor today, I needed to tell her about my fear of her abandoning me, as I had experienced being abandoned by Maree. I knew I needed to say something otherwise I wasn't going to let Courtney into my heart. Courtney said to me: "It's not up to me to leave you; it's purely up to you to decide that for yourself." I was so relieved and I felt loved.
The love and support I have received has been abundant. Here I am expecting Jezza to lead me, us, the relationship when I think I am to expect nothing from him. No conditions. God I am willing to go first and lead the way. I'm going to give it my best shot. If it's to be it will be.

10/1/00 7:30 AM : I wanted to go to his home yesterday. It was an impulsive decision. I told Liz my plans and we spoke about this for about 40 minutes while I watched her clean up. She was straight with me and said when she wants to do something 'out of the blue' and it feels right at the time, that's an indication to her that she knows definitely not to it because it's usually for all the wrong reasons. Bugger. I knew that was true for me. It was hard to accept it however, I am so glad I didn't go. Thank God for Liz. I gave Jezza the space to do as he wishes. The urgency has disappeared.

11/1/00 : After the pain free, scare free dentist appointment Marika and I went op-shopping and I bought three frames. Cheap as and they look great. I got out my paintings that were about my craziness around eating. Yes they need to be framed for they are a series about an important part of my life.

I want to write to Jezza. He's not in my life because he chooses not to. There are so many things I want to say to him about me. It could be great practise for a book. I thought last night how it's not that bizarre that I could be a writer, seeing that I've written most of my life either to my Mum, to my friends and to myself. I enjoy writing.

12/1/00 : Simone's gone back to her boyfriend. I thought yesterday that perhaps I failed her. She continually busts and I imagine some people would suggest she find a sponsor that works. I'm going to sound like Courtney when I say her growth may not be a reflection on busting but rather her willingness to grow. Whether Lana reads spiritual material or goes to enough meetings and to more people is, at the end of the day it's none of my business, its God's.

I'm getting a stronger feeling to write a book. Perhaps I could write a book about spirituality, however, there are heaps of books out there about that. People won't take me seriously anyway; I'm too young to write a book.

When I went to the toilet last night I had obsessing thoughts about Jezza and it is not doing me any good. I want it to be a healthy experience with him, not one of "I wish he were here." He's in my heart but look out if I run into him. I won't be hiding my feelings of love from him.

Marika just rang. I ran over and received a frame and a little jewel case from her. These frames get me so excited. Marika asked me if Jezza had rang. "No and I'm not even angry with him." "He's in fear," Marika said, "We know he's not calling not because he doesn't love you." That was reassuring. It's up to the Gods. I'm not going to push it.

13/1/00 : I started a portrait of Ruby today. I'm really excited about doing it well. I'm going to tell her to dress nicely for the occasion. She'll like the painting more. Yes, much more. Marika bought me another frame. The artwork I'm producing is improving and I'm getting excited about it all. I'm aware I only paint women. I guess I will move onto another topic when I'm ready.

I'm feel a little scrappy, I wonder if I'm okay.

I'm a little worried about money. I don't know why because I do have enough to get me through. I need more trust in God. And I find it interesting when I thought things were finally going to work out between Jezza and I, I wanted to give up doing anything for myself such as my job, art, singing and following my ideas. Isn't that scary and very unhealthy! Obviously I have a little way to go.

I'm aware I have not acknowledged I'm feeling let down that Simone is not going to stay at my place for the next four days to free herself from her boyfriend. She is going to go back to him and I feel like I have failed her.

I've let Jezza know my most intimate feelings and thoughts about him and I feel I have failed because he's not even talking to me. I had expectations on going to the twelve-step recovery anniversary with Dad and it's not going to happen, I feel I have failed.

I'm writing all this down to help release the crap in my head. If I wear my bather bottoms they will annoy me so badly. I'll put my g-string back on instead at least I will good about something.

14/1/00 : Liz suggested I create designs for linen; my own designs, my originals. I could start that today, not an all cover print, just simple pictures or writings placed in the middle or the left or right hand sides of the linen. I might go to a twelve-step recovery meeting today at lunch.

After swimming at Brighton Beach yesterday Aimee and I took went to Fin Bars. We sat on stools and giggled, cruised, sang and had a great dance. She might be moving into the unit above me, how fantastic. Met this guy, Steve; not Steven, only his mother calls him that when she's angry with him. He said to me: "You should be an actress, you've got what it takes." Aimee then said: "Yes, I've been telling her that for a very long time," which is true. It would be so cool to do some acting.

Simone just rang and she's nine days sober. She's realising she has a disease and how it has been affecting her. I really feel for her.

I told Jezza on his answering service that I loved him very much. Wow, I said it. He hasn't called me back. I think many times over in my head to give up. I really feel like a pest. I simply and truly love him. My love is growing deeper and deeper. Becoming freer and freer. Everyone I have shared this with have all said: "He's scared, keep going, he'll come around." I usually think I'm making it up that he feels the same as I. So I tell myself not to let him do this to me again. I felt when I spoke to him on that Sunday about my dreams, fears and hopes about me and us, that he felt the same way. I know he does want what I want. If he 100% wanted to be with me he would be calling? Perhaps there still is a part of him that doesn't want me. It may not mean he doesn't love me. I feel that he does. There is no question of the chemistry and affinity we share together. That's always been there for me from the day I met him. I'm powerless over Jezza. I have chosen to be committed to him and committed to being me. I'm just going to follow what I know and make it up as I go. I am willing to do what it takes in the name of love. I can't change him but I can certainly do something about me. I feel a miracle is occurring and I'm not giving to let fear run my day. If I'm being a fool in love, so be it.

15/1/00 : Liz has a friend who's just opened up a shop selling linen who may be interested in selling my product. My friend in QLD, Clarke maybe interested in supporting my product and Aimee believes that it sounds like a fabulous idea. Perhaps I could really do this?
I just rang Jezza with information about the Ambulance course and I'm shaking because I'm so excited for him and for me.

16/1/00 : Last night I was so excited I couldn't sleep. I probably didn't nod off until 2:00am. Lana and I also watched Australian film called 'Innocence', about first love and getting a second chance. I dreamt I was in my Hometown and Jezza's friend invited me to a gathering. One of his friends got too affectionate with me, which was not a problem. I gave him a quick push and told him to "fuck off." I fixed him. Jezza arrived and, my goodness, he was shocked to see me there. He gave me a quick hello and, before I he knew it, he was gone. Obviously he wasn't impressed with me hanging out with his friends. I felt like a stalker. Later in the dream I ran into my ex-boyfriend Max (I was his girlfriend of two years between the ages of 16 and 18). He was shopping in the men's clothes store and was looking rather spiffy. He was my first long relationship. I was telling Lana last night that I haven't experienced that nice feeling of being 'girlfriend boyfriend' since Max and Jarod. I'm talking of that lovey dovey, yummy feeling which now over five years ago.

With Jezza there is no one who has ever made me so alive and turned on even though we've never had a relationship. He didn't call back yesterday. I was angry with him and myself for contacting him. My self annoyance started to affect me because I was irritable with the kiddies. So I quickly got over it and got back to the moment, the children need me to be patient and 'there' for them. When I finished work I thought, I'm ready to pull the pin. I jumped into the car at 9:30pm and looked at my phone and there was a message from Len's friend Hock, to call him back. I did and he wasn't available. He has some of my things from skiing that I left at his place. I loved skiing. There was another message from Jezza apologising for not calling sooner because he's had a 'hell' of a day. Me thinks to myself, you just scraped in buddy, just as well I knew I had to keep pursuing. When I got home I was panting and raving to Lana using my hands like a puppet show to express my frustration with this man. I wanted her to say, 'yes, he's no good, it's obvious he doesn't feel the same as you, you've got to move on.' She didn't. All she said was: "Keep on your side of the fence, you don't know what he is doing. Perhaps you should slow down or you'll miss something. You didn't even ask him if he was okay today because you were going so fast." That's true, I thought. He was at the doctors. It was two hours later that I realised he actually apologised. I like that he can say sorry.

I got to speak to Courtney last night. She rang me and I blurted out so much stuff. Courtney said it feels like years ago that I was with Wayne. She's right, it does feel like years ago. She reminded me how important that decision to end the relationship. With Jezza I feel I love him too much. There is so much feeling inside me that I'm afraid of it. I'm so looking forward to seeing him. I have taken this Friday off so I can take Marika with me to my Hometown to see my cousin and his gorgeous girlfriend, Petunia. Aimee said suggested to be forward with Jezza and say: "I want to see you, I'm in town, would you like to catch up?" Look I need all the help I can get. I explained to Courtney how I see and relate to Jezza's position as a 'newcomer' and me as a sponsor. A 'newcomer' has no network, where as a sponsor has established a strong relationship with people who understand them and know them in and out and support growth, honesty and love. God has tricked me into thinking I'm leading the relationship so I don't do a runner. I'm aware I'm must pursue this and give it all I have on a day to day basis and it's God's will either way. I can't go wrong. This has been such a blessing in my life.

17/1/00 : Wayne just rang and said I was like a roller coaster. He's so good at looking at himself isn't he! I was a roller coaster because of many things, for example trying to make something be what it wasn't. He has a new girlfriend, obviously been seeing her since we broke up. They are compatible and Wayne has to state that we weren't and he's right about that. I was all over the place with Wayne, trying very hard to understand him and honouring me at the same time, which was tricky. I certainly have no attraction to him now, yucko, in the nicest possible way. If he were Jezza I would've been more eager and if he didn't want to make love to me for any reason I would've felt rejected too. That's how all of the men must have felt with me because I didn't want to have sex with them most of the time. I don't know how they stayed for as long as they did. Wayne wants to go to my twelve-step recovery home group. He has no sense of humour at all, that fellow. I was cracking jokes left, right and centre and most of them went right over his head. I don't know how I stayed with him for as long as I did.

Do you know having a relationship with Jezza doesn't feel like it will ever be. We don't talk much now. I don't see how that will change. It's been that way for years. Marika just rang and said Wayne's heavy stuff and I'm to let him go. Hock will be here in 20 minutes to drop my stuff off. Aimee moves in upstairs on Friday. I'm fearful and worried I won't come up with anything for my linen designs. I think I should get onto reading 'The Artists Way.'

18/1/00 : I remember picking up my old crappy bra from Jezza (about five years ago I stayed over at his place on a Saturday night and guess what I left behind?). Jezza had washed my bra. How embarrassing! I didn't plan on seeing him or being with anyone that night. It's always the way: when you least expect it you always wear the daggiest underwear. It's like when I'm walking down the street and I know I'm wearing un-matching, over loved, abused, used nickers and bra and I think I'm going to get hit by a truck and be taken to hospital where the doctors and nurses witness my disgraceful set of lingerie. The thought makes me cringe. Not the idea of being dismantled by a truck, but being humiliated by what the hospital staff will think of me wearing crappy lingerie. Jezza was so cold as he stood at the front door and handed me a plastic bag with the bra in it. Because I was so drunk on that Saturday night I did not remember what I did and I don't remember taking the bra off. I realised only in my sobriety that is called an alcoholic black out. I felt disgusting. He didn't seem to care and didn't say anything. He was so cold. Lana suggested that I ask him out Saturday night for dinner. I don't have too much cash floating around, but that's cool, God will supply and provide. I fear being rejected. We've never gone out to dinner before. I really have to stay focused on the moment today. Lana suggested keeping busy with art and having others around me. Wayne, who I am no longer with, threw me off with an unexpected phone call. He asked me if I did anything to his penis while he was sleeping because he can't work out what was creating him so much pain in his genital area. He's so sensitive to my sexual abuse, NOT! He's as cold as a wet fish.

It was so refreshing talking to Jezza. The night before I was going to give up because I was finding it too hard. I told him that I'm committed to staying and if anyone is going to run and break this up it's going to be him. "It's under control, it's under control," he said. Thank God. Then I said: "Good, because I have no idea what I am doing."

My beautiful cousin, Linus, said: "Do you know Jezza?" He was insinuating that Jezza is a dubious character who is a womaniser. Hmm. That didn't feel good. "Yes I do and I know he's been with many girls but we've never been together." I believe Jezza cannot take away anything from me. It's what I give. If he chooses to be with other women then that's his choice. I have done the wrong thing in my past and flirted with other men in front of him to get his attention and make him jealous. Wasn't that nice of me! I don't think I'll use that approach this time.

29/1/00 : I thought of God as soon as I woke this morning. I want to be with God this morning. I want to hear, see and feel each moment. May I listen, comfort, understand, have compassion, tell my truth, share my soul, believing every thing happens for my highest good. Nothing is done to me. No one owes me anything. I expect nothing from no one. People will be people. Everyone including myself will do their best today. Anything may happen. I am loved. May I be the instrument that God needs me to be. This is a new day. Yesterday has no bearing on the now. I'm on the couch writing. I have a blanket around my shoulders, the cooler is on, the kettle has boiled and it's 7:17am. I can be me today.

I will call Jezza for a swim at Jessie's, and have dinner with Jezza tonight and fit in anyone else who calls me today. God, today will happen let's go.

21/1/00 : This is what I want to say to Jezza. I want to tell you what it is I am feeling, thinking and experiencing. Thank-you for being in my life. I have come to face the fear in me that hurts my love. I have thought that I'm afraid of you. I am afraid of myself. Through knowing you I have chosen to begin to learn to trust, have faith and go within myself and love the parts of me I have hated and rejected. I have thought if I were perfect you would have me in your life. I'm only now learning I am perfect the way I am. I can't say what I want to say, because I'm so nervous that I want to spew. I say things to cover up my truth to pretend to be the person I think you would like me to be. I do and say stupid things. I do and say things opposite to what and who I am so you won't reject me. The only person who can reject me is me. I love you and to love me in the process has been, and still is, very difficult. What it is I want to say I have been scared to say because of your behaviour. I witness you acting distant, aloof, non-responsive, uncaring, inconsiderate and cool and it gives me every reason to believe I am not enough. I see those parts of you and I see them in me. When I am this way I am afraid of being vulnerable and afraid of others seeing my insecurities about myself.

At the moment I am learning to do many things, such as; to follow what feels right, to ask and trust the support I am receiving from the people in my life. This is not specific enough. When I asked you to kiss me goodbye I felt that you only kissed me to keep me happy. Something you didn't really want to do. I wanted, and have wanted before, to be sexually, emotionally and spiritually intimate with you last night. I found it very hard to accept that we were both extremely tired and that I had to wait. I have to wait until that falls together in time. I drove away saying to myself, he doesn't like me, he will not call me Sunday and he can't wait to get rid of me. These thoughts I carry upon my shoulders each day and when I am tired it gets the better of me. I parked in my Mum's driveway and realised that because I had expectations of spending the night with you I hadn't stopped to think to arrange somewhere to sleep. I chose not to wake Mum. It was my fault for not organising it and, so, in my delirious state I chose to sleep in the car in her driveway. Something I would not advise anyone else to do and, yes, I continually woke up from nightmares of being attacked. I told God I knew how insane it was to consciously choose to stay in the car. I asked my God to please protect me.

I had several dreams and there was one that gave me relief and a feeling of peace inside. I was in the car aware I was to meet you inside my home. I was reading something I had written a couple of years ago. I finished reading and you stepped out and yelled out, "Oi!" I smiled and yelled back that I had something I wanted to read to you. You sat in the car and you said: "Mandy wants to stop seeing me because she thinks I don't like her and I hope she does soon because I don't like her." I felt relieved to know that what I felt I knew, about you seeing other people as well as me, was true. I enjoyed you sharing that stuff with me. Then I said: "It is that I'm most afraid of; that you won't tell me the truth about how you feel because you don't want to hurt me and you're hoping I'll eventually get the drift and leave you. You said with a surprised look on your face: "You have gotten to know me for the past three years and you are still here." I said: "The only reason I'm still here is because I'm keeping my eyes off you, not trying to read your mind or guess what you want me to do and having a great support around me. Otherwise I wouldn't be with you." You paused, slouched back into the front seat, and said with great sadness, "I've been pretending and I do love you. I am afraid to love because I have experienced great pain in the past when I have loved deeply." I witnessed you share this and I understood the fear and sadness and the damage that pretending, wearing masks, not speaking and not being honest has done to us and to our love.

21/1/00 : Tuesday I ended up leaving a message on Jezza's answering machine at about 2:00pm Sunday and this is what I said. "Jezza, and (pause) I've needed to talk to you but I haven't had the courage until now. What I have to say is more about me than it is about you. I don't feel good about what is going on with us. I feel sad that I haven't been able to say what I've been feeling and thinking. I'm also sad that you can't share with me what you're going through either. I can tell you that whatever you're thinking and feeling I can almost guarantee that I've thought and felt it too. What I am doing is facing the biggest fear and that is being rejected by you and what I've discovered is that I cannot be rejected. I want to thank-you for being an important instrument in my life, I am learning so much. Last night when you were on your mobile I felt you were sending messages to another girl. I want to tell you that I felt for the first time, irreplaceable. I've always felt replaceable by other women and last night I felt good to be me. The kiss last night didn't feel right, there's something going on there, but I won't talk about that right now. What I'm trying to do is to love unconditionally. It's more about what I give than what I receive. I love you whether you're in my life or not. May I honour you by honouring myself. At the end of the day I just want you to know that I care. Hmm…okay, bye."

I was so ecstatic I ran over to the place where I dropped off Aimee earlier and told her what I basically had said to Jezza. I felt so wonderful and strong for saying what I felt had honoured myself. Aimee said she knew I would do it sooner or later because I can no longer sit with ill feelings. She's right. She was very proud of me. She said that it would take Jezza a long time to digest what I said to him and I said: "Yeah, probably a couple of years." She was surprised to hear on Monday morning that Jezza hadn't replied. I wasn't surprised. I felt disappointed. At times I think maybe he misunderstood what I was saying and took it as if I was leaving him, but that's God business. All I know is this. When I have not returned someone's phone call or letter and knowing they need reassurance it's because I was not free to do so. I believe its fear that holds him back from being and saying what it is true for him. I believe he deeply cares for me. I believe that when the time is right he will talk to me again when he is ready. I trust that he is in God's hands, as I believe I am. I am free. I have choices. I have cleared my slate and I am transparent. I cannot be hurt with my truth. I am not to be ashamed to love or to be loved. I have chosen to commit to being single and not get involved with anyone for my wellbeing. I need time. Jezza needs time. I am to write a book. I see myself speaking in front of large audiences. I want to sing, perform, stand on stage, paint and sell my designs.

22/1/00 : I dreamt about Jezza and at the end of each dream that I have of him I see and I am reminded of who he is and the person I love. I'm able to see through the macho stuff. I know him. The dreams bring me great relief. Without these dreams I would be scared off by his silence. I believe it's his way of protecting himself. I use to play games and test the men in my life and at the time I was powerless over myself for playing these games because of my ignorance of why I was being that way. I feel that Jezza has become that way. It's not to hurt me, it's so I can't come near him and hurt him.

24/1/00 : Simone slept over last night. I'm glad Simone feels comfortable enough to feel welcome to drop in when she's feeling distraught. I never felt that comfortable at Maree's. I try to create my home to be welcoming and I try to let her feel free to be herself around me. With Maree, I had her on a pedestal and I was nervous around her husband Harold. That can't just be about me. I felt very at ease with my good friend, Graeme. I did huge amounts of work on myself regarding feeling rejected by Maree. She was an extraordinarily courageous woman. I pat myself on the back for being so determined and persistent to travel a journey of wellness.

Last night I had the munchies. There's a lot of sadness inside of me and I'm carrying garbage from the way I was treated by Jezza. He doesn't bring the best out of me. I thought last night that being cool, aloof, silent and arrogant doesn't make another person feel good. I have been like Jezza, especially in my drinking days. I would have made people feel yucky inside like that to. Not good. He also said that when he has big nights out on the piss he usually spends his Sundays lying on the couch unable to answer the phone because he is so sick from his hang over. He hides for the whole day. My alarm bells went off when he said that. I have no doubt his drinking could be problematic. The time when I told him how I have felt for all these years, I'm aware now that he might've been half pissed or very pissed. More often than not he opens up when he's been drinking. I figure that I have been affected by Jezza. I don't look at him like a sick person and he knows that and I feel there's no way that he'll confront me. My therapist, Dr Wilmot, said that what I've done is really big stuff and that my focus now needs to be on myself, on my needs and wants.

25/1/00 : I'm sitting on the couch. Marika rang. It's time to stop and clear my thoughts. There is a lot going on and I'm feeing a bit rushed and overwhelmed by other people's demands upon me, if you get my drift. When I was talking to Marika, she helped me realise I need time out to do what I need to do for myself.

Elizabeth said to me last night: "Get your drawings together in the next seven days to be prepared to show the lady with the linen shop who will have returned from her trip by that time." I realised it was time to continue and begin my journey and course through the help of the book 'The Artists Way'. The book is currently sitting beside me. I'm to make no arrangements before starting work as from this Monday to Friday. I'm to concentrate on my drawing and my book. Note I don't know how, when or what the topic of the book will be but it's happening as I write. I'm writing a book. What I know and what I have experienced I feel must be shared with others. Aimee got goose bumps down her arms when I told her my insight of speaking to large groups of people. "You're not afraid of doing that are you?" she asked. "No I am not. I see it and I feel it. I gather that when it happens my heart will be racing so fast I will be unable to breathe for the first ten minutes." Aimee shared with me about what she said to her new guy, Ryan: "When you meet her you'll be overwhelmed and instantly taken aback, and I mean literally taken aback, not just by her legs that go up to her neck or by her beauty but what she will have to say and how she will say it to you." How I first met Ryan was by running into his house and into his room and started rambling excitedly about what I had said to Jezza on the answering service. In that moment I was full of life and excitement. Aimee later asked Ryan: "So did I describe my girlfriend well to you the other day?" And his response was: "To the tea!" I must have an impact on people. Marco would say to me once I sat down from sharing my experiences to the one hundred people at Landmark: "With the other people who get up and talk some people are naturally distracted by falling asleep and others are looking around with boredom. But when you speak I look around and everyone is listening and fully enrolled in what you have to say next. Everyone!" Now that's having an impact and I was only being myself and making it up as I go. I would be standing up the front with the microphone, feeling shit scared, full of emotions with millions of thoughts racing through my head. My passion was that I wanted the people to know who I was, as I am, perfectly imperfect.

I have Brett Whitley's book open on the coffee table in the lounge room. All I want to do is have all the materials, the time and space to create art. I've begun my artistic journey by getting out the 'The Artist Way' book for guidance and direction. I trust I will be shown step by step what to do. How fabulous and exciting. Time to read 'Acts of Faith'.

25/1/00 11:33 PM : I've done a progresso outline of my cousin Eugene dressed in a medieval out fit looking pompus. His face needs careful attention. I have the perfect frame and board. I found the perfect photo as I was looking for something entirely different at the time. When I saw it I wanted to paint it. Years ago, okay, two years ago I had my first thoughts then to paint it. This morning I painted cups with some of my writings on it and it's framed and it looks great. It's not of people! Yeh! It was lots of fun. I got the idea yesterday when I was sitting with Sam. He was drawing and I was flipping through a pamphlet from Noosa. I saw a picture I imagined would be great to paint. So today I opened up some of Lana's high pile of magazines and found an advertisement with cups in it and painted them with my artistic mind. These are the type of drawings I want for my linen designs. I'm going to get a watercolour book and start my designs and fill it up by Friday. Remember there is no time for anyone else but me.

I'm to follow up my singing, okay. Ruby knows someone who can teach me to sing and for some reason I didn't ask for the number when I was with her. I'm to get the phone number from her next time I am with her.

I figure I scared the pants off Jezza on Sunday. If I had received such a message from someone I wouldn't have called back either. Oh well. I needed to say what I needed to say. Do you think I can let it go now?

26/1/00 6:55AM : Saturday morning, while I was sitting on the toilet reading my books, two things stuck out in my mind. One was that I am an alcoholic and I feel that I truly forgot that. I am an alcoholic. Simone is still staying with me. Last night she shared about the idea of having her own place and seeing her boyfriend on limited visitations on the condition he is drug free. I felt this wasn't a good idea. I put forward the notion that her boyfriend is who he is and probably will not change over night. If he does it will be to have her back and then he'll quickly be back to his old behaviour because that's the way he is. I did feel that I wasn't approving of her new idea because all I could image what would happen would be only disaster. I want the best for her and I know that I was thinking I know better than God and I do not want to be someone who thinks that they know what is better for someone else. Sure I can point out possible danger but I don't know what her path is. I must be mindful and let her work out her own stuff the best way she knows how. I must focus on those things that are positive and what's working for her today. I had lent her $50 to help with finding a rental property. I asked for the money yesterday, she had it and returned it. She has been given the house key to my apartment; she is showing me she is a person of her word. She has used our phone to a minimum to be considerate towards Lana and myself. She is doing well and I want to focus on that and not what I think is best for her.

Wayne might be at my home group meeting this morning and that makes me feel a bit yucky. I want it to be able to go to a meeting where I feel most comfortable without him being there. I am not at liberty to say to him: "You can't go to this particular meeting." Go figure that he tells me not to go to the meetings he attends yet he feels quite okay to go to the meetings that I attend. What part of double standards does he not understand? What part of the words 'control freak' does he not understand? So I figure if I do feel too uncomfortable if he is there I can leave or choose not to share.

The kettle's boiled and I must continue my poo session on the toilet.

Wow, I'm over three years sober, how wonderful. I want to feel beautiful today. I'm going to wear my

232

new Indian skirt and top. I have God with me and a beautiful day ahead. May I be of service and stay close to God.

27/1/00 : What a heavy day I had yesterday, I didn't find it fun at all. It felt like I was at war camp. I went to my morning meeting yesterday and Wayne was there. I was asked to share. I spoke about the reading very quickly and mentioned I had been caught off guard and I'd rather listen. Glad I did that because the following speakers were great. I cried in Courtney's arms about how Wayne had called and asked me whether or not I did anything to his penis while he was sleeping. I felt at that moment how insensitive he was considering he knew it was my grandfather who liked me touching him inappropriately. Courtney was disgusted and pissed off that he was at the meeting after he had made such a big statement to me of not going to meetings that he attends, yet its okay for him to knowingly rock up to the one meeting I always go to. What a hypocrite and an arsehole he is. He stood at the main gate for a long time after the meeting. I chose not to walk past his way. We've arranged for a catch up at my place this Wednesday morning at 9:00 am.

Last night Simone and I went through some of the questions in a work book about alcoholism and after I had openly answered to one of them Simone abruptly said to me: "Oh my God, you can't be serious, you're scaring me, you're fucked." Well that's lovely. For God's sakes, for a moment there I thought I was stupid for not knowing something about alcoholism. I looked at her and said: "I'm looking at those questions with a completely open mind and I may think differently than you, it doesn't mean I am fucked." I want to say something to her as I feel angry about the way she spoke to me. I may not know all the ins and outs about alcoholism but I do know for me that I'm an ex-problem drinker and if I drink again, craziness will come back and I will become sick all over again. I think it's funny how she knows all the 'right' answers yet she's only 23 days sober and I don't know all the answers and I'm over three years sober. I just want her to know that I'm simply learning like she is and that I don't appreciate those things being said to me. I need encouragement the same as her and it doesn't make me, as her sponsor, an automatic wanker who is now doomed to pick up a drink because I haven't grasped the entire disease of alcoholism. At the end of the day, for me, it is in my Higher Power that stands between a drink and me. If I'm meant to drink, I will and if I'm not meant to drink, I won't. Either way God is with me in both cases and both are for my highest good. Just for today drinking is not what I want. Right now and my future is God's business

I started painting Eugene and I've surprised myself how well it's going. God, maybe I have a gift! I'm going to the 'big day out' with Hock today, fantastic, a break from meetings.

28/1/00 : I'm lying in bed thinking. The Big Day Out was exactly that. I talked to Hock about how I only want friendship and not to see my affections or if I accept his affections as anything more than friendship. It's important for him to know this, otherwise I feel of obligated to do what he wants me to do. It really makes me feel ill at ease and very angry. He told me how he really likes me and that he's very attracted to me. I was caught off guard by some attraction to him that made me giggle and shy away. He wanted to kiss me. I told him that a part of me wanted to explore kissing him, then I thought, Geez I'm still giving him hope. The issue is I can't see the future. So I stepped back into the car and said: "I don't want to confuse getting along and enjoying each others company with meaning that we're more than just friends. I only want to kiss you when I really, really want to kiss you and not for any other reason. I'd say that you'd only want me to kiss you when I felt like that and not because I felt I had to or thinking it might be good.

Am I right?" He nodded and said: "Yes." I also said: "I may never kiss you, but if I was going to I'd want to know that that's what I really wanted and until then it's a no."

I'm lying in bed and Simone has just come in and she's laying face down. I haven't said anything to her because as you can see I'm writing and I want to finish my writing. She can lay there and wait until I've finished writing.

I want to be with someone and only be involved with someone that I'm truly attracted to. That's what I want. I see that Hock has chemistry with me but I don't have that with him. I don't want to explore the possibility of us being together. I'm aware that I'm attracted to a friend of his and I know that we 'click' only because we like to party, anything deeper than that I don't know. I want the whole package, not just the looks or not just the personality. I'm to let Hock know that I do not want to explore anything further than friendship with him. I am committed to being uninvolved waiting for my God to put someone in my life who is for me.

Simon's upset. I'm ready to talk to her. I'd like to go to the beach or paint. Simone's leaving Tuesday. It's really good that she's discovered that she's not well and that she's not up to being in a relationship with her partner. She wants to move back home and keep it simple. I told her to do what is right for her. It's between her and her God, not me.

29/1/00 : My eyes are still glued together. Simone is up and about. I have no idea of the time. She was very frightened yesterday and she didn't want me to sponsor her any more. Through all of this I was calm and willing to let her do what she needed to do. She came to me later to tell me that she was experiencing paranoid thoughts. We talked about it and she came to see for herself that what she was thinking was not happening. I want to paint.

Lana called yesterday and I talked her through her fear about going to Bruce's (her ex-boyfriend from high school) parent's home. I suggested for her leave her phone number and address with them for him to call back if he chooses. She called back and had spoken to his mum for a couple of hours and the big news is, Bruce is engaged. That was a shock. I felt sorry for Lana. She'll be home tonight.

Simone is going home tonight. Spoke to Aimee and I found it very interesting how she said: "I knew that my relationship with my last boyfriend was not going to work out after knowing him for two months." I asked her why and she continued: "I remember clearly thinking to myself that I'm to finish my course first and then I'm to leave him." She ended up staying with that man for over two years and she knew she held on to him for far too long because of fear of being on her own and fearing making the mistake of leaving the 'best man for her' behind. Why I found it interesting is because it reinforces my motto, 'sometimes you know what you know and it never changes no matter how hard you try." With Hock I know I could become very attracted to his personality and his wacky spirit but I know that's not enough. I also don't feel comfortable about it because I told Len that Hock has no chance to be with me after he had told me of Hock affections towards me and here I am saying to Hock: "I just want friendship but who knows what the future holds." Aarh! He'll tell Len he has a chance. Bummer, that doesn't sit right with me. In the meantime, neither of them knows that I'm attracted to their friend Paul. I'm happy not to discover whether or not Paul is interested in me as I with him. I hold hope of running into him and in saying that I don't feel he'd be suitable for me because (like I've known him for years, not!) he doesn't understand why I can't have one drink. He loves his alcohol and drugs. He works long hours most days of the week and he gives me a feeling that he's a womaniser.

30/1/00 : I stayed up until 2:00 am last night talking to Lana. She wants Bruce; even though he's engaged she feels closer to him. She knows she loves him and she is willing to get on with her life and meet other men. It explains why he hasn't called or dropped in to see her. I shared with Lana the story about Len and Hock and how my motives all along were so I could get to know their friend Paul better. The first time I caught up with Len I organised for him and his friends to meet my friends on a Friday night, intending Paul would go and covering up my affections by setting Lana up with him. When we first met these guys, I spotted Paul and pushed Lana to meet him. What a load of crap on my behalf. I was too scared to let him know I was attracted to him, afraid he might not like me, and so to look cool I acted as if I didn't care. Good way to get someone's attention, not. Paul did not end up going along Friday night with his mates and that's how I started to get to know Len, hiding the fact that I liked Paul all along. Len constantly reminded me that all the girls liked Paul and I instantly felt dumb and ordinary because I liked him too. I kept this a secret to myself. It was difficult seeing Paul and being with Len. I had to be very careful to hide my true emotions. I had chemistry with Paul but I don't know if that was the case with him. So things didn't work out with Len because he wasn't tall enough and his head was too flat at the back. I found myself unable to look into his eyes. He had to go.

So the following weekend I went along to the Sane Bar around the corner from where I live hoping Paul would be there. He didn't turn up and I ended up having a great time dancing with Simone and Porcia. So I kept it in the back of my mind that if something is meant to happen with Paul then I will bump into him somewhere along the line.

Hock continues to ring because he has some of my stuff. I thought by going to the Big Day Out, I might have a chance of running into Paul. I'm sure Hock will tell Len that I told him a part of me wanted to kiss him and I'm sure Hock' interpretation will be: "She wanted to kiss me." No I don't know that because at the end of the day I'm afraid that Paul will think: "Oh, now she's after Hock, the tart!" Now I'm in a situation with Hock that doesn't feel comfortable because he doesn't get that we're only ever going to be friends. I know he's got it in his mind to work on me until he can get what he wants. He's manipulative because I've noticed that whatever I say he manages to turn my words around and upside down where I end up being stuck for words. I find that I'm put into a situation doing and saying things that I don't want to do or say because I'm afraid of looking bad and hurting his feelings. What is my saying? 'May I honour you by honouring myself first,' and at the moment that's slipping by the wayside. Strange really because on Sunday I said to him: "We are just friends," yet today I feel I have to remind him so he doesn't think other wise. Fact - he thinks he can have me as he wants me, he doesn't show me that he has heard what I have said and he gives me no personal space when I'm with him. He's keen and determined. He reminds me of Bob (the older guy in the fellowship who likes me more than a friend) how he held onto his fantasy that one day I would change my mind and want to be with him. I have the right to speak even if it is through writing messages on the phone. I have the right to say back off. Bob is physically smoochy and I'm going to let him know that I don't like it. I want to be able to speak my truth and not back out. I'm going to tell Hock again what the boundaries are, just one more time so as I can know for sure he really gets what I'm saying to him. I'm going to give him one last opportunity to hear what I'm telling him and if from then he doesn't catch on I feel at liberty to say nothing and not respond or do as Dr Wilmot suggests, 'make yourself unavailable.'

31/1/00 : Wow it's Thursday and I'm physically tired. Liz tells me she's spoken to this lady in regards to my linen designs, scary. I'll ring her and ask her how to go about it. My head is quick to tell me I'm not good enough and she'll see how bad my work is. Thanks head for sharing.

I got into a conversation with an older fashion sales assistant, Vicki, who told me there's an art gallery in Camberwell encouraging me to enter my art. I'm to ring the Camberwell council and get that organised. I'm afraid of failing and looking like a fool. I'll take my paintings to that fellow at the framing shop who planted the seed of hope of being an artist. I'll simply do what's in front of me. Ask for direction. God I'm willing to let go of looking good, looking like I know everything. My portrait of Eugene is looking very yellow. It needs more warmth, a bit of red.

I just want to sit on the couch and do nothing. I know what that is, it is fear. One way of moving through fear is putting in the action and the fear leaves once I've done the thing I was afraid of. I want to continue reading The Artist's Way. I find it very supportive and reassuring to continue being a creative being. I want to speak to Margaret from the fellowship how to write a book, she's written many books.

Mum dropped in yesterday by surprise and I spent four hours with her. She told me about Bob Earl. I may read about him, he wrote scripts without knowing how to write!

I asked Courtney how I would go about articulating to Hock what it is I want him to know. She suggested: "I ask for your friendship during this time, I need space and I cannot be available for perhaps two to six months. This is not a challenge, I understand where you are coming from and I am flattered." So I sent him this message at 2:16 pm saying: "Thank-you for the call, I won't have lunch, I need your friendship, nothing more. I need space and your understanding that I'm not available; please don't see this as a challenge. I will call you when and if it feels right to do so. Take care." His response was: "Okay, talk to you soon." I sent back; "Thank-you." His acceptance of my request felt so good. He messages me back within 10 minutes: "I don't understand, I thought we were taking it day by day." I didn't respond. Later in the day I questioned myself, perhaps I could've spoken too him, feeling baddish. Then at 9:00 pm Hock sends me another message: "Does that mean we won't be kicking the footy?" That's when I stopped doubting myself. I'm not to entertain him at all with any more responses.

I feel strong for not calling Jezza. It feels right for me not to call. I also simply don't want to invade his privacy. I want him to want to talk to me. Forcing him will not make me feel good about myself. For example when I asked him for a kiss and then asked for a better one, I didn't feel good about that. That's why I yelled out: "You didn't have to kiss me you know!" If he wanted to kiss me he would have. He had doubt. So I felt like a goose as he sniggered and shut the car door within seconds of kissing me. He's good at telling me how he feels, not.

I enjoy writing. I do feel like I'm writing to an audience, not just to myself.

I feel responsible for Lana's paranoia and assumptions of what she thinks I'm thinking about her. Sure I wanted her to go home on Tuesday as we had discussed deciding that was the best thing for her to do. I felt so much was going on in my head that I had to take time out to relax. I offered her food and said to her that I needed to lie down. She grabbed her stuff and left without saying goodbye. I'm powerless over her. I've given her my best up until now. I don't have to do everything for everyone all of the time.

1/2/00 : Just for today I enjoy loving Jezza from afar. That doesn't mean I have to be with him. At the moment I choose not to be and he chooses not to be with me.

I rang Carmen, singing teacher. Looks like I'll be having lessons fortnightly on Tuesday nights.

Talking with Debbie yesterday in her lounge room I imagined becoming nationally known for a personal achievement of some kind. What a crazy thought that is and how full of myself am I to think of such things that are so far fetched. It still feels it's going to come true one day. That's bloody strange that is.

MONDAY : I feel close to Jezza right now. For some reason I feel that right now he's feeling the same. I feel fearful about my art. I think I'm not good enough to design linen. Once Liz and that lady see what an amateur I am they will brush me aside as an uneducated dreamer with no true talent. I wonder if this is what people call being afraid of success?

I'm eating lollies for breakfast.

TUESDAY : I have therapy at 11:00 am today. I will tell Dr Wilmot about the anxiety attack I had Saturday morning and about the huge cry about being abused by one of Mum's boyfriends when I was a young kid, Mum being suicidal, Mum being taken to a psychiatric hospital for a month and so forth.

I have no interest in Rick, the guy I kissed Saturday morning. Courtney suggested that I'm to give myself a break from men.

Yesterday I felt close to Jezza spiritually and emotionally.

7/2/00 : How good it is to lay down in front of the fan and write. I want to paint a landscape with a Blue Wren for the Kiwanis art show, which I'm intending to participate in. I'm to go to Ekersley's soon to buy the big board, 1m x 1m, and some ink. Yes, I'm afraid of not being good enough. I want to frame the ink work of the sick woman and little child. Sitting on the toilet I thought: for the next month I will focus on doing these art works. Leave doing the designs for the linen until these are done first.

Carmen (the singing teacher) hasn't got back to me yet. My mind tells me that it's because I called her four days too late when I said I was going to call her. I will give her another call in the next few days.

I spoke to Dr Wilmot yesterday about my anxiety I've been experiencing when I'm at the twelve-step recovery meetings. Being in the rooms of these meetings bring about feelings of insecurity and the feeling of not being in control. Next time I experience anxiety I'm to practise breathing in and out through my nose, each breath lasting for five seconds. Dr Wilmot makes no big deal out of it. I really like his calm approach. Dr Wilmot suggests and supports me not to call Wayne. I'm to wait until this Saturday and if he's there again I'm to let him know that I feel terribly uncomfortable with him being present at my home group and I'd like him to find another meeting. If he puts up a fight and continues to go to my home group then will I choose not to go for the time being due to it being too much for me to handle. It's unfortunate that I may be too fragile to cope with Wayne going to my home group putting me in a position to choose to go elsewhere. I do feel this is the best action to take. Why I think this is because he always was on the look out to see if I was a sick person in the fellowship; he wouldn't know what that fucking meant anyway. I was affected by some very sick men in the fellowship when I was a young girl. I know what the affects are because I have experienced them and I do know who to look out for. He's just getting that stuff from his sponsor. He hasn't experienced it so he has no idea what the hell he's talking about. Dr Wilmot and I believe he's got a loose screw. Dr Wilmot has no idea what it meant when Wayne rang and asked me: "Did you do anything to my penis while I was sleeping?" My response to Wayne at the time when he asked me that question (not having spoken to him for over two months prior the surprise phone call) was: "I struggled to touch it when we were awake, what are the chances I was going to touch your penis while you were sleep!" Hello...ooh yuk! He grosses me out!

8/2/00 : The painting of Eugene is looking good but he's so annoying. The face, I can't stand doing the face. I'm sure I could do it if I had training. I actually want to enlarge his nose so it becomes 'the' feature, because it's so difficult. The background is red/orange and his over coat is dark purple, brown and black. I want to do little planes taking off around him, not sure. Just at the moment I'm frustrated with myself because I can't seem to get his nose right and I'm struggling to get the colours on his arms to match the colours in his face.

My gosh, my body is really out there at the moment. I'm bloating, carrying lots of fluid and my stomach feels all knotted up. It's so frustrating being this way and so I need some patience with myself, this will pass.

Rick wants to catch up. I forgot to tell him that I only want to be friends. He's going to another country in six months. He is a nice guy, as I find him to be an intuitive, gentle, funny guy. But wait for it, he's not tall enough!!

11/2/00 : I feel a little goofy sending a message saying; "Hi Jasey masey," to Jezza.

I read in this morning daily readings that having a go and failing are not as bad as not having a go. It also read to do what you love today and not to leave it until tomorrow. Waiting and having patience reveals the things we want when the time is right.

I felt so wonderful and magical the time when Jezza and I told each other how we felt and now it appears way too much for us to confront or handle. Isn't it easier to be with others that aren't so confronting? It was so spot on when Dad said: "You're stuffed now, you won't be able to have a relationship with just anyone and perhaps because of that you may not be with someone for a long time or ever." How harsh it sounds, but frightens me none. I'm in a space where singleness and living with my family and friends without a boyfriend feels right for me. I don't want anything, a relationship between Jezza and I won't happen.

I have to share some of the stuff I came to understand when I was talking with Dad. I can see the time I spend (so to speak) with men who are not potential soul mates (so to speak) is the time I could be spending getting to know myself. Since accepting that, yes, I do love Jezza and yes, he does love me, I am now in a space within myself to do those things that move, touch and inspire me. I have no fucking idea whether or not Jezza and I will ever be together. I simply don't know. I now don't expect myself to know how to bring a relationship about with Jezza. I was unaware that I hadn't told him that I'm here to support him in any shape or form. I sent him a message that was simply this simple: "Hi just want to let you know that if you need help with moving to Melbourne, I would be more than happy to help." Simple, isn't it? I complicate things. It feels like we stuff it up each time. When we're together (on the phone or talking face to face) we don't need to talk about the where we are going, as in, 'you are now my girlfriend' for example. It feels far beyond the idea of marriage. The emotions are beyond the mind. It's an endless feeling of yumminess and abundance, yet so fragile and so full on that it slips through my fingers. I have never experienced this before. I believe we don't now how to handle it, hold it or deal with it.

12/2/00 : I find it difficult with Jezza because I'm afraid of making him feel sickly uncomfortable. I'm afraid of not being considerate of him. I'm afraid of being manipulative. I think even about the last three messages I've sent him that perhaps he thinks: "What the fuck is she doing, I hope she leaves me alone." I wonder if I am to leave my job? I love being there. I will know when that time will be if I'm to leave.

13/2/00 : It occurred to me last night that perhaps the reason why Jezza continues to bring up the time we drove around the countryside in the middle of the night for hours looking for a toilet for me to go to was perhaps because that was the night he told me how he felt towards me. I remember being in the down stairs bar and we were standing at the back corner next to the boy's toilets. The place was well lit and it was there he began to say that he's always liked me. He said that I was very beautiful and that he finds it hard to approach and talk to me. I was overwhelmed with what he was saying. In the car he was like a puppy dog, giving me those loving eyes. I remember thinking: I've been waiting to hear this for so long and I can't feel a thing. All I could do was smile. I felt frustrated when I couldn't feel what he was feeling. I believe it was because I didn't truly believe him. I don't know. That night I assume we kissed, I can't remember. I can tell you that I bet I ran off in the morning as usual because I can't look needy or allow him to know that I really adored him. I think I invited him to come to Swan Hill and he said yes that night. I rang him the following day to see if he was still coming and he said no. I do believe that he said he couldn't remember much about what he said the night before. I felt crushed. The first five years of knowing he was on the planet I thought he was adorable, but we never spoke. I would have been 15 and he 21 years old. I couldn't even talk to him because he played for a local football team and I idolised him thinking he was a legend (if he could only read this now!).

Anyway he was also seeing a girl that he went out with for several years. I caught a couple of looks from him one night across the tables at a restaurant. Those eyes made me melt like butter. He was with a large group of people and I was with all the girls and we looked at each other throughout the evening. We were definitely flirting. He was still going out with his girlfriend. I had dated Max for two years and Jarod for three and half years during the time that he was with his girlfriend of many years. It wasn't until a Saturday night when I was playing pool and he was watching that we spoke to each other in a nightclub. I had no hope in winning the game of pool. My nervousness over took the game. He approached me and in that conversation we both found out that we were finally single, roughly for six months. I was 21 and he was about 27. He was wearing a suit that night. He remembered me from the football games that I went to. He said he couldn't concentrate what the coach had to say because I was standing there amongst the supporters during the quarter breaks. I always went out during quarter time with Dad, not to listen to the coach but to be near Jezza. Unfortunately that night when the nightclub closed at 5:00am Jezza held my hand and I ripped my hand from his clasp because I didn't want him to think he could get what he wanted just because he wanted to. I didn't want him to think that I was a slut. Jarod would call me a slut privately and publicly. I'd allow myself to get close and then I'd think 'see you later mate'. Why? Because I wanted him to know I was not a slut. I moved to Melbourne, he worked on weekends, so I couldn't stay Sunday mornings because he had to work. I didn't know what to do with myself anyway, so taking off in the mornings was a choice I felt safe with. It took me a while to allow myself to kiss him. Sometimes we'd fall asleep in front of the heater watching rage with him holding me. He always was very hospitable. Oh the first time I kissed him I was so drunk that I couldn't remember the next day and I did that two weekends in a row. I hated myself for being that way and for not remembering. I felt great shame and embarrassment. I never felt good enough. I always dressed well and looked good because I thought I was not good enough to be respected or liked by him. I played many mind games out of fear. We both did. Where are we now? I'm in Melbourne again and he's still living in that small country town. He's not talking to me at all, even though I told him I loved him. When I spoke to him about how I felt for all these years and that I do love him, I asked if he felt the same. His response was, "yes". He said: "Now that we are here it's not so hard, is it?" What he said to me felt so right at the time. He said that it was so difficult for him to lie beside me one time when I stayed over, he stressed about it all night and fell asleep two minutes before having to get up and go to work. So, we love each other like no other on this planet and he's not talking to me. I'm waiting for his call.

14/2/00 : I need to ring Courtney today about going through my personal inventory on my past sexual relationships. It's time to clean up my act and get honest about my behaviour and motives in my relationships with men.

16/2/00 : I'm not 100% well today.
I need to do something about the art show. I'm running out of time. It probably won't happen. I don't have the confidence. I'm afraid of not being good enough. I'm afraid how I'll feel if nothing sells. Mum's pieces of art are worth buying, she is the true artist, not me. I just make it up. Dad doesn't think much about my art.

21/2/00 1:35 PM : I had my first singing lesson last night, absolutely amazing. I'm breathing from my tummy for the first time. I don't have time to write. I feel I'm unable to say all the things that have been happening.
Where I am at with Jezza is at peace. I actually cried on the phone whilst leaving a message about letting him know I was sitting on the bathroom floor. How I was confused with fear and I couldn't get out of it. Also saying that he said I could call him if I were upset and that I was afraid of his judgement of him thinking I was psycho. Next day I sent a message letting him know I was feeling at peace with myself, so that he wouldn't need to worry. Tuesday I sent another message whilst I was practising for my first singing lesson. I was singing 'Foolish Games', sung by Jewel, and I began to cry. So I reminded him that we agreed that if he wanted out then he would have to verbally let me know. Guess what? He hasn't sent anything back or replied, which is what I expected. I do love Jezza and I enjoy loving him.

22/2/00 : The author of 'The Artist's Way' writes in her book to write all the negative stuff that is in my head as part of the morning pages. She says I'm not to read back over it, if I want to I simply will. Here we go...I think I don't have a toned enough body for singing. What a wank thing to believe, that I need a toned body to sing. I find make up on women is becoming more and more unattractive to me. I see make up as a mask, yuk! I don't know how men stand it. Yes, I think and consider whether or not my motives are healthy in regards to Jezza. My mind tells me I'm a stalker, just hanging onto the old times of my past. That thought pops into my head each day and it brings fear with it. I really don't want him to feel that is what I'm about. I suppose if that were the case he knows he can let me know. I do think and believe that my paintings aren't so good. I am unsure about getting my art works together, however doing what I can do will lead to having it done by the due date.
I've been practising my singing by lying down on the floor, that way I'm able to breathe into my stomach. Practising and singing Jewel, Foolish Games, it occurred to me I wanted to share with Jezza that the first half of the song I feel I'm looking at him and the second half it's him looking at me. So I got up and sat on the toilet and started to send him a message about why I ended up with that song. I'm sharing my life with him. He gets to know me without having to do anything. I feel free and what I'm doing feels to

be a natural thing to do. I don't know what he'll be getting from what I'm doing. The positive would be that I value him and I value me. I'm being consistent, reliable and probably a good pain in the arse.

26/2/00 : I was in a large bookshop with my girlfriend and while we were looking for the book, 'In the Meantime' for her to buy she said out of the blue: "I can see you being on TV. Seriously!" Wouldn't that be cool if it were true? A part of me wanted to believe her.
I'm writing a letter to Jezza.

27/2/00 : My head tells me that I'm hanging onto the past and Jezza's moved on and so should I. I've been sober over three years and I speak of love with passion, curiosity and some wisdom and here I am loving someone who is not giving me much back in return. Not only do I run into the continual thought that I'm a messed up, dependant, needy, psycho who is holding onto the past because I'm thinking I am nothing without him but I see this is starting to interfere with my writing and my painting. About my letter to Jezza. Will he understand? Does he really give a shit? Is it too boring and jumbled? Last night I did some writing and I believe it is really boring. I'm looking at my writing as a short story now, that's Lana's idea. Of course I'd have to let Jezza read it to see if it's okay for him to share it with others. But because I'm looking at writing a book, I feel I'm losing track and sight of the purpose if I think I'm writing to him. Also, I have to complete works of art. I think about them. Nothing is happening. I got the ink, I'm afraid I'll splash it everywhere. It's something I don't think I can do in the house. I remember it was Jezza who pointed out to me that Van Gogh did paintings at home, so I can do the same. Courtney warns me to be mindful not to 'people please' Jezza in hope of having him like me

28/2/00 : I have the money for Scott. I'm debt free! Can you believe it?
I feel nervous about going to Shepparton. I'm afraid of seeing Jezza. I'm afraid of being ignored. I really don't feel up to it, carrying all this tension. I'm thinking I'll give the letter to him this weekend. The man's not talking to me.

1/3/00 : I do wonder when I'm going to get my paintings done. What I'll do is take down my artwork and do some at Linus's. I don't know if I'll get time to create.
      The letter I'm writing to Jezza is twenty-nine pages so far. I have lots to do, although I don't really want to leave the house. I want to write and see if I can finish the letter so that if I want to go to Shepparton I can drop the long arse letter off to him while I'm there.

ANOTHER DAY : Let's see what my dragon in my head has to say. Jezza is going to give you another brush off and how foolish are you going to look and feel? He's not going to be interested in your letter. He doesn't even want to read it. There will be another girl there so he'll treat you like a 'nobody', like he always has. The only reason he won't tell you he doesn't love you or feel the same as you is because 1. He doesn't give a shit 2. He doesn't think you're worth being honest with 3. Can't get the guts to say it to you, otherwise he would've said: "Please leave me alone." Jezza thinks you're a real twot and so do I.

11/3/00 : I haven't written in a bloody long time. Still haven't begun reading the book, 'The Artist's Way'; I don't know what it's going to take.

Bob will be having lunch with me today. Had coffee with Margaret after the breakfast twelve-step meeting and it's really lovely getting to know her. Margaret is a writer for Penguin Publications. She is so delightful and fascinating to listen to. She tells me to give up thinking I'm a slut as I was forgiven the moment I walked into the rooms of the recovery meetings. When I was 22 a voguish looking, 75year old woman, who I admired for her spiritual wisdom held my hand and read: "You are very intelligent and highly creative. You will be very successful and wealthy doing something you love and you will find love at 29." My first reaction was, '29, that's seven years from now, that's so far away!' I was barely sober, in debt, engaged, hated myself and intelligence was not something I thought I had; stupid yes, intelligent, no way. I haven't forgotten that moment, it was beyond what I thought would be possible yet I knew I would wait to see if her words would become true.

27/3/00 : I've been working on my book and I think it's really boring and I'm sure I'm only repeating what someone else has published before. I have no educational background. Thinking this way prevents me from writing. I resigned from my job last Wednesday. I had an insight two weeks ago, on the Thursday, and realised that I have the opportunity to live with my Dad now that I am not with anyone or have any children. I haven't lived with my Dad since the age of seven because of Mum divorcing my father. I thought (up until this moment) that if I lived with my Dad I would hurt my Mum's feelings and that living with him would never be allowed. Being an adult I can choose what feels right for me. This thought made me cry. I thought immediately that if I were to return back to my Hometown, where I swore I would never live again, that God would have to give me some pretty big signs. I'm happy living where I'm living and the wonderful family I'm working for. My heart wants to give it a go so I told God to show me signs to solidify my reason for such a big move.

ANOTHER DAY : I gave Jezza the 35 page letter on Saturday. Met his mum, dad and cousin, they are really nice people. I spent two and half hours with them. Jezza hasn't called me. I'm not worried. I trust he's dealing with it the best way he can. I sent him the lyrics of my song, 'I only want you', to him for him to put a tune to it. He told me he's afraid of being involved with anyone. He was talking about me. I understand that feeling so I'll keep on doing what I'm doing. A beautiful affirmation is that Jezza and I are already having a relationship with one another. We are already here. This is it. It doesn't get any harder or better than this. I wonder if I can let him know that. I want to say: "You are afraid of getting into another relationship, fear of being hurt. We are already having a relationship with each other as we speak. This is as good as it gets."

11/4/00 : Yesterday I finally let go of it all. I feel Jezza doesn't care. He doesn't like me, doesn't feel the same. I didn't tell the girls. I'm sure they know something is up, especially Lana. I just can't talk to her at the moment. What can she say, really? I've given the man a letter that exposes me and I have received nothing in return, as if he hasn't read it. I'm moving to Shepparton. That's for certain. I'm very excited. Lots of stuff is going to happen there I can't look Lana in the eyes. It's like she's waiting for me to tell her something. Simone didn't drink or kill her self as she said she was going to on Saturday. I'm letting her go, I can no longer be her sponsor. She has no regard for me what so ever after what she said to me on that day. I was hurt that she didn't call to let me know she was alive. I let Courtney go as my sponsor. I no longer want the feeling that she's on a pedestal or that I'm answerable to her. I want to feel like an adult and not continually feel scared about sharing how I feel or what I think in case she disapproves of my choices. I want to feel absolutely comfortable with her and I feel that by having her as my girlfriend. Seeing her as an ex-problem drinker, to be able to talk to one another at the same level, I believe I will feel that we are both on even grounds this way. No one is better or less than any other. I believe only my Higher Power knows everything and works through everyone no matter where they are at in life. Portia has decided to let her sponsor go because of her inner struggles feeling like a child and having to do as her sponsor tells her to do which puts her in a position of feeling incompetent and the fear of being wrong. I support her to focus on having good friends in the fellowship, one ex-problem drinker sharing with another ex-problem drinker where both are not answerable to another. She's thinking about it.

I sent out to the universe a request for a laptop computer to be able to type up the book.

12/4/00 9:50 AM : I've written 20,000 words so far. I trust God's working through me. There's a lot to cover, to explain and to work out. Mum will be a great help. I need to ask her if it's all right to use her computer. I'm a little afraid that my book is too messed up and will be a flop and this writing is to just get all the junk out of me.

So let's go. My head tells me that Jezza doesn't care and that he's really confused about what I've given him. I think that he's probably wishing I didn't call him or text him. He probably wants me to leave him alone. I think to myself that he wants me to piss off because I'm not getting the message to do so.

1/5/00 : Rejected!! Joshua, this guy I met three weeks ago tells me last night that he does not want to get involved with me or anyone for that matter. He also told me that could change, but hey do I believe that! I've noticed that I've been crying more than usual due to the unworthiness I feel about my art being on display. Knowing Joshua has also brought up within me the same destructive and self-abusing thoughts I experienced being with Jarod. I'm glad I didn't have sex with him. I felt at the time that he was genuine and so I allowed him to know who I am. I'm thinking that I did and said too much. Where to from here? Well, I don't feel good about catching up with him at the moment. My feelings are hurt and so I'm angry. I want to hurt him for not wanting to be in a relationship with me. He came over late last night at twelve midnight and my alarm bells went off in my head. He is experiencing blackouts and behaving wild whilst drunk and it really concerns me. Weekend benders are a worry and the fact that he triggers old emotions from the days of Jarod need to be noted.

I'm not a slut. Yes, I'm emotionally all over the place at the moment. My spirit knows he is not good for me. I hear, 'let go' in my mind. I didn't want to share with him any more after he said he didn't want a relationship. Yes I believe I was too much, too full on, great. I need to know if my man will be there for me, emotionally, mentally and spiritually. I'm to protect myself and to do what is right for me. I need not to beat myself up.

17/5/00 : I'm to begin my writing again. I'm finding that I'm laying in bed longer than I usually do. It's getting hard to get out of bed. The purpose of writing is to get the negative stuff out of my head. Hey there's plenty, let's go. I can't write a book. I'm not old enough. I haven't studied. I haven't got a clue what to write or how to write a book. I'm a phoney and I won't be successful.

Jezza is scared of me. He thinks I'm a screwball. Lana thinks I should go visit him. It's too soon. I'll wait until I move to Shepparton in June. Another four weeks until I move and I can wait. What if Jezza gives me the cold shoulder? I'll feel like a fool. I've taken it too far. I tell him too much. He's not interested in poor, messed, psycho girl like me with a poor Dad, poor Mum or a dirty living, loudmouthed cousin. And what about me giving the letter when I had told him prior of kissing someone else? He won't understand. I don't understand. Joshua the other guy I kissed who I got physically close with, no sex thank God, he's got herpes. Great!

I want to sing. I want to be a fantastic painter, person, leader, performer, speaker and lover. I want to be in a relationship with Jezza without feeling that I don't have a life because I want to be loved by him. If he's not meant to be, then I can never change that.

18/5/00 : I have my astrological chart reading today. What's up with my clenching jaw? I use to do that about four years ago when I was full of resentment and anger during my drinking days. Why am I doing it now? I'm wanting to get to Shepparton and I'm feeling impatient, maybe that's what the problem is; probably. I'm going to rewrite my book into something that is moving, touching and inspiring. I'm afraid I won't get to write my book, that I'm no good or someone else has done it. Bla, bla, bla. I won't be different. I need to find my own style. God, shall you show me? I know I have a particular writing style, maybe I'll ask the people around me. I wrote 13 songs/poems last night. I'd love to put music to these words and sing my own style, instead of wanting to be like other people. I want to know my voice and sing my own songs. I know my head tells me I can't sing and that I'm just dreaming. I'll get over that. I want to do bold paintings using colour and texture as well as keeping them simple; paintings that will capture the eye and set off the room. That's my style. Yes, I'm open to doing a course. No I'm not. Come on. Okay, I'm open. I want to learn how to use different mediums, just to learn how to be an artist would be nice.

I've put on a little bit of weight; not that noticeable. I can feel it. I've been eating lots of yummy foods that are full of fat and sugar. I've been indulging. I'm okay with that. I'm going through different experiences and they bring up emotions and thoughts of insecurity and not much self-love. So I've attacked food. I'm not to fear the need to indulge in food. I'm not to fear weight gain. I'm to embrace it. Fearing overeating only magnifies my eating and it then gets out of control. When I accept my overeating disorder the sooner it passes because what I've noticed it is the fear that makes my eating go out of control. I recognise that food is bigger than me. I accept that food has already won the game. I'm to trust my Higher Power, to accept that I'm overeating. This is the only way I know how to find relief from the torment of fighting food to get back to my natural size, the way my Higher Power made me to be.

28/5/00 : I sent this message to Jezza Saturday morning around 9:30 am.

"Good morning Jezza! So sorry about the multiple calls last night. My housemate was drunk and got to my phone without me knowing. I'm okay and I'd like to talk with you anyway to get clear with what is and isn't happening between us. To keep it simple, I've been trying to say for the past 10 years that you're the man I love. I always have and I always will. You got into my heart somehow and I'm glad that you did and I've always hoped that we'd get a chance to be together and I have no clue how to make that happen. I just want to know if being with me is what you want too. You know if it's not I won't reject you as my friend, I may go a little shy and red faced though! Would you mind responding in some way in the near future? You know how frightening it is to blurt out stuff like this to the person who really matters."

His response was at 2:00am Sunday: "I'm on holiday." I asked: "Great, where?" His answer was: "Apollo Bay." I then called his phone and there was no answer. I then sent another message: "Are you travelling around Australia?" No more responses from him. I attempted two-three other messages that I ended up clearing and not sending because they were angry and hurtful. I reminded myself that I cannot make him talk to me or tell me what I feel I need to hear. I sent my last message at 3:30 am saying: "Have fun what ever it is you are doing."

SAME DAY : When I was awoken this morning by my gorgeous girlfriend, Portia, at 7:30am, I felt I woke up with a hangover. It quickly passed when I remembered I chose not to send hurtful messages to tell Jezza.

ANOTHER DAY : Just called Jezza and left a message telling him I've been pretending and that I stop myself from calling him all the time because I'm afraid of being invasive and that I wondered what he thought about the letter: was it too much or was it beneficial? I also mentioned in the message I sent to his phone about wanting to be with him, telling him I'd like to hear what he feels or thinks about that, welcoming him to call me anytime day or night. I feel relieved and still afraid of his judgement. At times while I was talking I paused for periods not knowing what to say. I said I wanted to be with him even though we've been physically apart most of the time. But it's my heart that wants this (thinking this is all fantasy, he never thinks of me). "I'm being genuine," I said. I'm the one who holds myself back. Right now I'm thinking that I wrote and gave him that letter months ago, and I'm still hanging on. The chatter in my head is loud. My head is now saying that I don't even ask how he is, that I don't care about him, that I'm only interested in myself and my obsession. Jezza said I could call him anytime that "the line is always open to call." So am I being intrusive?

18/6/00 : I have a singing lesson tonight at 7:45pm, aarh! I'm convinced I'm a hopeless singer. I'm scared to go. I feel like I'm not good enough. I haven't been practising enough. I have myself to blame.

I've put on a bit of weight. I feel uncomfortable in my jeans. I'm not depressed about it. I'm aware now that it is important to drink more water and eat fruit and vegetables.

21/6/00 : I've got out the Artist's Way. I signed it where there is a declaration to begin the work that is suggested. I'd love to live off my artworks. That would be fantastic. I'm willing to start. Ruby mentioned her sister wanted a painting for her boyfriend. So I painted a slip shot of the Island of Capri in Italy on three wood panels. I really like them. I'm putting $200 on it. If she doesn't want it, I'll keep it for myself until someone wants to buy it for that price.

What a fool I am for writing that letter to Jezza and then giving it to him. I know that would've been an overload of information for him to digest. Deep inside I don't want to see him. I dread running into him. How do I be? How can I apologise for being who I am? I simply don't want to. Why do I need to feel shameful about being open and honest? I feel I'm physically hiding though. I'm putting off going to Shepparton. Jezza has taken off around the countryside to get away.

I can hear Aimee moving around upstairs. Ruby moved some of her stuff in last night. I felt a little sorry for myself and angry that Lana has my good friend to live with and has taken up my fantastic nanny job with Liz and David with their gorgeous children. I'm aware of the selfishness in that. I accept it as letting go of what I've known and I'm a bit scared of the unknown future. I'm grieving.

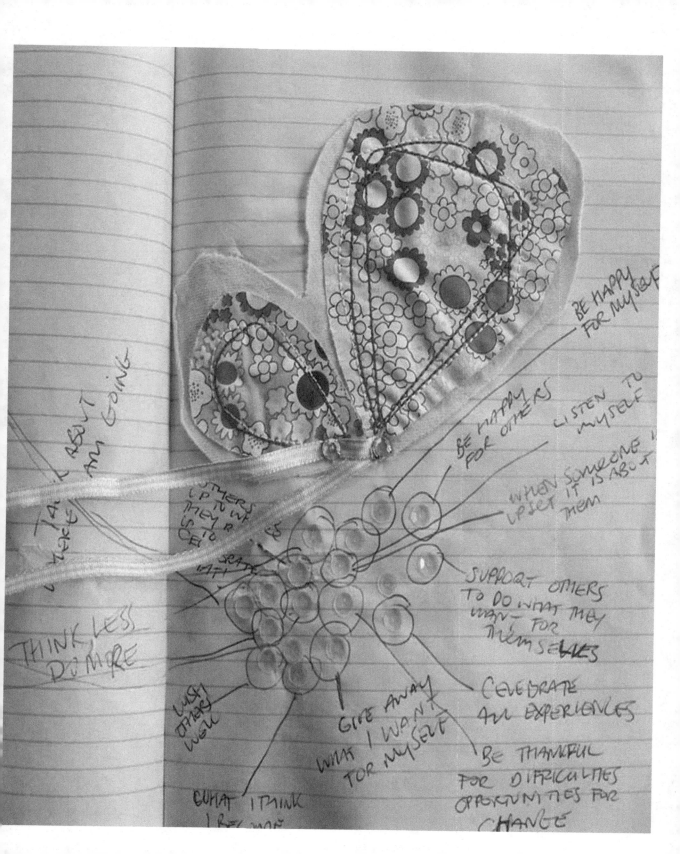

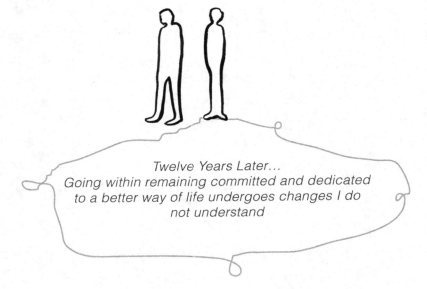

Twelve Years Later...
Going within remaining committed and dedicated
to a better way of life undergoes changes I do
not understand

OLD THOUGHT: I must keep others happy to be okay
NEW THOUGHT: Following what is right for me makes me happy

I feel so sad to know I risked my sobriety to keep a friend of mine happy. How did I do that? I ate food soaked in wine. The alcohol would have been cooked out of the food, however my body certainly didn't like it as I felt sick in the following morning and it screwed with my head. For me, to drink alcohol is to die. I cannot afford to forget where my drinking took me, what it did to my body and my life. When I drank, I drank and drove; I put myself into situations where I could have been raped when I walked home alone down the city streets in the dark. I went home with strangers, they could have been rapists, murderers God knows what, all because when I began to drink alcohol I could not guarantee I would make good safe decisions for myself and more often than not – I didn't. When I drank I lost my ability to choose. When people who don't have a problem with alcohol do not lose their ability to make sane and sound decisions whereas I did.

I was so caught up with upsetting my friend I over looked the danger I put myself in – eating food with alcohol in it (even though the alcohol was cooked), it could have triggered my mental obsession to drink and I over looked her insensitivity toward my disease of alcoholism. It's a shame I felt so responsible for her feelings, so much so I couldn't allow her to be upset with me. I felt responsible to make her feel better instead of letting her work that out for herself. There obviously was a misunderstanding between us, that's all it was and yet I put myself in danger to solve the problem.

In the alcoholic home I grew up in I felt responsible for my parents' unhappiness. I just did. I thought I could relieve their pain if I bent over backwards to make them happy again. At the time I just felt if they were happy I would feel happy and free of the weight of guilt and badness I felt when they weren't happy.

I shared with Marika my uncomfortable experiences I was having with Wayne. I was extremely angry with Wayne waking me through the night; it was causing me such tiredness during the day that I could hardly function in my job. Marika commented how awful I looked and I told her about Wayne waking me up during the night to have sex with me. I didn't want to be having sex with him when I needed my sleep. I really needed my sleep and even though I would ask him to quit waking me he would wake me wanting sex. GRRR!

Marika understood exactly why I was allowing this to happen. She knew I felt guilty and afraid if I didn't have sex with Wayne because I was living under his roof. I felt I had to have sex with him to keep him happy or I feared if I said no he would threaten me to move out. I would have nowhere to go.

To be honest I don't know if I had the courage to stop having sex with him but I did decide to find somewhere else to live quick smart in the meantime. Marika helped me to begin to understand I didn't have to have sex with someone just because they were helping me out, in this case, putting a roof over my head. The relationship fell to bits when I moved because I made the decision he wasn't to stay over night in my new place. At the time I thought it was because I would feel uncomfortable having a guy stay over when I was living with another friend. Now I know it wasn't that, it was the fact I didn't know how to say 'no' to having sex with someone when I didn't want to be sexual with them. So it was easier to not have him stay over where I wouldn't have to face the problem where he was waking me up during the night to have sex when I didn't want to.

I was abusing myself and I didn't know it. I have had experienced suicidal thoughts as the result of letting someone else do things to me that I don't want them to do. I would turn against myself. I'd find myself curled up in the shower, bed or bedroom floor crying or in a state where I stare and go blank about everything. I knew there is something terribly wrong with this picture and I was convinced it's me.

Well in one sense there was a problem with me because I was curled up on the ground thinking it was better to kill myself than go on with the pain heart and badness in my head. However I'm not wrong or bad if I want others to respect my body, respect my decisions that I make for myself. Yet, I'm the one who needs to know, accept and understand that, not the other person. Other people will say and do what they want however I always have a choice how I choose to respond to what others say and do if it affects me. If I don't like it I need to do something about it. I didn't know at the time that I was being affected by Wayne's sexual behaviour. He was pressuring me to be sexual with him and there is something not right about that and something more not right about why I thought he was okay and I wasn't. And this is how I was affected by his sexual behaviour.

Keeping others happy didn't make me happy, if anything it creates a horrible pain in my heart because to keep someone happy instead of understanding others make their own happiness sets up relationships where I miss out and the other gets all. It becomes a lose win situation instead of a win win situation. Keeping others happy at all costs also sets me up to stay silent about how I really feel and if I'm not being real about my feelings then others do not know who I really am and neither do I. So instead of thinking 'am I able to keep the other person happy' maybe I can focus on what can or can't I do without placing in myself in positions where I feel hurt, harmed or threatened. Am I taking care of my needs first? Do I feel comfortable about what is being asked of me? I believe if I follow what feels right for me it is the right way to go.

OLD THOUGHT: I won't say anything my love will stop others from harming me
NEW THOUGHT: Breaking my silence can teach others it's not okay to hurt & harm me

How many times have I skipped over feeling my feelings or seeing situations as they really are because of going to the extreme of seeing only good in a situation when there was some really bad stuff going on as well?

My cousin Linus began to treat me in a way, which was unacceptable to me. I continued to focus on how good he was to me and that how he was treating me would change, I thought I just needed to be extra loving and understanding to help our relationship along. I didn't write about these painful times in my journals. This illustrates to me how much I didn't want to face the reality of what was going on in my relationship with him.

He grew marijuana in their backyard. When I would visit them and his girlfriend, I felt I was committing a crime because I knew about the illegal activity growing in his garden. It didn't feel good to be around people who were growing a plant to make drugs out of it. I was sober with the sincere intention of living an honest life and going to their home could lead me to feel I was jeopardising what meant the world to me - being sane and sober.

I picked up the phone and called Linus to let him know I had decided to keep away from his house while they grew marijuana. My girlfriend sat with me in the lounge room as support. I let him know it made me feel extremely uncomfortable knowing he was doing something illegal and I felt I was breaking the law by being around it when I would go to his home. The conversation heated up very quickly. He became extremely angry about my decision and threatened to cut my thumbs off if I told anyone or chose to keep away from his house. I remember crying and feeling very afraid. This was not a joke, he was not mucking around, he was deadly serious about his intentions if I didn't do what he wanted me to do.

Did I see this relative at their home again? Of course I did. Did I accept they weren't going to remove the marijuana plant and do what felt right for me? Of course not! Did I tell them it was not okay to threaten me? No, I believed my cousin loved me; that he was just going through a bad patch – he'd been so good to me in the past, he wouldn't really cut my thumbs off – would he? Looks like the threat worked.

From that point on I chose to do what this family member told me to do in fear of what they might do to me if I didn't. If I didn't go to their house anymore, I would risk finding out if the threat was real, something I wasn't prepared to face. I chose to say nothing to him about how I felt threatened, controlled and petrified of what harm he could cause me if I upset him. I let him think it was okay to treat me this way through my silence. When I did what he wanted me to do, I let him control me. I put his needs before my own; I failed to look after myself, put my safety first and treat myself as important. It's sad to say, this is only one of many experiences I had because of my fabulous ability to not pay attention to painful experiences and only see the good in others and situations. I refused to see the reality that what I was allowing this family member do to me was hurtful and frighteningly harmful.

I failed to accept the person whom I loved was changing from being loving to being abusive and because of this wonderful super-duper positive attitude I had I exposed myself to more abuse by him. By the time I thought it would be a good idea to really see the full picture, that yes he had been good to me in the past, however that does not mean I excuse him when he treats me badly.

It's the fine line between accepting things as they are, and taking the appropriate action in the right direction. I learnt from my experience that when I'm treated in a way I feel is hurtful or harmful to me, it is up to me to take full responsibility for letting the person know about it, if I feel that's the right thing to do. I left it so late to get real with him, that I entirely missed the opportunity to work things out as things became out of control. I later placed an application for an intervention order upon my cousin where he refused to have mediation and chose to take an undertaking at the court for a period of a year. I don't know if talking to him earlier about being affected by the way he was treating me would have prevented it from going to court. I'm guessing perhaps I would have chosen to exit the relationship sooner rather than later to protect and look after myself if he chose not to change the way he was treating me. And then again, as the result of open and honest communication I may have helped him see how his behaviour was affecting me and perhaps it could have helped him. Who knows, all I can say is, now I have learnt the importance of being open and honest with others, because as strange as this may sound – OTHERS CANNOT READ MY MIND! My silence lead him and particularly myself, to believe for a long time that the things he was doing and saying were okay when they were not.

OLD THOUGHT: No point following my dreams, I'd be no good at it anyway
NEW THOUGHT: Focus on the joy of dreaming & start living them

I had no idea how much impact the book 'The Artist's Way' was going to have upon me. It was the beginning of creating the life I love today. It was the book, which gave me the permission to be creative, the part of me I have struggled to be connected with. When I began reading this book, I could not relate to the people written about in the book. I felt the author wrote a book about and for extraordinary people who were capable of being writers, screen play writers, actors and successful artists. I could not relate to these people back then. I was a nanny working for extraordinary people and did I not see myself as an extraordinary person or become extraordinary by following my dreams. I really thought I was a dreamer reaching for the clouds.

I felt like a fool for giving new things a go. I felt stupid for taking my creative self seriously. I believed others' would think I'm a fool, wasting my time and probably watch me fail in the end anyway so why bother.

I'm so glad I accepted these feelings and thoughts as they were and persisted to follow my creative journey anyway. I wouldn't be doing what I do today if I had chosen to believe I was an idiot for doing things I loved doing. I wouldn't be doing what I do today if I believed it's not worth doing what I love because there's no money in it or that I'm no good at it anyway - being creative or following a creative path. Today I believe the creative path has played an enormous role in my happiness and has allowed my self-esteem and self-worth to grow. I've had many problems with my mental, emotional and spiritual health and being honest about what I love to do and giving myself the permission to do those things has certainly helped with these problems.

When I become worked up, such as feel anxious or stressed, I find myself walking to the cupboard, picking up a big block of clay to dig my fingers in, the tension begins to lift. I love it. I'm able to clear my mind and create whatever my fingers desire to create. I'm calmer once I've given myself the permission to be creative and I'm able to think more clearly. It's just lovely. What helps prevent or calm my emotional upsets is by being creative such as; working on this book little bits at a time, usually while my child sleeps, making clay sculptures, painting, cooking something new for my partner and I, dancing for the hell of it, or skipping through the house - why not when no one is watching! Like my mum tells me "life is too serious to be taken too seriously!"

The Artist's Way' taught me not to focus on the outcome, however focus on the purpose and leave the outcomes to a Higher Power or life itself. It's great to think this way because it helps me to just get on with what is in front of me instead of being stopped by the worry of failure. There is nothing to say great things won't come or dreams won't be found from following the joys of my heart. Giving things a go has lead me to live my dreams and experienced lots of joy and peace. This is one very good way to create a healthy relationship with myself. I can learn to depend upon myself to encourage myself, to think positively about myself, to love myself for giving things a go and celebrate who I am along the way.

SACRED CREATIVE FOCUS
WHAT DOES A HEALTHY RELATIONSHIP LOOK AND FEEL LIKE?

A healthy relationship to me looks like allowing each other; the right to make mistakes, the right to make our own decisions, the right to be treated with sensitivity, the right to have our own feelings, the right to have our own thoughts, the right to be encouraged, the right to privacy, the right to real support, the right to reach out for help, the right to rest, the right to do the things which bring us joy, the right to choose who our friends are, the right to explore new possibilities, the right to spend time with loved ones, the right to be healthy, the right to say 'no', the right to say 'yes', the right to be ourselves, and the right to have fun.

To create healthier relationships with others I begin with myself. How I am loving, trusting, respecting, forgiving and accepting myself. Is my relationship with myself going well or is there room for change to make it healthier. It's quite hard to nurture my relationships if I am not nurturing the relationship that I have with myself. If I'm having a hard time with myself I'm sure others will too. I find when I get myself right with myself it is so much easier to know how to get it right with others.

SUGGESTED CREATIVE ACTIVITY

I can see how I am treating myself. See the Appendix: 'How is my relationship with myself going?' I fill out the questionnaire to see where I am looking after myself and also to see where I might have some room for growth? Do I encourage myself to be good to myself? Do I encourage and support others to be good to themselves? Do I encourage myself to do what is best for me and do I encourage others to do what is best for them?

Having just filled out the questionnaire above, I draw, sketch and/or cut & paste the image/s that reflect how I treat myself. Then I imagine how I would look or what I'd be doing, thinking or feeling if I were treating myself really well in all areas of my life. What would that look like to me? How would I feel and what, if any, changes could occur in some of my relationships if I did treat myself really well?

SUGGESTED MEDITATIVE ACTIVITY

I sit quietly with my eyes closed imagining I am sitting with my legs crossed with my hands resting on my knees. As I look up I see myself sitting in front of me. The 'Me' who I am looking at across from me is my 'wise self' who knows how to treat me really well, with great love, kindness, compassion and understanding. I then hear my loving 'wise self' talking to me, encouraging me to look after myself. I listen very carefully to what my 'wise self' is saying? If I can't 'hear' anything I then have a guess as to what my 'wise self' would say. To take this further I imagine my 'wise self' encouraging me to look after myself in all of your relationships with others. I like to focus on one person at a time and write down what my 'wise self' has to say to me about each one.

COMMITMENT STATEMENT

I .... am willing to put aside everything I think I know about myself, my life, my past, my future, in order to have an open mind and a new experience with knowing what healthier relationships look and feel like. I am open to the possibility of knowing what healthy relationships look and feel like, receiving new thoughts, and living a new life.

MOVING FORWARD TO BEING WHO I REALLY AM
WEEK TEN : FORGIVENESS OF OTHERS & MYSELF

INTRODUCTION TO THE SACRED SHARING

LIZ AND DAVID SUCCESSFULLY FOUND A NANNY TO REPLACE ME. IT TURNED OUT TO BE MY HOUSEMATE, LANA. I PACKED MY BAGS AND ALL MY THINGS AND RETURNED TO MY HOMETOWN TO LIVE WITH MY FATHER. DAD WANTED TO WAIT UNTIL I ARRIVED IN MY HOMETOWN BEFORE HE BEGAN TO LOOK FOR A HOME FOR US IN WHICH TO LIVE. I STAYED WITH MUM DURING THE TIME BOTH DAD AND I HOUSE-HUNTED. THIS WOULD BE THE FIRST TIME I WOULD LIVE WITH MY FATHER, JUST THE TWO OF US. I HADN'T LIVED WITH MY DAD SINCE THE AGE OF SEVEN WHEN MY PARENTS DIVORCED.

JUNE 2000 : People don't see me as a loser. I'm so hard on myself. I haven't asked for more faith, more direction or for clarity. Well, I have asked for more clarity, and Sunday I received it. I'm here to write a book and sell my work. Something I read in 'The Artist's Way', "God, I will take care of the quantity, will you please take care of the quality?" God, will you please take care of the selling of the book? I'd like to talk to Bruce about his friend who is a renowned and successful artist to ask him how he got started. Maybe I'm being lazy in the areas that matter. Or am I being hard on myself, seeing that I'm doing a great job at the present moment. Wherever I can help I am there. I follow up.

I just want to say that I want to send Max a message of love and support. The thought of that makes me nervous. An employee in his business died in a working accident yesterday. He had worked for him and his father for many years. I have no idea how he's feeling but I know he's hard on himself at times. I wanted to say something to lighten his burden, but unfortunately nothing is coming to mind other than he's a beautiful man and that he's in my thoughts and prayers. During this difficult time if he needs anything, I'm here.

TUESDAY MORNING : I'm cold and I'm sitting in front of the heater. I couldn't fall asleep last night. Mum shut the door and I felt that she was upset with me so I couldn't sleep until she came back to the bedroom. I dreamt that a lady wanted a nanny and offered twenty-eight dollars per hour. My resume was all over the place and I tried to show them that I certainly was worth that amount per hour. At first they were only offering sixteen dollars per hour. She then mentioned cleaning, etc etc, and I said: "There's no way I'll be doing extra duties. I'm a nanny not a cleaner." I had to get that straight. Do I need to let Wesley House know I'm not interested in Residential Care? I'm only keen on the Day Program? Tamika said they were two separate jobs. I'm not going to work for a pittance.

Things to do: buy the paper and find jobs. Max is calling me today in regard to going to the pictures together. I'm looking forward to going. I won't take up soccer. I can't afford it. Perhaps there's indoor soccer? I'll talk to Max about that. There's plenty for me to do. I can go house-hunting today for Dad and I. I stopped writing and started to daydream, thinking about the kids at Wesley House. Yes, I'll go and have a look.

Jason crossed my mind. Well, I'm keeping it simple with him. I sent him a message asking how he's going. His response was: "I'm going okay," and my response to that was: "Thank God for that!" And I left it and he didn't further any more communication from that point. I realised that's all I could manage. He didn't ask how I was. That's fine but I'm not pushing it any more. He knows I'm here. He knows how I feel. He knows what I want. I know he's not doing anything about it. I'm not angry, hurt or embarrassed. Frustrated, yes, when it comes to wanting to be involved with someone else. It feels like a 'never-going-to-happen' situation because Jason is who I want and love and that's how my heart feels and I can't tell my heart what to do. Acceptance is the only way to go.

Catching up with Max is testing the waters to see if my heart will fall in love with him again. I don't think it will. I'm finding a really good friend in him though. I hope I'm in some way spiritually and emotionally helpful to him. God has me in his life for a reason as much as he is in mine. I want to write a chapter on, 'I can't tell my heart how to feel.'

Have I started painting? Have I started writing the book? Hey, I could write in the mornings when Mum is not on the computer. She loves sleeping in. I've started netball. I'm continuing singing. Dad's now learning how to sing. I can call Carmen today to talk to her about guitar lessons. Hey, my singing teacher suggested to me a while back that I play an instrument as well as sing. Good going. Now there's STAG (My Hometown Theatre Arts Group) to suss out.

So I remember why I've come back and that's to focus on my creativity. Guess I got distracted. I know Maree would've taken the time off work to do her book, having faith in God to provide. So that's what I'm going to do. As I have a medical certificate from Dr Wilmot, I can spend time writing my book. Also, I will paint my paintings and sell them and that will be my income.

I dreamt of buying my bed last night. The bed I wanted was old, I liked it but my friends and I shopped around and found another larger bed. Both beds were king size. I wanted the largest size. I wanted something of value and worth. I also dreamt about the money I had. Dreaming whether I had enough to buy the bed I wanted.

Today Dad, Linus and I are having singing lessons. We're all going to Melbourne to do this. We're leaving at 10:00 am. It's about 9:20 am now. I haven't done my homework check as yet from the book 'The Artist's Way.' I know I didn't do all my morning writings. I think I missed four of them, 'cos I started on the Friday not on the Sunday. I didn't go for a walk on my own for half an hour. I didn't take myself on an artist date or spend five dollars on myself. I don't feel too bad about it though. I realise I can do it this week; it's progression not perfection. So I talked to Kevin and he assures me that not working this week is okay. He repeated to me saying it's time to spend some time on myself and not on others. He says I give a lot of myself to others and it's okay not to at this point in my life. That's coming from someone who knows me and who is a successful businessman. I feel secure in taking up his advice, mainly because it feels like the right thing to do. I don't think I'll stay at Ruby's home though. I just want space from Lana. Perhaps Friday night I will, 'cos Lana won't be there. I just feel yucky about it all. I think Liz and David are taking their family away Friday, or maybe it's the Friday after. I've needed a break from being a nanny to concentrate on my life and what it is that I want for me. I will miss them. I love and adore the kiddies.

The netball last night was a success, fucking fantastic! Linus is a champion, un-bloody-believable! I rang and cancelled his singing appointment. The man keeps his integrity with me. All we need is a consistent male in the team.

Great, my head tells me I can't write a book. My head is telling me I'm not good enough, that I don't know what I'm doing, etc etc. Let's do some affirmations.

26/6/00 : Well, I've already started the day by calling Louise and Kate in regards to netball on Sunday nights. They, and Debbie, will get back to me. Louise is afraid of not having enough gear to wear to play.

I can give her something for her feet and legs that won't look too geeky. So far there is Tamika and I. I need to call Aimee, she might play on Sundays whereas Jessica can't. Hmm. There's lot's I'm doing today. Linus and I are shopping for clothes for the game. Wait till Eugene hears what Linus's doing! It's amazing. I'm to buy a netball and organise bibs for the teams. The indoor netball organisation requires two more teams for the competition to go ahead. How can I round that up? Surely I can think of more people to play. The boys are hard to find I suppose.

Being an adult I want to ask Max if it's okay to hang out together. It's okay to do that. I will go to a twelve-step meeting and have breaky with my buddies when I'm in Melbourne. I'll call Tom to ask if he can pick me up in the morning to take me to the meeting. The boys I'm going out with on Friday night will be sleeping anyway after the night out. Why waste time sleeping when I could be socialising? I will say something to Max about last night in regards to what he said. I'm not putting up with bullshit. No way! I'll set that straight.

Debbie is excited about commissioning me to create a large painting for her—abstract and full of colour. I'm excited too. I need a subject, something to work on. It's good that she'll pay for the material; saves me from buying them. I'll get the plank of wood that I want to paint on from Linus.

I need to get going because there are so many things to do for Centrelink. I'm a bit nervous about the interview but I'm basically okay. It's not until 1:30 pm. Two things I didn't buy because I'm poverty conscious were the Footrot Flats cartoon book and the cookbook, only eighteen dollars altogether. I'm stopping myself buying those things that interest me because I'm afraid of running out of money. Today I'll allow myself to buy both those items if it feels right at the time. The money from Ruby I'll bank into my account. Two hundred and seventy dollars will go nicely into there.

I want some advice on how to write a book and how to begin. How do I creatively let it flow? I want to do that.

Gosh, Kate (girlfriend from my school days) surprised me when she was talking about soul mates. She understands the journey of others and an understanding what soul mates are about; not just having one but it's possible to have two or three. She is amazing, and my lesson is to never ever assume. I do a lot of assuming. I'm terrible.

I've got the heater up full bore because it's so chilly in here. Marika rang; she's a sweetheart. I'll call Max today and I'll let him know I want to do a couple of things before we return to my Hometown. Maybe I can go back with Aimee. I want to see Marika and the 'Breaky with Bill' crew and perhaps pick up my stereo from my Mum's brother. I enjoyed having dinner at Linus and Petunia's place. It was much better than I imagined, plus Linus complimented me on my ability to play chess. That's surprising, I just enjoy the game. I've practiced with Sam, and I guess that has helped me. Now I want to write a letter to Sam to let him know how my chess playing is going and lift his day. I want to write to all the kiddies I know. They are all treasures. Keep on writing, okay.

Spoke to Courtney yesterday and she helped me to see what I'm prepared to do for Wesley House. I'm willing to work during the day with the children so I can stay focused of the other areas in my life. I'm writing a book, continuing singing lessons and guitar lessons, and I'm catching up with my girlfriends. It is also important that I keep my weekends free to go to the football, to go camping, to travel to Melbourne and to keep on painting.

I want and need a job that has some routine so that I can keep appointments and keep track of what I'm doing. Time to do a poo!

Courtney suggested that I ask the Universe for clarification around my purpose for being in My Hometown. I'm to ask what my purpose is for coming here and what is my universal purpose? I know it's much more than I can imagine. It's so much more than I can feel, see, and hear right now. Courtney said that I don't have to take up something right away, meaning work-wise just because it's been offered. What I offer is probably not what they want. That's cool with me. I may only stay here long enough to get a house with Dad. I'm too excited about renting. I'm hoping I can stay here at Mums a little longer to work something out. I'll call Kevin up to let him know we've found a house in Lake St. "Position, position, position", he says. Maybe he'll be interested in helping out. I know he'd love to give me some advice. I enjoyed singing with Josie last night. I never would have reached the notes she sang a couple of years ago or before I started to learn how to sing. I sang higher notes than her! I realised, by singing with Josie, that I have progressed and I could see how much I've come to learn from my singing lessons from Shelly.

4/7/00 : Nope, I really doubt myself as to whether I can really write a book. I can't even start. My head can't decide where to start. I'm doing lots of good deeds for others.

I haven't decided whether I'll go to Melbourne tonight or not. It's the money. If I had the money I would go. Maybe I'll need to go to bring my bed and couch home. If I get this place in Bella St then I'll call Kevin and ask him to bring my bed and couch to My Hometown for me. I'll go to Melbourne for that. So today I'm making it up as I go. Kevin may not be able to shift my stuff this week. I'm writing very neatly aren't I?

My dream last night was very clear. Rocko was in it and I wasn't allowed to taste his yummy chocolate peppermint ice cream. I was annoyed that I was to marry Rocko. Everyone was so excited. There was a dominating ethnic woman—what she says goes. I was excited at first to marry someone but then I felt afraid for my future because I knew I couldn't pretend for too long that I loved him when I didn't. I was thinking in my dream that I loved Jason and I couldn't imagine being intimate with Rocko. So I went to him when he was lying in bed with me (Helen his ex-girlfriend was with us as well, hmm, how strange!). I told him what I was thinking, after mistakenly calling him Jason, and said I couldn't marry him because I didn't love him. I felt so relieved. Rocko was okay about all of this. I woke up thinking of the significance of that dream and the other dream of being paid twenty-eight dollars per hour. I feel that my personal worth is becoming more important to me instead of making sure others' needs are being met before mine. The dream about shopping around for the best quality bed and having enough to pay for a king size suggests to me I want the best for myself.

Wesley House has not yet contacted me and that makes me think that perhaps I didn't get the job. With that though, I felt immediate relief. It is an indication that the residential position I was interviewed for is not for me. Courtney's voice is clear in my mind saying; "You don't have to take the first job that comes your way." I need to fill out the unemployment benefits diary

I bought a paintbrush yesterday, yet I'm reluctant to paint. It's painful not painting. I've been singing around the traps, the shower, the car, inside my home, etc etc. I haven't been practising properly, I need to sit down and practice my singing in front of the mirror without the music. I want to have enough money to play guitar, sing, and pay for my therapy in Melbourne, as well as pay for my mobile phone and art materials. If someone likes my art maybe I'll sell it to them depending on how much money they have to pay for it. That sucks, doesn't it? Yep! I need to focus on painting first. My thoughts yesterday were, 'Paint what you want to paint and paint because you enjoy painting—put aside the money. Write because you enjoy writing—forget about the money. Sing because you like to sing—forget who will listen and who will judge.' The only person stopping me from doing all of this is me.

I have left my job. I have left my home in Prahan. I have lived well with Mum. I have been getting along great with Dad. I have brought Dad along to singing lessons and survived. I have created a netball team on Sunday evenings. I have enrolled Debbie to commission me to paint her a painting. I have sung and walked with Josie (an old neighbour of mine) early this morning.

I am hungry. It is windy and cold outside today. I'm organising a home with Dad, interviews for jobs and stuff with Centrelink. I have been here less than two weeks. I have travelled to Melbourne to see Stuart (Eugene's good friend who is home from England) and I've been a good friend to Max. Went with Dad so he could collect his last items from Joyce's home (his ex partner).

ANOTHER DAY : Arrh! The coffee's cold. Tamika rang yesterday to explain her quick exit at work so that the children wouldn't think I was favoured in anyway. Before she could tell me about that I shared with her my admiration toward her in regard to the work she does. Guess I had it good at my last job in the sense of cash; even a two-and-a-half- thousand-dollar bonus at the end of the year. Golly gosh. Stay focused.

I'm thinking in my head instead of writing. Why aren't I writing a book? Good question. Because my head tells me I don't have enough to say. I'm 'not inspired enough and nothing is going on to help me create such a large volume', which is bullshit. I probably have a colossal amount of information I need to share. I thought this morning that I need to give away what I've got in order to keep what I have. To help me to stay spiritually, mentally and emotionally in tune with life, the book needs to be written. Okay, so I'll pick up the beginning of the book that I wrote while I was living in Prahan. That's a good idea. I'm feeling excited about it already. I forgot that's one of the reasons why I moved here to My Hometown.

6/7/00 : Good Morning! I spoke with Graeme and he told me, 'Yesterday's history, tomorrow's a mystery, and today's a gift, and that's why they call it the present.' I'm here for a reason. "God, you've put me here in My Hometown for a reason and I trust in You that all will be well if I continue to do what is in front of me." I'm not in Melbourne. I'm in My Hometown. I have been focusing on what I don't have and missing out on the beauty of what has been given to me.

My Dad is rapt that he has a new home to live in. He wants to work so that I can paint, write, sing and learn guitar. "You've set that up, haven't you, God!" Dad understands and reminds me I'm not here to fill up my time working for others. I'm here to write a book, paint, and do many other things. Talk about being spoilt. I'm only afraid of looking poor while I'm on unemployment benefits. I need to get over myself.

I hate that real estate guy. He pissed me off. I'll let him believe he's done Dad and I a favour if that makes him feel worthwhile in his world. "I need to be thanking you God for providing Dad and I with a home that we like and for providing Dad and I money during these changing times." While I'm focusing on what I've left behind I'm avoiding what needs to be done now for my future. Writing a book is a crazy, out-of-this-world, idea for me. Painting is just a waste of my time as I see it. No one is supposed to take me seriously. I'm just joking. Going through a phase. I'm being ridiculous. Let's get distracted by the bad. My unhappiness is running the show. I forgot I'm not running the show, God is.

There's an advertisement in the paper for a female vocalist. I'm curious; it's what I want to do. I'll know how to sing well enough sooner or later. I forgot that what I want is a microphone to practice with. To apply for this job seems like a dream. It would fit into my life very well; it's a job that's worth my time. Will I ring Shelly? Hmm. I'll read the article again. I want to know who's advertising for the position. Well, it's got me thinking.

ANOTHER DAY : Thank God it's Friday. Mum's talking to me as I write. She's stopped now. I've started a painting and I'm thinking its crap because it's too simple and boring. I'm copying it from a photograph. I'm using ink, oils and acrylic. I started my book. I've written two thousand words and I'm thinking it's not very good. I'm so positive, not. There was a position advertised in My Hometown News for a lead singer in a band, I'm thinking I should have a go. I'm not that good yet. It would be great. I practiced singing by myself yesterday while I was painting. I was in my element. It's good to write on the computer because I'm learning about grammar and how to spell correctly. It's quite fun and the writing is coming easily.

That guy from the real estate rang about the house. Dad will be excited. He didn't tell me whether we had it or not, maybe there's some conditions I don't know about. Who knows?

I'm happy not to work for Wesley House as a residential carer. That's an indication for me that that particular job is not for me.

Scott didn't call last night. I'll call him today and see where he is. He might still be in My Hometown; he might've assumed that I was in Melbourne. I'm glad I didn't go to Melbourne because I actually needed the money.

I'll go down to Melbourne if Kevin can bring my bed and couch up. That'll be good. I may get to the morning meeting, that would be nice, and I may have time to go to the women's meeting.

Geez, my head tells me I can't write a book and that I can't paint, or sing. It continues to natter at me, all the time. I feel better today, full of life and energy. It's amazing how a little bit of attention to those things has a positive impact on me and how I visualise myself being a part of the world around me. Oh, I don't like my hair. It's yucky. I need a new cut and colour. I can't seem to do it lately. Its three weeks since I had it cut. I'll book myself in on Saturday if I'm in Melbourne with Aimee. I'd like that a lot.

What else is there to write? Saw Max last night. Hung out with him at his house. I took ice creams with me. We played pool, watched Big Brother and Seinfield and played cards. It was very enjoyable. Some yummy feelings emerged while we were having fun and lots of laughs. I don't want to do anything close or intimate with him unless I know within that's what I really want. Not because I'm feeling horny. That's not a nice thing to do and not something I want to do to him because he doesn't deserve that from anyone, especially me. I would only want to be intimate with Max with my whole heart and soul involved, without any 'ifs' or 'buts' reserved within me. I need to keep in mind he may not be interested in me at all and I may not be interested in him at all. Jason is present in my mind and soul. Nothing ever will match it. The feeling I get with him is truly amazing. I'm enjoying getting to know Max again, believe it or not. I am taking things slowly with him. That feels good and there's no pressure. Not like the pressure I put onto Jason or the others. And that's okay with me. I have an incredible amount to offer and I can do this in my book. God works through me and uses my hands to paint. God works through me and uses my voice to sing.

ANOTHER DAY : I feel like I'm losing it. Afraid of not having the money to live the life I want here in my Hometown. I'm afraid that I won't have enough 'get up and go' to do the things that move, touch and inspire me. I feel lost in this small world. I feel hopeless, without faith and without hope. I'm fearful of being nothing, having nothing. I'm not enough to write a book. I'm not good enough to sing well. I'm not enough to live happily and to be full of laughter. I'm missing the joy and freedom that's available to me right now. I'm afraid of not having a job that's suitable for me. It's all around money, and I'm afraid of not doing: not doing art, singing, my painting, my writing. I'm fearful of failure. Getting stuck. Looking bad and poor like a loser. Eugene hasn't got a house and he's three years older, happy, in love, and has a great job. Good for him. Aimee has landed a high paying job and I instantly felt like a loser and a loser forever. My thinking stinks. My outlook stinks. My lack of faith stinks. My self-hatred stinks. What doesn't stink is the work I'm doing from 'The Artist's Way' and continuing singing lessons with Dad. I've invited Josie to come along.

Went walking with Josie this morning at 7:30 am. That was enjoyable. Sang songs with Josie and talked with her Mum. Spoke with Aimee's partner who has invited me to Aimee's surprise birthday party on the twenty-first. I'm undecided about going to Jennie's thirtieth birthday party in Melbourne; whether or not I can afford it, or whether or not I really want to. I'm afraid of spending money that I need here to get started.

This is my third week off from work. Wow, how time flies. I was so passionate and involved in my life at the beginning of the year. I wish I had sustained it. I was flying so high I could touch the sky. Well, I could have a go at singing every second Thursday at the pub. Dad said he was proud of my singing. That's surprising because I thought I was quite horrid. Carmen said that my technique was good. I wonder what that really means. I will get out of singing what I put into it. I'm putting some effort into it. The wonderful thing is that I'm continuing it, having stickability and determination. It takes great courage to take up singing lessons. It takes great courage for me, anyway. Took courage for Linus to play netball knowing he hasn't played any kind of competitive sport in his life. "Thank you God for helping me find people to make up a netball team." Mum and I are about to clear out the cupboard to put in the good crockery and throw out the crappy old cups and plates.

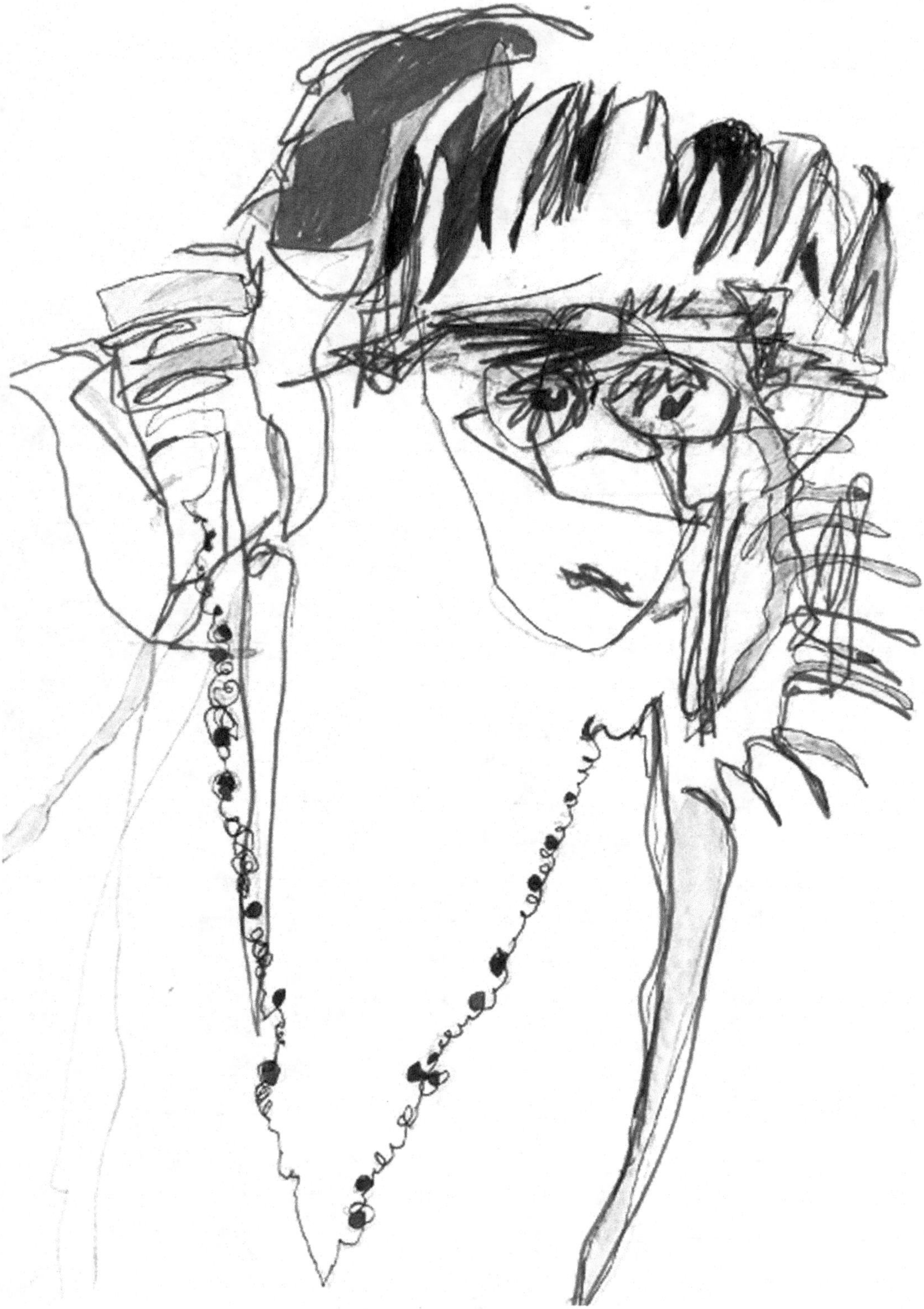

Twelve Years Later…
Going within my true self emerges through
what I create, what I think, what I say and
what I do

OLD THOUGHT: I'm in trouble if I don't' get permission
NEW THOUGHT: I'm my own person who can make my own decisions

I can see I chose once again not to write about another painful experience I had with one of my cousins. Was I waiting for them to quit their silliness and snap out this crazy phase they seemed to be going through? They hadn't always been like this, had they? Surely their old self will rise to the top and save me from having to do anything about it! Surely?

I met a male friend of mine at the local pub. We were talking and laughing before this cousin stormed up to us and reefed the table up, reefed the seat I was sitting in from underneath me and forced their arms around me lifting me off my feet. He carried me across the pub (it was a large pub, full of people on a Friday night) to the other side, telling me he didn't like the guy I was talking with and that I wasn't allowed to talk with him again. I was standing on my feet by this time, shaken by the experience. The cousin put his arm around me; we were side by side as he pushed me toward his mates and partner. I didn't want to be with these people. I felt bad about leaving my friend just sitting at the table not knowing what the hell had just gone on. I dared not say a word; I was scared what the cousin would do to me if I did.

Time passed long enough for me to sneak away and return to my friend who had waited patiently for my return. In shock, my friend asked, "What the hell happened? Who was that person?" "He is a cousin. Forget about him." I then I continued our conversation as if nothing had happened. My poor friend. I do wonder what he really thought about what he'd witnessed. Come to think of it, I saw him many times after that and we never spoke about the abuse toward me that night. However, I haven't seen that friend in a long time. If I do see my friend again I will ask him if he remembers that night and if so, I will ask him what his experience was like, and to apologise for pretending something terrible didn't happen when it did.

My survival strategies kept me silent about this particular cousin's behaviour, which caused me pain. I remember thinking to myself I should talk to him about what he'd done to me in the pub, however I talked myself out of speaking to him about what my experience was because I felt, if I did, he would be offended. I felt he would be unable to handle my anger toward him for threatening and humiliating me in front of others and that perhaps he would hurt me again for mentioning it. So I avoided any possible conflict and when I saw that cousin the next time, I appeared to be unharmed and didn't say a word about the experience. Worse yet, I smiled and acted as if nothing had happened. There is an expression in Al-Anon, which describes very well what I did - I pretended there wasn't 'an elephant in the lounge room' when there was a mammoth staring right at me! Deny, Deny, Deny! I thought I could get away with not facing what had happened.

Because of this thinking, I felt I didn't have any options. It didn't occur to me to talk to someone about it. It didn't occur to me to get help regarding this situation. Nothing occurred to me more than keeping the cousin happy - rather than to keep myself safe.

I understand now, twelve years later, as the result of being affected by his abuse, I protected him from facing any legal consequences of his unacceptable behaviour, and supported him instead. The fear of what he could do to me kept me in this relationship for another five years. Did I get away with the avoidance of being honest about how I was being treated? No I didn't. Did this cousin's 'crazy' phase go away by not facing what he did to me? No, it didn't. Did the treatment toward me improve as the result of turning a blind eye? No it didn't.

So I sent them an email. I shared with them what happened, what it was like for me then and what it is like for me and what I failed to do to look after myself. I felt it was important to take responsibility for decisions I had made which exposed me to family violence. My experience had shown me I allowed the behaviour to escalate because I didn't take the abuse toward me seriously. When I began to talk to others about what I was experiencing, I began to learn I deserved to feel safe, to be respected and treated with kindness. Today I am committed to being free from the effects of growing up in an alcoholic home, being an alcoholic, and being affected by another's sexual behaviour. I believe some of the effects are perfectly illustrated in 'Out of the Shadows'. I became willing to let go of the old idea: 'When I'm abused by others I'm not to take it seriously and to forget about it'. I felt at the time I needed to write to this particular cousin and to record the experience as I remembered it and to let them know I had made a decision I felt was best for me. I said goodbye to him without his permission.

Jarod also had a habit of publicly humiliating me. One time at the nightclub in front of our friends he become angry about something and poured his drink over my head. As I didn't know how to handle this abusive behaviour I laughed it off by wetting and pulling my hair back into a high piggy tail returning to work behind the bar. Or another time when I was walking away from the nightclub crossing the street he screamed out "You're a Fucking Slut" in front of everyone. It felt embarrassed and humiliated at the time, and I would tell myself I wouldn't go back to him, and yet I would allow him to sweet talk me back. I would then feel more embarrassment and increased humiliation when others would see me still with him. I didn't know I was in an abusive cycle in which many people find themselves.

It was extremely difficult to finally leave him to believe I deserved a loving relationship that I deserved to be happy. I listened to many songs on the radio, which gave me hope and inspiration to believe things could be different for me. I read self help books such as, 'The Road Less Travelled' and 'Super Joy' which challenged what I believed and what I was doing. But most of all I aspired to have what other women had: freedom, peace and love in their relationships. I believed if they could find a guy who treated them well, who trusted them, and supported their choices, then so could I. No-one could have forced me to leave, and trust me, many tried and all failed - including me. I left him many times and I was powerless over his seductive 'sorries' and begging to have me back. I longed to be loved and I wanted to believe that this time he was going to be different, every time he proved himself to be the same. But the next time I held onto the slim hope he was going to be different.

My Dad gently pulled me aside one day and explained to me that if the day came that I was serious about leaving him to not talk to him again. He related it to his drinking. "I don't have one drink of alcohol, because if I have one I think I can have another one and then another and then another. So if I don't pick up one drink I can't get drunk. If you leave him, don't take one phone call, don't have one conversation then you can't get caught up into the next and the next and find yourself back into the relationship you want to get out of." That made sense to me. It was some time before I thought I could really leave him, however when that time came, that's exactly what I did. If he rang I would not talk on the phone. He waited outside my house. I let him sit in the car and I stayed inside. He smoked outside my window during the night. By not engaging in any conversations with him I also was placing myself in the situation where he could try the "I'm going to kill myself". This stuff would make me feel bad and guilty; he had the knack of always making me feel bad and guilty because deep down I believed I was, until I didn't anymore. Five years went by before I felt safe to talk with him. I knew all feelings I had for him had passed and when we talked I just felt sad for him. He hadn't changed at all and I felt I was a completely different person. And that's because I was.

With both my cousin and ex-partner I didn't have their permission to do what I needed to do. I gave myself the permission to do what I needed to do, knowing I could get into trouble with them for it. Neither of them liked the decision I made and yet I allowed myself to take the chance that the decision I made to keep myself sane and safe could be a mistake. I've learnt its okay to mistakes and it's my right to make my own decisions without the approval of others. It's my right and responsibility to create peace, happiness and personal safety in my life.

OLD THOUGHT: People who have hurt me deserve to be punished
NEW THOUGHT: Forgiveness of others and myself sets me free from anger

I believed if I forgave someone for the harm they caused me it meant I accepted and condoned what they did to me. When I felt hurt, harmed or threatened by others my natural response was to pay them back for the pain they caused me by not forgiving them. It was only fair that they should suffer and be punished for—what felt to me at the time—a crime. However thinking and feeling this way filled my heart with anger and hate.

When I was about 14 and sitting at a table with my Nana, I was horrified when she criticised my cousin's haircut. I always felt she treated Linus extra special and I felt jealous about that, however when she attacked his haircut I knew it really hurt him. He'd gone from being the golden boy to being the bad boy. I didn't tell her how I felt of course. I chose to make a pact that I wouldn't talk to her again and get her back for being such a bitch.

At a self-improvement course I attended I realised—when I couldn't believe people would stop talking to other people for years—which I hadn't spoken with my Nana for

10 years! I made the brave move to get real with her and tell her why I stopped talking to her, so I could be free of the hate and resentment I was carrying around with me.

It was great. I called her, shaking with dread, and told her why I had stopped talking to her because I believed that she was a bitch, instead of letting her know at the time that I felt I needed to protect my cousin from being hurt and that was the only way I knew how to do that at the time. Her response, "Oh, I didn't even notice you had stopped talking to me." First I thought, 'You've got to be kidding me! This proves you don't care!' However, it then occurred to me, the only person I had hurt was ME! She continued. "Resentment is like a seed. When you plant it into the ground it grows into a big tree with branches and leaves. Resentment begins to affect every part of your life." As I bawled my eyes out I knew it was true. I also realised I had missed out on a family older female's wisdom for all those years because I didn't know how to talk about my feelings.

It doesn't make sense to hurt others in response to being hurt. How do I separate the difference between another's wrong and mine if we both believe the other is to blame and both hurts are justified? Where does it stop? When does the justifying stop? For me, it was when I grew tired of hurting.

I deserve to live free of hate, anger and constant sorrow and one way I found through the examples of others and what I've read, was to find compassion and understanding toward that person for the way they have been or the way they are. It does not mean I am saying what the person did was okay, quite the contrary. Once I can forgive someone for what they have done, I can make a choice about what is best for me in the situation. I can choose to say to the other person 'I understand why you did what you did, however, it is not okay or acceptable to treat me that way'. If the other person does not agree, and thinks their behaviour or treatment toward me is okay, I am free to respond in a way that is right for me. It's up to me to choose how I can be in my relationships with others. Forgiveness opens the doors to choices and having choices creates the feeling of freedom.

"Dear Pop,

I'm going to have another go at writing to you. I'm writing to you because I feel I understand a lot more about the effects of someone else's unacceptable sexual behaviour.

I've come to understand it was not because I was beautiful that you sexually assaulted me. I did not make you or cause you to sexually assault me. I had nothing to do with you sexually assaulting me. I was a child and I was defenceless. I understand your compulsive lusting drove you to violate my human rights. I believe your sexual illness of lust drove you to do this and it was never about me, it was just about your sexual illness. I take no responsibility for your wrongful and unlawful actions toward me. However, I take full responsibility to ensure that I recover from the effects of your unacceptable sexual behaviour you imposed upon me.

As a child I didn't understand what was happening. I believe now you were so sick with lust you maliciously sexually assaulted me while my father was in the same room. I believed at the time what you were doing to me wasn't bad because it was the only way I could understand why my Dad didn't say something. I believed my Dad would have said something if he thought what you were doing was wrong and because he didn't say something I thought it must have been okay. I thought I was wrong for feeling sick. I've had a conversation with my Dad and I believe him that he did not know you were sexually assaulting me while he was in the same room. Dad explained to me you became a very sick man, which caused you to do things, which were not okay. I believe this to be true.

In the past when others have treated me badly I tolerated it. I felt I was bad if I were to walk away from relationships or situations where I felt dominated or where my rights were being violated. I accepted feeling sick when others were violating my rights and I believed there was something wrong with me for them to do this to me. You violated my rights and dominated me when you lost the ability to control your lust and I then allowed others to meet their needs at the cost of violating mine as the result.

I forgive you for the horrible things you did to me. I understand you were sick with sexual illness, which caused you to do things, which harmed me. I feel deeply saddened I missed out on having a beautiful bond between you and I.

I understand I have been powerless over the affects of your inappropriate sexual behaviour ever since. I am grateful I am being shown one day at a time to learn how to create genuine emotional closeness with others, an opportunity you missed out on. I understand I have a long reconstruction ahead of me. I'm okay with that, I have the opportunity to experience love that some never do.

I like to imagine you are in heaven healed from your sexual illness and I see an old, wise, and gentle man smiling in the sun warming up for the first time. I believe you were not a bad man, just a very sick man.

Your grand-daughter"

See Appendix: 'Are you affected by someone's sexual behaviour'

SACRED CREATIVE FOCUS
FORGIVENESS WITH OTHERS AND MYSELF

Forgiving someone opens me up to healing from a past hurt, whether it's recent or in the long distant past. When I haven't forgiven someone I continue to feel pain about what was said or done. The pain can feel like many things such as betrayal, anger, rage, depression, sadnes, numbness, regret or shame just to name a few. When I am unable to forgive I carry this pain around with me. The memories of what happened or didn't happen pop up to remind me I have not let go of the pain and still in the hurt. Now feeling hurt I find to be annoying to say the least. So I find when I'm tired of feeling hurtful feelings, tired of talking about what happened, tired of thinking about it enough I become willing to move toward forgiveness. I ultimately do it for myself because I am the one suffering. Whether I like or not, if I'm suffering it's up to me to do something about it - if I want to.

For me forgiving someone doesn't mean that I agree with what someone has said or done. It's not about condoning or accepting unacceptable behaviour. It's not necessarily about taking responsibility for others or about being weak or a push over if I am able to forgive.

Forgiveness can show me humans can get it wrong, really wrong, because we are human. Forgiveness can show me how to see a certain situation or person in a different way than I did before. Forgiveness can show me parts of myself I have not forgiven. Forgiveness can show me new ways of handling certain situations or how to better take care of myself. Forgiveness can show me better ways to communicate, or how to make new decisions. There are endless loving outcomes, which come when I'm shown who, what and how to forgive.

I can step out of the dark and into the sunlight. I can feel relief. I can have a full and open heart. I can be brought back to the present moment trusting all is okay and will be okay once more. It's great to be free from the old thoughts that make me feel bad about others and myself. It's wonderful to free, joyful and grateful. And when the tide has turned I feel that little bit stronger and wiser. Forgiveness is something I do for me because I'm worthy of love and I can start forgiving myself by doing the things I failed to do in the past. Forgiveness takes me to know a greater awareness of how to reconnect with life, with others and myself.

SACRED CREATIVE ACTIVITY

I found writing in my journal very helpful. I noticed through my writing that I wasn't very good at communicating to others when things upset me, or how I felt, or why I was upset, or what I'd prefer to see happen, or show I did understand or say what I needed to be okay. So I spent time practicing how to say what I mean, mean what I say and without saying it mean. Sometimes I told stories, wrote letters, created a poem or a song or created art to understand what I failed to do and say which set me up to be resentful or fearful. I found using the following format helpful to know what I really needed to say to someone I felt upset with as a step toward practicing forgiveness. I often found giving others and myself a chance to work things out to be reward as I got to know others and myself better. Even if the other person didn't like what I had to say or agree with me, I felt inner confidence grow as the result of speaking up and being real. An amends to myself you could say.

When you (do, say, think)..
I feel (how)..
because (reason)..and I'd
prefer (what I would like to happen)..
I understand that you (see, feel, think)....................................
however, I need (what?)...

SACRED MEDITATIVE ACTIVITY

When a friend loses someone, store-bought sympathy cards can say what I struggle to say. Songs are the same when I struggle to forgive someone. Listen for a song that in some way is about forgiving the person who hurt you. Allow yourself to feel the words and let the sound hit your heart and if you really want to get carried away, write a letter or poem of forgiveness or even about the willingness to forgive.

COMMITMENT STATEMENT

I .... am willing to put aside everything I think I know about myself, my life, my past, my future, in order to have an open mind and a new experience with forgiveness toward others and myself. I am open to the possibility of forgiving others and myself, receiving new thoughts, and living a new life.

MOVING FORWARD TO BEING WHO I REALLY AM
WEEK ELEVEN : WHAT DO I WANT TO DO AND BE IN LIFE?

for better... me
... go to QLD
... ore. AGAIN!

to face it & do
Everything that hap...
for my highest go...
how painful and fearful
first & before anythin...
and I shall follow

"I'm afraid I de...
it's over." (I just did...
were not the eyes I ca...
hair was not dark eno...
...ng. Too much.
I want to paint, sing,
explore, play, laugh, sa...
- wrong or right. Preter...
has hurt me   Thanky...
that acc...
deserve...
I know
too m...
to know...
I f...
per...
...wh...
...the...
I l...
thin...
& that...
only you to b...

...RT
...estrianw...
do

...enb...
...d

-NO-

...you.
...A

whether you're in my li...
to give without anything in ret...

INTRODUCTION TO THE SACRED SHARING

DAD AND I FINALLY FOUND A PLACE FOR THE BOTH OF US TO LIVE. NOT TOO FAR FROM THE CENTRE OF TOWN AND CLOSE TO THE LAKE WHERE WE ENJOY WALKING AND TALKING TOGETHER.

ANOTHER DAY : Good morning pages. I'm doing it back to front this one time. I'm going to get up at 5:00 am. There is no hope and I have no will in me to wake up at 4:30 am to write this, so I'm writing it now at midnight. I tell ya that with Jezza it's just an uphill battle. Stubborn as an ox, scared as a rabbit and cold as a cucumber. I wish someone close enough would say something to him, get into his ear, and speak on my behalf and tell him to snap out of it. Really, he spills his guts to me when he's had a few beers and when he knows I'm not going to get close (chances of that happening again are limited) he shuts down. Maybe I wrote something in my letter that put him off, set off his alarm bells. Maybe I'm immature at times. Maybe I said things he didn't want me to repeat. The things I have repeated are never exclusive to what he's told me. I'll never tell anyone the stuff he's told me because that's confidential. I have no desire to break his confidence. I didn't specify what I have repeated. I'm guessing and making things up until he tells me otherwise, and seeing he's not big on talking, I'm in a bit of strife there. Like I said before, it's all up hill with Jezza. I do remember saying sorry and repeating what his friend said to me, "The girl to win Jezza's heart will need to have balls and she'd be the luckiest woman in the world." I don't think or feel that other women have gone through this; at least not to this length. Maybe they have. I don't know. From the conversation we had I felt I was truly irreplaceable in his life and visa versa. As I write this, my thinking tells me that, if he were drinking, it all could be to the wind and that he doesn't remember a thing. That's not that fantastic. The only one here having the relationship is me. At least I'm learning about patience, tolerance, trust and love, which are the greater treasures in the life that I'm living. I am the fortunate one who is growing enormously through this experience and I wouldn't swop this love for the world. I love him and that's all I can feel and say. If that's the worst thing, then I'm not doing too badly.

So I'm off to Melbourne tomorrow at 5:00 am so I can make it to my old home group (twelve-step recovery meeting) at 8:00 am. I'll get to talk to my friend Courtney, Tom and many others. I start work at 10:30 am with Liz and the kiddies. I have no presents for the children. Oh well, I'm poor as buggery. My love is my gift. I'll bring Portia home with me, God willing. She can come and watch Linus and I play netball for a buzz. Oh, Mac hopefully went with Dad tonight at the meeting. Hopefully they'll both come to the Euroa meeting on Monday night.

MONDAY MORNING : I don't know the date. It's a glorious day outside. I have no idea of the time. I will need more paper to write on, I'm down to only a couple of pages now. Someone's up and making a coffee. I don't know whether it's Dad or Porcia. What can we do with such a perfect day? This is an unfamiliar winter because the weather is beautiful, and it feels like spring. Porcia's birthday is the same as Eugene's, the same year as well. I caught my thinking when I woke this morning and in my mind it searches to see if everything is alright, to check to see if there's any pain or stress or worries to worry about. Isn't that interesting? I hate waking up remembering a loss. The last time I felt that was over Wayne, yucko! I'm tired and a little fluey. The game of netball I played last night was not the best. I need to make sure I'm well rested and focused before I play. I got angry with the umpires and that's not good for a grown woman.

ANOTHER DAY : Well, what are some things Porcia and I can do today? We can call Jane to see how she's going, I'll check to see if I owe her any money from the time she stayed at my place in Prahan. We can go walking, swimming, visiting members, going to meetings and suss out my Hometown Theatre Art Group. I can go to Centrelink and pick up a new diary, paint, sing, call Carmen for more music sheets for the guitar and collect the organ from Mum's place for Dad to play with. I need to look around for furniture for Dad, call Jessica and talk to her about walking in the mornings and call Aimee to ask if she'd like to come. I've been thinking of taking Vinyl the dog for walks, I'll need to call Warren and his girlfriend first, seeing it's their dog and not mine. Maybe Warren's girlfriend would like to come walking with us girls? I can continue to put down ideas about the book, call Dr Wilmot about changing appointment dates, and request receipts for Medicare. Oh, my thoughts just changed to, 'Am I avoiding what truly needs to be done?' For example, writing my book and painting, those thoughts are getting very loud inside my head. Are they loud because I'm focusing on what I haven't got, instead of what I am doing? Probably. What 'something' would ease my mind to feel productive, fulfilling and satisfied? If I could put something in daily toward both my art and writing I would feel relieved. So setting up an art area would be a good place to start. It is laziness, not just fear, which stops me from doing what needs to be done. If materials were there for me just to pick up and do, it would encourage me to paint. I need to call Louise to take a photo of my 'crazed woman' for Linus's tattoo. Debbie dropped off the wood for the painting. We need to find oil paints somewhere. I think Echuca might have them, seeing that my Hometown doesn't, how pathetic. So I could start designing for Debbie's big arse painting. I sneezed and a big goobie landed on my doona, yuk!

WEDNESDAY : It took me ages to fall asleep again last night. It's so annoying. I'm going to have to buy cough drops to soothe the throat. Aimee will be here at 8:00 am. We're going walking together. Its 7:30 am, I slept in, oops!

I found a guitar tuner in my cousins' guitar bag. I sent a message to Jezza via the phone asking how to use the goddamn thing, because he was telling me last night that what I needed was one of those. Believe it or not he responded four times in a row. Wow, growth! I can never pick whether he'll respond or not, or for how long. I practiced on the guitar. I actually dreamt I was talking to Jessica, telling her I needed more guitar music because I'm bored with what I already have. Playing guitar has become second nature to me now. It's fun. I'll be able to show the kiddies my new guitar skills. I'm writing very fast. I wish I could write faster so that I get everything ready before Aimee gets here. I wonder where we'll be heading off to this morning?

Big trip to Melbourne yesterday, singing was really fun. Even Dad enjoyed himself. I got up to a high note by using my back muscles. Everything is slowly switching on. I need to practice. What I put in is what I get out of it and, at the moment, the time I spend on singing is not that great.

My bloody left eye is bugging me. I have to keep it shut, bloody bastard. I can work on the book today. Now will I type or write? It's hard to know. I feel that writing is smoother and free flowing. When I type it seems a little stiff. I don't know. Twenty-five minutes on the clock.

Drank some water today. I didn't drink much at all yesterday—not good. I read some of my book last night. I'm not supposed to because in 'The Artist's Way' it's suggested not to read or watch TV. Damn it, I forgot. My brain is so cunning doing that to me. How the hell am I going to fall asleep at night if I'm not to read or watch TV for the week? How am I not going to read the website to look for work if I'm not allowed to read? Maybe that's an exception because it's job hunting. I doubt it.

Well what to scribble down now? I spoke to Portia and Louise last night. That was enjoyable. Louise says it's always a world lifted off her shoulders when she talks to me, although at times I feel like I'm treating her like a fifteen year old. Interestingly enough that's one of the reasons why I got so emotionally upset with Peter from the real estate because I feel he treats me like a child. How insightful. I'll keep looking at that one. I'm sure I treat Jezza and other people like that too at times, especially my Mum and Dad. That sucks! Today I'm going to be aware of the way I speak to people, to consciously listen out for when I treat people like they are children.

SATURDAY : Talked with a restaurant owner last night about a position available for me behind the upstairs bar. Sorry, but it doesn't interest me for ten dollars per hour cash in hand. I'd have to declare it, being an honest person and all. I don't feel empowered working for such a man. So it's a no. Next! Caught up with Dianne last night and that was nice. She needs a new job; she's like me— a creative soul. I encouraged her to write. She too would like to write a book about her life. She is a survivor of sexual abuse. Through talking to me, Dianne worked out she needs to encourage her aunty to say something to her daughter-in-law about what happened to her so that they can protect her grandchild. I simply said, "It's principals before personalities." She agreed. It's pretty yucky stuff.

I have a pinching nerve down my leg. I asked Melissa to look up in Louise Hay's book 'Heal Your Life' to find out what a pinching nerve means. It means that I'm holding onto old childhood traumas. Firstly, if I knew what that was it would help me to release it. I've had a few traumas in my childhood such as, the interference from my grandfather, my mother leaving my Dad (Dad was no longer living with us), changing from a school of nineteen kids to six hundred kids at the time of my parents' divorce when I was seven, being physically, emotionally and mentally neglected by my Mum, Eugene leaving the house when I was fourteen so he could go off to University, going out with a emotionally and mentally abusive man for three and a half years and what I did to myself through drinking. Trauma was evident when I started starving myself at the age of twelve and wanting to die as a little kid. I wanted God to kill me in my sleep. I would rock backwards and forwards on the lounge room couch for three to four hours at a time, I remember doing that when I first got my period. I'd rock myself to sleep each night and I always had the fan on because I was so petrified of the dark. It was rather awful. So I could be hanging onto any one of those things. How would I let them go? Some stuff to take to Dr Wilmot, my psychiatrist.

I sent a message to Jezza yesterday afternoon at 5:00 pm to ask if he wanted to catch up for drinks. Guess what? No response. Surprise, surprise, surprise! I was really nervous sending it. An older friend of mine suggested I invite him to catch up. She commented that I have no self-confidence and I didn't disagree or feel bad about that. I'm powerless over it. I'd rather not feel nervous or panicky, but it happens. She then said, "You must really like this guy." Yep, she got that right.

So being Saturday I might see Mac at the meeting at lunchtime. How confronting for him. I know how it feels. He'll have a hangover for sure. Poor bugger. Debbie rang me with her concern about her ex-boyfriend. She commented three times on how wonderful it was that I was so understanding; it made her feel good or better about her ordeal. I relate to her ex-boyfriend because I think he's a problem drinker, although it is up to him to discover this for himself if he has a problem or not. I'm no guardian angel, God will work through me if need be.

I must go and make pancakes for Dad and I. I enjoy doing that. Did we get jam? Just asked Dad. Stuff filling out the rest of this page. And blah, blah, blah, blah, blah, blah, blah. Going to the footy today. Jezza will be there—how exciting. I'm going regardless of what he's doing!

SUNDAY : I'm feeling like giving up hope that Jezza would want to be with me. It hasn't been a bad innings. I've stuck it out for seven and half months, constantly being open, loving, and patient. Louise asked, "Is that enough for you? Is that what you want?" After those questions we chatted for another fifteen minutes about stuff and I began to wonder.

Usually when I have a sleep, the next day to me is a new day and I'm usually okay with where I am at with Jezza. Today holds a new tale of letting the whole thing go. It feels like the right way to go. If I say anything to him I want to stick to what I say, no manipulation or mind games to get what I want. I've moved to my Hometown and he was one of the reasons for my return. He wasn't the only reason but certainly part of the reason. Perhaps I need more time to think about it before I tell him or send him a message to say that I've come to the conclusion that I have no idea what he wants. 'It concerns me that you avoid me and knowing that makes me feel awful. I'm letting you know that I'm lovingly letting go of the idea and hope that you want to be with me as I do with you.' From saying this I am hoping that it will encourage him to say something. It's called, 'Reject him and he will come running.' That sucks. That's not how I want to do it. I don't want to give up hope and the idea that he does want to be with me. I feel if I say anything I'll ruin it for myself, the way I'd let Jarod go, and then I'd change my mind every time; that's torture. Come here, go away; that kind of thinking and behaviour is awful. I'm afraid if I say goodbye I will want to change my mind and go back on my decision. I probably would. I can't read that man's mind or heart, but when I do, it always seems incorrect.

I've been here three weeks, it's time to begin the book, paint and focus on singing and playing guitar. I don't want to dilly dally any more. I need to buy myself…no I don't, I bought pizza last night. It was really yummy; that was my treat.

According to 'The Artist's Way' I need to call a friend who thinks the world of me, do an 'artist brain' for an hour then spend two hours by myself for my artist date. Hey, the 'artist brain' can be my singing; I would feel better prepared for my Monday lesson. Get out my tape and go la la la. We have new neighbours. Saw the boys and their wives out last night; Dale, Peter, Mick (he's now a father) and Bill (these are the men I grew up with). All married men, well, Pete's about to be. He scored an unhappy soul and his last girlfriend was the same. Poor Pete - Louise and I are happy to be single. It's a free and easy feeling of no responsibility or hardship. I feel too young to be married I'm only twenty-six, not forty-six.

MONDAY : I was so reluctant about waking up because it took me ages to fall asleep last night. It's only just 8:30 am and I'd like to leave for Melbourne by 10:30 am to get to our singing lesson by 1:00 pm. I'm to call Kevin to see what he's doing about the couch that he has of mine. It's a beautiful day. I'll go down the street to find this beautiful song 'Misty Blue' it's such a lovely song. Dad's making me a lovely hot coffee. I'll let him know we'll leave half an hour earlier.

I must say, my head tells me I'm hopeless at singing, that I've failed at practicing and that Carmen will be disappointed and she'll know that my progress is really slow and think I'm terrible. I still don't have a song to bring for practice with her. I'm so unprepared; I'll probably grab a song from the little collection of what I do have and it'll just have to do, eh! Hopeless, hopeless, hopeless!! Actually, right now I need to think of some affirmations around this. God sings through me. I'm a natural born singer and I sing like an angel (all in good time). I'm developing my own voice that God has created in me. I need not fear because it's a beautiful voice. I have many things happening in my life and singing is one of them. Now that I'm settled in my new home with Dad, singing can be arranged. Change occurs through God. God changes me when He is ready. There are many teachings and things to learn with singing and my voice is developing over a period of time. I sing in the shower, in the car, around the house, down the street, in the supermarket, and with friends in their homes. I practice each day. I practice my breathing and the use of my body every day. That takes time. Everything takes time. Practicing for me is new and frightening. I won't do it perfectly. I will have done it gradually.

I have one more page to go of positive things to say about myself. I have a beautiful home and a wonderful Dad who is great to live with. He's generous, thoughtful, caring, courageous, willing, patient and loving. I have a bedroom that I really enjoy coming home to. I have a lounge room that's enjoyable to sit in and has my paintings hanging on its walls. I have a guitar to play and to practice music with. Hey, I could grab some music somewhere; I can do that. I don't have to wait until my next lesson to pick up new music. Wow, that's great. I'm actively participating in 'The Artist's Way' discovery course on a daily basis. I'm singing every day. I have gorgeous friends who love and support me. I have meetings I can go to, and pubs and clubs I can dance in. There are people to meet, art to paint, clothes to wear, a clean new car to drive, plenty of knickers and socks in the drawer, a stylish hair cut and I receive lots of lovely compliments about my beauty that continually fly my way. I'm the luckiest woman around!

TUESDAY : I have my phone bill to pay and also my car registration, bugger; two big bills and not much cash to get me by. My Dad will support me if I need the money. I have a christening this Sunday and on Monday I have singing lessons. I need to ring Dr Wilmot to rearrange my therapy session for a visit on Monday. Ruby rang this morning at 9:00 am and woke me up asking me how I am going living here. I get stuck with that question. I'm adjusting to the rather large change.

Oh, it's a little chilly with the fan going above me. I really like my bed. Dad bought me a double electric blanket and a fluffy doona. I have the doona cover that he gave me on my bed and it all looks and feels great. I'm very fortunate to have these things. I feel at home in my new bedroom. I like it more than any room or bed that I've had before. I'm very happy with it. I have my paintings up now and they look good on the walls. I've been busy everyday that I've been here in My Hometown. There are a couple of friends that I still haven't seen. I'm enjoying learning the guitar enormously. I look forward to my lessons with Shelly. It feels so good to learn.

Dianne rang and I asked her who I could talk to about getting help in writing a book. She suggested I get myself a tutor because it's been her experience that having someone to help her in that way with the book she is writing has been great. I need help with my writing so that I continue to do it and that I have guidance. I don't have to do it on my own. I'm willing to be helped. Isn't that fantastic?

I rang Liz and spoke to the kids. Sam told me I don't have to give him a present for his birthday. I feel sad I don't have any money to buy him a gift. I'm afraid I'm going to run out of money. I accept that is normal when I'm on unemployment benefits. Most people on unemployment benefits would be afraid of not having enough money. If people on unemployment benefits could manage their money and their lives, most wouldn't need financial assistance, would they? It's a hard call. It forces me to budget. I don't want to budget. I don't want to stop doing the fun things in my life because of the lack of finances. Look how self-righteous and ungrateful I'm being! I'll take up Liz's invitation to look after the kiddies on Saturday night. Dad can come by train on Monday morning and drive home with me—what a wonderful idea! I'll ring Liz and let her know my decision, I'm sure the kids will love it; I know I will. It would feel good to do that. Max hasn't rung me. I'll call him today to see if he wants to go to the pictures with me.

WEDNESDAY : I hope I don't have to do anything today. I do need to fill out the conditions report for the house that Dad and I have moved into. I want to complete my painting of the 'Fully Fledged Birds' that I've started. I've lost my train of thought. I dreamt I was leaving Melbourne and before I left I was sitting closely to Courtney in a twelve-step meeting, Wayne was there, watching us. I felt good about myself. I felt a feeling of growth within me that tells me that I'm moving on from something old to something new.

Gee whiz, I have the toilet runs today. My tummy aches. I must be letting go internally and accepting the change.

Anyway, in my dream I found the man I just married in a crowd of happy people and ushered him behind the buildings where there was an open grassy paddock and where we could hear the happy talk and laughter by the girls in front of us. It was nighttime and I was excited because I was allowing myself to be silly with my husband. He was a little apprehensive. He didn't know what I was doing. I was behaving a bit out of the ordinary. I enjoyed doing it. Next thing I knew I was lying in bed with my husband and I kissed him passionately and he turned into my Dad. I didn't like the kiss because I had biscuit in my mouth. I rolled over and felt disappointed that I married my Dad and that didn't feel right. I didn't have those kind of feelings for him 'cos he's my Dad. Being a newlywed I knew and thought I needed to tell him straight away that I can't be married to him, even though he'd be hurt. It's better to be honest about it now rather than doing it later because I'd have to do it some time and I wanted to do it now.

Before I fell asleep last night I remembered being in love with Max, I was helplessly in love with him—how I just adored him. I remembered kissing him in his parent's lounge room. He was lying on me and my legs were apart and it was so heated. He would chase me through the house and catch me and we'd have sex wherever he caught me. It was when being together was so exciting and fun. Sometimes I didn't enjoy it. I didn't have a voice back then. I couldn't say no. I pretended to have orgasms. I did that with all my boyfriends, not with the men in my sobriety though.

I sent a message to Jezza last night informing him I have moved to My Hometown, I've moved into a house with my Dad, started guitar lessons and started up a netball team and that I'm scared about being here. I haven't heard from him as yet. Surprise, surprise, it doesn't surprise me. I need to allow myself to feel that it doesn't matter. I used to be hurt by that stuff and I wouldn't bother him. No more riddles with that man. That's something that has to be changed. We used to talk riddles all the time. That's changed now. The last time we spoke riddles I became very upset and hurt. I rang him when I was very confused and afraid. He didn't talk to me for three months because it scared him. I haven't spoken to him for about four months now. I would've scared the pants off him due to the thirty-five page letter I wrote to him, the song I sent, how I told him I was writing a book and my new idea of us already having a relationship. I did really well. So his messages are short and sweet to basically let me know he's alive.

THURSDAY : I couldn't be bothered to write because I was woken by Marika. I've written down the people I need to ring on my ring list.

Yesterday Mum and Dad were talking to me about commitment and basically said that I'm the leader of the netball team and it'll fall to the shit house if I don't go or make the effort to be there each week.

When they put it that way I'll do anything to be there for the team's spirit. Let me lead the way.

So I figure this: that I know what it's like not to get what you wanted. Look at this year for example in my relationships with men. Joshua brushed me off with the scare of genital herpes—lovely; George didn't want to kiss me for unknown reasons—great; and Jezza hardly talks to me or responds and I've spilt my guts to him about my soul. Oh, what a feeling! And Max tried to kiss me and have sex with me and I said,"No way! You're a drunken man, and you wouldn't kiss me if you were sober, so forget it." I invited him to the pictures and still no call since Saturday's events. So I meant a lot to him didn't I! Next time I'll go for Ross even though his legs are too skinny. I'm too big for him. He's given me the eye saying, 'I like you a lot, doll face'. I wonder if that'll wear off now that I've gotten close to his mate Max. Keeping in mind if I did attempt to kiss Ross I'd feel and see myself as a slut, through his eyes. Now that's my low self esteem, fragile me. So I know what rejection feels like and it's not that bad. It's better than being with someone I don't like, yukko! At the end of the day I don't know if I like Max enough, I would've kissed him by now if I did really like him, surely.

I'm going to the pictures with Gary tonight. Do I want to go? Not really. Why am I going? 'Cos he asked me to and I said: "Yeah sure." I'd rather go with Max any day. Am I wasting my money going? Good question. I'm going to Melbourne by the looks of it and I'd rather spend my money on that trip while I'm there. Not on a movie I'm not keen on seeing or being with a person I'm not that interested in spending my time with.

I'm going to do an hour's work of painting, then guitar and singing. I need to look at writing. Get it going! It's at Mum's, so now I'll fill the page with scribble. Yes, keep on scribbling.

Perhaps Gary would prefer to drop by and stay for a chat. Oh no, I've written two pages, bugger. Another whole page to fill out.

I'm not looking forward to filling out my form for the unemployment benefits and asking for rental assistance or telling them I received two hundred and seventy dollars in my bank account. They'll deduct more money off my allowance and I'm stuffed then, aren't I? Bugger.

I wonder if Ruby's sister liked the painting? Probably not. I'll collect it from her and bring it home. I'd like to see my painting hanging on my walls. The painting is of a place in Italy that I can't remember the name of, damn it, damn it, damn it! I'll have a shower this morning, put some daggy art gear on and paint. I'll feel better if I strum the guitar first. I think I could ring Dianne and ask if I can come and visit tonight. That would be more fun, more satisfying and fulfilling. Sing-a-longs with her husband John, and she is waiting for my call back, so there big bear. Living with Dad is weird. How about I commit myself to being thoughtful, considerate and gentle with Dad today?

FRIDAY : The cat's meowing. Caught up with Scott last night at his hotel room. Chatted with him from 9:30 pm to 12:30 am, mostly about where I'm at and marital dynamics. It was great. He doesn't understand Jezza or Max being without a girlfriend in their prime years. He thinks there's something very wrong with that. I explained my behaviour, when I'm in a relationship, that when I like someone I have difficulty with my mind because it tells me I'm a slut, cheap, and an easy woman. He said maybe I am and so what? It doesn't mean anything. His interpretation of that would be I'm easy going and fun loving. My interpretation is I'm worthless and I am nothing. Maybe it comes from the combination of the sexual abuse, having alcoholic parents, a neglectful mother and my extremely dysfunctional relationship with Jarod.

My girlfriend Doreen, who I worked with for three years as a manager of a large supermarket, supports the idea that I will experience a loving and romantic relationship again in time. She repeated several times that Jezza is very scared and has himself to deal with and that I need to push and push. I told her that I disagree with idea of pushing him. I don't want to be a stalker. She said that something is going on with him and it's not about me and that I need to help him get over it. I said, "Okay but how?" She didn't know either. She suggested I call him. I laughed. "He won't answer the phone. Watch this." So I picked up my phone and called his number and, bloody hell, he answered his phone and we chattered on for fifteen minutes before the phone cut off. Bugger. Doreen was signaling me to organise catching up with him but I couldn't. I was too rapt that he was talking to me to take the risk of asking him for a catch up. I didn't want to scare him away. I know that I'm not that powerful. It's the fear of being rejected. I sent a message and suggested a catch-up for a jam session and his three worded response was, 'Be in touch.' My immediate thought was, 'Yep that'll be another six months away'. Oh well, we did well to talk. He at least and most importantly digested most of the letter and all the other stuff I've sent him. I know this because he was able to allow himself to talk to me. No more riddles, how wonderful. We spoke easily on the phone and at times I was nervous. I couldn't believe I was talking to him. I picked up the guitar and he helped me pick to a song by REM. He mentioned that the song I'm learning is a difficult song to play, a song he has only just picked up. He was amazed that I was playing and singing to that song so soon I think. He said the reason for not travelling much during his time off was due to lack of finances. I was relieved to share my financial hardship and having friends around me who are financially well off and successful in their careers, brings up feelings within me of going backwards and going nowhere. He related to what I was saying. It felt so good to have someone finally understand how I feel without trying to change me. I got he was experiencing the same thing as I. I felt okay to be where I am in life knowing that I'm not the only one.

MONDAY : I put the paintings up in the lounge. Max didn't call yesterday—that's not very nice. Well, it just doesn't feel good. One minute I'm lying half naked in bed with him and then the next he's trying to kiss me along with the yummy touchy feely stuff. I'm holding back and not allowing him to kiss me or do other stuff. I'm not ready for it. I didn't want to for many reasons. One was that he was drunk and I didn't want to kiss him whilst he was drunk. I don't want myself becoming emotionally involved with him when he's not emotionally involved with me. It's not a nice feeling for me. For me it matters, and I need to matter to the other person who's involved with me. I don't feel safe otherwise. Fair enough if I've been in the relationship for a period of time and have built some kind of foundation with that person. With Max and I there are no foundations that have been placed at this point and at this stage we're still building on our friendship. It's because I care for him that I didn't want to do anything more than snuggles. I want to feel inside of me the feeling of love. I want that love to grow. If it doesn't, then it doesn't. Kissing him willy-nilly is not being responsible. I want to be accountable and feel good about the decisions I make and make honest choices. It didn't feel right to kiss or have sex with him.

You know, I wonder after my horrible experience with Joshua that I've got to get real about the danger of alcohol and one night stands. I was knocked off my feet when Joshua took back what he said the night we met. I had based our friendship on drunken words, words that had no grounding or meaning the next day. To top it off he said he had STDs. That was frightening and terribly uncomfortable. I'm so glad I didn't have sex with him. Jessie, my older girlfriend in Melbourne, felt very strongly about not giving up her body or sharing her inner self with strangers so intimately. She believes that they don't deserve it and that it is too dangerous, physically, emotionally and mentally. I agree with her, especially on an emotional level. I'd like to talk to Max and tell him where I am at with all of this so that he has the opportunity to understand where I'm coming from. He matters to me. I matter to myself, and the friendship I have with him matters to me. To have our friendship, we need to talk. Things will and can go amiss too easily. We're worth more than that. I feel pressures from his family and the past pressures from my friends and family because they all feel he'll be lovely for me and I for him. I'm carrying this on my shoulders. I'd love to make everyone happy, especially myself and Max, but the thought of it falling to bits and Max being hurt by me again, seems like too much of a risk; one that I'm not willing to take. So I need to look at the break up. I've taken on the story that I'm responsible for Max and that I'm responsible for why he hasn't had a girlfriend since breaking up with me nine years ago. It's not possible that I could be that powerful to stop someone from having relationships with other people. I'm thinking now about these negative unloving thoughts that I have of myself when approaching intimacy, and whether or not it comes from the unhealthy relationship that I have with Jarod. It is important for me to have the understanding and acceptance around that for me. I need a deeper level of understanding, closeness of the emotional, mental, and physical connection, and more importantly, a spiritual bond to feel fulfilled, safe and able to connect to on a real and loving level.

I'm about to have a go on my guitar. Had my first guitar lessons with Shelly. It was for free, fabulous. I didn't expect that. She says it'll take at least three months before it starts to sound like anything. You know me. I'm already thinking that I'll show her. I didn't ring the kids for their birthday yesterday, how forgetful I am. Oops...I'm the terrible one, bugger.

16/7/00 : You are so divine and beautiful, such a charismatic person and full of energy. You have a beautiful joy for life. You are talented, intelligent, spirited and truly amazing. I encourage you to follow your heart's desires. I want for you everything your soul desires. They are at your feet and only a breath away. The unimaginable is about to occur. Follow your love. Be there. Trust it. All in good time. God will deliver things you'll need to address and do. You handle yourself and others with such love and compassion. Follow the voice within when it calls you to write. Follow the voice within that calls you to paint. Follow the voice within that calls you to sing. Follow the voice within that calls you to learn. Follow the voice within that calls you to play. Follow the voice within that calls you to love. Follow and trust. Trust and follow. God has you ever so close. He won't allow you to skip a beat. Miracles, my sweet; you are God's little miracle. You are so important. Have loads of fun, love always, Granny. (I wrote this letter to myself imagining it was from myself at the age of 80).

19/7/00 : I'm reluctant to start writing...I will write all the same before Aimee turns up at 9:00 am. Slack, I'm bloody slack. My boobs are tender and my period's two weeks away (probably only one week away but let's allow for a week's lateness). I created a beautiful poem for Aimee last night before I fell asleep peacefully and soundly. It's her twenty-seventh birthday today and I've witnessed ten years of birthdays with this girl. I strongly remember her eighteenth and what a night that was!

I went to a meeting at Girgarre with Mum and Dad last night. Dad drove, he liked that. How wonderful it is to go to twelve-step recovery meeting with both of my parents. It felt like a real family occasion, something that truly matters to me.

I've had thoughts this morning about the book and wanting to write. I'm always thinking of what to write in it and what I will say. How I will structure it and so forth. Then it occurred to me I've been thinking like this on a daily basis for some months now. Perhaps I'm really meant to write a book! It's difficult to take myself seriously. "God help me to continue with my writing." Maybe the computer is not the way to go. Maybe handwriting is. My handwriting seems to flow smoothly. I feel that when I'm typing, it is not as smooth. It seems stilted. So now I'm aware that I'm to write a book. God speaks to me daily about this and I'm ignoring it. I haven't really given it a go for a reason. Not ready until I am ready. The days I really feel like writing are when I experience insights and new understandings about what I didn't understand before. I just think that everyone knows what I know and what I have to say has already been written in another book. These are the big blocks that stand in the way on my writing. MY HEAD TALKS TOO MUCH! I'm not painting. I'm being lazy.

20/7/00 : Dad's been silly this morning. He dreamt he was a politician with his cousin. I dreamt Dad dragged me into the sea to swim like a speedboat. I was limp. I couldn't be bothered. Prior to that I was standing on the beach with all the movie stars. They had makeup on their faces that looked like masks with their perfect hair. This old, fat lady came up to me and I wet my hair with the wetness from her body. I liked her. She was herself, an absolute dag. Meanwhile I was thinking, 'Do guys really like stuff painted on women's faces? I surely don't.'

Liz rang last night. David's in hospital. I'm to go with Liz to help out with the birthday party on Sunday. She'll be stressing out, poor Liz. I'm looking forward to seeing the kiddies. I'm taking music so we can sing and dance together, I'm sure we'll have lots of fun. I have no gifts. I have no money. How sad. My little bubbles of joy, they can cope without gifts from me.

Aimee's coming over here again for a walk. Yesterday through talking we/she worked out that she's worth more money than she was taking at the salon, and that they had already cut her hours back before beginning her work there. The boss doesn't want Aimee to do makeup in the shop due to the insecurities of her sister. The owner couldn't meet the money and Aimee said thanks and goodbye. She's already organised a haircut and colour with my girlfriend Louise. I need Aimee's business cards so I can hand them out to get her clientele going. She needs to give me another haircut, particularly if I'm promoting her as a fabulous hairdresser. Look out, here I come! How much fun will that be! I've already started without the cards or the haircut. And me, well, yesterday I did minimal guitar practice, my fingers are sore; I actually lay in bed playing guitar on my back in the dark. I wanted to send a message to Jezza but I didn't. I bought a CD, Brandy and Ray J, and I practiced my singing, something that I've done three days in a row now. Carmen suggested I listen to the tapes of my lessons with her more often. So here I am singing and listening to my singing on the tape each day and I can see the results of doing that and playing guitar. So results will happen by practicing. I'm offering Aimee singing lessons for a haircut and colour. Bartering is great.

ANOTHER DAY : I need work to earn some cash. I do need some extra cash to get me through. Fifty bucks for two weeks is a joke.

Dad's cutting wood, poor Dad. It's cold outside. Louise will be here at 8:30 am. I have half an hour to get ready. My throat's not good; psychosomatic I believe. I read about that in 'The Artist's Way'. The only book I'm allowed to read, bugger. Boring. I have been tempted to read and watch TV. It doesn't push me to do other things instead of those two other creative suckers. Another coffee for me and I'll get dressed and then I've finished my pages for today. Keep on writing.

ANOTHER DAY : I played guitar nearly all day yesterday. Wow. I'm still shit! No, just kidding, I really enjoy the guitar. Aimee and I went for a walk at 8:00 am and it was great listening to her. She stayed with me until 10:45 am, we even played guitar and sang songs together.

Portia might be coming today; her Mum's getting in the way. Let go, let God. I'd love her to be here, she's able to stay here until Saturday. I'll drive back in time for the morning meeting to see all my friends.

Jessica and I played the guitar for a while and it was fun. She even got up and did a dance! She said she could picture Jezza singing John Denver's song, 'You Fill Up My Senses', to me. It's actually called, 'A Song For Annie'. Jezza actually did sing the start of it once for me last October, gee whiz, how time flies. I haven't kissed that man for a long, long time. I'm talking not last year or the year before that. It must have been around April or June in '99. That's over two years ago. Wonder what he makes of me returning to My Hometown? Go girl. Probably feels damn uncomfortable with me in town. He'll make sure we won't run into each other. He's Mr. Cool. Shocking, absolutely shocking.

Anyway, I'm putting off my painting and writing; of course, if I produce anything I might fail and be a loser! What about the saying Aimee said yesterday about 'Having fun in trying, enjoying the journey and doing what makes your spirit soar'?" You never know maybe I'll do some of that this week. Or maybe I'm enjoying being on my holidays. First week I had off and this week is the same. The three weeks in the middle were stressing and I was doing something along the lines of moving home every day. So no wonder I'm inactive with getting into my work, I could commit myself to writing as from Monday or next week.

24/7/00 : I've just remembered my dream. I sent a message to Jezza telling him I wanted us to meet. I was down the street with my friends. Then he arrived with the whole football team. (They were out for a big night on the piss to celebrate something and they were all rather drunk.) I walked away without telling him what I was doing. I was asking Louise how to get to a certain place. As she was looking up the street directory I noticed I felt uncomfortable about not talking to Jezza. He was standing with a close mate of his and they didn't look happy or interested in talking to me. They waited, they were there, all the boys were waiting and I felt like a nuisance. I knew, normally, if it were another friend, I'd run over as my happy self and explain what I was doing, but with Jezza it's different. He walked away with the team. They obviously felt they had waited long enough. I didn't chase them or try to catch up with them. I felt more like they could've waited until I had finished what I was doing so I thought to myself there was no need to feel bad. I sent him a message: 'I love you' so that he knew how I felt. I felt let down and disappointed and wondered if what I did was not right but I felt okay about it all.

I do wonder if I did give Jezza too much information all at once, and if he read parts that he interpreted to be different to what I meant, and which then stopped him from calling or seeing me. He's not excited to talk to me or to see me. That's what I think and feel. Actually, that's what came out in my dream. He doesn't have to be excited. God knows what's going on with him. I know he's on his own island, which is a lonely place to be. Lots of thinking would go on. Lots of ideas would be stuck in his head to protect himself from being hurt. I am not powerful enough to change that or help him see anything more than he already can. I know God is though. I trust, and put trust in God's hands, that when I get that internal tap on the shoulder to contact him I will follow it. My soul is connected to the Universe, which is almighty and powerful. It knows when it's time for me to speak and what I need to say.

I know some beautiful people in my life who do like me very much as a person and who think to pick up the phone to call me or to come over to talk to me but haven't been able to do so, because of their own fears. They being rejected by me and I know this because they have told me. If my friends do this, then Jezza possibly would too. That is comforting for me to know. So it's not me that they don't like. It's the fear in their imaginings that tells them I won't like them if I were really able to get to know them. They are in fear that they'll be wasting my time and that I will judge them and then think badly of them. That, to them, would be something they couldn't cope with. The fear list goes on and I know it does because I do it in my life, particularly with Jezza. At the end of the day we're all the same.

I reckon it was so cute that, when I stayed over on the 'Notting Hill' night, he was awake until the time he had to get up to go to work. He was frozen and unable to move. I was exactly the same way. He didn't touch me and I didn't touch him, lying beside each other in his bed on our backs. I was thinking, "Touch him. No! He doesn't like me!" I love the thought now that he didn't or couldn't touch me because that tells me he really cares about me and he didn't want to upset me, and also because I matter to him and the thought of being rejected would be too much. That went for me too. I forgot that Jezza hadn't been drinking and I know how nerve-racking it is to do anything sober especially in the company of someone you like. The question was asked of me, "What has been the most joyful moment with him?" I know my most joyful moment was talking to Jezza telling him and reading to him something I wrote two years prior saying how I truly felt towards him after all these years. I told him if anyone asked me who the 'One' would be I'd say, 'Jezza.' The phone call was the most beautiful and mystical spiritual feeling of oneness, bonding with God, the Universe and Jezza. I shall never forget that feeling. Jezza felt the same toward me and said; 'Now that we're here, it's not so hard is it." God got us there and it's been somewhat of a challenge and frightening to me ever since. "I lean on my faith, and God, I trust in you that you are leading the show and I pray I will be ready when the calling is there. I will and I am doing the best I can and that's all I ever have—ME."

25/7/00: Portia is leaving today, I'm pretty sure anyway. All will be well in her life with God. I will remind her that God is with her wherever she goes. I do not know what is best for another human being. I will support her decisions. I will remind her I am here if and when she needs me. I will not say to her, 'Told you so' if she does bust. This home is open to be her home anytime. That feels much better. When she leaves it gives me the time and space to be with myself to sing, play guitar, catch up with Mum, do my Artist's Way course, artist's date, suss out My Hometown Theatre Arts Group, paint the birds and write a paragraph for my book. That'll be good for me.

I'll let Liz know I will be in Melbourne to look after her kiddies. Gee whiz time flies. I'll need to speak to Mum. The extra money in my pocket is what I need to travel and pay for my singing and guitar lessons, food and other items.

Perhaps once I've finished with writing today, Portia might want to paint before she heads off home.

I really need to know which way I'm going to take the book. What it will be about? 'Follow what you know and make it up as you go'. It does create lots of freedom and lots of other people have liked the title, 'Follow What You Know And Make It Up As You Go.' I do too. It's me to the tea.

Hey, the play I was thinking of, I could have that cute guy called Victor in it. He's 'out there', and a gorgeous looking fellow. You need people like that in a play; brings people along. Aimee will do the makeup. I'll be the director. Tamika will perform and Dad could be in it too. I could write it and put the people in it and then meet once a week. The crew could give pamphlets out and we could perform it at the Yahoo Bar. Sounds good. I'm a little excited.

I'm needing to do a poo. I suggested to Portia that we do a painting and that I'm here if she wants to come back and I feel better for it. I've accepted her decision to return sooner than planned. Gosh, I need to do a poo. Quick, write, and hurry up.

A walk would be lovely, it's now 11:05 am and the train leaves around 2:30 pm. So the play, the script is something I can start writing or begin looking at. Sounds great, heh?

I'm to ring Debbie about the painting. I need to have a shower and get ready. I need to finish off this writing. I'm rushing and I'm thinking, 'Quick!' I feel I have nothing more to say. I need to do other things other than sit here scribbling. Have I spoken of Jezza today? I don't think so. Yesterday as I was walking I had that period pain feeling in my tummy. I put my hand on my right ovary and I felt and thought my eggs are for Jezza. I'm waiting to have my babies with him and it was a delightful and beautiful feeling. I knew it sounded a bit much; something I wouldn't say willy-nilly to him or anyone, but it felt real to me.

Glynn sat me down last Saturday and told me not to see myself as a slut any more. She said I am not that. She believes I had been forgiven the moment I walked into the doors of the twelve-step meetings. She explained to me that the male's organs are 'out there', willy-nilly, they are exposed and that's the way it is. For us women, she explained that our organs are inside and are to be protected; women need to protect our womanhood with great care, particularly as a sober woman. This is something I'm doing that I have worked out for myself. I feel good, whole, clean, and sane when I'm not running around chasing a man or having a man trying to get inside of me. The last guy who tried that was, I've forgotten, no, Joshua and he didn't get to be sexual with me and I'm so glad. I don't want to do that anymore. Here I wanted to be with Jezza and I kissed someone else on his birthday. That's not very nice. My motive for telling Jezza I kissed someone else was not to have any secrets between us and to bring comfort to him if he were kissing someone else but was too afraid to tell me so. Now its five months down the track and I'm feeling sad because that would've been warning bells for him. Then I give him a thirty-five page letter when he knew I kissed someone else. Now that doesn't seem right. What would stop him from thinking that I'm still kissing other people? The feeling would be for him, perhaps, that he doesn't matter much to me. I did see Joshua for a couple of weeks. I'm not a bad or unclean person but if I'm talking about commitment with Jezza then my actions aren't meeting my words. Do I need to make an amends to him? Perhaps, hmm. This could be the 'big' thing standing in the way. He wouldn't want to be with someone who's kissing other people, as much I wouldn't take Jezza very seriously either if he had done what I had done. I can't write a letter. Talking to him I find is too difficult and a message through the phone may not be clear. Or, I could wait until the day I run into him. Yes, I could explain it in a letter and drop it off. That's something I could do. The nerves in me are still racing. It's a good thing that I'm nervous, it suggests action needs to be taken.

26/7/00 : I've been woken by Carmen. After yesterday's phone call to Jezza (which I didn't enjoy very much at all) I've come to the conclusion that I'm affected by Jezza's drinking. It's hard for me to write it down. I'm not in a position to say he's an alcoholic although I'd like to. My hand feels weak. I must not want to write this. I've shared with Dad my thoughts and he sees that I've been affected by Jezza's drinking also and it would make sense if he were a problem drinker. He's a different person when he's drinking and when he is sober. I find he is very hard to talk to when he is sober because he closes up. The information my girlfriends have given me is that he stays out late until stumps at pubs and clubs. I've been treating him like a newcomer in the Fellowship. I see myself in him. Aimee says he looks lost and Doreen says he's troubled and lost in fear. When he went to the races in Melbourne alone, he called me up when he was drunk. I didn't meet him because he was so pissed. He has called me numerous times after midnight. Each time it's when he has had many, many drinks and at three and four o'clock in the morning on weekends. His comment, "I can't believe you're still talking to me", suggests he knows some of his behaviour is inappropriate. His personality changes when he is drinking and when he is not. I've been dealing with Dr Jekyll and Mr. Hyde and thinking the whole time that there was something wrong with me; that it was something I had done that made him hot and cold. I have become responsible for his action and inaction. I've been trying to work him out and that, in itself, tells me I am affected by his drinking. I do need a twelve-step recovery program to help me heal from being affected by his drinking. I do need help. If I don't my life is in danger. I can't afford to be affected because I could pick up a drink over it and God help us if I do that. It also explains why Jezza can't see why I could be an ex-problem drinker because he sees his drinking as being normal. It explains why he didn't understand my apology because he probably can't remember any of the stuff he has told me about himself because of being drunk. It explains why he is very closed-minded and has stuck with old ideas and there's nothing I can do to change it.

I am powerless over his drinking. I'm so sad, yet relieved to know this. It's hard to accept because Jezza and I may never be together now that I know how badly affected I am by his drinking. If, by a miracle, that we do come together, it is a long way away because the first profound miracle for him would be for him to become aware he has a drinking problem - IF he has a drinking problem. The next step is to do something about it, for example, go to a twelve-step recovery meeting to admit he has a problem, then travel the journey to recovery which is another miracle because only three per cent of all the people who walk through the doors of a twelve-step recovery meeting arrest their illness, if they have the illness and if they have the capacity to be honest with themselves. If that all goes well, he and I, through the grace of God, could have a chance of having a loving relationship.

The only way from here as far as I can see, is for me to get the help I need for my own sanity because I know I am affected and I know that my thinking is insane regarding Jezza. I need to detach from Jezza with love, and hand him completely over to God's care. I only have myself to carry on with my life one day at a time and do what I need to do through God's eyes. I know I'm going to be busy. The time with God and myself shall not be wasted. If I can live for today then my tomorrow is my mystery and miracles do happen. God is all-powerful. There's a reason why God has had Jezza in my life. Nothing is wasted. I am grateful for Jezza's drinking because I have become humbled enough to see that I am not God. I can see now that I need a twelve-step recovery program that helps those who are affected by someone who drinks. I need the twelve-step recovery program also because I grew up with alcoholic parents and there are no observers in an alcoholic home; everyone is affected and that includes ME!

There are blessings all around. If Jezza is an alcoholic, there is only one way for him to go and that is down if he continues to drink. It's not my job or role to work out whether or not Jezza is an alcoholic. It's my job to figure out if I'm affected, how I'm affected, and what I am going to do about myself. I am powerless over another and over another's drinking. Looking at Jezza will not fix the damage in me. Looking at myself and seeing what I have done and continue to do is the first step to real change. I do know that alcoholics without treatment go insane, end up in hospitals, jails, or die without help. "God I pray for Your will in his life. I love him and I trust You that whatever happens from here is meant to be."

I'm questioning my working role on this planet. I've had five to six weeks off now. I worked last weekend as a nanny and I thoroughly enjoyed being with Liz and her two gorgeous children. I'm in a position to ask if I can work this weekend. I have a singing lesson with Carmen on Monday and therapy with Dr Wilmot on the same day. I'm in need of money for the trip and the expenses involved. I have incoming bills and registration for my car to pay. I need not panic.

I didn't accept the invitation to work for Wesley House as a residential worker. From time to time I question my decision as to whether or not that was a good idea. If I asked myself the question, 'Would I only say 'yes' to that job for the money? The answer would be 'yes' and for me, that is not a good enough reason to work there. I ask myself the same question in regard to the work that I do for David and Liz being their nanny and my answer is 'no'. They mean more to me than money. I feel useful and appreciated and the love I have for them and their children gives me an inner reward much greater than any dollar could pay for. I have a choice today and that is my choice whether I work or not and it is my choice where I work. Today I can ring David and Liz to see how everything is going. If I work Saturday night I will not be able to go the footy game that same night. A sacrifice I'm willing to make. I can go next week or I could go to Melbourne Friday afternoon if I choose to, to catch up with friends in the meantime. Yes I will call Liz today and get onto that. This feels like a good thing to do. If I'm meant to go there to work, God will make it happen because it's in His hands what I need to do and where I need to go. How wonderful.

Twelve Years Later...
Going within to share my deepest concerns with
my Higher Power to build my self-worth and
through this devotion I became my own loyal and
trusted friend

OLD THOUGHT: I'm a nutcase when it comes to relationships
NEW THOUGHT: I'm willing to focus on living my life honestly

I was totally obsessed. I wrote a 35-page letter to Jezza for God sakes! That took such a long time to write and this kind of thinking filled my days, my months and years. I thought and thought and thought. I enjoyed thinking about it. I enjoyed fantasising about Jason when I was driving, on the toilet, talking to others, watching movies, reading books, eating, falling asleep, sleeping, walking down the street, whatever I was doing he was there with me in my head. And that's all he ever was, in my head. I spoke about him as if I knew him! I perhaps had a day's worth of conversation with him in the 14 years of "loving" this guy. How much could I know about him to love? Not much, but the stories in my head were so fantastic! Have you ever seen the movie 'Notebook' or 'Titanic' or 'Twilight'? To me we were like the lovers in those films, who needed conversation because we were soul mates!

No, I didn't have a problem with intimacy! LOL I knew all about intimacy, I watched it in the movies and I experienced it in real life. We had the passion, the intensity, the fire, the spark, the chemistry, the longing, the longing and some more longing. All the right ingredients for real love. I worked out what he needed, what he wanted, and what he was all about with a few hours of conversation with him and most of them were while he was drinking!

I had trouble with intimate relationships because I had no idea what the hell intimacy was. I thought intimacy was when I thought someone was hot looking, someone whom I felt all tingly for when I thought of them. If they gave me a little bit of attention that meant a true and deep intimate relationship! The true ingredient for my passion, my undying love for Jason was being ignored and rejected. I didn't consciously know this at the time. I just fell head over heels for him and that's as far as I ever really got until I realised 14 years later I was affected by his drinking.

It's the one thing I cringe over when I read through this book. I know I have written many other things I could be cringing over, but none of that compares to the awareness about how screwed up my thinking had become when I thought I was loving this guy. I was stalking him, I don't know about loving him and I certainly didn't love myself.

With him and so many others I have been attracted to those who hurt, disregard and abandoned me. I'm always left in despair, sadness and loneliness. It is the key ingredient for my attraction to a guy. If I know I cannot have them, whether it's because they are too young, or drink too much, or have eyes for other women, I'm theirs. I'm all theirs. If a guy turns out to be someone whom I know wants to stay with me, who wants to commit to me, my attraction fades and dies every time.

I remember being about 8 or 9 years old and I was really attracted to this boy, a few years older than me. He liked other girls too and he told my Mum that having 20 girlfriends meant that, if one leaves, he still had 19 left.

In grade six I really liked a kid in my class, he was very popular and I chased him and couldn't have him. He stayed good looking.

In year eight I fell head over heels for a tall, dark, and popular guy whom I adored for many years, but he got with another girl when he was with me, which was announced by his mate in front of the students in the schoolyard! I wanted to die twice! I found him to be gorgeous and I pined over him until I met my cousin's friend Max.

I just thought Max was the ant's pants and I was with him for a few years. I kissed another guy and he wanted to stay with me. I knew I had him for keeps and I didn't find him attractive anymore and that's when Jarod caught my eye.

Jarod was a DJ, I thought he was popular and very cool and I wanted to be with him instead. I'd hate to know how many girls he got with while he was with me. I loved him and stayed attracted to him for years after I finally ripped myself away from him.

Dylan, I knew he really liked me. He was so sweet. He wrote me beautiful letters to reach to my heart and soul. He was kind, open, honest and good looking to top it off. As much as I strongly desired to stay "in love" or attracted to him my feelings would fade without grace. Disgust would fill my whole being like a tsunami. When I'd break up with Jarod I'd go back to Dylan to try and be with him again and every time I'd go back I'd break his heart. How I treated him was just awful. I just couldn't help the inner disgust I felt which I thought at the time was because of him. Twelves years later I found out - it was me.

After Jarod I hated men. They were going to pay for pain "He" caused me.

I had moved to Melbourne at 20 and there were a few really lovely guys that I met. Many actually. However I remember one really nice guy. He was tall with wavy dark hair. I have no idea what his work was, however he owned a lovely cottage style home in Williamstown and I knew he really liked me. I felt it like I felt it with Daniel. He had invited me over for dinner, which he cooked and I remember standing in the loungeroom thinking to myself 'as soon as he knows who I really am he is going to hate me. I cannot keep up with pretending to him I'm someone he'll want to be with. What a humiliating experience that would be. I could feel the disgust rising within me again and made my decision not to go back and that's exactly what I did. I never saw him again. It is only twelve years later that I wonder if I had the capacity to be loved and to love what would it have been like to share my life with men like that.

I moved to Queensland and fell for another guy from the Philippines and he liked to be with other girls too. I left him even though I was still attracted to him.

I met Shaun, the guy I got engaged to when I was 23, and he moved to Australia from an Island to be with me. My attraction toward him faded off during the week I knew he was moving to be with me. My attraction came back after I left him.

I always stayed attracted to Jason, and yet I could never be with him, I never got to be his girlfriend.

No matter how hard I try I am unable to actually stay attracted to someone who cares for me, someone who is committed to be with me. I'm as powerless over this as I am when I have a drink of alcohol. When I had a drink of alcohol I couldn't choose not to have another one even when I didn't really want to drink. I'm unable to change the way I am with this stuff too, and boy, I have tried and tried and tried and the result is the same every time.

Although there is one difference this time than all the other times, I have surrendered to this simple fact: I am powerless to change my inability to love or stay in love with someone who genuinely cares for me (someone I know who only has eyes for me and I feel they are committed only to me). I accept this about myself. I accept I no longer have the answers. I have waved the white flag; this relationship, love, attraction stuff has kicked my ass to heaven and hell and back again. I have quit the fight and the fantasy and the fury. This is exactly what I did when I realised alcohol was killing and wrecking my life; when smoking was no longer a joy but a hell; when food ruled my thinking and stripped me of any happiness or connection with myself; when another's drinking brought me to my knees yet again. Each and every time I came to see all my efforts to change these things with my own (and others') brain-power we had failed. I surrendered to each of these dilemmas, I quit the fight and reached out for spiritual help, my last frontier, my only hope.

When I surrendered in the past with other things I had lost choice or power I was freed from the suffering and taken to new ways of living. There are no guarantees with this sex stuff, love stuff, relationship stuff or that I will even be shown a way through it. This may be my lot in life. It could be the direct result of growing up in an alcoholic home where I was at times emotionally, mentally, physically abandoned. It could be the direct result of the effects of unacceptable sexual behaviour from my grandfather, a sibling, a few of my Mum's partners and from society as a whole. Maybe it's a combination of those things plus experiencing my parents' divorce and the fact I developed the disease of alcoholism and eating disorders. At the end of the day, knowing all of the possible reasons for the way I am—unable to be attracted to someone who cares for me-has not and does not change how I am. That's why I've chosen to reach out to spiritual help according to my own understanding of its source. For the first time with this stuff I do feel a genuine inner peace from knowing how powerless I am over the way I am and that I can turn to a source of spiritual strength and wisdom. I can stop chasing answers and stop trying to force solutions. I can stop hiding this from others and myself, having done so for so long. Finally my heart just goes "Ahh, what a relief"! I can now get back to focusing on what I can do and what I love doing and just see where life takes me. I accept my human limitations and I am willing to live my life to the fullest, meaning, doing what I love and communicating honestly with others and knowing myself better.

How funny to experience hope when there is seemingly none!

OLD THOUGHT: Someone else's drinking doesn't affect me
NEW THOUGHT: Alcohol affects others & that can affect me

I felt so chuffed when Jason would call me and it didn't matter what hour during the night it was or how much he had drunk. I felt so special, that he was thinking of me. I believed it was a sign and evidence that he really liked me. I was desperate for his love

GOING WITHIN TO GET OUT

and attention I took anything he gave me and I went to every effort not to stuff it up. When he was drinking he would tell me how much he liked me and how wonderful he believed I was; how long he had longed to be with me. When he was drinking he said the most loving, caring, and wonderful things to me, about me and about us. These moments were bliss, they were few and far between, sometimes years would go past as I waited for another special moment between him and I.

I searched for his approval of me. If he liked me it meant I was a good person. If he didn't like me or want to talk to me I felt it was because I was a disgusting person. I saw him like he was a mythological god, and I saw myself as a 'nobody'. He was my Supreme Reality.

I confused feeling sorry for him with loving him. I saw him as helpless and hopeless, which meant he needed someone like me who could love him unconditionally, to bring him back to life. All I could see was that no one could love him like me. I was endlessly patient, understanding, tolerant and amazing. I was the missing link in his life and all I had to do was prove it to him by never being upset with anything he did. I would not feel offended by the late phone calls while drinking or the no calls for months when sober, or when he broke his promises, or changed from a warm personality to a cold one, or for ignoring me in public, you know, I was an angle, how else would he really like me?

I overlooked the effect that alcohol in Jason had on me, and I tried to make sense of what became a mad situation. One time when he was drunk, he told me he felt the same as I did, committed to be with me and that he would drive to Melbourne the following day to see me. I called him the next day to see if he were still coming to see me, as he promised and he spoke to me like I was some kind of idiot. He had rice to cook! He wasn't going to drive 2 hours to see me! I was shocked and I felt disgust toward myself. I wondered what had I done to make him change his mind and treat me this way?

I was so confused as to why he would change toward me the day after his drinking. I feared his criticism. I feared his rejection. I tried to control this 'coldness' that he'd slip into after demonstrating how much he really wanted and liked me by acting perfectly. I just thought if I could just say the right thing or do the right thing he wouldn't be upset with me. I took full responsibility for his treatment toward me, his change of mind, his broken promises, and his ability to be hot and cold. He couldn't do anything wrong and everything I did was wrong. I blamed myself for the way he was. This became a sign to me that I was affected by his drinking.

Instead what changed him from being warm to cold, or Dr Heckle to Mr Hyde depended on whether he was drinking or not. Alcohol did this to him; it was never me. I was not responsible for the effect alcohol had on Jason. Alcohol was. I was never a bad or worthless person just because he was 'cold' or didn't keep his promises or when he failed to call me. Jason was responsible for this not me. Whether or not Jason liked me was not a sign that I was a worthwhile or valuable person. However because I felt responsible for him, his attitude, his choices and behaviour I failed to see what alcohol did to him. I failed to see what alcohol was doing to me through him.

As a kid I felt responsible for my parent's sadness or anger. I would do all I could to change their mood, change the way they treated me by sometimes cleaning the house, or not showing I was upset by smiling instead, or keeping all my worries to myself. I was neglected at times when I needed love. I was emotionally abandoned when they were suffering from their own disease of alcoholism and other stuff. I grew up believing I was worthless and disgusting, and when Jason showed me some attention I confused that with being loved when, in actual fact, it was the effect alcohol had on him.

It's amazing how quickly I changed once I acknowledged that I was affected by Jason's drinking, and realising I was the one who needed help. I did reach out for help immediately once I realised I was powerless of the effect his drinking had on me. I felt a great weight lift from my shoulders, my heart and mind, I felt free. I understood why I took on so much blame and responsibility. Mind you he never asked me to take on the role. I did that. Jason never asked for my help and he actually never ever criticized me, drinking or sober. I struggled at the start to take my eyes off him, thinking I had worked out what he needed to do and where he could get help, believing he was an alcoholic. However, the effect his drinking on me wasn't going to change overnight, but with time it has. I don't know if Jason is an alcoholic. That's not for me to decide. All I needed was to discover how to change and find peace and happiness once more. I discovered it was about focusing on myself—not what he could do—but rather, on what I could do.

See Appendix: Are you troubled by someone's drinking?

OLD THOUGHT: If I do things I enjoy doing I will be a loser
NEW THOUGHT: Doing joyful things creates a doorway to amazing experiences

It was a big risk to leave my secure job and my little flat in Prahan to return to the country town I grew up in. I didn't go back with a job waiting for me. I went back to continue to do things, which brought me joy and peace of mind such as; painting, writing, singing, playing netball, and doing the suggested activities from 'The Artist's Way'. I was committed and open to remember who I really was.

I didn't have much money to do the things my friends were doing. I couldn't afford to buy new clothes, or any clothes for that matter, and when I did I went Op Shopping or asked friends if they had clothes they didn't want any more. I felt inadequate around those I knew. I feared I would never become anything; never make any money doing what I was doing, the things which brought me joy. I feared I was in fairytale land. I had no one around me following the same path as I—only stories from the books I read. It was hard to find people in my life that understood what I was doing and many times found myself feeling alone. When asked by others what I was up to I felt vulnerable having to explain while feeling like a loser. I had less material and employment status compared to others I knew who had good jobs, good cars, good clothes, who just had it good. I was on unemployment or sickness benefits filling my days up with what seemed to be pointless hobbies. Looking back I now understand that my capacity for employment was severely limited because of my anxiety levels.

All I had at the time was a feeling it was the right way to go. I had experienced feeling better within myself when I acted upon doing those things, which brought me joy and happiness. The author of the book 'In The Meantime' started out with nothing and she became a very successful published author and spiritual adviser for women all around the world. One of my friends I knew in my early recovery lost everything from drug and alcohol abuse and went on to become a published author and started up a foundation to help others. The author of the book 'The Artist's Way' shared other people's personal stories about how they created success from their creative journeys. From what I could tell, it started off with one decision in the right direction, a day at a time. They all had their struggles and hardships; they got through their tough times by walking through their fears, and I believed if others could change their lives I felt I could too.

It started to make more sense to me to do things I enjoyed doing because these things brought me joy and that's what I believed I was meant to experience while being on this planet. I thought what's the use of having all the money and material items in the world if what I was doing didn't create happiness or peace, the two things I felt had been out of my reach most of my life.

Beforehand I felt I had lived most of my life living in a way, which would suit and please others, to prevent them from judging and rejecting me. I rejected myself for those who didn't have to live in my head, or feel the painful feelings in my heart in each passing moment. So, what was I going to choose? Was I going to choose what others thought was best for me, or what I felt what best for my happiness? I chose to follow what felt right for me knowing it could have been a mistake. When I became aware I was to write a book I asked Life to help me to keep writing and in doing so I had the opportunity to challenge the old thoughts that told me to stop kidding myself in order to keep writing.

Like writing and many others things I chose to do for the joy of it created new doorways to amazing experiences and a new life. What I didn't know at the time, I was developing a new sense of self-esteem and confidence by doing the things I valued and enjoyed doing. I went outside my comfort zones and met new people, and those new people opened more doorways of unimagined possibilities for me. I focused on choosing those things, which felt right, a feeling of joy, and therefore leaving more space for opportunities to come my way.

SACRED CREATIVE FOCUS
WHAT DO I WANT TO DO AND BE IN LIFE?

It's question time…What does it mean to move forward, forward from 'what' and to 'where' and why do I even have to think about where I am heading anyway? Well, I worked out that what I think and how I feel directs what I do and what I do creates the life I live. In essence my thoughts create my life. When I challenged what I thought, what I believed and became willing to explore and remember the things I enjoyed doing and became aware of the things that I wanted to find out more about I simply began doing those things. In doing those things, one thing lead to another and I am now living a life surrounded by wonderful, beautiful people, and doing things I thought I would never do, never be good at, and yet I'm doing them. I'm so glad I desired to move forward from what I knew, and dared to dream to where I would like to be and started to care about myself and where I was heading. I wouldn't be writing, or creating, or sharing my life with others as I do, happily and easily if I hadn't dared to dream and have a go.

What if I was meant to do things, which really excite me? What if I am meant to be doing things beyond my imagination? What if the decisions I make today do create living an incredible life being the greatest vision of who I am tomorrow? If I'd like to know how to get to a place like that where do I sign up and where do I start?

I start right here and right now - today. Every day from here on is the day to begin living the life I only dreamed. When I work out what I like and what I imagine liking, I can begin to make decisions that will take me to do those things and in doing those things create the life I love. And how do I find out what I like? I ask myself more questions from my head and I let my heart do the talking. I follow the joy and excitement in my heart, it knows the way, all I need to do is trust it. That's a big word – TRUST – one day at time anything is possible!

Starting today, I can also begin to acknowledge the things I do well and the wonderful qualities I possess and count the things and experiences in my life, which I can be grateful for.

SACRED CREATIVE ACTIVITY

To be in touch with who I am I can begin to remember what I liked doing as a child and what I loved dreaming about and who I imagined myself to be by drawing a picture, cutting out words/pictures etc about those things. Then I can write down what things I would do in my life if I had no fear, all the money in the world and all the freedom to do it? It can be a list of those things great and small. When I've finished, I ask myself, can I start doing some of those things I would love to enjoy or even begin to investigate how I could go about achieving some of the things on my list?

SACRED MEDITATIVE ACTIVITY

Now is a great opportunity to think about the people I believe to be fantastic/amazing/inspiring/uplifting or simply incredible and write about what it is I like about them. It could be someone in my family or a writer, actor, sports star, neighbour, teacher, friend, inventor etc. Then I like to list the qualities I believe they have? I do this before I consider the next step.

A counselor once asked me to write about the qualities I saw in someone I really liked and admired. I wrote down a list of various people I admired, mostly were spiritual teachers and comedians. They said to me that those qualities, the great things I can see in those people are probably the qualities I also have. When I see the flaws in others they are usually the flaws I am blind to having myself and I believe I can and I have been blind to my own qualities, gifts, talents and attributes. It's just easier to see stuff in others than to see it in myself.

If I am going to grow toward being who I really am by moving toward what I really want to do in life I begin by getting out of my comfort zones! I can do this by doing one thing I've been too afraid to do or have resisted doing and do it, then write about how you felt before, during and afterward.

COMMITMENT STATEMENT

I .... am willing to put aside everything I think I know about myself, my life, my past, my future, in order to have an open mind and a new experience about what I want to do and be in life. I am open to the possibility of becoming the greatest vision of who I really am, receiving new thoughts, and living a new life.

MOVING FORWARD TO BEING WHO I REALLY AM
WEEK TWELVE : LIVING MY DREAMS AND HELPING OTHERS LIVE THEIRS

LIFE CARRESON ... EON EDNEON

INTRODUCTION TO THE SACRED SHARING

"MY INSIGHT ABOUT BEING AFFECTED BY JEZZA'S DRINKING CHANGES MY DIRECTION WITH THE BOOK. I NEED TO ASK MYSELF WHICH ANGLE WILL I COME FROM NOW? HMMM. PERHAPS SOMETHING ALONG THE SAME LINES AS, 'IN THE MEANTIME' OR 'FORTY DAYS AND FORTY NIGHTS MY SOUL OPENED UP'. THAT COULD BE A GOOD APPROACH. I COULD WRITE AND LET AN EDITOR HELP ME WITH THAT. I'LL CREATE THE FIRST DRAFT OF THE BOOK AND LET GOD TAKE CARE OF THE QUALITY. HEY, NOW THAT I'VE LET GO OF JASON, PUTTING HIM ASIDE I FEEL READY TO WRITE!"

27/7/00 : Woken up by Linus calling this morning. I dreamt about writing a letter for a baby, a special child. I dreamt she would read the letter when she was much older. Two guys called Jezza and Matthew were out the back in footy training. I walked out there and there was a guy who told me of a girl who fell off the back of a truck and was killed by an oncoming car. I asked if her name was Julie and he nodded his head to confirm that it was and I told him that I knew her. We were all a little shocked and it felt like a really small world.

I knew Julie in the Fellowship in real life. The last time I spoke to her was when she called me up when she was pissed. She thought I said at a meeting that I could have anyone I wanted. She thought I was gay and arrogant, that everyone knew. I told her she must have misunderstood what I said, which happens, and that if people want to think I'm arrogant and gay, then that's their choice - something that I am powerless over. I told her whether or not people think I'm arrogant and gay doesn't change the fact that I'm not gay. I might be a little arrogant at times though, I am human. I arranged to meet her at the women's twelve-step recovery meeting two days later but she didn't show up. A few months later I heard that she was killed on Swan Road by an oncoming car.

Dad's going for a walk with Linus and the dog and I'm here writing my morning pages. I feel I'm missing out. I'm committed to these writings. Instead of chatting with Linus when he first arrived I could've finished the pages of writing I feel I have to finish. Someone just rang and hung up. I'm feeling paranoid and I wonder who it was. Oh well, they'll ring back if it's serious.

I have a rotten feeling down low in my heart. I told Dad that I felt grief and sadness in relation to Jezza. I said to him that I didn't know why. I felt like I had said goodbye. Dad then said: "It sounds like you're at Step One, where you come to accept that you're powerless over the drinking in Jezza and that your life has become unmanageable." The Second Step is 'Came to believe that a Power greater than ourselves could restore us to sanity'. Gee whiz, what come up for me was; I'm not the insane one here! Meaning that I'm okay, except when I take my eyes off myself and look at him and what he's doing. He's the one with the problem when his personality changes! I think I'm a candidate for the Fellowship which one?. Unreal! Here I was cruising along pointing the finger at him the whole time and not seeing myself in the same picture. I've been treating him like a child when he's a grown man. I finally get he's a grown man who can look after himself. I am a grown woman who is responsible to looking after herself. I know I am affected by Jezza's drinking. Jezza calls when he's been drinking and shares with me about how he feels towards me and I respond by doing the same. I find the next day he is different and distant and I am left wondering why he isn't as affectionate, open and honest as he was the night before. The promises he makes when he calls when he's been drinking never come true and I'm left thinking it must have been something I had done wrong to make him distant and not affectionate towards me. I would go on the next days, months and years, living my life believing what has said to me while he was drinking was true, when I now know that what he has said was under the influence of alcohol that most likely, it was forgotten or were just drunken words. Bloody fantastic! What a joy killer, bugger me. I love him. I still feel in my heart that he has deep and true feelings for me but I'm not safe to be around him when he's been drinking.

This is a whole new ball game. I'm grateful that I've finally come to realise this. I now know how I feel, and I know I love Jezza, and this is my truth. I'm now handing it over to God. The program suggests that I make a decision to turn my will and my life over to that Power greater than myself. The Fourth Step is talking and writing stuff down to God and myself about my resentments and hurts I experienced with Jezza. From there I take it to Courtney, whom I trust greatly in the Fellowship, who is also my beautiful friend who understands and knows a great deal about me. I feel that I'm ready. I don't feel I'm rushing. I want, and can, handle doing what needs to be done for my recovery. I know for me I don't have to wait forever to apply the program into my life. So I need to talk to Courtney.

I also need to hand in my form and fill out my diary for the unemployment agency - I am four weeks behind. There's a lot to fill in and write. I can handle that. Nothing could be worse than in 1993 when I was at University doing my first year of Bachelor of Nursing in Melbourne when I was having private conversations with God about how many ways I could kill myself painlessly and successfully. God did help me through that one so He can help me through this one too. I only need to ask.

One of my thoughts when I was walking to the toilet: 'We don't focus on those who don't want the help, we focus on the ones who do.' Jezza is not asking for help from me. That's okay with me. I'm the one who needs help and I'm the one who needs to do the asking, not from Jezza, but from people who understand the effects of alcohol. I accept where he is at and where I am. I am to gently pass him by and focus on the people in my life who are reaching out for me to help them.

Sophia called this morning about her fridge that Dad recently bought her, to inform him that it's not working properly. For a year old fridge, that's shocking. So Dad and I will pick it up, return it, and buy her a brand new fridge. Sophia's very frightened and lonely. It probably wouldn't hurt her to attend twelve-step recovery meetings regarding her relationship with her daughter. I will ask if she'd like to come with me.

I thought about Liz and how she truly appreciates my love and helping hand with her children. She felt relieved when I offered to be there with her on Sunday to help out the birthday party. We had a giggle about her being like Con. She's never spoken to me about seeing herself in that light before. Being geographically away from the family I find it easier to be myself when I'm there now. I don't feel like I'm working for them I feel like I'm part of their family.

It's my friends' third sober day today, he's needed lots of help. He's been reaching out. There's that saying that I hear around the Fellowship where it says that it is my responsibility to be there for those who reach out for help. I am wondering about time out for myself and when that will be. Knowing that I know so many people and having helped many others is beginning to consume me. I don't have any time to scratch myself. I need to allow time to do the things that I need in order to do my creative recovery. Hey, perhaps I could get some money off Debbie to buy the oil paints while I'm in Melbourne. I'd love to start that painting. I'd like to do something now. Time to say goodbye.

28/7/00 : Wow, how yummy was it to be with Ross this morning. My head talked so much, as normal, but I didn't sleep between the hours of two and four or seven o'clock onwards. Yutta, yutta, yutta, it went on about how foolish I was not to take note that Jezza hadn't called me for three and a half months. He didn't even read my letter for a while after he received it and when he did, it took him a very long time to get through it. I sent a song his way and messages on his phone and he would not have had any idea what they would've been about, because I sent them in relation to the letter, thinking he would've read it by the time I sent the other stuff to him. Bloody hell! I really took on his drunken words, as being set in concrete didn't I? I should've known better. I'm grateful that I now know what I'm dealing and that I know I've been affected by his drinking. I was ignorant and I must look after myself. No good beating myself up for not knowing something I didn't know I needed to know. It got me this far. It got me to my Hometown. It's been a great catalyst.

I'm aware I need to look after myself with my interactions with Ross. I can be affected by his drinking too if I'm not careful. I like him, I really do. How yummy, I just wanted to touch and kiss him all night. I even dreamt about it, but I couldn't in real life because I was too afraid of his rejection. I still am. What I resist persists. It's what I give, that matters. I woke him up early just because I wanted to. I couldn't lay there any longer with my eyes wide open. I cracked some jokes and that's when he brought me closer to him and we kissed and it was so yummy, very yummy. I trusted him and felt safe enough to do that with him. He was sober. Being sober and alert means to me that he was present to me. That's when I realised it's important for me to know that when I'm intimate with a man, whether it's emotionally, physically, mentally or spiritually—he needs to be sober. We rolled around in his bed. He had a tightish white t-shirt on the same as me. He was wearing black boxers and he didn't do any quick or unsuspected moves or push me to do anything that I didn't feel comfortable with. He did comment that I was being a little nervous and I quickly informed him I was being shy. He smiled, he liked it and so did I. I enjoyed it for what it was. I thanked God for giving me something very beautiful this morning. I didn't think I'd be finding myself in this position so soon. Max is his friend; I can't help how I feel. It feels good too. I didn't feel good with Max that time I was lying in his bed. I like Max as my friend, as my cousins' friend. I have no sexual desire with Max. With Ross it may only be that 'yummy time' that quickly flitters by. I want more of it though. I want more of him. I know I get my hopes up and then nothing ever happens. But how's me saying only last week that I'll wait forever for Jezza if I have to! That was before I realised I was affected by his drinking. Bugger. So last week I let him go and left him in Gods' hands.

Why I can be with Ross so soon is because so far he has let me be close. Jezza wouldn't let me be close with him and probably for a very good reason. All Jezza can offer me is friendship. Four days later I ran into Ross at a pub and all my girlie parts got excited and so I asked him if he'd like to do something together some time and he replied with a long "yessss". I must be aware firstly that he doesn't believe that I am an ex-problem drinker. He's a big drinker. Sad really. Doomed before it's really begun. Do I just like big drinkers? Bloody fantastic, just my luck! They're great people only when they can have their booze. In saying that, alcoholism will destroy anything in its path. Apparently that's what I'm attracted to.

Sophia says that I'm attracted to that type of man and that it's time I lifted my standards and need to look elsewhere. I'd like to know where. She said the last man left me decimated and I grabbed hold of him without listening to myself first and I took on his facade and I didn't see the real creep underneath and that is what pulled me under. She was spot on. It took me a while to work out who she was taking about. Dad was there and he knew straight away who she was referring to. Both Wayne and Joshua fit that description. Yucko! I must call my doctor to check that I don't have sexually transmitted diseases from Joshua, even though I'm sure I don't. Joshua wasn't a nice character. Sophia reinforced that I need to slow down because, in one way I'm very confident, yet in another I'm extremely insecure and I need lots of nurturing by my partner. That's me to a tea. That's my past. I'm grateful to her mentioning it because those experiences with those particular men are for me to learn from. I'm not to be 'all or nothing' in these circumstances.

She also said I need to do whatever makes my heart sing. Let me tell you that kissing and being held and touched by Ross made my heart sing. I cannot know what he feels but last night he let me in on a few secrets and one was that he doesn't like chasing the people he's attracted to because he's afraid of being rejected. Well, we have that in common. He's also very sensitive so we have that in common as well. We both like Scrabble and that's always a good thing. "God, I like him and you know he's not a physically huge man where I get to feel very feminine or petite and that's okay with me." Wow, there's some growth. His body is yummy. I actually like his bowed legs, his bum, mouth and chin. I just think he's yummy. He and I had a sparked from the word go. I thought nothing would happen with him and because I loved Jezza when I first met him, you know, when I thought that 'I-would-wait-for-Jezza-forever' motto, Ross became 'off grounds' to me. I wasn't comfortable with Ross being Max's mate either. At the time of our first meeting, I told my feelings to shut up. Wasn't that good of me to do that to myself? I love the way he dances. Bloody hell, love is so blind or should I say infatuation is so blind. Dad said yesterday that now I've let Jezza go I now don't know who's around the corner and looky, looky here. The only thing is that Ross is going to England in three weeks time for three weeks and he may not come back. There's a strange feeling inside me about all of this. Maybe I'll be a catalyst for him to stay here longer.

30/7/00 : I'm at Lana's house and it feels uncomfortable knowing that Aimee doesn't live upstairs any more. I feel a little sad about the change. Things have changed, life moves on. I'm picking up my Mum at 9:30 am at the train station. I'm squeezing my writing in; I didn't do my writing yesterday morning. There is no way I am going to miss another writing.

I loved being with Liz and her family. I love them dearly. I love putting the kids to bed. I'm returning on the eleventh in August. David and Liz are going away for a couple of days, just the two of them. I'm so happy to be asked to look after their kiddies and I love saying yes when they do ask. People pleaser sneezer? No way, I love them dearly, I am blessed to know them and to be loved by them. I love my work with them because it isn't work for me to look after their gorgeous children.

Lana waxed my under arms and nicker line. I feel very clean. I didn't bother with my legs; they don't need to be waxed.

I like Ross. I have self-doubt and insecurities. I looked at the emotion 'insecure' and it means: 'inward, consumed with self, for example; paranoia. Secure means 'safe, okay, at peace with oneself and the world'. So insecure is not being at peace with the inner-self and feeling unsafe. I wonder if it is an alarm about the other person when I feel this way. The reason behind my insecurities is because Ross is being a human and a young twenty-seven year old male from England, I can trust him to do what young travelling males do, which is to lie, manipulate, withdraw, lack commitment, be self-indulgent, and I can trust he'll get with other women. He'll probably find me too confronting. I look at the people he knows, the places he goes, the alcohol he drinks, and the woman he lives with. He's in a transitory phase in his life and it screams out danger to me and I'm not going to ignore it. So if I feel unsafe then there is a good reason for it. I'm somewhat disappointed because I'm attracted to him.

Marika said last night: "Don't follow your fanny, follow your head." Then I remembered, 'what about the heart?' Let's go with the heart. God is running the show. God is not judging. God is love, all forgiving and giving, trusting and knowing. Am I grateful for the yumminess I have experienced with Ross, knowing that may be all it will be. One moment at a time and nothing more? Am I willing to stand in a place of unconditional love, without judgement and selfishness, to give care without strings attached no matter what the outcome? Yes I am. Am I willing to accept Ross and myself the way we each are, putting each other into the care of a Higher Power, being mere humans and knowing that we lack so much? Yes I am. Am I willing to accept this journey as it is and willing to accept me as me and do what is at hand for me today, to have loving thoughts of the people I'm with and of Ross? Yes I am.

1/8/00 : Graeme from Queensland would say, 'It's about having the right mental attitude.' I'm not looking forward to working all day with Kevin. It feels too much. I'll do it today and see how I go. If anything, he's helped me out in the past and this is the least I can do. I don't have any cash on me. I wonder what I'm going to eat today? Kevin is going to Queensland in a couple of weeks' time. I've been invited to go and I just might do that. I'd love to say 'Hi' to my friends up there. I would have a ball. Money, hmm. I need some from somewhere.

There's a lot of banging going on outside, how annoying. I need to nurture my body with water - more drinking water and less coffee. It will be better for me in the long run.

Dr Wilmot suggested I continue my sabbatical. He said; "Don't rush back to work unless something fantastic arises." Wow, that's fantastic! He suggested to me that I think about study for next year and to continue what I'm doing for now. He commented that it is wonderful what I am doing and asked me a couple of times if I am happy. I am happy. I had a big change last week realising that I'm affected by Jezza's drinking. That's a big pill to swallow. I know I wanted to write a book, but since that understanding, I haven't wanted or thought about writing a book. It does change things. My acknowledgment of my persistence in trying to love Jezza unconditionally changed my life. He hasn't a clue about this. I'm meant to be in my Hometown doing what I'm doing. I gave it a go with Jezza and now I need not think that I did not give it my best shot. I'm a winner for having a go. It hasn't removed my insecurities, bugger.

With Ross, I'm very attracted to him. I have this way of thinking that isn't constructive. I can make a conscious choice about this. There's the three A's - Awareness, Acceptance and Action. I'm aware that I question and doubt what Ross says so that I can reject him before he rejects me, lovely—not! I accept I'm doing this. I accept I'm scared of being hurt, disregarded, left behind, joked about, not cared for and abandoned. I accept that I doubt, worry, judge, hesitate, assume and rush things. I accept I do all of this to protect myself. The action I'm committed to do is to firstly focus on what I'm doing and giving. Let it begin with me. Leave his life and drinking to him because it is none of my business. Listen to the facts, assume nothing and if doubtful I can ask. Action is; let go if he walks away. The Dalai Lama says it's the attachment to something that we have that creates unhappiness. It's the ability to receive and to freely let go freely that creates a happy life. I'm to be grateful for what I have in my life today. Expect nothing in this day and all else will be well in my day and in the world. I have great abundance in my life and this is why I'm the luckiest person sitting on this floor. I'm alive, well and a bloody spunk!

2/8/00 : Donna came around this morning and it was great to see her. She's reading, 'How to Heal Your Life' by Louise Hay. It's a very intriguing, helpful, and useful book.

Well, what do I want and need to write this morning? I'm going to spend some time doing my homework in the 'Artist's Way'. I failed to do half the tasks last week. I failed to do something on my own as a 'date' for two hours by myself this week. The best I did was the trip to Melbourne by myself because I'm consumed with others any other time. The past week and three days I have been focusing on others and my creativity has suffered. I feel like I'm behind. I feel I've left myself behind. As I'm writing I'm aware that I'm powerless over others needing me and what I can do is say 'no' at times when I feel I need to do something for myself. Put me first to do the things that I need to do. Hey, because of the lack of creativity in my life, it may have led me to be over concerned with Ross, which left me carrying feelings of sadness. My astrological reader, Jenny, said that if I don't allow myself to express myself creatively, then I turn inward and become unhappy, even depressed. This is probably why I have had such difficulty in letting go of my demands and expectations of Ross. I want him to fill the areas in me that aren't being fulfilled by me. That's why I felt so unsure and insecure. It's not him. It's me. What a relief, oh, I feel free inside. I feel good, happy and joyful. I hope I haven't done any damage to my friendship with Ross. It's okay if I have. I can explain myself the next time I see him if it feels right to do so. If I don't hear from him by Friday, then the chances are I'll see him at the pub at lunchtime where Linus and I have lunch and play pool. I don't expect anything now. Gee whiz, I like him lots, he's so cute. I realise he's a human being and he is nothing more and nothing less. It's what I give to myself and what I choose to give to him that matters to me.

I need to grab my guitar off Mac and chat to Shelly to see if she can give me more music to play and also fill out my unemployment diary. I need to call Ruby and apologise for forgetting to call her yesterday. I need to call Jessica about the idea of walking at 7 o'clock in the mornings. I need to call Debbie about her painting. What is it she'd like me to paint? I'd like to begin sketching for that painting. I need to organise some time to pick up a desk, glass pieces and perhaps the drawers from Ruby's parent's home. That could be fun and hard work. Oh, Eugene, my cousin in England is on the phone talking to Dad. He's probably asking about Mum's surprise fiftieth birthday party, to which I've given no thought. It's a little difficult for me to get going on it knowing I have no money to help out. Maybe by September things may change, even though I can't imagine so. I dreamt last night that Eugene had died, I cried deeply for my cousin's death. It was very sad. That's it for now.

3/8/00 : I had very intense dreams last night. Before I fell asleep I meditated and saw I was on Oprah talking about my book. I also envisioned Ross kissing me first and that was significant and reassuring. My concern was that I had made the first move to contact him. Meanwhile, in my mind I'm thinking he doesn't find me wonderful enough for him to bother with. He suggested we go to the movies tonight and I shall wait excitedly for his call to see what we do. In the first dream I had I was in a violent relationship, being beaten by my boyfriend and I knew at the time who it was and now I cannot remember. It may have been some movie star. I seduced him to have sex with me and he suggested to do it on the car and I thought, 'No worries' anything to stop him from beating me.' I had created a painting of three people that I was trying to sell. A friend scrubbed one face off and we could all see in the painting (what was meant to be hidden from my abusive boyfriend) was that one of the persons was strangling the other so badly that her eyes were going cross-eyed. "No", I screamed, "He'll kill me seeing what I've painted because he knows it's him in the painting." It was my way of sending a message to someone to help me from this mad man. Brad turned up and I said, "You buy the painting and I'm out of here. It's over. I have four of my big male mates here to protect me." He knew there was nothing he could do. He was found out and so he gave me one hundred and ten dollars for the painting and walked away. I laughed inside knowing it wasn't worth that much and relieved that I was safe once more. I remember Jock Huddly in one of my dreams with his long curly hair saying to me, "You look clearer than the last time I saw you." That was a wonderful compliment. We measured who had the longest hair between two other girls at our high school reunion. Louise fucked up the truck delivery. I couldn't close the truck door that had swung open and before I knew it, the room was full of old school mates who selected me to get up and be the first speaker and I thought, 'But of course'. There was a clear message that Brad said to me in the earlier dream. I hope I remember it during the course of the day.

I did this amazing painting of Bob Marley last night. I need to finish it, well, part of it. Dad doesn't want me touching much more of it. He called it a masterpiece! He gave me permission to sell my paintings at one thousand dollars apiece. The message was loud and clear. I got the Universal permission I was asking for. Other Universal messages I've received have been: I'm not to view myself as a slut, I am a very attractive woman. I am to sell my paintings at a high price and continue my sabbatical until the end of the year. They are all wonderful messages.

I just realised that the room out the back of the house is the art studio I have been asking for, for all these years. I can do all my artistic things there at my own leisure. It has been sitting under my nose the whole time I've been here. I do wonder about my intelligence when I miss obvious things like that. I'm going to bring up the little black couch from Kevin's shed and put it in my studio to make it warm and snug. 'Trivia Night' on this Saturday at 7:30 pm and I'm not keen to go, but I'm willing. It will be doing something different. I'll ask Louise, Max and Ross to come and join the table of ten others. I'd feel better if they came; it's twelve dollars a head. I don't know if I can afford it. I'll go by myself, I'll ask and see what they say.

4/8/00 : My hair feels gross. I put it in dread locks and I felt rather insecure about it when Ross picked me up to take me to the pictures last night. I had a massive insecurity breakdown when he dropped me off at home. I felt so bad about myself. I'm still recovering. I have an emotional hangover this morning.

I dreamt of another war, this time I was fighting aeroplanes, shooting them down to the ground.

My jaw is out which represents, (from 'You Can Heal Your Life' by Louise Hay), anger, resentment and a desire for revenge. I feel terrible. I'm hoping I'll feel better soon. I couldn't get my head and heart around last night. Nothing bad happened; it was just a little uncomfortable. I wasn't my normal self. There were conversations with Ross that I didn't click onto like I normally would have. I joked about nearly everything that was said and I just felt plain awful about myself. I abandoned myself. I didn't like myself at all.

I'm not looking forward to anything today. I have a few bills to pay and Lana didn't return my sad and lonely message that I sent her last night. I want to wash my hair out. Linus, Dad and I normally go to the Pub for lunch. Ross says he goes there too. I wonder if he'll be there today. I wonder if all the stuff I thought up in my head was true. The assumption I made was that he was put off by my home because it lacks furniture. I was thinking that he was dying to drop me off to get away from me. I thought that because I didn't care about the deeper things that mattered to him, meaning we don't really connect, and because of that he will never ring me again because he doesn't like me.

Where does all of this stuff come from? It's like a bad rash. I just want to be liked for me. It is a lot to ask from a stranger. Do I like me for me? Am I enough? Am I accepting of myself? Do I accept that I put my hair in dread locks just because I wanted to? Can I accept my home, my Dad and my situation exactly the way it is? Can I accept that I felt lousy about myself? Can I accept that I didn't go into the deep and analytical stuff that I normally go into? Can I accept I was talking all the time? Can I accept that he didn't appreciate my hair? Can I accept the fact that I was uncomfortable and feeling daggy, and feeling responsible for Ross's feelings towards me? Can I accept that I'm a human being who is not perfect? Can I accept that I am powerless over Ross? Do I believe God has another answer and another way for me? I'm willing, to like myself. I also want him to like me too and I want to feel good again. I ask God to remove my self-reliance. I have hurt myself' I'm sorry for what I put myself through. I am willing to live in the present—to do God's assignments for me today.

4/8/00 : Stayed over at Ross' last night. I took along two Scrabble games, chips and dip. I enjoyed being with him. It was fun. I was feeling good about myself. For the first time in many, many months I had my first hair cut by Aimee. I was feeling good after spending a couple of hours with Doreen talking and singing to the music in her car driving around town. I had my legs waxed and I painted my toenails; I looked gorgeous in a high, long sleeved, wool, tightly-fitting black jumper with my beige Indian skirt with long black boots. I was feeling great. My spirits were lifted when Doreen shared with me about angels being in my life. Also, that she had her first spiritual awakening with me while we were driving a couple of years ago, and she saw a flock of white geese as a sign of hope. She said it's taken her a couple of years to understand the spiritual world and to apply it into her life. She then passed it onto her sister, the knowledge of the new experience, who is now showing Doreen affection more than ever. She shared with me how she told others about my 'time-out' drive around the outskirts of my Hometown. Now there are heaps of people going for the same drive for peace and reflection because of Doreen. That's so funny. I still do that drive. I only did it this morning with a smile from ear to ear.

Let me record this: I asked Ross to kiss me and, yes, he did. He was a little taken that a twenty-six year old woman would be shy about taking off her top. My comment to him was, "It's not a bad thing to be shy. Maybe it's a little silly and this is me and that's how I am." (Like, too bad if he doesn't understand). Note: I haven't shared with him about my sexual abuse or my deep-seated difficulties with intimacy or my high paranoia about my body. I chose to keep these personal issues to myself. I couldn't see why it was important for him to know so much about me so soon. I wasn't sure whether or not he could manage such information about me. I felt maturity was definitely lacking on his behalf. We went to bed and we got down to our underwear. I noticed a beautiful green flower tattoo on his shoulder and asked what it meant to him and his reply was, "When I get to know you better I'll tell you about that." I thought, 'That's cool, it's your tattoo, your reasons and I understand that.' He started to take off my g-string and I said; "Oh no, not until you get to know me better." I was smiling. I thought that was funny, but I meant what I said. Then he says with a screwed up look on his face, "That's more painful than sticking needles in my eyes." With that he jumped off me and laid 'over there' on his side of the bed and continued to say, "You come over here to my place, get naked with me and let me lie between your legs and then tell me we're not having sex. Why do girls pretend they don't like sex?" After a quiet moment he asked if I were upset and I said, "Yes, you're awful for what you have just said to me and you're down to only one point." Silence. Righteous. He follows through with, "We're both adults here. You may as well go home if you're not going to talk to me and have your back to me." I lifted my body up onto my elbows and looked at him square in the eye and said; "You're the one who wanted to go to sleep because you're not getting sex tonight. I think you've forgotten I'm a human being with emotions and not a robot or just 'a root'. I want to know what happened to rolling around in bed together, having fun? Don't you know you don't have to have sex to have fun and be intimate with another human being?" He kisses me on my forehead and says goodnight and flicks off the switch. I had by then emotionally detached myself from him.

I went through different feelings and thoughts. Yes, I was awake most of the night. I chose not to leave because that's what I used to do with other guys if I were upset, so I saw if I did it this time too, I'd be repeating old behaviour. He hogged the doona all night and the only time he touched me was when I told him in the dark that I was feeling uncomfortable so he put his arm around and drew me closer to him for at least five minutes.

Knowing I was going to take a long time to fall asleep I made a decision to talk to God the whole time. I had a great chat with God—I actually really enjoyed it. In the morning I got up and got ready. I had a cuppa and sat on the couch and took myself mentally through the twelve-steps from the twelve-step recovery program. Doing that helped me come back to the moment, freed me from the fear that I was enduring and to know what to do with myself in a situation where I was feeling uncomfortable. I was feeling awkward and unsure and just not right about his reaction towards me for not wanting to have sex with him, and my reluctance to tell him previously about where I was coming from. I then proceeded to tidy up the mess in the lounge room that we had made, because that's what I would do for any friend of mine. I made the bed that I slept in and tidied our mess in the kitchen as I would for any friend of mine. We found ourselves standing in the kitchen at the bench and I said the following, "I need to say something to you." He nodded. "I failed to let you know earlier that I did not come over here for sex. I can get that anywhere if I chose to. I failed to be straight with you from the beginning. I like you more than a friend and you actually matter to me and I think we want different things here. I knew a while ago that I liked you more than just having sex with each other. I know it's a bit heavy for this time in the morning." He smiled and said gently, "Leave it with me." I returned his smile and I was not hurting inside. I felt clear. I felt comfortable and had a safe feeling knowing that he knows he doesn't share the same feelings as I do and that I'm okay with it. I felt relieved about it.

Last night while lying on his bed while he slept 'over there,' I thought to myself that this is my body; these are my organs to be protected just like how Margaret had said. I will choose who will enter my Pandora box. I will not be made to do anything that doesn't feel right and especially not out of guilt for not meeting another's needs. Telling him I liked him wasn't embarrassing. It was real and honest. I chose to give and share that information about me to him with no expectations on the outcome. That was me being real. I didn't have to pretend. It's when I pretend to be someone I'm not that actually hurts me.

My jaw is sore and I believe it represents anger and resentment. I dreamt of Jarod twice last night, I was talking to him about Ross, the guy I was lying next to while I was sleeping and standing in my truth. He was telling me I was cheap and easy. I felt and knew otherwise and told him so without any real care about what he thought. It's what I knew and felt that mattered. I am not a slut.

5/8/00 : I'm to ring Shianne Wednesday evening and Simon sometime. Shianne was hurt that I didn't call her when she gave birth to her son. I want to clear that up with myself at some stage because at the time when she sprung it upon me, I got very upset. We were at the pub having a coffee with Aimee when Shianne sprung her upset towards me. To cope with the fear and hurt, I went to the toilets and cried. Shianne said she wasn't fussed that I had a very strong reaction to what she had said to me. I did have a strong reaction. I felt like a really bad person and I didn't have a response to what she was saying to me. I did call her after her child was born. I did call her numerous times and just didn't get through for some stupid reason. She told me that she loves me as much as she loves her other close friends. I couldn't believe it and I told her I never knew that was how she felt. I told her I never felt good enough for her and that I've never felt close to her because of it. She was shocked and continued to reassure me that she never thought those things about me. She's never questioned herself whether or not I'm a loving girlfriend for her and vice versa. I continued to cry and we hugged and I cried some more. At some level I felt the feeling of being abused.

When I first arrived at the pub to catch up with Aimee and Shianne, all was okay. The next minute Shianne was very upset with me and I couldn't find any words to defend myself or think quickly enough to stand up for myself in response to her accusations. All that was required was a word called 'sorry' and letting her know I had called her many times. But I froze and said nothing and ran off to the toilets instead. I had actually left a few recorded messages on her answering machine and she knows that now anyway. I'm afraid now I feel insecure or 'littler' than her. I reacted to her as a child does to a parent when they are in trouble. I did nurture myself by going to the toilets and I allowed myself to have fifteen minutes time-out with God because I didn't know what I was doing. My emotions took over and I couldn't think. Shianne came into the toilets and she sat and waited for me to gather myself. That was very sweet of her, I expected her to leave, but no, she sat and waited and that's when I came out to face her with my eyes full of tears and still with nothing to say.

We all had a ball last night. Shianne and I didn't get home until 4:00 am. Gary likes me a lot. He wants to tell me how he feels, a hit and a miss I'm afraid. Last night I had a thought. Ross, if he is not ordained for me, then he'll be powerless over not having deeper feelings for me. He won't be able to meet me on the same ground. It's impossible to feel what is not there. Not his fault, it's just the way life is or, shall I say, how love is. It cuts through the feeling of rejection and I feel acceptance. God put him in my path to learn something and for me to receive some affection and love. It was beautiful and I thanked him for it while were being close, knowing that closeness comes and goes and knowing when its time to detach. To become free to receive, to give, and knowing everything comes and goes and nothing is personal.

6/8/00 : It took me twenty minutes to wake up this morning. I'm walking with Aimee at 10:00 am. I'm going to have a chat about Shianne, about what to do. I'll be calling her Wednesday evening; hopefully there'll be a twelve-step recovery meeting on during the day. Today I have a guitar lesson at 7:00 pm. I'll have to practice my singing from today till Friday before I head off to Melbourne to look after the kiddies. Dad's up. I hope he'll make me a cuppa. He's been having difficulty sleeping. I've written four post cards as suggested by the tasks in 'The Artist's Way'. I'm looking forward to reading the next chapter in the book. It's exciting. I haven't recorded my money expenditure as yet. No good. I'm pretty slack. I haven't completed my diary either for the unemployment benefits. Aimee fills it in with one hundred per cent honesty. Mine's not that honest. I'm just filling it in. I'm not looking for work, with as much enthusiasm as perhaps I should. I'm not sure. I don't have the internal nudge to look for a job. I'm trusting that I will when I'm meant to. Doing a course is probably something I can do in the meantime. I'll speak to Aimee today about it. I could go to TAFE and suss out some creative courses, such as sculpture, that would be fun.

Yesterday while I was showing Mum my fantastic painting of Bob Marley I asked her for her opinion: whether or not the painting needed some improvement. She mentioned some ideas and the big thing was I wasn't offended like I normally would have been. I was willing to learn and I wanted her advice so I could make my painting look one hundred per cent great, not only ninety-five per cent great.

I just want to say I am sad and disappointed that Ross has not contacted me in any way since

Saturday morning. Some of my girlfriends, the one's with whom I've shared my experiences that I've had with him, such as Louise, Shianne and Aimee, all felt that he would call me. But he hasn't. Deep down I know the chances are slim. Like I've said before it would take maturity, courage and humility to call. Those things I believe he has not quite developed yet. So I understand him not wanting to call me because it's easier not to. There's nothing he can do to change that. He's not my soul mate. I should say if he's not my soul mate then he couldn't really meet my needs emotionally, spiritually, mentally or physically. He would be inadequately equipped because he's not ordained for me. I would be inadequately equipped for him because I am not ordained for him. It's my ego that would feel good if he called. The man lacks substance and he won't gain it overnight. He knows I'm not an immature twenty-four year old and that frightens him. It would frighten me.

I'll need to check my insurance to see when it runs out. I believe that will be soon. Louise's Dad said I've changed, and become more beautiful with age and that I look like a model. Louise truly looks up to me and I to her. My jaw is out and it's time to look at why. It represents anger, resentment and wanting revenge, but with whom?

7/8/00 : Toastmasters are on tonight, a public speaking group, I'll have to go there and find out whether it's for me or not. The fan is on and I can't turn it off, by choice. I would be warmer if it weren't on, but I can't bring myself to turn it off. Today Gary is taking me to the pictures. I'm happy to go. I know he likes me more than a friend. I'll let him confess first before I say anything to him about it. In 'The Artist's Way' it says to accept 'freebies'. So that's why I'm looking forward to it. I need to call Jessica and speak to her about walking because I'd love to walk with her.

I had my first guitar lesson last night and Shelly says I have a natural flow with it. She's even given me some U2 and Oasis music to practice; fantastic. I'm looking forward to playing it. Okay, I'll turn the fan off because my fingers are freezing. I mentioned my Bob Marley painting to Shelly and she was thrilled and said she'll commission me to do a painting for her. I need to speak to another artist to see what they ask for money wise when they are being commissioned to do a painting, because I have no idea. I'm wrapped about doing some artwork for her. I've sent off a message to Debbie about going to TAFE to see if they sell oil paints. I can't find any in my Hometown. I'm going to see what course they offer there. I've thought of art, language, acting, and sculpture and a course sounds like a good thing for me to do. Apparently while I'm on the unemployment benefits the courses are free. Liz says it's fantastic what I'm doing and that it's very positive.

I'm working for Kevin on Friday for six hours. I can do it if we start early. I'm excited about seeing the kiddies (Matilda, TJ and Maude) this Friday. I adore them and they adore me; we'll all be so thrilled to see each other. I'll bring Matilda's favourite song by Nelly with me as a gift. Mat's will love that. I have washing do and unpacking.

Dad wants to go shopping and I have no money to shop with. That's life.

Portia rang me last night. She's twenty-four days sober today and she's putting in the footwork. She's so gorgeous. I love her to bits. Mac rang me yesterday as well and he'll be feeling crook today. He's out at his Mum and Dad's. He'll need to pick up his things at some point from the 'boys'? house. I went to bed thinking of Ross and I found that tiring. Things have worked out for the better—they always do. At times it doesn't seem that way. It's a matter of seeing it from the light of love, the light of acceptance. "God I pray for Ross and Max, both I see as suffering from emotional pain at some level and that would include

Jarod and Jezza. I pray for Your Love and Your will in their lives. I am thankful for the love and lessons they have given me."

8/8/00 : Dad came along with me to Toastmasters as a visitor. Dad and I really enjoyed ourselves and we're going back for the next meeting. The room was full of lovely people; they were interesting and provided useful information in their speeches. It felt like a safe place to be for me to learn how to speak publicly. David speaks in front of hundreds of professionals and I'm truly amazed. He must be a little nervous.

Shianne rang last night and apologised about her behaviour the previous Saturday afternoon and that evening. I'm glad that I got a chance to encourage her to go to a twelve-step recovery meeting where there is a Fellowship of people that can help her. I was taken aback with her honesty; a level of honesty I haven't heard her express to me before. Yes, there is a level of awareness that she hasn't seen yet, but all in good time. She can see that she can't support her husband the way others want her to, in regards to his addiction. I did the best I could to explain that her husband needs to look after his own problems by getting help himself. I suggested to her that the best way to support her husband is to find support for herself. It is now in her hands if she chooses to get help. She will obviously take or leave my suggestions and that's okay with me. The important thing is that she called and let me know what was really going on for her and that is a beautiful thing.

One of Linus's friends informed me of an employment position that was opening soon—helping people who have schizophrenia. I'm happy to work in Melbourne at the moment but not in my Hometown. The job sounded good because it's more about encouraging others by involving themselves in activities. It's fifteen dollars an hour, casual rates; it sounds okay. It's being involved in the psychological field and I would need a certificate to do that kind of work. He said he'll let Linus know when he finds out more information about it. Gary likes me and so does Chris, the radio guy. Funny how it's all hit and miss. I could send him a message letting him know all I can offer is friendship.

What I want and need in a man is height, good looks, a strong and healthy body, yummy eyes, great hair, intelligence, humility, character, spirituality, and maturity, a funny sense of humour, an open mind and honest heart. He needs to be caring, healthy-minded, and have close friends around him and who has integrity with the people in his life. I want him to be compatible with me, loving, thoughtful, considerate, emotional, self knowing, fun to be with, easy to be with, not controlling, accepting, sporty, creative, spontaneous and manage his life and money well. I understand that what I need in a partner is rare. But to have that in a man and to have that man in love with me at the same time would nearly be impossible. I'm going to be the black board out of Mr Squiggle, "Hurry up, hurry up."

Dad's about to get up. I want a coffee. I'm going to play my guitar, practice my singing and organise photos of my artworks for my art folio. How exciting. Turn this bloody fan off, it's freezing! I offered Aimee to come along to a twelve-step meeting this week, which means I have to go, good! TAFE is another place I can get to today.

9/8/00 : It's unpleasant waking up in the mornings and feeling low, sad and bad about Ross. I even have difficulty going to sleep because I'm thinking negatively about him and about what happened between us. I judge myself as being weak because he's not someone I knew well or got to really like and I'm still affected. I remember someone asking me if I found him mentally stimulating and I said yes at the time because I liked him. But if I honestly ask myself that question now I'd have to say, no. I didn't find him mentally stimulating at all. When I have spoken to him in the past these thoughts would run at the back of my head. He's a high candidate for being a problem-drinker, he's a man on his own island; he's reserved, he's a perfectionist, he has to be looking good all the time (which I know out of personal experience indicates a level of insecurity) and he's very young-minded. His aim in life is to be a professional party animal on weekends. He drinks copious amounts of booze. He lives with a spiritually sick woman, associates with a very sick men and tells me I'm not an ex-problem drinker. That's like telling someone after they have disclosed they have a terminal disease, such as cancer, that they're making it up and it's all bullshit. I pulled away from my friends, Monica and Mason for that exact same reason; they didn't believe that I was an ex-problem drinker. So I knew in my mind that Ross had a long way to go to mature and grow. There are other ways of finding out whether he felt the same as I and it's called talking about it. I failed to talk about it, and how I felt. Linus knows what he said to me in the bedroom. Linus said next time he sees Ross he'll give Ross a hard time about it. I'm powerless over what Linus chooses to say or not say. I can ask Linus not to do or say anything. I know he'll want to say something to protect me. I'll leave that in God's hands. I sense the true reason why my friend called me the other night was to find reassurance from me that I   wasn't going to tell others about her kissing another guy, especially while she is married; more so than apologising for their behaviour. I can understand that's where they are at.

So why do I feel this sadness with Ross? I do not know. God knows. I'm aware of how I feel. I accept it and the action I take to heal this pain is to not look at him to blame and know that we both wanted two different things. Being straight with Mac last night was my way of being responsible and healing the part in me that was hurt by Jezza's inability to be honest with me about how he was feeling towards me. I told Mac I do not like him more than a friend and that if his feelings grew to be more than that then we would have to end our friendship. Why? Because I feel uncomfortable with someone who likes me more than a friend when I do not feel the same. I cannot meet Mac's needs and he cannot meet mine and that's the way it is.

Linus says there are so many men in my life he can't keep up. Oh, my goodness. I'm not running out of men in a hurry. I'm single by choice. I'd like a really good looking guy to be very wonderful and, well, to fall in love with me. That would be great. If I'm going on my journey and become successful, I will most likely be attracted to someone in the field I'm going to be working in. I won't be held back by a man. God won't allow it. The challenge is to be free of financial poverty, which feels like the hardest thing for me to break.

I've broken...God has broken my drinking, my smoking, my drugging, my stealing and my eating disorders. That's all been made possible. So anything from here is possible when God is running the show. God is abundant and joyous. I'm to enjoy my day. I'm to explore. I'm to be open. I'm to get ready for what God has in store for me.

Right now I'm to get ready and head off to Melbourne. I'll take Dad down the street to the library. I can sing. I'm going to sing my lungs out in the car to practice my singing skills and build my confidence. It's mind over matter.

Linus wants to put an artwork of mine on his arm as a tattoo. I'm doing a painting for both Shelly and one of Mum's friends; things are happening all around me. I will clear things up between Kevin and I.

10/8/00 : Hey book! How are you today? Go on and ask me how I am. I feel like crap. I ate fattening and sugar-filled foods all day yesterday and drank plenty of coffee. Yeah, not good. I'm carrying yucky stuff about Ross, yucko. I feel heavy-hearted. I wish it would go away. I suppose the upset with Ross only happened a week ago. I did get my hopes up. I feel sad and let down and I'm fearful that Linus will say something to him. Ross will be going back to England soon. I feel so heavy this morning. Today I can eat healthy refreshing foods that will help lift my mood.

I am not looking forward to helping Kevin today. Wait for it, I reckon he likes me more than a friend. He's not telling me so that he can keep me as his friend. I can feel it. If there's an opening in the conversation today I'll tell him about my gut instincts with him. I'll bloody say something.

I had the worst sleep last night. I'm not used to sleeping with anyone any more. It's not just Ross. I didn't sleep well in Lana's bed. I don't believe I fell asleep until after 2:00 am and I woke at 6:00 am. My gut feels big and have I got anything good to say? No, fuck off! I don't want to be here doing this heavy-duty work with Kevin any more.

Okay kiddo, snap out of it. Pull yourself together. Today when you've finished the day's work, tell me then if it's not for you. During the day remind yourself the money you earn today will pay for petrol to get home, your singing lesson and your guitar lessons for the month. The weekend work with the kiddies will go towards your car's insurance. On Monday you'll hand your unemployment form in and drop your tax paper off to the accountant. Okay, now your finances are on the way.

Mac rang you yesterday. He spoke to you about how he felt about going to the rehab in Wagga Wagga. It's a big step for a scared man.

Yes, you have five minutes to finish writing, put on your shoes, and grab your bag and guitar, race down the stairs and jump into your car. Get to Kevin's shed and off to work. Remember to smile at others, remember to wave and say hello to others with every chance you get. Remember to ask how Kevin is going. Notice the beauty in the day and don't forget to take your phone. Be grateful for what you have.

Ross is okay. Give him to God. Remember things have worked out for a reason. Okay, last Friday night was not a pleasant experience. You don't emotionally shut off like you did that night for the sake of it. YOU honoured him by honouring YOURSELF. You didn't blame or point the finger. You didn't lie or carry on. You stayed in your truth and told him that you really liked him more than a friend, risking not having him at all. You just weren't in it for the sex because he matters to you and because you matter most. You're a loving woman.

11/8/00 : I'm looking after the kiddies this weekend. I love it. Sam came down stairs, grabbed two bowls and poured milk into the cocoa pops. He made breakfast for both himself and his younger sister Stephanie. How fantastic! I've never seen him do that before! He had this idea while I was having a shower. Stephanie says to me: "Sam said that you were going to get mad at him for making our breakfast and you didn't!" She had the biggest smile on her face, full of great surprise. Sam is now going to let the dog out and get dressed without me. We'll see how he goes. This is a big thing. Stephanie is grabbing her Barbie gear. They are so gorgeous. Sam looks so spunky. He's wearing his choice of clothes today, I only suggested he wear a skivvy as well. Stephanie made sure she had matching undies and singlet to match her Barbie outfit. They're so delicious this morning.

I've asked Lana to drop off the magazines so we all can do collage together, that way I get to complete my homework for 'The Artist's Way' and the kids get to join in and have fun whilst being creative. They love cutting, ripping, pasting and smearing. Yesterday I waited for the kiddies (children I looked after in Yarravillie a few years ago) for an hour before I chose to leave. I left at their front door, three packets of lollies and my Nelly CD for them to sing to. They will love it. Sam wants to head off to Chadstone now; the sooner the better he reckons. I'll ring the shopping complex to find out what time the bowling alley opens, good idea 'Ninety-Nine'. I must drop off papers to Liz's Mum and organise piano lessons for the kiddies for tomorrow morning. Perhaps I could reward them with a movie on Sunday.

I'll send a good luck message to Max because his soccer finals are on today. I don't know what he thinks of me dating his friend. He can think whatever he wants. I've known him for some time. Our friendship is strong enough to carry us through any hurdle such as dating his friend, surely. If not, then that's okay, that's life, that's other people's feelings. Kevin said that I have nothing to worry about. I needn't think I've done anything wrong. Lana says Ross is a tosser; I have to agree. He did act like a tosser. Both Lana and Kevin said that Ross's ego was hurt and that he did only want sex and it's great that I found out sooner, than later. Len didn't pressure me into having sex or pressure me to kiss him. He was happy to go without sexual intimacy until it felt right for me. Now that's a man with esteem and self-confidence. Ross said to me that he wasn't very mature, obviously he wasn't. The heaviness has lifted.

I've hurt my body by over-munching on junk food for the past two days. Today I'll be selective and gentle with my body when it comes to food. Time to go and take the kids out for a great day of fun.

12/8/00 : I'm waiting for my water to boil. I had another eating day yesterday. Thank goodness I stopped eating at 8:00 pm last night. Yep, I had junk most of the day. It is concerning. As soon as people start mentioning I've lost weight, I feel bad for receiving the attention and my thinking goes into, 'I can eat whatever I want whenever I like.' This is not true. I like my body better thinner. This food thing is scary to me. It gets out of control and when I try to control food, the more I try to control my eating—the more I eat. What I resist will persist. Acceptance is the only way out of this way of insane thinking for me. It's the only way I know how to calm it down. I need to accept that I'm eating more than normal for me. It could be overeating for so many hidden reasons and that's a psychologist's job to work those things out, not a job for me. So I'm going to carry a little extra fat and that's okay with me. I'll focus on who is with me and live in each breath that I take.

The kids and I are going to do some drawings for their grandmother today. I have flowers for her. I'll blow up some balloons to make it really special just like a party. She will love it. I loved my day yesterday. They are so adorable. They both left voice messages on Marika's answering service. Marika will love it. Stephanie and Sam loved the movie Marika gave to us to watch. My cute little munchkins.

Today the maintenance man is coming over to fit the washing machine at 9:00 am. At 10:00 am the kiddies have piano lessons and Max's team play at midday today at the Bob Jane Stadium in Albert Park. During the time the kids are at piano, I'll prepare snacks then we'll go and play at the big wooden playground where we'll indulge ourselves. Sam will love it. Straight after piano lessons, we'll go. I'll also need to get dressed, dress the kids, and tidy the house. There are things I need to do and places to go.

I called Dad yesterday morning to say hi. I'd like to go to the Prahran meeting tonight, but it makes me feel nervous thinking about it. I also promised Kevin I'd go to the pictures with him tonight. Surely after the meeting we could go. It's only an hour meeting today; we could catch an 8:30 pm film.

Oh, I better bring in the papers before I forget. I need to race to the toilet. Yippee my body is functioning again. I'm back to normal. I'm walking with Ruby this afternoon. Great, my body needs some exercise. Sam's running around upstairs, hmmm… What am I going to wear today? I might wear my shorts, white top and Nike jumper. That'll work. I don't want to wear a tracksuit today.

13/8/00 : The maintenance man offered to put in the new expensive washing machine while Liz and David were away. He sounded very convincing that he knew what he was doing. I was doubtful for a while and he said he could put it in without stuffing anything up. My mistake, it turns out that by him installing the machine and not the appointed mechanic the warrantee may now be invalid. To top it off the washing machine is still not working for some unknown reason and the door doesn't open correctly. Plus he scratched the shit out of the marble floor, which I didn't notice until five minutes before they got home. I fucked up. I didn't feel good about this at all and I can't turn back time and I can't blame him, which I'd love to. I should have said 'no' and trusted my instinct to not let him mess around with it. I hope he realises what a stupid thing he did when he speaks to Liz this weekend. Liz's Mum even thought it was a good idea. I couldn't know the unforeseen consequences of allowing him to install the machine, thinking he was doing the family a favour.

Ross's relationship with his father is only a few visits every so many years and that picture comes up strong whenever I think or see him. Ross's drinking concerns me especially when he says: "When I have one I cannot stop." Really! God knows what he is doing. He has removed Ross from my life for a very good reason and maybe that's it.

14/8/00 : Feeling good, even about the unknown sadness I feel toward Ross. I'm going to be busy between now and Wednesday. I've been invited to a gallery this Wednesday night and I want to go. Take up the opportunity that is there. Shelly says I don't have to do anything, only to go along and see these things. Whether I'm ready to present my art to others is my decision and not something I can do before I am ready. I must learn how to crawl and then walk, she says. It's just what I needed to hear. Tamika offered the idea of looking after a girl for three and a half days a week for three hundred and fifty dollars—that must include sleepovers as well. That's not a bad income. For me I can't allow it to get in the way of any of my activities such as guitar and singing.

I'll call Warren to find out the name of the person I have in mind to play the part as Sir Gerwain in the play I want to put on. Tamika's going to be the cursed sister, Linus can be the woodsman and all we need is a King, a Queen, some women and some knights. Aimee said she will do the makeup, hair, and perhaps will be another woman. Debbie could be a woman too. Tamika was thinking that the kids from Wesley House could make the backdrops, create donations for food, etcetera. It can be a charity evening and the funds could go to Wesley House, and if the kids put a bit of work into the play they, in turn, would feel good about that.

For Mum's birthday we could get Mac's musical gear for karaoke or even he could perform for us and sing Frank Sinatra. This is good thinking—using what we have to get us through. I know many wonderful people who'd love to help, including Scott, I'm sure he'd be happy to make donations to our play. We'll advertise his business by being a sponsor. He'd love that. Organise costume hire and offer free advertising. Good thinking 'Ninety-Nine'. So many things to do. I'll certainly keep busy. Perhaps I'll call the crew tonight to catch up somewhere to talk about it further—dinner maybe. I won't be here any other night. I must be back for this Sunday netball match in the afternoon. I need to find an outfit for the wedding in Queensland that Liz and David have asked me to come along to. I also need to organise Mum's fiftieth birthday today. There's no time to waste. I'll need to decide on a venue suitable for the party.

15/8/00 : I sent an express parcel in the post to Liz for her birthday. Dad and I visited Uncle Albert and Aunty Gayle yesterday and we gave Bethany some beautiful flowers just to say we love her. Uncle Albert showed me a photo of himself dressed up in the most spectacular clowns outfit with his next-door neighbour when he was a kid. Uncle Albert has never bothered to ever show me anything before in my life. They work together. They're a great team. Bloody hard work though.

I had a long and gritty talk with Dad about the way I run my life. He's not happy how I choose to live half my time in my Hometown and the other half in Melbourne. He feels I'm not living up to my end of the bargain. It was hard but I reminded him that the reason he left Joyce, the shop, and his home in Kerang, had nothing to do with me. It took him a fair while to comprehend that what I was saying to him was true. I told him my life is not going to be run by anyone else and that I'm changing. I feel I've paid my dues by running around meeting everyone else's needs my whole life. Right now it's time to do what is right for me. Do what feels good for me. I believe if I do what feels good and right in my heart then I'm doing my Higher Power's will for me. I told him also that with the pressure that's put onto me to be or do a certain thing, he will find I will only rebel and do the exact opposite. That's the way I am. I hate having his expectations placed on me. I need to know I have a choice and I chose to do things because I have the freedom and the want to do it. It was a new way of talking to him, yet it was important for me to know that he understood what I am about and what I will and won't do. I told him he basically needs to get off my back and needs to concentrate on living his own life to allow me to be the person I am and that things will be okay because it's all in God's hands.

Howard came over yesterday at a time when Dad and I had only just arrived home from our walk, and in that time, I had called Mum to drop around as I wanted to spend time with her. As Dad was walking out the door I asked Howard to leave so I could spend time with my Mum. I noticed he was on edge, looking lost and insecure and I didn't know what to do with myself. I felt a little bad for asking him to leave but I just felt that uncomfortable having him around. I do know he likes me a lot. How I know this is because he disclosed his feelings to me several months ago. I can't stand it. I'm not going to analyse it. I know I would have been people-pleasing if I had said nothing to him. This is my home and I have the right to govern who is and isn't in it. If Dad were here then that would be okay.

16/8/00 : Sophia's insights and new information for me gave me goose bumps and the hairs at the back of my neck rose as she spoke to me (which, she says, represents a psychic reaction to the truth). She says it's a radar from the Higher Knowings' guidance. Wait for it. Intuition is the purest form of intelligence. Sophia said I am very intuitive and that Dad needs to trust my gut-feeling about Howard. She said I am to help the sixteen-year old girl because I have a good feeling about it. My radars, God's guidance and intuition, can never be intellectualised. It explains why sometimes I shut down or go mentally blank when I'm with intellectual people. I'm to trust myself. Carmen has been saying that over and over to me—to trust myself. I didn't like Jenny's boyfriend. He is not a warm person. I found that he changed and became very hard and distant like a drifting piece of cardboard. I felt like a little girl.

Courtney says that she's always wanted to play pool, as well as buying and riding a motorbike. She told me that I don't have any of the traits of sex/love addiction. I felt relieved because if anyone would know, it would be her. She did say though, that many of those people who have been attracted to me, show traits of sex/love addiction, more than the norm. It would take up five minutes of my headspace to deal with these people and they have no right to do that to me. I felt sick to the guts when Gary sent me a message about boning me with his car, which didn't make any sense (after his first attempt of calling my mobile). I couldn't be bothered dealing with crap like that so I didn't reply. I need to make it clear with these guys, Tom included, that they have no chance of being with me. I feel that Gary is still hanging on even though I've sent him a message saying I have no feelings toward him. I added that I treasure him as a friend; I should not have said 'treasured'. For me, I would get what the other person was saying and accept it and let go of the fanciful idea of being together. I get paranoid if I behaved like Gary with Max or Jezza. Note that I've let that go completely; I don't entertain the idea of being with Jezza at all. I haven't said anything to Lana about it, it doesn't feel right. The idea of working for Wesley House feels good.

17/8/00 : It's a beautiful day today and I have lots of things that need to be done. I heard myself talking in my sleep last night saying: "Don't tell me you moved for nothing or that you're too old because that's just an excuse, you've got to give it a go." That's a straightforward statement. I meant it. I discovered in my dreams that I need to drink plenty of water.

I want to buy some new sneakers—the blue one's I saw yesterday, I don't know if they'd be any good to wear. They would go well with my skirts, shorts and tracksuit pants. I don't know how much they are. I can't allow myself to splurge.

Today I'm to sing and practice lyrics. I'd like to catch up with Ruby, I feel comfortable singing with her.

My tummy has been upset since last night after the Indian food. Chris took me out to dinner, the radio guy. I spent about twelve dollars on beer for him and the games of pool we played. He paid for the delicious meal. I need to allow myself to spend on entertainment. I have one thousand dollars in the bank. I laughed when I saw the amount, looks like I won't get much from social security this week. I like having money in my bank. I feel yucky in the tummy—it's gurgly.

I spoke to Howard last night and told him that I like him as a person but I cannot ignore the fact that I feel terribly uncomfortable around him. I also said that I need space from him and that he's not to drop around unannounced. I supported him to call by phone if he needed to talk with Dad and organise a catch-up outside my home. I apologised for not saying anything earlier when I could have, and putting him in an uncomfortable position due to the lack of communication on my behalf. He was understanding and was mainly relieved; he was happy to talk about it. I believe it was easy because I trusted the nudge to call him when I arrived home from being with Mum. Mac's been calling us to let Dad and I know where he is at and what he is doing with the rehabilitation. He's doing one step at a time and he's doing well to do that much.

I began taking Portia through the Steps yesterday. She wanted a sponsor so that she could be shown through the Steps. So I offered to take her through the Steps and discovered that she's wanted me to but was too shy to ask. God showed us how and we began. We started the Fourth Step together. Two hours later I let her know she can finish her list on her own and to call me if she needed or wanted to.

18/8/00 : Mum didn't like me saying 'no' to her yesterday. She tried a guilt trip first, then thought bullying would work and then how about 'coming over to my place to talk,' she says. I don't think so. I don't feel safe in her territory. She walked through my home door and stood over me as I sat at the kitchen table. I didn't waiver on my decision deciding not to meet up with an ex-boyfriend of hers who showed strong signs of attraction towards me in the past. I find it totally unacceptable that he has made comments about my beauty and then wanting to meet me when Mum and him were seeing one another. She accused me of being disrespectful, to which I said: "That's your judgement of me saying 'no' and you are putting your friend's feelings before your own daughter's safety." She walked out in a huff. Yep, go, I'm not chasing you. She also threatened to kick me out of her home if I ever chose to visit her because she believes I don't respect her friends. It didn't bother me so I let her know by saying: "Kick me out Mum, I don't care; if I don't like them then I probably don't want to be with them at your place anyway." She didn't know what to say when I asked her how she felt about his comments of me when he was looking at my photos. Her response was, 'uncomfortable' and I told her that I felt ill then, and that I feel ill about it now, and that she cannot intellectualise my feelings. She didn't like that either because she didn't like my tone. I explained to her that it's simply the sound of my anger and hurt, they are just my emotions. She made a comment about how I'm saying 'no' a lot to her lately and I came back with, "I wasn't allowed to say 'no' as a kid, and as an adult, I can say 'no' as many times as I like." She didn't like that one either. One picture came to mind. It was that she ignored her sickening gut feelings when she walked in on my Pop ruffling my covers when I was only six months old.

I feel I have been an unprotected child because Mum's interests were more important than the safety of her children. One of her boyfriends called me up when he was pissed and sexually abused me over the phone commenting on my breasts when I was only thirteen years of age. So, no, I do not want to meet a man who is a drunken thirty-year old who's keen on my Mum, who's not interested in getting sober and who fancies me, fuck off!

19/8/00 : Aimee is going to drop around at 10:15 am so we can go together to clean out a hairdressing shop for her to run in a couple of days. I'll take along my stereo; can't clean without music to sing and dance to.

I saw Ross last night leaning up against the bar with his mate. Louise was holding my hand pulling me through the thick crowd. We exchanged hellos and he kissed my cheek. His mate then thought he'd have a go as well, and leaned over and grabbed my hand. I instantly pulled away saying 'no' to him three times (obviously he didn't hear me the first two times.) I smiled, looked at Ross and continued on my way. I don't kiss just anyone. It was my small moment in saying Ross matters to me and I'm happy with whom I am but I do not want to talk. Remember it was left in his hands to do something about us and he did nothing with it. I would've loved to chat, I wish him the best of luck, and I leave him in God's hands. If I'm meant to say anything to him then God will set up another situation for that to happen. Otherwise I'll spiritually send my blessing to him.

I saw my girlfriend, Emily, from Queensland in my dreams signing up for a course at Melbourne University. She looked ill and she looked at me and said, "I've been drinking vodka." I said with great concern in my voice: "You look so ill, do you have a problem with the drink?" I was woken by my alarm. I also remember saying to her: "I knew I was going to see you." I've been experiencing many synchronicities and they have been leading me to audition for a play called 'The Beat' put together by the my Hometown Theatre Arts Group and the rehearsals are on today. It feels too soon to begin acting. I'll find out where it is and cancel the time I selected to go to audition. I'm too frightened. I don't know if I can cope with the rejection, especially after the incident with the real estate agent, I don't think I'm strong enough. I'm cautious about how I present myself to strangers while I'm feeling so vulnerable.

I must ring Wesley House this week about working with the new kid. I need to sit and pray. I'm to be still and know what is right for me to do. It's tempting to take up any kind of work that comes my way. I must remember that Dr Wilmot told me to only take up work that I really want to do. I'm finding that distractions are all over the place.

Tom wants me to go into business with him. It's not my thing at the moment because I'm focusing on art, singing, guitar, and playing. I played the guitar at Louise's party last night. Mac commented on how amazing it was to see me catch on so quickly. He says I have a natural knack. Linus rang Dad last night whinging that no one's doing anything for his birthday; he doesn't know that I've organised a little surprise party at the pizza restaurant with his mates and netball crew.

20/8/00 : It's Linus's birthday today, he's twenty-eight. His party last night went really well. Seventeen people rocked up and Eugene called at the restaurant from London and wished him a happy birthday. It was a moment I will never forget as Mum ran over to see Linus's reaction to hearing Eugene's voice. Linus was stoked. The chocolate and orange cake didn't last long...poor Petunia missed Linus blowing out the candles. She was on the toilet at the time. It was so easy to organise the evening and it was such a success. That was a practice run for Mum's 50th surprise party I'm organising for next month. It's a shame I haven't heard from any of Mum's family; they all live three hours drive from here. I'll ask Mum's sister to get it together with Mum's family and she can let me know how many are coming. I can't afford to make STD phone calls to chase them up. A part of me wants to scrape them off the list, bugger the bastards. I'll let them know there are at least five spaces available for sleeping including the floor here in my home. There are fifteen people coming so far, not bad. I'll organise Eugene's money for Mum to go on a trip away, a dress for Mum for the party and an experience of a lifetime to jump out of an aeroplane—all of that will cost about five hundred dollars. There's no time like the present.

I spent two hundred and twenty dollars on a beautiful black evening dress for Mum and some stunning earrings and matching necklace. I had the money.

I'm working for the kiddies this Saturday and I'll be able to go to Melissa's going-away party and pick up the remains of my stuff at the flat in Prahan. I believe I have an appointment on Monday with Dr Wilmot. I cancelled my audition with the theatre group and the lady on the other end of the phone suggested I go along and have a look what goes on. So I took Dad and Tamika to hold my hand. Blow me down, Tamika and I ended up singing and dancing to the song 'Dancing In The Street' as an audition for a dancing role. I received a phone call from the director to say that Tamika and I were successful and explained we would have had many more dancing roles had it not been for the large amount of talented people who she'll be putting in the show. I don't care, I am thrilled to be in it and my heart feels complete knowing I've made the first step towards performing on stage. I feel whole about it. I belong on the bottom, I feel safe to work my way up. Tamika is rapt and I'm rapt all over.

21/8/00 : I'm not full of spark this morning. I do hope this changes. It's dull and boring feeling this way. I had a restless sleep. I dreamt a young woman came into my home without being invited in. I asked her to leave and of course she wouldn't, so I ended up calling the police but it was too late. She had her hands around my neck strangling me. I must be wary of danger about to come my way. I'm to trust my instincts and not to rely too much on what I can see. I'd like to buy some sneakers. I can pay for the pathology and one hundred dollars towards the phone bill, three hundred and eighty five dollars for rent; so out of six hundred dollars I'll put some on the incoming bills. I gather I won't get too much from the unemployment benefits. I may need to hand the diary in on Friday in Melbourne. Sunday afternoon would be a good time to do some shifting. I can't be bothered shifting Lana's stuff as well. I don't know how Kevin does it.

I'm finding concentration difficult today. I'm not looking forward to guitar practice. I think my strings are out of tune. I'm excited about going for a walk with Dad. I feel ready to talk to Mum again. I want to go to TAFE to buy paints for the art works for Mum's friend and my guitar teacher. I'm looking forward to seeing Carmen to tell her about the auditions and that I sang and danced getting a dancing role in the show. I'm looking forward to ringing Doreen about my paints and organising a catch up with her this coming Wednesday. Great, I have enthusiasm for these things. I will do these things that create joy within me. I will also read Chapter Nine from 'The Artist's Way', which I've suggested for Howard to read. He's been suicidal because of the depression he's going through. He accepts that he has it, so what he did was resign from the job that he's tired of doing and is now having time off and he says he feels wonderful about that.

22/8/00 : It's quiet in the house. It's been a fabulous morning. It's already 10:30 am, and I've been talking with Lana. It's easier to talk with her when she shares about herself and her life, instead of hanging onto what I have to say all the time. Dad noticed Tamika's partner's drinking the other day while visiting her. I didn't and hadn't noticed the drinking until Dad pointed it out. The three times that Dad's seen him; he's been drunk (during the day), including a Monday night! Dad asked me how Tamika tolerates it. Well she does come from a drinkers' home. It's amazing that she's coming along with me to the theatre group, netball, and wanting to be a part of the play I want to direct. God's got it all worked out. I never imagined I'd be helping Tamika in this way, but it's wonderful that I am.

I can go along to a twelve-step recovery meeting tonight after rehearsals. I'm hoping that the meeting will only go for an hour. Must pass on Aimee's business card to the theatre group. They may need her hair and makeup services. Mum just dropped by and dropped of Liz's Mum's writings. It was easy to deal with her because she was being proactive and not waiting for my initiation on what to do. I must make others feel uncomfortable being themselves seeing that they are waiting on what I have to say first so they know how to be. I hate that in myself. I'm like that to Liz. I wait to see how she is and what she has to say before I do or say anything. I do it to Con sometimes, Aimee as well, and with other authoritative figures in my life. So it's about acceptance around feeling uncomfortable around 'scary' people; the ones from whom I feel I need to seek approval. I pray for healing around that stuff. I pray for self-approval. My God approves of me all the time because His love is always there for me, non-judgmental, all knowing all the time. I don't know. "God please let me know what action I can make when I'm around people who I feel insecure around. I abandon myself when I doubt myself. I accept other's ideas of me, instead of staying as myself for myself. How can I change? I am willing."

I'll need to call the restaurant and confirm that twenty-five people will be seated at Mum's birthday dinner. I wonder if Eugene has put the monies in my bank account for Mum's present. I will need to organise that next week. I want a big pin board so I can see my projects, the things I'm to do, and where I'm at with everything. I'm such a Bizzy Lizzy.

Doreen's coming around to drop off my pants she mended for me. She's gorgeous to do that for me. I'd like to drop in to see Aimee at her hair studio to see what she has in mind for the salon and to thank her for generously cutting and colouring my hair.

23/8/00 : The last time I looked at the clock it was 2:00 am, I just couldn't fall asleep; it was awful. It wasn't a problem waking up. I bloody couldn't wait to get that over and done with. It's the third time that that's happened to me when I've needed to get up early to work for Kevin. I just can't fall asleep during the night before the working day. I have to drive to Melbourne and start work at 9:30 am. No, that's not fun. I have most things I need already packed into my bag. I'm ready to go. My mind just wouldn't shut up last night. Fucking arsehole, bastard, cunt of a head. So lucky me, I've probably had three and half hours sleep. Fuck, I need more than that. I'm not impressed.

I sang in front of twelve people from the supermarket I use to work at last night at the Indian restaurant with my guitar. Doreen encouraged me to do it, so I did. I couldn't play very well; my middle string's broken. The women said that my singing was really good. My voice has improved a great deal because I couldn't sing most of my life and here I am helping Maria strengthen her singing by giving her the tools Carmen has taught me. Once she learns how to sing, my oath, she will be great. So I gave some hints in the meantime. The lady who owns the restaurant said she knew a band looking for a female vocalist. It would be funny if it were the same people who had the advertisement in the paper I saw the other week. They sing heavy rock, I don't know what songs that would be exactly but I'm willing to have a go. I wonder if they would be willing to train me. They used to play at the Aussie on Saturday nights. It would be so much fun singing in a band. It's in God's hands. If I'm meant to sing then I will; if I'm not then I won't. I'm happy to go where God takes me.

I got up and danced on the chair that I was sitting on once the meeting had finished. The director put on music and told everyone to get up to sing and dance to have some fun. Assuming that the eighty people that were there would have done so because they're actors and singers without any inhibitions, I jumped up and danced. People laughed at me, especially my girlfriend Tamika. I couldn't believe only one other person did the same as I. I thought everyone was going to join in. The guy at the door who was helping run the meeting said, "Wasn't it you who cancelled your audition?" "Yes," I replied with curiosity about how he came to know that. "It's always the extraverted ones who are the shyest!" He says with a smile. I noticed a tall, handsome guy who walked past me at the beginning of the meeting. I observed him as I sat quietly for that moment on my chair. He looked about twenty-four years old—too young. I'd like a guy who is about thirty to thirty-five years old.

24/8/00 : I had a great sleep here last night at Lana's place. Lana and my girlfriend Ruby are moving out today and tomorrow I'll have a good reference from our estate agents; fabulous. I'll visit Marika today. Carmen's performance is next Thursday, which fits in perfectly because I'm taking off with Liz and her family to Queensland the next day.

Ruby and Lana have both left the house; I'm here on my own. Kevin and I watched 'A Knight's Tale' together, we loved it—absolutely loved it. He doesn't have much fun. I drove from my Hometown to Melbourne between 7:30 and 9:45 am; we worked until 5:30 pm. We showered (individually of course!) and completed the day with dinner and a movie at the pictures. It felt so good. I loved Heath Ledger's role, loving the woman pure and true. She wasn't perfect and he loved her no matter what and loved no other. I know it's the movies, but I want someone in my life to love me pure and true, like no other, and I want to love that man pure and true, like no other. She tested him, just like I do. I no longer see my tests as necessary. I test men so I can pick out the fakes and the phonies because not anyone will have my heart and soul. I will allow someone in soon enough and that someone will have my heart, freely and soundly and he will treat it with great care and know that it is God that holds our two spirits together. What will not hold us together will be money, possessions, rules, 'have-to's' and obligations. I am delicate and

336

sensitive; an angel. I will wait for my angel. I will not be impatient. I will wait for a man with a beautiful heart and soul; one who will not need to destroy my heart to have his satisfaction. "Hi there! God, it's You who keeps me single and free through such busy and changing times. Nothing is wasted. Nelson Mandela says: "We people are not afraid of failure, we are afraid to shine and it is our duty to God to shine." I love that. Thank you for reinforcing that today."

Dad doesn't like, or feel comfortable at Toastmasters (public speaking group). I feel it too. "God please direct us. Let us know if we are to stay for the people or go for ourselves and find safer grounds to let our spirits soar. There is significant difference between me shining in the theatre group compared to Dad and I not shining at Toastmasters. It lacks heart and spirit. I can put my energies into better use. Say no, then perhaps we can choose again if we want to." I need to go and do a poo. My footsies are frozen.

25/8/00 : Good morning! Feeling a little resistant getting out of bed. I went to bed early, around 10:30 pm, and the girls arrived home five minutes after I put my head on the pillow. I didn't get back up to be sociable. It took me a further hour and a half to fall asleep, that's why I went to bed early in case I found it hard to fall asleep. I was to meet others after the twelve-step recovery meeting. I couldn't find a park after twenty minutes of searching for one. I was tempted to call Tom to see what he was up to because I was feeling the want to go out and find a cute boy to fix my loneliness. I came home before 9:00 pm and did some of my homework out of 'The Artist's Way'. Yes, I discovered, I was feeling a little lonely and sad about how things have changed with Jezza after reading my morning pages as required as part of the tasks in the book.

Portia puts her Mum before recovery and tells me I'm not going to understand the feeling of losing a Dad and the hurt and grief of her Mum. I didn't say much to her yesterday. She apologised for the way she was, "There's no need to apologise," I said, knowing she's the one living in hell. She got me with her clever words where I had nothing to say and whatever I said came out wrong to her ears. I understand it's only so she can drink some more. I'm powerless. I don't have the power to change her. She knows that and she knows why she keeps busting. I have the same disease. I have the same emotions and thoughts. I am no different. It helps her to make me different and separate so she can keep on drinking. I'm the one who needs meetings. I'm the one who needs sober people around me to stay sober.

Today everyone will be out of the flat. A time has come to an end. I have tingly feet. I'm off to see Liz, and the kiddies today. I hope the fridge magnet wasn't too overboard that I sent Liz in the mail for her birthday. I wonder what we're doing today? I'm going to wear my daggy pants. Liz hates my shoes; so do I. I didn't find a pair of sneakers yesterday. I found a gorgeous bag though. It was one hundred and nine dollars. Too much for me to spend, so I left it in the shop knowing that one day, I will have money, just not right now.

I'm playing netball tomorrow. I have Melissa's party on tonight. Kevin and I are picking up the desk, table and chairs depending on whether or not Lana wants them. I have my guitar teacher's painting to start. I could start it on Monday. I would feel better about that if I did. I need a big corkboard.

It's 7:33 am. It's time to finish this off, get dressed and go. I'm afraid what I have to wear isn't good enough. Yes I'm silly. It's a gorgeous day outside. I could get Linus to write a play. In the meantime, by the looks of it, Ruby may take a bloody long time to put hers together. The guys and I would have fun with Linuss' play; we could be waiting forever for Ruby to get her act together.

27/8/00 : I missed a morning writing yesterday. When Margaret explained to me that when she criticises another group or member, what she really is doing is breaking the first tradition of the twelve-step recovery program. The common welfare of the Fellowship must come first, all members are important, all meetings are important. Judging and criticising any of those things is not in the best interest of the twelve-step program. I want to write to Portia an email. I have some things to say to her. I can still help by being honest and truthful with her. I need to vent.

Lana rang informing me that the wedding I'm going to with Liz and David is black tie. I need to find a beautiful dress to wear. I need casual sneakers and a dress shoe. I need to buy a canvas for my guitar teacher's painting.

Gee whiz, I became very stressed yesterday. I didn't expect Gary and Chris to rock up at netball. Linus's friends were there also supporting us. I felt sad because I have lovely men who would die to go out with me and I feel disappointed that I don't feel the same toward them. I feel guilt for not having the same emotional attachment. It reminds me of what I don't have—a boyfriend. Somehow it feels like I've failed. I know I haven't in reality, but my emotions tell me otherwise. I enjoy being independent, free to do what pleases me. I see some kind of weakness in me for wanting, or even having, a relationship, but also see failure in singleness. They are all negatives. If I turn my thinking around, it's by choice that I am single and I have inner strength to be with myself until the time that I may meet someone that I feel whole and complete with. When and if that happens it will be God-sent and I will be grateful for such a love in my life. I will feel blessed.

I need a calendar to hang on the wall to put my daily activities on. I need to restructure and cut out the things I do that are time-wasters. I'm cutting out my participation with Toastmasters. I'll keep going to the theatre, continue looking for volunteer work, give about four hours a week to the kids at Wesley House, and continue creating artworks.

I need to wash my car and give it a good clean out, wash my clothes and clean out the laundry. Put time aside to paint and time aside to write. I need time to complete the tasks in 'The Artist's Way' and I will do that today. I need time to write these things down and I also need to fit in exercise and my weekly artist date. I have not succeeded in doing the 'artist date' (a two-hour period spent by myself doing something that is rewarding and joyful to me) for the past ten weeks. That tells me something. I fail to spoil myself, to allow insights, and I hinder creative imagination during these times. I am committed to change and nurture myself today.

28/8/00 : My guitar teacher gave me her guitar. To buy new they are around four hundred dollars. I didn't know how to say thank you. I couldn't believe that she gave it to me. In return I'm to do her a painting and I hope I do it really well. I hope I don't let her down. So far I've had three free lessons. I hope it'll be an expensive painting by the time I'm finished with it.

Oh, I feel crook in the guts right now. I have a few things to do today and I need to have them done before 3:00 pm, that's the time I meet Wesley House's coordinator and a guy called Terry about volunteer work. Tamika wants me to work with a young girl called Angela. She's sixteen and she's apparently very creative. I believe we could help each other.

Went to a twelve-step recovery meeting at 8:15 pm last night that helps me from being affected by alcohol and half way through I was asked to talk, but I chose to sit and listen. I will continue to listen until I feel comfortable, safe, and ready to talk. I am sensitive knowing that others know my parents. I can only

338

trust that some may use it against my Mum and Dad even though I know it's an anonymous Fellowship. So until I really feel its okay for me to share, then I will but only at that time. I enjoyed it very much. One thing I overheard one woman sharing with another was, "Call that person you are angry with in the morning and after a good night's sleep. We are better for ourselves and for those we want to discuss things with when we have rested." I'm not feeling close with my Mum. I feel estranged from her. I feel different towards her and it feels wrong, I don't feel good about it. At the same time I do not want to force myself to be nice, so in the meantime I'm wearing the shame of not being an affectionate, overly helpful, caring daughter. I feel sad about this and it's gotten worse for me. I'm afraid of her dying and then I'm left with this guilt for not being close with her. In the reading at the meeting it talked about withholding sarcasm and being quick with the tongue (criticising or speaking badly to others). I don't enjoy being that kind of person so why do I choose to be that way? Choose another way.

Dad brought in a hot cup of coffee, yummo. I'm already feeling sad that I'm finishing 'The Artist's Way' in two weeks time. I don't feel I've done enough of it. I'm a workaholic. I've worked that much out. I'm not great at having fun, especially by myself. I used to be great at it. I'm willing to change. I'm afraid of doing something on my own. Fear means False Evidence Appearing Real, as Marika would say.

Okay head! You've got lots to say tonight, I know what you're like. You keep me up until 3:00 am and wear me out for the next day.

Yes, Liz rang about speaking to an artist that she knows. It's great and scary but you need to remember what Carmen said, and that was that I don't have to do anything I don't feel I'm ready to do and I'm to do only what feels safe and right for me. Ring Liz when it feels right to do so; God will present an opportunity. Yes, cancel your name at the door for Carmen's show for tomorrow; you've got a great memory and you will remember to do it. Portia and Mac are in God's hands. God is big enough to look after them. Keep Friday free so you can begin the guitar teacher's painting that day. Have fun and go shopping with Mum tomorrow for her party dress. Buy what you can afford. I can't call the man Mum loves to invite him to the party, because I can't get my hands on his phone number. "God please provide the phone number if you want him to come to Mum's birthday party."

Angela is God's child. "May I be myself when I'm with her. May she learn to love and trust herself."

There are lots of things to think about. I have an upset tummy. I haven't called Helen to congratulate her for getting married. In regards to Mum's surprise birthday party, it doesn't matter if her Mum has told her about it. Everything happens for a reason, that's just life.

Is there anything else you want to share, head? I'm afraid of over doing it. This is as bad as it gets. Well, remember when I couldn't stop eating? I went to great lengths, such as reading the Bible to find relief. The internal pain of anxiety, grief and fear was so overwhelming. I was starving, purging, lying to others and myself; I stole from others (food, money, clothes and alcohol) and I people-pleased everyone to have love and acceptance in my life. How I used to dishonour myself by not meeting my own needs and wants and not trusting my gut feelings. Not saying 'no' because I wanted to keep others happy. God has me in his hands. I need not stress. I am not running the show.

29/8/00 : For the wedding that I'm going to, I won't buy a dress. I'll ask if I can wear something of Lana's. I need to save my pennies. One reason to work for Liz and David is to earn money, not to spend it. More importantly, I need money to buy something for Mum for her birthday party. We're going shopping this morning. I think it took me around four hours to fall asleep last night. It makes me angry.

I think to myself what a waste of time lying in bed doing nothing. I don't have time to waste. I could be doing something constructive. I didn't want to work at that early hour in the morning. Dad went to bed early so I felt I couldn't do anything in case I would wake him. This insomnia is driving me nuts. I believe coffee would be a contributor to the problem. It surely wouldn't be helping.

I don't know what I'm going to wear down the street today. I want to wear something nice, stuff looking like a scallywag. My eyes are weeping.

Well, I'm so busy I haven't had time to paint my guitar teacher's painting. It's not good enough. Today I have time to buy the materials for it. I'm not looking forward to spending so much money on everything. "God, help me buy bargains today, okay buddy?" My guitar teacher shared that she gets depressed on weekends. My advice to her was simple. I suggested for her to accept it and say to herself, 'This is okay with me. I've been like this for a long time. Why do I expect myself to be any other way?' Last night I couldn't sleep due to stress, no other reason. Nothing seems to be helping. I need to follow up all the little duties for me to feel relief from the overloading things I need to do. I am committed to not letting anyone interfere with my Friday. I'll call Lana and ask her to come Saturday, not Friday night. Friday I'm dedicated to keep it free just for myself, to do what I please. So, I need to get the little things organised so I have nothing to do other than paint on Friday.

I look forward to seeing Angela on Tuesday morning. We'll be going to Nathalia together to do art and pottery. I'm looking forward to meeting Pauline who has the art workshop there.

I'll have a shower this morning and put some music on. Enjoy drinking a cup of coffee. Easy does it today. I'll need to drop off Ruby's plants to her that she left at the flat. I'd like to do that before I do anything else; if she is not home then I'll sit them on the veranda. "God, I offer myself to you to build with me and do with me as Thou wilt. Please relieve me of the bondage of self, that I may better do your Will…" I can't remember the rest. I'm okay now. I feel at ease. Not stressed; all will be done in good time.

30/8/00 : I haven't called Liz about going to her friend's exhibition. I haven't yet cancelled my name off Carmen's list for her show tonight. I still could go, take a girlfriend with me, and come back Friday. Don't know if I have the money, hmm, I'll think about it.

I started painting again yesterday and it felt good. I decided to sign my pieces of work with my whole first name instead of having it shortened. It was a suggestion by Jenny's boyfriend who's completed an Arts degree to have the same signature on every artwork I do.

I'll need fifty dollars for petrol and twelve dollars for a ticket if I decide to go and watch Carmen perform. Can it be done? I could bring Marika home with me on Saturday. She might like that.

I slept well last night. I've found reading 'The Traditions' of the twelve-step recovery program very helpful for my everyday living. They are something I've been needing in my life; to be able to read and understand them. The only thing is, I need to concentrate because I find them not that thrilling. What happens is I'd rather become sleepy than continue reading it.

Ring Aimee for a haircut; maybe Aimee might want to come to Melbourne. There must be someone who's keen on going with me. What about Debbie? Keep on writing. It's not quite dark enough. Hey, if Debbie comes we can buy some paints in Melbourne together. Now that's thinking. I need to make some phone calls and get things organised.

Rehearsal was good last night; Tamika and I were chosen to sing solo if they wanted us in the chorus, no, I mean one of the solo lines. We didn't get chosen the second round and that's okay. We have to go along Monday at 7:00 pm and Wednesday at 6:00 pm for dance rehearsals. The dancing choreographer asked what experience Tamika and I had and my response was, "Just disco dancing, like what we do when we go out." The choreographer of the show looked very concerned. I thought it was pretty funny.

I'm a little slow with it all today. I haven't gotten up to open the curtains and I'm not easily filling in the pages. I have yet to begin my homework with 'The Artist's Way'. I need to do them today and tomorrow; otherwise I won't get them done over the weekend.

I told Linus about what Nana had done, telling Mum she wouldn't be going to her surprise fiftieth birthday party. I couldn't keep it to myself. I didn't need to spoil it for Linus or Petunia because they thought Mum was none the wiser. I've spoiled it for them now. I wanted to share it with him that our Nana is nasty and cruel. I wanted to whinge and criticise her so I told him, hmm. Well, I can always organise something else for Mum another year. She still doesn't know the finer details of the evening. I can't be bothered today, I wonder if it's a nice day outside. It's around 9:45 am, a good time to get up and make a cup of coffee. Yes, I'm drinking enough water, I've put on some weight, not a great deal but I can feel it. I haven't gone overboard on the food but I did overdo it three weeks ago.

31/8/00 : Tamika's partner asked me to take him to a twelve-step recovery meeting, and if not, could my Dad take him along. I was afraid to say the wrong thing; I was frightened of scaring him off. It's like I've forgotten that I'm an ex-problem drinker and how it harmed me. He asked for help and I know that takes a lot of courage. I suggested Dad would pick him up Monday at 7:00 pm and take him to the Euroa meeting. Tamika's partner knows he drinks too much and that he's not going for Tamika. He wants to go for himself. He knows he hangs out with drinkers and he doesn't feel good about it. I never imagined in my wildest dreams that he would ever ask me about the program. How it came about was when I brought out my guitar (I bloody chipped it and I'm not happy about that) and we (Tamika, Debbie, Jessica and her new partner) sang songs. Debbie could not believe that Tamika's partner was singing. I got a bucket of warm water with disinfectant to soak his feet in. He had bad fungus on them. Maybe it's because of the kindness and care I gave him and the efforts I've made involving Tamika in netball, theatre and my play. He has certainly softened toward me compared to how I've known him to be in the past. He comes along to watch Tamika play netball. He went out of his way to buy batteries at the supermarket for the camera at Linus's miniature surprise birthday party. I've noticed the small changes in him. God works miracles.

I'm enjoying reading the 'Twelve by Twelve, Steps and Traditions'. It's very useful. I feel out of touch with what to say to other problem drinkers such as Mac and Portia. I'd like to go to a twelve-step recovery meeting tonight.

I saw some sneakers that I liked for one hundred and fifty dollars. I asked Dad if he could buy them for me. I felt like a goose telling Liz I was scared of calling her artist friend. She simply asked me if I wanted to go and visit his exhibition, it was no big deal and she said she didn't understand my fear. Oh well, I'll drop by Tamika's and ask her if she'd like to come along to a twelve-step recovery meeting (those affected by alcohol). I've organised my haircut and colour with Aimee and I feel good, relaxed and not stressed. Not like last Monday, Tuesday, and Wednesday. That's how I am when I return from Melbourne, like it's a big rush and I'm running behind schedule. There's too much to do and not enough time. It felt so good to paint and I will do so again today if I can. My studio is coming together slowly and looks kinda cool.

1/9/00 : Today's the big day where people will be coming from Melbourne and Swan Hill to celebrate Mum's fiftieth birthday. The only things I need to do are to put the cake together, borrow nail polish and a black cardigan from Tamika, organise Dad to pick up Louise and do my Mum's hair for the evening. Oh, and also pass on the earrings to Linus and Petunia to give her on the night. Some lovely red lipstick for her would be the way to go. I hope to remember to read what I've just written down to know what I've got to do.

I have a twelve-step recovery meeting to attend today but I don't know if I'll go. I don't want to stress out about tonight in any shape or form. I'm a little worried about money and whether I'll have enough. It's been an added expense in my poorer days and I trust God is providing what I need, so it's all good. I'll also call my cousin back. I'd love it if she could come and party here with me in my Hometown. That's something she hasn't done before.

I need an opportunity to talk to Tamika about the effects of living with a drinker and invite her to a meeting with me. It's a cloudy and windy day and I'm happy that all is well and okay. I'm happy with the number of people who are coming. I may only have twenty-one attendees, not twenty-five, due to some cancellations. If I get all that's required done this morning it will relieve me of all stress.

I'd like to sit down and practice the guitar today; I'll take it to the girl's place for a jam session. They'll still be at Tamika's if I get there soon enough.

I need to remember to buy Dad a Father's Day card and something little for him. I'm walking with him in the morning and shouting him breakfast; that'll be fun. I'll wear my blue trackie pants, blue top, and my awful sneakers. I'm down on my luck looking for a pair of sneakers for myself. Maybe I'll find something today, who knows? Most likely not.

Debbie is a spiritual woman who is in tune with the spiritual world. Debbie, Tamika and I all have similar, if not the same, spiritual understandings. How unique and wonderful that is for us. I had a great time with the girlies last night, getting ready to go where the swingers reside. We then went on to the Aussie and Yahoo bar. I had a ball dancing with Tamika.

3/9/00 : I just want to say it's okay to say no to my Uncle if he asks to live with Dad and I. It's simple. I don't feel good about him living here. I get the feeling he'll ask if he can.

I have a black head under my nose and I'm going to squeeze the hell out of it when I finish writing. I don't feel good about not filling out the unemployment benefits diary. It should've been completed and handed in by now. I didn't do my writings yesterday because I didn't want to go into my bedroom and get my writing book and pen, where my Uncle was sleeping. It wasn't worth it. I'm picking up an uncomfortable vibe from him. I always have since I was child. It—the feeling—has never changed.

Mum's fiftieth surprise birthday party at the restaurant was an absolute success in every way. My favourite part was going over to Mum's and doing her hair, preparing her for the occasion. I had her convinced that there was only going to be Dad, Linus, Petunia and myself who will be there by telling her throughout the week that everyone invited had cancelled. It's called damage control after Nana spoiled the surprise. She looked beautiful in her elegant black dress with diamanté droplets. She was breathtaking when she walked up to the very large table of her friends and family—all twenty-six of them. Linus came up to her as soon as she arrived at the table with her mouth open to the floor and put on her earrings and necklace bought by her girlfriend (my guitar teacher) and Linus and Petunia—the one's that she had chosen at the shop but I told her I couldn't get them due to financial shortage. Louise was taking photos left, right and centre. Mum felt like a movie star and I felt like a million dollars. Mum, Dad, her two cousins, one of my cool aunties, Louise and I, all went along and boogied down at the restaurant 'til 1:00 am. My Uncle and the cool aunty are such groovers and I discovered that they met when my aunty was twenty-one and my uncle was twenty-eight and they have been married for eighteen years. They're such a good match. They have chemistry between them.

I ran into Jarod at the Yahoo bar. I wanted to talk to him. So we stood there and talked until the place closed at 3:00 am. No one thinks that's anything fantastic. Friends of mine who were there were giving me the 'What-are-you-doing' face. I thought to myself, 'I'm an adult woman and this feels right for me to speak to this man. I feel safe and okay about it.' It's been five years since I last spoke to him. Jarod's hair is receding. He says he likes his comfort zones along with his ouzo and cokes, and smoked away with Winfield Gold cigarettes. He tells me I have a good head on my shoulders and that I'll do well no matter what I do. I told him I've been single for some time, because he asked. I've noticed I feel strong when I tell people that I'm single, hmm. He understood I needed the five years of silence between us to get through what I needed to get through. Iggy, his friend offered me a cocksucking cowboy (alcoholic shot). Jarod was quick to say to him, "No, mate she won't have it." I liked that. He gave me the 'puppy look' many times. It did absolutely nothing for me. I wonder if that day will happen where Jezza will give me that 'I'm innocent' look and it will do nothing for me? It's such a ridiculous facial expression. It worked for him in the past with me but it's so yucky now. It's like I'm to fall over heels because of it. I felt good about myself as I spent time with Jarod, not because of what he was saying to me, but because I could see how far I have come and that I know I'm a good person. He is now my friend and not my enemy. God has me where He wants me.

4/9/00 TUESDAY : I'm spending time with Angela. Yesterday she played up and was self-destructive. The feeling I got was that she was grieving for her therapist. Dad said that she's very fragile and she becomes very attached to people and to things. I trust that God knows what He's doing with me in her life. I hope I am of some use to her and to God. Today all is well. I'll take her to Nathalia to see Pauline for three hours if she's available for that amount of time. I'll take along some apples. I wanted to bring the guitar to have a jam session but we can listen to the radio instead.

I painted a little painting yesterday and it felt good to do. I did some singing as well and I belted out Amanda Marshall's, song called 'Rain'. I had the tape where I sang the same song with Carmen; that session I began to cry. I have come a long way. My voice is maturing and I find that encouraging.

What am I going to wear? I thought I could throw on my Calvin Klein trackies and my black skivvy with my white jumper. Oh, I can pick up my mended cord pants today. I'm going to need Dad for more cash for my shoes. I'll pay him back when I return from Melbourne. I aim to get the newspaper to do my homework for the unemployment benefits.

I learnt a new song and strummed with my guitar teacher last night and I'm very excited about it. I look forward to practising the song. I know I'm being a perfectionist with my guitar playing. I feel good about that because that's the way I am. The reading in 'The Artist's Way' is good in the eleventh week. I write because I want to. I paint because I want to. I sing because I want to and I play guitar because I want to. My value as a person is not contingent upon money. The value is what I give it from within.

I need to do a poo. I can borrow a dress from Lana for the wedding, how wonderful. I need to do my hair today because it's looking a little shabby. I'd like to finish off the sides of my two paintings. I can begin my Mum's friend's painting. I need more white paint from TAFE; hmm, what else to talk about? It's time to fly and get moving. I need to do Dad's errands today.

Kevin dropped by on his way to Queensland for his holidays. It was good to see him and see him do something spontaneous. We walked around the lake and he bought us foccacias for lunch. We sat on a big wooden cart that looked like it was from the Flintstone's. We proceeded to swing on some swings and then he took me for a spin in his new 'beaute' ute. It's all good.

5/9/00 WEDNESDAY : I feel bad that Tamika saw me wearing brand new sneakers after she shouted me lunch, knowing I'm low on cash. I felt guilt and shame, like a bad child, and I caught myself justifying why I bought them. It felt like I had lied and she caught me out. I had to keep reminding myself that I am adult. I made the right decision for myself. I am not answerable to my girlfriend, despite the fact that she bought me lunch for the day.

My pink toenails look pretty; they match the pyjamas Liz bought me in Noosa. I look forward to singing, painting, and practicing the guitar today. Sometime during the day I'll go to the bank.

Working with Angela at Wesley House does consume my mind. I need only be there for a few hours on Tuesday and I'm not to get too involved; easier to say than to do. I'm a little resistant at times toward Angela because she, at times, behaves like a spoilt child. The therapist picked up that she's not travelling well. One could say that she's unpredictable every day. There's a lot of focus on her reactions to things.

Next door has 'I Remember You', a beautiful song. My hair is all over the place. Kevin is sending me many more messages on my phone than usual. I'm weary of Kevin despite what he tells me, "I'm a friend to him and nothing more." Sorry but he can't hide the 'more than friends' emotions because I don't feel comfortable being touched by Kevin or his new comment, "You're beautiful." I used to have many men around me because I liked the attention and it was great for my bullshit ego. Now I don't like the uncomfortable feelings inside of me that I experience when I'm around them. I don't particularly enjoy being around men I'm attracted to because I change and act strange, and I feel yucky because I think I'm making them feel yuck, the way I feel around blokes who like me.

I found Ross very immature and inappropriate that Friday night in his bed. Not many men truly attract me and when they do they lack substance. I've heard someone say at a meeting once that the acronym for fear is Fuck Everything And Run, or Face Everything And Recover.

It's great that Portia shared with me what she was feeling and thinking the last time we caught up in Melbourne shopping for sneakers. I told her about my new understanding of the first Tradition; having feelings that I'm separate and how I invalidate others with criticism and judgement. Portia says she admires me for what I have done, whatever that is. She doesn't feel good about herself and she finds it hard to understand why I like her and how I could have possibly liked her in the past. She says I give her hope.

I need to pray for Angela. God has me in her life for a purpose; it's important I don't become distracted. I need to remind myself I am a volunteer. I will let her know I'm not about being tough. I'm not going to pretend that she doesn't scare me or pretend I'm God and that I'm super-human. I'm about being me, about being real, being honest, open and caring. How she chooses to react is her business. How I choose to react is my business.

6/9/00 THURSDAY : It's a beautiful day and I feel good to be sitting on a chair in the sun and writing. I've decided to go to Melbourne Friday morning. I'll call Lana and let her know. We can have a catch up in the morning; have a cuppa in Williamstown. It's great that she's moved there, it's such a relaxing, friendly place and I love it.

I ran into an old girlfriend of mine, Sarah, whom I met in a nightclub in my Hometown at the age of eighteen with her Mum. She had her two gorgeous children with her also. The eldest boy has grown into such a little spunk. I look forward to dropping around and being a part of their lives. He's so cute. Ten years has gone by so quickly.

I feel I need or I could write with some descriptive, passionate words to describe my life. It's not my thing to write like that. I'm straight down the line. I found myself singing a butterfly song about Angela in the car yesterday. I made it up on my way home from my casual walk down the street. It's a part of my tasks in 'The Artist's Way' to do a 30-minute stroll. Angela's having a party at 2:00 pm today, I'm not going; it doesn't feel right for me to go. In a way it feels like I'm rebelling against supporting destructive behaviour. I enjoy our one-on-one time together. I lent her two CD's with the songs 'Let it Rain' and 'Angel', along with a letter with angels on it; to encourage her to listen to music that will touch her soul, not corrupt her mind. I do hope she'll return them. I can only cross my fingers. In the action of me lending those things to her I hope to pass on an unspoken message of 'I have trust in you' and 'I care'. The other idea behind it was to encourage her to be with her Higher Power, the one that loves her, to help soften her, to break down the hard walls. I wonder if I can teach her how to appreciate and look after what she has. It's not going to hurt the ones who have created such pain in her. I'm willing to work on it.

I went to a twelve-step recovery meeting (affected by alcoholism in others) last night and I was wondering why I was there. I'm at peace, I've come through the shithouse, but I have a message to carry to the women who are there, who are new and who may need hope. They, like I, become too focused on the other person. I'm like that with Liz. I find I'm a people-pleaser around her. She knows I'm growing while I'm away in the country. I'm not so predictable as I perhaps used to be. I hope I can be more like myself around her and her husband. He's so intellectual, it's sometimes extremely uncomfortable being around him. I don't stress about it. I accept it and know my feelings of being uncomfortable will pass.

As I was sleeping I was woken by a rustling at the end of my bed, a scuttling in an 'L' shape. I froze, I couldn't move, I was petrified. I opened my eyes—they were bulging by this stage—somehow that's to help me see more of the monster in my bedroom. I couldn't hear anything so I leapt to the light switch and flicked it on and saw nothing as usual. It sounded like a scurrying mouse. I checked under the bed and nothing. My last dreaming thought was, 'I'll call Portia on my mobile.' That's when the noises began. I felt a spirit beside my bed creating the noise and I felt it didn't want me to call Portia. I'm not into spirits by the way, it's just how it felt and it was a strong feeling.

7/9/00 FRIDAY : I'm off to Melbourne today. Yes, it did take me until after 1:00 am to fall asleep and I've woken at 6:30 am. I wasn't agitated as I am normally because I accept that I don't sleep well the night before I go to Melbourne to work with Kevin. I will have a quick shower this morning. I don't know which jacket to take. Decisions, decisions.

I had an absolute ball with Angela yesterday. I lent her my cousin's guitar to practice with. We went through my childhood drawings, which was a scream. The crazy thing was, that while we were laughing about how I had written out the lyrics to the song 'What About Me' to give to my Mum when I was seven years old, on the radio another girlfriend of mine requested that same song to me! My radio jockey friend, Chris, played 'What About Me' on air at that exact moment! I showed Angela the dance routine that Tamika and I were shown at rehearsals, she was amazing and we are an amazing team. I thoroughly enjoy being with her.

Just thinking if I need to take anything with me for Monday, but no, I don't. I'm afraid I'll forget something for the trip. I don't have enough room in my bag to fit all the clothes I've selected to travel with me. A process of elimination is in order here. Do I have time to continue writing the following two pages? I do want to get up and have my shower. I don't want to forget anything for my trip. Filling out the unemployment benefits diary is very important. I do feel like a robot when I write. It's not poetic at all, thinking that I should write poetically. I will miss my guitar and painting while I'm away in Sydney. I can take my voice with me everywhere I go. I so look forward to seeing the kiddies. I forgot to call Debbie. Lana's cousin starts work at 7:00 am. Keep on writing and fill up the pages.

I met another young girl from Wesley House and I felt that she was so fascinated by me. Her eyes sparkled and glowed when she was looking at me telling me I'm very funny, over and over again. Her spirit was glowing. I could see it. The other adults, or workers, should I say, were just being boring typical adults. They were outside having their hard-earned smokes, talking between themselves. It looked boring. So I brought out the stereo, turned up the music, and began to sing and dance with Angela and the other young girl. I felt like a ray of hope for these young girls. I felt I was an example of a happy, fun-loving person who is free and able to do so without any substances or approval from others. God has brought me to my Hometown for so many reasons. I'm so glad I followed my heart to come here. All is going well and my spirit is soaring. I'm being creative, useful and happy. All my needs are being met. I'm a blessed and fortunate person. God has brought me a long way. "Thank you God, let's go and do your work, buddy."

8/9/00 : It's nearly my birthday, only a couple of days left, I'll be twenty-six. I'm leading up to my twenty-seventh year. I'm bloody nearly thirty! How time travels by so quickly. I'm at the Quay West Hotel in Sydney with Liz and her family; all is going well. I adore the kiddies. We have so much fun together. Sam's currently up watching TV and Stephanie is sleeping. The kettle's boiling. I'm going to make myself a delicious hot, sweet coffee. I wonder what we're going to be doing today. I'm afraid if we go swimming that my hair colour will fade, and of course I don't want it to.

Yes, it's difficult to write and this pen is fading and I'm a boring storyteller. I haven't worried about what I write or how I write since I started writing four years ago. I suppose now I expect some effort in the imaginative area as seen in 'The Artist's Way'. Well I'll keep writing.

I'm afraid what I'm wearing tomorrow isn't right. I have a couple of outfits to choose from. I need to accept that what I have is good enough, remembering I'm here ultimately working and helping out and that I'm not the centre of attention. I'm a beautiful person and God loves me; all will be well. The main thing is that I'm there with and for the children, even though I'm seated at a separate table.

What will I do for my birthday on Tuesday evening? Perhaps I could organise the girls and other friends to catch up on Friday or something. My birthday bashes never turn out well. Only a couple of friends end up coming. It's so embarrassing; it's not so much now, but it used to be so devastating. I'm hanging out with Angela the morning of my birthday.

I forgot to collect the material I promised Pauline (Angela's art teacher). Oh well, I can call her and ask how much she charges to make a canvas. I also didn't tell Debbie which paint I love using. I can send her a message via the phone to let her know.

What will I say to fill in the last page? Oh, I forgot to call Mum for her birthday yesterday, I'll send her a message via the phone. I'm boring. Maybe I don't allow myself time to write and time to write poetically.

At this moment I just want to finish and snuggle up to Sam.

I think I dreamt of that guy I liked, Ross, I don't remember what happened. I do remember Tamika saying this, "Oh, you're here to help me out, not to work!" My reply was, "Yes, that's right, I've been in pain and I've worked out how you get out of it." There you go. My toenails are straight, clean and healthy. My hair is all over the place and I look forward to washing it.

9/9/00 SUNDAY : It's the wedding day and I've decided to wear the glitzy, high neck top with Lana's flowing black skirt. My legs are hairy but I don't think many people will be looking. How important is it?

I just had a thought about the program that helps those who are affected by alcoholism in others, that I can share my wisdom and strength there. I thought I didn't belong and had nothing to offer because I haven't spent much time in the meetings. That program is the same as the original twelve-step recovery program I attended, and I've been using the slogans for years, for example, 'How Important Is It', 'Easy Does It', 'First Things First', 'One Day At A Time' etcetera.

I can't share about my current pain because I'm not going through any and that doesn't mean I'm useless, a fake, or a show off. It means God has worked miracles in me. It's time to share with others how I came from feeling bad to feeling peace. It's called sharing hope. I use the program that deals with being affected by alcoholism in others more than I realise. Another reason I participate in those meetings is so I can be an example for my girlfriends who are affected by drinkers in their lives. They don't find it easy to go at all; they're young and they believe they have all the answers. In the meetings is where I show my humility and down-to-earth nature. I'm quiet and rather shy.

My Dad is a humble man. I'm discovering more and more how patient, tolerant and intelligent he is. God has blessed me with a beautiful father, considering his father was a sicko, a paedophile. My grandfather was a very sick, sad man, and it's amazing how my father survived and turned out the way he has.

The room I'm sleeping in looks out over the Sydney Opera House and the Sydney Harbour Bridge. It's a truly beautiful and spectacular sight. I'm a little distracted by the kiddies. Stephanie and her tinkling coins follow her everywhere she goes.

I really want to be with a guy who is as good looking as Pete Sampras. Yes, I suppose I want to lift my self-worth and self-esteem a little. Later, when I'm more confident in my ability to sing, play guitar, paint and write, I will most likely associate with people on higher ground; not that they are better than I or anyone else, but they are generally well groomed, intelligent and financially stable. For example; a guy who 'hoons' around town in his hotted-up car is really not my type, nor is an over-sexed guy who's full of ego and pride. No thank you, that kind of man is not my kind of man. I'm happy to be with my friends, family or spending quiet time by myself, rather than be with, or be worried about someone who's not for me.

I've noticed I'm more creative with the kiddies. We play, draw, swim, tickle, giggle, sing and dance a lot together. We know joy from our heads to our toes. Liz says the kiddies have been fighting at least four times a day along with Stephanie's daily tantrums. During the time I've been with them they have had none of that kind of behaviour. I've perhaps been able to help them focus on having fun and the more important things—such as making the most out of every moment together.

10/9/00 MONDAY : It's been a lot of fun here in Sydney with the family. The wedding last night was wonderful and everyone looked fabulous. The groom wrote and sang a beautiful piece of music and played the piano for his new wife. I found that wedding ceremony and reception traditions very romantic, full of fun, dance and song. I wish I could have that kind of amazing celebration as part of my culture. I wonder how I could make my wedding as beautiful?

I'm so at peace within. I remember going away with Liz and David's family for the first time and needing morning readings on the toilet. I would rise earlier before the kiddies to squeeze in time alone to sort out my thoughts and feelings to cope with being with them. I was full of nerves twenty-four-seven. I had to work on food management to avoid overeating, going to sleep early and having to call someone each day to help me through the day. Today I don't need to do that. Even when I'm not perfect and make mistakes I find I don't worry as much. I find Liz isn't on my case as much. Perhaps it's respect towards me. She treats me very well, like a visitor to her home.

Her mother thanked me for being at the wedding. She said that me being there made it more special. My eyes welled up with tears and they dropped like pearls from my eyelids. Liz's mother said that I felt like family to her. I told her that she is a part of my heart family. She lost her whole entire family—over seventy members—at the age of seven in the Holocaust. Today she is an inspiring, delicious seventy-one year old woman, full of substance and abundance. As Liz would say she's a very 'strong' woman. David told me twice that he wants me to come back and work for them and be a part of their family as I once was. My response was with a big smile, "All in good time, Davids."

My inner calling is to be in my Hometown. I feel right to be there. If they go overseas I hope I can tag along, that would be awesome, considering I've never been overseas before. People in my life remind me that in London families are calling out for Australian nannies and they pay extremely well. But it's not my calling to go there. I love the kiddies. I love sitting in the back seat with them. I enjoy the snuggles, the giggles, and their resting arms and legs over my body. Stephanie gives me lots of 'moosh moosh' squeezes and they are so yummy.

Yes, just to change the subject, I'm avoiding Kevin because his attention toward me rose while he was away on holiday. I don't cope well with extra compliments and messages from him, I feel he likes me more than a friend and I feel unsafe.

Stephanie has jumped under the covers at the end of the bed, giggling between my feet. How could I not love my job with these guys?

11/9/00 : IT'S MY TWENTY-SEVENTH BIRTHDAY!! Yippee! I will create my own happiness today. It is my choice to see fun, be fun, see love and be love wherever I go. I need not wait for it to come to me from others. I need not search for it either. My joy and love is abundant. I'm alive right now. My Dad is gorgeous and he is the first person I will see today to celebrate my birthday morning with. I can go and buy my birthday cake, candles and perhaps some party items. I'm spending half my day with Angela and I'm very excited about that. I've put some clothes in a bag for her to wear if she likes them. I've also got her a plectrum for her to play guitar; I've lent Eugene's guitar to her for the meantime. I'm giving her the heart-shaped chocolate that I received from the wedding. I will wear something that I will feel good in today, something bright perhaps—something happy. I will get going soon so I have enough time to check out which movies I want to see tonight. I'll invite my friends and family to come along and we'll go for pizza. Lots and lots of fun for me and everyone today.

Oh, I'd like to write out my poem for Angela. The one I wrote originally for myself, because I need to and have the desire to. I pray it's all okay to do so. I refuse to treat her the way the other workers do. She is human like me and everyone else. She is no different. She holds up the 'Help me sign'. I will give her my love as freely as others have given it to me. I am the lucky one to have made it through the other side—through the misery.

Portia rang up drunk saying I was the most beautiful person in her world. She was crying very deeply apologising that she's come to the end. She was saying goodbye for good. I'm glad she rang me because it tells me God wants her alive. If she does go to God, my heart will sing for she will be surrounded by unconditional love instead of mental and emotional torment that she lives with day in and day out. Dad suggested that I let her know she can stay with us again, to tell her it's okay to be sad and that she will surely die if she continues to live with her Mum. I rang my Mum straight after Portia hung up on me. Mum explained that Portia was in full alcoholic flight. I rang Courtney for double reassurance to see if there was anything I could do and she reaffirmed what Mum had said. I am powerless over Portia and the alcohol she drank and what state she is in. I'm glad Courtney reminded me that I'm not a professional psychiatrist or therapist and I'm to extend an invitation for her to go to the twelve-step meetings to deal with alcohol and the disease. I can encourage her to seek out grief counselling in regard to losing her father, and therapy for the abuse she has suffered in her childhood. She's the one who's responsible for doing the work. I hear that she's not telling anyone her daily stresses and I believe it will be exactly those unsaid things that will bring her undone. I will ring her today and say hello to see how she's going. I will extend my hand of love to let her I know I care and that she's not alone. God is with her right now. "Thy will be done. I am willing, ready, and here to do God's work."

14/9/00 THURSDAY : It must have been from the stress of organising parties and fitting in all the things that needed to be done that created sleeplessness. I'm not crash hot on working with Kevin. It's not the worst thing. I find the work so exhausting.

Eugene rang me this morning to wish me a happy birthday. How sweet. He's tried calling me a few times but couldn't get through as I'm never home.

I'm thinking of choosing a photo of a statue and painting that for Mum's friend. It's time that I painted on calico instead of wood. The board I'm painting on for Mum's friend is not one hundred per cent straight. I wonder if that's good enough. I need to get my hands on my guitar teacher's painting and create ideas for Debbie's painting, hmmm. I'm lagging behind. If I really wanted to I could put a hook on the back of the painting of Bob Marley and hang it up. I could touch up the painting of the birds and hang that up too. I need more hooks around the house and new curtains for Dad's bedroom. His room is very dark and it need not be that way. I could bring in the furniture that Ruby dropped off. I'm enjoying the time spent with Mum at the moment.

Its spring and it makes my heart sing. It fills every cell in my body with joy and the wanting to make love to a man that I love. Gary and I drove around yesterday. I dropped off some beautiful deep orange coloured poppies for Max's sister at her work. We drove out to Nathalia and visited some of Gary's friends at the supermarket. We casually walked along the river with yummy ice creams in our hands and when we had enough of that, we laid down on a blue crossed-patched quilt by the river and rested. After regaining our energy, we drove home again, got changed into shorts and a t-shirt, and kicked the football down the park by the lake. From there I went off to dance rehearsals. I need to find the schedule sheet and I need to stick it up where I can see it.

No, I have not completed the unemployment benefits diary and yes, I am hopeless. I do feel good about the voluntary work at Wesley House I do there and, yes, I need to look into TAFE courses for next year. That would relieve me of the unemployment benefits requirement stresses.

ANOTHER DAY : Another gorgeous day. I'll call Gary to see what he's up to. My singing has improved immensely which is great, and I don't feel like getting out of bed. I'll grab the guitar and have a strum on it. I do need practice although I'm a little rusty. I need to keep learning the songs my teacher gives me. Ruby has moved to our Hometown. I felt it was the most nurturing thing for her to do, I'm glad she's returned. I'm happy and free. I've suggested Gary look into working with the kids at Wesley House. I believe he would be great with them, especially the boys. I feel that the short introduction he has had with the two boys the other day indicated that they liked him instantaneously.

16/9/00 WEDNESDAY : I didn't get up at 5:00 am to go to Melbourne. I chose to stay in bed until 8:00 am. I missed going to the 'Breaky with Bill' meeting in St Kilda. I didn't return home from the pictures with Rebecca until after midnight. By the time I fell asleep it wasn't enough sleep for me to drive to Melbourne on.

I want to take down the photos I've hung up on my wall. They don't look good any more. Trying to make my bedroom look 'girlie' is somewhat a struggle for me. Maybe I need to swivel my bed around and I could put my stereo on the drawers Ruby gave me, what a good idea!

I may bring Portia back with me if she wants to come and sober up. She's alive and God's working his miracles with her. I had Simone call me for the first time since five to six months ago. We chatted for about an hour and a half. She's suffering from loneliness, which is a part of untreated alcoholism. The disease isolates the person from others. So I've organised to catch up with her at the Parkdale meeting today.

Keep writing. I've gone blank on what I was going to say. I gave myself an extended week on my 'Artist's Way' course. A flitter of fear came over me and said, 'I probably won't finish the course'. I will continue the week twelve on Tuesday or Wednesday. Speaking to another member I found out there are nude drawing classes on Tuesday's every fortnight for fifteen dollars with a fabulous teacher whom I'll call to find out the next class time. How fantastic. The nude drawing classes at TAFE are on Wednesday evenings when I have rehearsals on at the same time and so I won't have the time to be there.

I could return from Melbourne by 5:00 pm in time to show Tamika the dancing routine she missed out on. My life is full of fun and excitement. Wesley House asked if I were available Monday for volunteer work, it would be wonderful if they employed me on a casual basis. I haven't filled out my unemployment benefits diary. I'm so naughty.

I'm happy with the work I'm currently doing for Liz and David. It appears to be a beauty of a day outside. Sunny or not, every day to me is beautiful. I do not know what the hell I'm going to wear. I do want to cook up a storm for Dad's breakfast. If I get on with my life it enables me to leave my Dad with himself, which encourages him to do something for his own life. He's getting a lot out of the book 'In The Meantime'.

Gary invited me over to his place at 2:20 am. That's not just being friend's stuff. My feelings aren't that attached; to fall in love would be nice but it's not happening with him.

16/9/00 SUNDAY : It's 7:00 am and Gary sent me a message around 5:00 am on my voice mail. He was drunk walking home from the nightclub. Maybe he headed off to his friend's place that is around the corner and it makes sense when he said it would be quicker to walk to my place than his. I'm not in love with him. He has his hopes placed on me having 'more than friends' feelings towards him. No butterflies flutter within me when it comes to Gary. That's the way it is.

I'll head off to a twelve-step recovery meeting today. It starts at 11:00 am. I'm free to be with my Melbourne buddies.

I enjoyed being with the kiddies last night. Sam is watching cartoons. My cousin Linus did this as a kid. He got up before anyone to watch the cartoons. Poor bugger for having to go to school where he was physically bullied. I don't like how many kids are not protected from unsafe children in school. I went through great anxiety and fear at school because I was afraid of the teachers and the other students. It was so unnecessary. I would prefer to teach my own children if they had to go through what I went through.

It's taken me a while to write down the first page. It's not sunny outside and I see not a cloud in the sky. It's breezy too. I wonder what I'm going to wear. My cord jeans need to be taken in more. They are still loose because they hang too low on my body. I'd like to draw with Sam this morning while he watches cartoons to help stimulate his highly creative mind.

Louise, who had lost her tickets with the falling of Ansett, is feeling much better. Acceptance is setting in, she's discovered she is powerless over the situation and, yes, she lost four hundred and forty dollars but she realises that she is alive and well. It's not a disaster compared to the horrific tragedy in New York. I'm planning to do what God has planned for me to do today. I get a feeling that Liz and David will ask me to stay tonight to look after the kiddies. If they ask, I'll say yes.

I wish I had something interesting to say. I suppose I need to remember that this writing is for me and not for anyone else. If it's boring then so be it. The Parkdale's women's meeting yesterday was absolutely fantastic. I experienced a warm, loving spiritual presence wash over me there. It reminds of the women's meetings I religiously went to in Brisbane. They saved my life.

Maree crosses my mind as I write. I caught my thoughts yesterday and it simply was awareness around the book she's written, and how I feel she's not open to all possibilities. She's not at the level of spiritual understanding as the writter for 'In The Meantime'. I noticed she didn't mention any other family members other than her two boys in her book. It sounds like she hasn't healed all relationships with other members in her family. She can't cope with her family members. I need to write about what I know because I'm being presumptuous and ridiculous because I haven't read the whole book! Last night I reflected on the way I am about the topics of love, relationships, and life; I believe it is a part of me as naturally as Sam understands numbers and constantly thinks of them.

17/9/00 MONDAY : I'm happy, I'm so happy. I gave Lana a cuddle this morning. My life is so good. I am so spoilt. I used to be such a misery guts and today my heart sings with joy and bliss. Things have fallen into place for me. I have the best of both worlds working with the kiddies here in Melbourne and voluntary work in my Hometown. I'm a captain of a netball team, I'm a dancer in a play, I participate in pool competitions, I'm learning guitar and singing, I'm painting again, I have a psychiatrist who lowered his hourly charge so I can still afford to see him and lots, lots more.

I dreamt of my Mum, her Mum, and some other family members. I don't remember the story as I think of seeing my therapist today at 11:00 am. I wonder if there is anything I can ask or share about that my therapist could advise me on. Nothing springs to mind, so I'll wait and see what comes up out of sharing with him.

Lately I've found writing a slow and timely process. I'm not poetic.

I ignored Bob's efforts to say hello and his want for me to acknowledge him. He doesn't get it. I've told him to his face to back off and not speak to me. I even asked two male members to talk to him about keeping away from me, as his friendship is unacceptable and not appropriate in my life or in the Fellowship because he is in love with me and he's fifty years old. I'm in the program to recover, not to be harassed by men who fancy me. I know he loves me because he told me so. I thought I could handle being his friend (I did so for over a year) but I feel so uncomfortable with him that I cannot have a friendship with him at all. I felt so smothered by him following me and hanging on every word or move I made. Yet here he is saying hello and looking for some kind of response from me. At the coffee shop where members go to catch up, he sat in a position so he could see me and tried numerous times to catch my eye. I made an effort to avoid any eye contact whatsoever. He, of course, sat with my ex-boyfriend Wayne, who couldn't help himself by yelling out my name across the room over two tables of people to say hello to me. I really don't want to have anything to do with him. I was so decimated after that relationship with him, so exhausted, I allowed him to take the wind out of me. I cringe when I think of, or see, him. He didn't hear my mumbled 'Hello," Damn it! I didn't want to look at him. So he screamed out again and I gave him a thumbs-up and a smirk just to shut him up. 'Fuck off' were the words I wanted to say.

At the beginning of the meeting, my friend Tom, whom I haven't seen since moving to my Hometown, told me to speak to his hand when I crossed paths with him saying hello. I thought he was joking as I walked into the ladies room, I was busting. I came out and looked for him, but he had left the meeting before it even began. He was another man who told me he really liked me. At first I found it hard to say I didn't like him the same way, so I left it open when I said to him that I only wanted to be friends for now, and maybe as time goes on my feelings may change. Uh, uh, uh, no that is being dishonest and living in fear. So I called him a week later and explained that what I said wasn't the case and I left hope for him to be with me so that I could keep him as a friend. I apologised for not being straight with him and told him I don't have those special feelings towards him and if that meant he didn't want to be my friend any more I told him that was a risk worth taking. He laughed it off and said he already got over it. How silly did I feel? He called me back and said that wasn't the truth and in actual fact he still liked me a lot and said if I discovered that Jezza doesn't want to be with me, then he would. Hmm, I don't think he got that I don't have any special feelings toward him. A part of me felt tempted to be with him because he sings and plays guitar, he was fun-loving, tall, a good looking fella, very successful in his career. He was a well established man, who took me out to dinner to high class restaurants, let me drive his brand new Mercedes, kicked the footy together, taught me how to fly and dive a kite and had a cool blue ute and lots of other great things. When the love isn't there, all these things don't matter.

I'm tired of being with someone just because they like me or with someone who is nearly the right person for me. It's hard to say 'no' to someone who's really close to the mark and trust the Universe and my God will send someone who does fit with me, knowing it's meant to be. So I guess when he told me to speak to his hand he wasn't joking and he was hurt I hadn't called him in the past two months. I didn't call him because I chose to back away. I didn't want him to believe he was next in line to be my lover knowing that I had let Jezza go in my heart. A couple of months without contacting a friend is not a big deal, if you ask me. He certainly has high expectations and demands upon me and he can stick them right up his arse. He's not the only person in my life. I have a life and he isn't it, and if that means I made Jezza feel the

352

way I felt with Bob, Wayne and Tom then I can stick it up my own arse for being an inconsiderate arsehole.

It's an important lesson for me to learn that just because I like someone does not mean the other person has to meet my expectations and demands. It's not in the rulebook that other people have to be and do what I say. It's goddamn arrogant of me; it's selfish, inconsiderate, and immature. Love is love and nothing more, nothing less. Loving someone in my understanding is to love that person exactly for who they are, the way they are, and where they are at in their life. NO CONDITIONS. To have conditions is to chain someone down and to claim someone as yours and that is not love; that is fear.

19/9/00 WEDNESDAY : I missed a day's writing yesterday. It's easy to do when my writing becomes boring. I was thinking about if I were to be working with Angela as a residential carer, she could come along to netball, to the theatre, to my guitar lessons and participate in activities that I'm involved with as a compromise. It's a low-paying job considering the work that is involved. I could do it if I didn't have to sacrifice those things in my life that are important to me. It could be a job I could do until the beginning of next year and I would then go on with my art course that would run for two years. Marco was delighted and relieved to hear that I was painting again. "You're an excellent artist," he said. Mr Intelligent would know. I believe I know what I need to do. I ask for clear direction and guidance in regard to my idea with working with Angela. I feel I have time around this decision. I'll throw my ideas to Tamika and her co-worker to give me some feedback.

My guitar teacher brought up the topic of unemployment benefits and how people who bludge the system eventually get caught. Aarh, my heart started racing. I immediately began to think I was a bludger! Had I just been in denial the whole time? Then I remembered that I nominate all of my working hours and the money that I earn on the forms that are required to fill out. I don't know if she was giving me the hint about being 'careful'. I don't feel any need or to be particularly worried, I'll take it on as she's encouraging me to work. Dad reminds me I was willing to do three days work with Angela. I realise now that with all the good and right reasons to do the job, I feel nothing inside my heart to do it. God, does she need me or do I need her? For some reason I want to go and see Sophia. I remember her saying; "You are needed to care for this girl." I'm afraid of her acting up and then of me becoming drained, stressed out and then being unable to do the things that make my heart sing. I even thought then she could come along to meetings with me if need be. Live the life for me. Angela says I'm very intuitive; that I'm very in touch with myself and with who I am. Does God believe we can do this? I could give it a go and see how it goes even for a week. I may be surprised. I feel the need to talk to Angela about it. My fears are around it at the moment and that may be inappropriate. Yet she is the person I'm looking at sharing a house with. It may be what she needs as long as I can continue to do most, if not all, of the things in my life.

I may have to put more effort into doing things that I love doing. I'm to take my creative urge and inner desire more seriously. I'm afraid I won't write my book and that I simply won't be a successful singer. I'm angry that I haven't begun my book. I may not be that dedicated to being a performer or an actress. I can't be hurt or rejected if I don't paint the paintings I committed myself to do for other people. If I write the book then I'm in a position to be challenged by someone who knows more than I do and I'm afraid of looking like a complete fool. I'm afraid I'll be caught out that I don't have any idea about what the hell I'm talking about. If I procrastinate about singing then I avoid being expected to perform and then I won't have to end up being a bundle of nerves. I have made others responsible for me. I'm afraid of governing my own life, of being the 'boss' of my own life, so to speak.

I hurt Gary's feelings last night by being a smart arse about him being a new car salesman. He sent me a message on the phone telling me so and I replied with an apology and so he sent another and another going on and on about it and I consider that taking it too far. I'm thinking enough is enough. I've said sorry, now drop it kiddo. I feel that he's attracted to me and because of that he's affected by my comments more than usual. He's told me he's happy to be friends and that he doesn't have any extra feelings towards me! Isn't that great! Although it's little things like this that turn out bigger than Ben Hur that set off my alarm bells. I need a bit more space from the guy.

Louise is off to New Zealand to see her ex-boyfriend whom she met and went out with in London. I'll call her at some point and see how she's going. I have a job interview with Wesley House on Monday in relation to being a carer for Angela. There are some things I'm already confused about and things I view differently. The woman in charge questioned my maturity, after seeing me dance and sing with Angela. Her fear is that I hype her up and that can be dangerous in her view. I see it as lifting her spirits and creating joy in her life. Tamika shared what the manager's concerns were about me. Tamika has great confidence with my approach with Angela. I do treat Angela as a normal human being and not as a damaged kid. Tamika feels that it is dangerous to treat Angela as normal because I could then fall into the trap of expecting her to be normal.

Dr Wilmot really simplifies things for me. He helps me to bring everything back to, 'Who I am is okay'. He says things like; "Well, that wasn't so good, so perhaps you can do ... next time." or "All I see is you're being yourself." Dr Wilmot has brought out my self-confidence. Confidence can be nurtured and supported for it to grow within someone. If someone truly believes in hope then maybe another may begin to have hope in their own lives. Miracles can happen. Angela is a miracle. I do wonder if a part of her acting out toward others is a way to help her stay with Wesley House? I wonder where she goes after Wesley House? Also why is it paramount that she be surrounded with peers? Why? What's the rush? We can't stop her wanting to die. We can't stop the pain that she feels. We can give her examples of hope and reasons to live.

I have a lot to organise. Stop writing that way. I need to take doonas, pillows, my guitar and clothes to Nathalia and have it all ready to go this morning. I suppose I don't have to go to a meeting. But it was such a fantastic meeting last Friday that I simply can't miss this week. I need to drop in my employment benefit form and hope they don't ask for the diary, because I believe it's due. I could get Dr Wilmot to write a letter allowing me time off from looking for work because the pressure to find work is too much for me to cope with, hmmm, keep on writing.

Mum and I left a message for Eugene and sang happy birthday to him, which would have been at 5:00 am where he is at overseas. Yes his family is mad. Fabulous! Angela has been fantastic all round this week. I shared with Angela's full-time carer that I'm being considered as an additional carer at Wesley House. I'd prefer to be called 'a source of inspiration' rather than a 'carer'. A 'carer' suggests that there's something wrong with her when there isn't. She simply reacts strongly in certain situations due to her difficult upbringing. She is human; a young, sixteen year old girl. I'm swimming with her today at 12:00 - 2:00 pm, great stuff McGruff. I'm always dreaming and thinking about my role in her life and I'm experiencing continual conflict with Tamika and the organisation, including myself. I could be obsessed or I could call it that I'm passionate about something I believe in. What I do with Angela enhances my life because we are creative monsters when we're together. I find its great fun being with her.

Let's change the subject. Great, what else is there to say? I played a good game of netball last night as a goalkeeper. I surprised myself in my ability to defend. It's fun. Linus's taking over my role as captain this season, which I believe is fabulous. I have other commitments so I can't lead a team.

It's sunny outside and I'm sitting in bed and I want to finish my writing. I saw Howard at the meeting and I was angry to see him in my home when I returned from Melbourne. I asked him not to be in my home because I feel uncomfortable around him. I was furious. I didn't say anything to him yesterday when I had the chance. I will remind him next time I see him. I'll talk to him privately. My home is not to be visited by him. It simply makes me wild, especially when I've requested that he's not to and then he does so anyway. I simply asked Bob not to talk to me or make any gestures towards me and he does anyway. I told Tom I'm not keen on him and he's acting like a hurt boyfriend and now he's not talking to me. I gave Wayne no attention and he continues to loudly say hello to me every time he sees me, and it fucking pisses me off! If I didn't say anything to these people then fair enough. But come on, I've spoken to all of them very directly; no hidden messages. "FUCK OFF" are the words that are going to fly out of my mouth soon at them and I will continue to do so until they fucking get the picture!

22/9/00 : Yes, I'll have a shower this morning, wash my hair, wash my skin and say good morning to Pauline who has been up since 5:30 am. I'm going to be surrounded by beautiful, artistic, talented, spiritual women today. God's got me where he needs me to be.

Angela and I enjoyed swimming yesterday. She was scared about getting undressed in the changing rooms. I was gentle and patient with her and I didn't make a fuss about it. She continued to beg to find out why I didn't want her to tape the music. I still haven't told her because I don't want to put the idea into her head about taping music by Eminem. At the moment she's choosing to play the music I've lent her. She's practising playing the guitar and only one song at a time. She's quick to learn and I find she's like play dough because she's teachable, due to eagerness and willingness. I lent her a book of mine called 'Love Is Letting Go of Fear'. I really want to give her the books 'Heal Your Life' and 'In The Meantime', I believe she would love them a great deal and learn about loving herself and the process of life. She'd love them much more than the other book I lent her. Not to worry, like I said to her, she can take and tape what she wants and leave the rest.

While we were down the street another girl from Wesley House walked by us without noticing we were there watching her. Angela's face went white with fear. I don't blame her because this girl is an extremely angry young woman. Angela shared with me once that one of the other girls is misbehaving and she wants to be another way. On the way home she had a craving for lollies so I stopped off at a milk bar and she bought four dollars worth. I laughed at the size of the bag. I'm sure the managers at Wesley House would think it was a bad thing for her to do, but like I said to Angela, that four dollars worth of lollies is much better than choosing to swallow forty-eight tablets of paracetamol, which could actually cause great physical damage or death.

It reminded me of my very early days in recovery when I come to accept 'first things first.' Put down the alcohol, then I stopped taking drugs and trusted when the time was right I would let go of smoking. They all went in their own time not when I demanded it. I always want to do it NOW instead of when I am truly ready. Angela says she's quitting smoking on the eighth of October with her friend. At least they want to better things for themselves. I do wonder if it's because of my influence. I must be a strong role model. Someone they like who doesn't smoke. 'If she can do it, then so can I' might cross their minds at times.

Dad's coming out here where I'm staying with Pauline for Sunday lunch. I'm full from dinner last night; it was a delicious mix of salads, smoked tuna, rice and curried egg, yummo. I look forward to catering for the women again today. I must ring Marika and ask her how to make scones. She knows how to make the biggest and the most yummiest scones in the world. I remember her coming from Melbourne with her partner Gerry and she made these ginormous scones and scooped the jars of jam in bowls and cream up to my nose. It was such a treat to have such amazing and beautiful people in our home. I always felt safe with them as a kid and it was like Christmas when they arrived. Just to sit or be near them was a treat.

I need to go to the toilet. I needed to go throughout the night and I didn't go because I find it hard to do so in someone else's home. One time when I was living in Mackay in Queensland staying at my fiancé's friend's home, I was so petrified about going to the toilet. I was too afraid to go in case my fiancé's friend heard every sound I made. I got a towel to wee on. I knew at the time what I was doing wasn't quite right, but I was so crazy in my head at the time, I preferred this option. I prayed to God to help me get out of the bed and get me to the toilet. He did and I didn't tell anyone about that. Why would I? Who does things like that?

The kookaburras are going for it outside. They're loud as hell. I still have that lump down my throat. If it continues I'm going to have to see a doctor about it. It feels like food stuck in my oesophagus that needs to be washed down by a drink of water. I'm thinking its cancer of course, hmm.

Pauline says that my writing would be very therapeutic. She also thinks it's fantastic that I continue to write each morning for myself. I failed to inform her that I got the idea out of the book, 'The Artist's Way'. I don't know what else to say… Pauline says I'm a breath of fresh air and she encourages me to visit her at any time. What else can I say other than writing has been a struggle of late?

Gary continues to send messages to my phone. For someone who considers me only as a friend damn well includes me in his life A LOT. I'm very wary and cautious of him at the moment. Oh, I dreamt of Kevin being naked last night and that he wanted to have sex with me, YUCKO!

23/9/00 : I dreamt of Maree, her husband Harold and her two boys. I spoke to them as I would anyone and told them I was uncomfortable around them because I sensed Maree's sensitivity. Her hair was long and beautiful. I was unaware that my hair was the same as her old hair cut. In the dream, the reason she stopped talking to me was because I was in denial about being unaware of men's attraction to me. I felt shameful and had a sense of being sexually abused. It felt like stuff I haven't worked through yet. She had a name for it in the dream but I can't remember it now. I was mucking around with the boys and I woke myself up from talking in my sleep. Harold showed me the new stock he bought for his new business, a whole bunch of wheelbarrows. I found it of no interest but it felt good to be a part of their lives again. The boys must have grown to be much taller now. I felt I was an important part of their lives—they were very important to me.

I feel this rift between us. That I cannot seem to change, after all these years I still feel like I've done something wrong. Why else would I be nothing to them now? I suppose she wrote me a letter and I chose not to respond. I didn't like how she wrote without any emotion. She just gave me facts about her success with her art exhibition and her book. Which I think is fantastic. I was jealous at the time, because she was a person who spoke from the heart. I was shocked to read a letter from her that had little heart in it—so little that I threw it in the bin, like it was a blank piece of cardboard. I felt awful. She didn't go to any length to see me while I was in her town. I even offered to go out of my way to see her so she wouldn't have to go anywhere, but no, a half an hour visit was even too much for her. Something is up and she ain't telling me. So I rang and left a message at their catering business, knowing Howard would definitely receive it. I no longer had their home phone number. I let her know where I was staying and how I was nervous ringing and knowing that her accomplishments were confronting for me as it brought up great jealousy. I explained how it has helped me look at myself and to get on with my creative abilities and for that I am very grateful. I congratulated her on her successes and told her I missed her and her family and that I send my love. I heard nothing from her. I even put all my phone numbers on the message for her to call if she wanted to. I cannot change her. She has her reasons and I trust she is in God's hands and maybe one day I'll let go of the story that there's something wrong with me that keeps her away from me.

In my dream I dreamt of being in a war and people were being captured and Scott was one of them. He was a kid I grew up with at High School.

I don't feel well at all. The cold I have is getting the better of me. My muscles are stiff, my mouth is dry and sore, and to top it off my nose is stuffed with mucous.

I told the partner of the short course portrait teacher that I would like to have a naturopath reading this morning. I have always wanted one. So let's do it and get it done and then I'll know what I feel like doing after that. I need to be aware of what my body needs and pay more attention to it.

I'm to make scones, tuna salad, curried eggs and crackers with mixed salad on top for the hard working girlies today. I could make a chocolate cake.

24/9/00 : I don't know where I put the rehearsal time sheet, bugger. I need to see if I can take Tamika's partner to a twelve-step recovery meeting. I wonder if I can cancel just one night of rehearsals to take him to a meeting if he wants to go.

I'm at home in bed. I'm flushing out the cold I'm carrying at the moment. I can't remember if I'm to ring Wesley House or if they were to call me today. I'll wait most of the day and if they haven't called by late afternoon then I'll call them.

I dreamt about Lleyton Hewitt this morning. I had my guitar fixed and there were four of us walking the streets of Melbourne on some dangerous mission. He was walking along beside me. We didn't say a word to each other for some time. It felt nice to be with a man I felt attracted to. I thought to myself, 'There's no need to talk all the time; sometimes it's okay just to be.' I thought he'd like that about me. Then I asked him who won the footy and began to chat. It felt a relationship between us had just begun.

I feel like falling asleep. I wasn't attracted to Gary, I was attracted to the person he was, but I was not attracted to him physically. So I will wait until the man for me comes along. Kevin rang last night. I'm very sensitive with my male friends. I'm convinced they are attracted to me and that makes me feel yucky inside. I had a thought that it's all about me, just self-centred stuff. They are good blokes and I have been straight with them. They'd have to be stupid to try anything with me. I've told them I'll cut them out of my life if they do anything that's inappropriate and disrespectful. That'll be that. Harsh, very harsh. Well, I know I'm not comfortable with Marco knowing where I live or knowing my phone number, hmmm. What is that telling me about my relationship with him? I question his motives and I trust he wants more than a friendship. I trust he is still manipulative, cunning, overly sexual with me, and overly analytical of what I say and do. Really, I already have a psychiatrist in my life and I don't need an unprofessional person giving me advice and telling me who he thinks I am. I've laid down strong boundaries. He knows if he crosses my boundaries again, he'll lose me as his friend for the second time. The first time was when I visited him at his office when he was a Barrister. I was going out with Wayne at the time. He asked questions and concluded that Wayne wasn't going to last because he wasn't intelligent enough for me and he sensed I didn't love him.

My Dad reminds me never to take other people's masks off. Let people do that for themselves. He was right, but I didn't go to see him for him to take off my mask. I wasn't ready to see that yet or ready to deal with that at that time. It wasn't that his words upset me. It was when he touched my breast deliberately for a feel that horrified me. I thought about it and I shared it with other female confidants and decided enough was enough. I didn't need someone in my life who was disrespectful toward me and my body. I was sick and tired of the games of the mental torment, fighting for who I was and forcing my boundaries upon him. That's not a friend; it's just bullshit that I no longer wanted to take any longer. So I rang him when I was sitting with a bunch of members from the morning meeting. He didn't answer but his answering service did and that was good enough for me. At least I could say what I needed to say without being interrupted. I thanked him for being a friend and all that we've been through together. I told him I no longer can be his friend due to him crossing personal boundaries with me and enough was enough. I asked him never to call me again. I told him I care about him and I wish him well on his journey through life. Soon after that he rang. I deliberately didn't answer the phone. I knew it was him and once again he did not listen to me. Surprise, surprise! What part of, 'Don't ever call me again' doesn't he understand? I didn't even listen to the message he left for me. What for? When something is at an end, as 'In The Meantime' would say: "Wash your hands and let it go and don't look back."

Well, a year passed and he called me out of the blue, I didn't know it was going to be him. I was partly relieved to hear from him, it reminded me of the good old days. He asked for my address and I simply said, "It's been nice to talk to you again but I don't feel comfortable with you having anything more than my mobile phone number at this stage." I said, "Let's take it easy and talk over the phone in the meantime." He was okay with that. I haven't heard from him since and I haven't called him. For an intelligent man he can say some really stupid things. I told him I would catch up with him if and when I feel like it. He's not sweeping into my life that easily. I need to know for myself how far he has come along in terms of personal growth since the last time I spoke to him. Inner change takes time; there are no short cuts or quick fixes when it comes to one's inner life and soul. Miracles and insights occur over time, and acquiring the skill to put them into living action, requires more than just saying words.

I've had a thought that if Wesley House put me through rigid questioning to know my skills, abilities, and acquired knowledge, then I have the right to ask some probing questions of my own about them. I need to know how they are going to treat me as a fellow colleague. I'm not interested in being manipulated in any shape or form. I'm not interested in being asked too much of me; I don't see myself as a slave and I don't see my job as my god or the biggest thing in my life. I will not sacrifice my truth for their approval so that I can have money in my hands. I'm not interested in being overworked and not acknowledged for the good I contribute.

I read in the 'Twelve-Steps and Twelve Traditions' that being annoyed by someone is the underlying feeling that I am superior to the person I am being annoyed by. Well, didn't that put me in my box! When I bring myself down off my pedestal, Gary doesn't seem so bad, nor does Kevin or Howard. I can have my awareness around my boundaries and what I feel comfortable with and practice keeping my eyes off them and seeing them as equals. The other side is that the men I really like, I see them as being more superior than myself. Very interesting, and that does not make me feel very good inside. See ... Jezza. I put him on a pedestal and I made myself feel sick and embarrassed about who I was. I feel embarrassed about what I've said and done and I'm embarrassed because I don't see myself as an equal human being compared to Jezza. I did that with Maree.

Speaking to Graeme yesterday he shared that he knew Maree before I did and that she was mixed up with a group of people who supported victims. He saw that these people were controlling and got carried away with their egos. He said that when I really needed Maree she failed to be there for me. When an alcoholic reaches out to another alcoholic, we do our best to help. He said her ego wouldn't allow her to help. I knew of her sponsor, but that's the only person I knew of in the group that Graeme was speaking about. It's like a newcomer walking into the controlling group of women I know in Melbourne. It's what I did and it's taken until now to see it. Graeme still remembers the day that my heart was so broken and there was nothing he could do. So she did want to control me. He said it was fantastic that I took the courage to break away from her to do what was right for me. He says it was a blessing. He said I've changed tremendously and I'm a very courageous woman today.

My Nana wrote a belated birthday card stating a new beginning between us. That's incredible. Miracles do happen and I feel like the luckiest person in the family. Most of them are missing out on the love she has. I made her out to be a cow when I witnessed her criticising Linus's haircut when he was about fourteen. I felt helpless to defend my cousin when I could see that he was heartbroken by her judgemental words. He was always the wonderful one in her eyes, so when she put him down about his Mohawk hairdo (his individuality) he was devastated. The only power I had was to never talk to her again to show her she can't treat my cousin that way. It wasn't until I participated in a self-improvement course that I saw I hadn't spoken to my Nana for ten years. I made her wrong for all those years. I took the time to write a letter and I called her a couple of times and no answer on the other line. I swore she knew it was me and didn't want to talk to me. The second course I participated in I had the opportunity to call her from the institution. I was shaking with nerves and my heart nearly pulsated out of my chest when I heard her voice. I introduced myself as her daughter's daughter and she sounded pleased to hear my voice. I told her I decided when I was thirteen that I was never going to talk to her again for being nasty to my cousin. I told her I told everyone that she was a bitch and I hated her guts for everything, I even blamed her for the pain my Mum went through in her recovery. I apologised to her for hating her and for not talking to her. You know what she said? She said, "Oh, what you've said to me is very brave but, sweet heart, I didn't even notice that you stopped talking to me." Well at first I thought, 'You heartless cow,' but then I realised the only person I had hurt for the past ten years was ME. She then went to explain that being resentful toward someone begins like a seed that's been planted in the ground. That seed grows roots, a trunk with branches and many, many leaves. Resentment infects all relationships in our life if we allow one resentment to go unhealed. It was at that moment that tears dropped from my eyes and the ache in my heart was raw. I 'got' for the first time that what I had missed out on for the past ten years was having an older and wiser woman in my family giving and sharing her inner wisdom with me, something I never knew was so important to have until that moment. So to have my Nana send me a card for my birthday and wanting to begin a new relationship (after making the mistake of telling Mum about her surprise birthday party) is a miracle.

Hey, Dad's home from work because it's raining, he's going to be thrilled about that. He cut and badly bruised his hand yesterday, so he needs a rest. Must go now, he's walking through the door as I write.

26/9/00 : I looked through my Brett Whitely book and it's inspired me to paint. I want to be free to paint as he was. I want to play around with a portrait of Mum's face on the big board with ink and paint. I want to paint a picture of the bathroom and I can begin today.

Brett's studio wasn't clean and tidy. It was a store house with a concrete floor with a pole he swang on and a couch. The back of my house is perfect for an art studio. I could paint to my heart's content. No wonder I don't want a job.

Everything has calmed down. I accomplished the netball by getting it up and running. Linus doesn't want to play netball unless I'm in his team. I'm now dealing with period pain. God's worked this one out by keeping me at home and I'll have great insight about my art, ouch! No wonder my pages got boring, I'm lacking my artistic inspiration. Completing a chalk portrait of my Mum I can see with my own eyes that I can draw. It is evident I'm good at it. A new idea that sat right within was 'I can start painting now'. I don't need to go to school to paint, I have a woman in my life that can teach me art and her name is Pauline. She has workshops I can attend. I can see my confidence is already building. The visual arts course is no longer in my Hometown. I believe it's moved to Wangaratta. Another thing I had in my head was I believed I had to be high on drugs to be a great expressive, free artist like Brett Whitely. Well, I can't get on the drugs any more but I can be free within my heart to do my artwork. I may need time to allow myself to explore and play. I need to have some fucking fun with it. I need to take my focus off what others might think of me. I need to paint because I love to paint, because it's fun to me and because I want to look different through my eyes. Fuck working for an organization. Be a woman who holds an art exhibition without having a degree behind her. Be an example of being talented, gifted and without an education to back me up. My works are enough. They are fantastic. I don't need an institution to tell me whether or not I'm good enough to be an artist. Like Sophia said, "Who said I'm not to be the next Picasso?" I love linear work, I love texture, I love colour, and I love nature. I'm sensual. I'm imaginative. Sophia said I had a creative mind and I'm highly intuitive and there is no need to feel incompetent or inadequate. I'M ENOUGH!

26/9/00 : Feel like I was going a bit nuts yesterday obsessing about Jezza then about the young kid at rehearsals. I realised later it was loneliness which triggered off the lustful thinking of Daniel and the loneliness that triggered off missing the illusion of what could have been with Jezza. I have been vulnerable in my mind because I have been unwell for five days - going on to six. I thought two to three days of it was enough, usually that's how long it lasts. Feeling isolated and cooped up inside made me prone to stinking thinking. When it gets going—the negative thinking—it's very hard to slow down. I feel bad about being dependent on unemployment benefits for over three months. I'm afraid Centrelink will make me do all sorts of things; for example; working somewhere where I really don't want to spend my time. Perhaps it's time to see Dr Wilmot about this. I do not plan to be on it forever. No way, it's just for the time being.

I'm catching up with Doreen at 11:55 am, I have netball at 6:50 pm and Debbie will call me today about dinner tonight. I painted yesterday and I really enjoyed it. The second painting needs more work. I want to do an ink figure. Whitely is clearly my inspiration. My head tells me I'm a phoney. I love how he's free to express, to play and explore. He knows what it is to paint, to create. I love the way a painting looks and the way you can build a room around it. I'm very happy I passed my paintings on to people who treasure my work. Adelene put her painting in the shed of her parents place. Shianne did the same. The message I got from that is my paintings are crap and the only reason they were hanging onto them was because they did not want to hurt my feelings. I got that they weren't worth anything. I felt very sad about it. Warren loves the painting I did for Shianne. He told me this only this year, ten years after giving it to her. I've told him to buy it from her but he hasn't done so. I have promised him a painting and I haven't followed through; the same with my guitar teacher and one of Mum's friends. I need to take myself seriously, otherwise no one will. Many people see my talent.

I wonder how Clint is? He's a young, local artist here in town. He is a friend of Pauline and he knows my friend Warren. His works are displayed in the Yahoo Bar. He's twenty-five. I'm sure we'll run into each other sooner or later. Emotionally I'm feeling better; my thinking has calmed down a few notches. A shower this morning would be nice and a big glass of coffee will go down just as good. I need to call Liz about the weekend, and Carmen about singing lessons. I feel she's dropped off the planet. I haven't been singing this week because of my cold. Louise comes home soon. I'll call and ask her when.

28/9/00 : I'm horny for Daniel, the nearly-nineteen-year old. The boy's on heat at that age; he's cute, he has a great body, he's sporty, soft, gentle, touchy feely and very yummo. Rebecca informed me that she tried to make a move on him but it was clear that he did not feel the same toward her. I waited to see if things would work out with Daniel and Rebecca because she had told me she liked him. I didn't let her know of my attraction to him because I believe if Daniel and I were meant to be together then I would have nothing to worry about; time would tell me soon enough if he felt the same as I. As soon as she told me he wasn't keen, I came up with the idea of inviting him over to a mutual friend's home where we all were going to watch videos. I thought there was no harm in doing that—not like anything was going to happen! I just wanted to see him. I called him on Rebecca's phone and pretended I was someone wanting to buy his van, he fell for it up until I dobbed myself in as being a phoney buyer. He guessed my name straight away and it was all very fun and exciting. While we were at Rebecca's I discovered he was only eighteen! Damn it! Damn it! Damn it! We ended up sitting together and he couldn't keep his hands off me and it was then I decided he was a sleaze. I always fall for that type. I felt disappointed. I couldn't help but notice we were measuring and studying our hands and feet. I liked what I was looking at and I liked what I was feeling inside my heart. I felt bad though that he was being affectionate in front of my girlfriend Rebecca. It wasn't part of the plan that he would do that so soon. I just wanted to see him and suss him out a bit. So I continued telling him to stop touching me because I knew Rebecca would have had hurt feelings, with good reason. I felt very embarrassed by his affections; he was so open in front of everyone and displaying his kindness toward me. I wanted to kiss him there and then and tell him how much I enjoyed his caressing on my leg and hands.

By the end of the movie he was hugging me, like he couldn't let go. As we were walking back to the cars in the dark, I instinctively ran and leaped on him and wrapped my legs around his waist. He whizzed me around and it felt like the most natural thing to do. I was overjoyed as I screamed to the bright stars above. With ease, because he's six foot four, he carried me over to the bull bar of a 4WD. I loved that part. I felt light as a feather. The moon was shining directly above as he gently laid me on my back. He was going to kiss me and then my head screamed, 'AARH! He's EIGHTEEN years old! You can't kiss a boy that young. What would everyone think? I'm afraid of really liking him and him not liking me, or giving two tosses about me and me looking like a fool. I'll be embarrassed and humiliated by being rejected by an eighteen-year old, egomaniac that I am. I figured that once he had me he wouldn't want me. I want to be with someone who wants to be with me. I'd love it if he wanted to be with me as my boyfriend. I'd allow him to be free to do whatever we want to do. I'm afraid of him seeing where I live. Yes it's the poverty/fear thing and feeling rejected by his judgement. I hate feeling insecure.

Oh, now I remember what Sophia said, that I'm attracted to the dubious kind. She told me that I need to take things slowly with someone because I'm highly insecure. I felt a little offended when she said that, but it's true, I am a very insecure person. I'm thinking now that he probably doesn't give a toss. Thanks for sharing, head. I'm the one with all the judgements. I'm stiff, rigid and I carry many hang-ups and fears. At the moment he probably only sees me as being cute, but wait for it, wait for the psycho dragon to raise its ugly head: "RUN FOR IT DANIEL, RUN FOR YOUR LIFE!" He's young, like play-dough. What's my thinking around this one? If I don't give him what he wants straight away then that will make him want me so bad and he'll realise how special and wonderful I am and that will guarantee he won't stray on me. Somehow, I believe this one is a fairytale I made up a while ago. This fairytale is the one that stopped me from passionately kissing this young hunk. It's obvious I'm in lust and so is he. There is no love between us. For him to know what I have to offer in such a short time is not possible. Am I able to let myself be free—to do what makes my heart sing in the moment—or am I going to stay in fear and miss out on the fun, hmm? Time to let go of the bullshit head stories. I know who I am and what I want and that's what matters. Eyes onto myself and off him. Daniel sent me the same text message that Rebecca sent him last Saturday night. It was a naughty sexual message, which he did not respond to when Rebecca sent it to him. I responded. He called me from a phone booth because his phone ran out of credit. I rang him back on my mobile for another twenty minutes and that's a long time for me. I told him I wanted to kiss him and he asked me why I didn't. I explained firstly that Rebecca liked him and I didn't want to hurt her feelings any more than I already had and also because of the fact he was so young. He asked if I was okay with it. I told him I've accepted it's okay that I'm attracted to an eighteen-year old. He sang to me and it was so sweet. He wants to see me this Monday night when I return from Melbourne. I think I'm in over my head now. He probably thinks he's in for great sex with a twenty-seven year old. It brings up FEAR. I feel I don't have any control because I've set this up and I can only trust that he just wants sex.

So can I get involved knowing this fact? I'll have to get over the intense insecurity of being abused. Lana said that I have no resemblance to being an 'easy woman'. I'm so afraid of him thinking I'm a promiscuous woman, but why? What's 'easy?' I mean nothing to this person. How do we get to know people? I'm afraid of thinking and saying too much to spoil the heat of the moment. He turns me on. So I'm all sexual. I know nothing about him. I don't really care to know too much about him—now that's interesting. I'm the one who thinks he's easy, so does that make him cheap and nasty and less of a human? Actually no, I don't like him any less because he's had heaps of girls. It's his ego that thinks he's so good for being with all these girls, so it's more his insecurity and hormones that he wants girls so much. As for myself, I don't need sex or a partner for my ego or to feel like a complete person. So eyes onto myself again. I need to be mindful of how I think about him. I'm the culprit. What he does is none of my business. Who he's been with is none of my business. I'm not being loving of him or me. There's nothing wrong for wanting to be physically close to a big, tall, handsome man. It's my judgements, my criticisms of myself that hurt me. He's done nothing wrong to me, or by me. Here we go; it's the Jarod stuff. After all these years the wounds he made are still there. If I don't want to do the Hooty Dooty then that's my business. I will say no if I want to, mate!

30/9/00 : Daniel had been drinking last night and this is the conversation we had that I will remind him of in case he has forgotten. Don't ask me why I didn't think of reminding Jezza what he said whilst under the influence of alcohol. I would've known that I was going on words he'd forgotten. I'm so silly. Anyway he started talking about massaging me all over my body and I courageously said, "You scare me when you talk like that." He asked why and I followed on to say, "Because I don't know if you know but I'm not

362

one of those girls who have one-night stands." That was easy to say after talking with Lana earlier who gave me the confidence to say what was important to me. Lana reminded me that it's okay that I'm not okay with sex straight off the bat before getting to know the man who wants it. I had all these meanings to my ideas. I had judgements about myself thinking that I must be an immature twenty-seven year old for not being comfortable or confident about sex. I had judgements around not being fully healed from the sexual abuse by my grandfather, the neglect of an unwell Mum, the dysfunctional relationship with Daniel and many other things. I expected myself to be superhuman. So I needed to be up front and clear with Jarod so I wouldn't get myself mixed up in the same uncomfortable situations as I did with Ross, Max or Joshua. Daniel's response to what I shared with him was, "That's great because I want you to be around for a while. I'm a one-woman man and I don't go after girls who already have boyfriends." I was so relieved. I brought it up that if he lied to me about anything, would he tell me the truth later? He repeated he just wouldn't lie. He was so sweet and adorable. He wants me to be his first girlfriend. He wants to do everything and anything for me and I only have to ask. The puppy dog I've asked for has arrived. I hope he doesn't go back on his word. I don't think so. He asked me to be gentle with him. Talking like this so soon scares me so I said to him, "Let's not rush, okay?" Daniel says, "We'll get to know each other and if things don't work out then that's okay, but I want you to know that I want you around a long time."

I'm worried about what Tamika will think of me dating an eighteen year old. She probably won't approve, maybe lots of people won't agree. The question is—do I feel it's okay with God and me? That's what counts at the end of the day. If it's okay with me then I'll be okay with allowing others to react how they feel. I admit that eighteen is young. Yet I still like him, my heart likes him and that's life. My heart is ageless; I'm young at heart, that I know. He thought I was sixteen when he first saw me at the introduction meeting at the theatre group. I was dancing on the chair in front of eighty other people, maybe that's why. We could have so much fun together. He thinks it's great I don't drink, drug or smoke to be who I am. He doesn't drink much and I told him his drinking is none of my business and we were both relieved. I look forward to see what's going to happen between us. I cannot wait to get to know him, to kiss him, yummo.

1/10/00 : He's intelligent. He's an excellent musician. He's mathematically minded. He's studying nursing which is made up of science, anatomy and the element of compassion towards others. I wonder if he chose to be there or landed in it like I did when I was eighteen. I'll have to ask. His family are business-orientated people, very structured. They have a bond, they're very caring and they seem to work as a team. Daniel has three sisters. Now that would explain his gentleness and his ability to openly express his emotions. I like how he is open and free to speak his heart's desires and needs. Yep, I'm watching to see if it is all it's made up to be. I'm cautious and weary. It was so yummy to hear him say, "Can you lick my toes? I miss you; I can't wait to see you." I cannot know if this is genuine because I don't know him very well. I hope it is. I'd love it to be so. I'll give him the benefit of the doubt and take on what he says as real. I'll trust he is human and he'll do as human does. Because of my caution I'm not as free with words as he and that's okay, there's plenty of time to fill in the gaps. My attraction grew when I heard and knew that was an intelligent man and had the ability to stimulate my mind, to teach me things I do not know. He has something to offer and that's important to me. He's in lust and crush mode. I'm in that too, with the awareness of being that way. No doubt he'll know that for himself. So it'll be interesting to see this unfold; pretty frightening for me. But I'm bloody excited about it. At the end of the day, I can't wait to hold him, to touch him, to put my fingers through his hair, to kiss his delicious lips and lie naked together.

Dreamt of being naked with him and we were wrapped in a blanket and it felt GOOD, very yummy. I need affection. Yet it must be genuine affection. He could, and can, have all of me if he is as beautiful as he shows himself to be. If it's fake I'll know sooner or later and that'll be that. He also may not like me so that'll be that also. I'm sitting in the sun on the porch at Lana's place.

I hope Liz has my purse, otherwise I'm in trouble. I hope it didn't fall out of the car. Louise found that her attraction to her ex-boyfriend fizzed while she was with him over in New Zealand together. He was rude to her and didn't want to talk with her about anything. I believe he was emotionally shut down. When we fail to know it's okay to talk about what is real for us, misunderstanding occurs and then we feel separate from the person by being dishonest. Louise chose to lovingly detach from him by keeping strong and honest with herself to get her through her holiday alive and well. It's all we can do at times. It's not her fault he was the way he was. He wouldn't even understand it. It was no reflection on how he really feels, silly man. I relate. I've been a silly woman and I still can be.

I can go and see Marika and call Portia. I have a singing lesson at 4:30 pm. I need to find out if someone can tape videos for Liz's Mum. I'm going bra shopping with Lana this afternoon. "God, I forgot that you're running the show, not me, oops!"

2/10/00 : Wow, yummo! We shagged in the car last night and I loved it. I enjoyed being with him immensely. It was great. It was free and easy, so comfortable, so natural, very close, like we've been doing it for years. Man I was tight down there, probably because I haven't had sex in a year. It was very pleasurable for him and for me. We laughed, mucked around, and talked while we were being intimate, funno! Eighteen, shmeighteen, he is perfect for me for now. He fits and sits well for me and with me. My heart was a YES. My head had a few hurdles to get over, telling me I was cheap and tacky. He allowed me to share my negative thoughts about myself and he didn't pressure me into anything. I'm the one who led the way at my own pace at my own leisure. Who'd imagine an eighteen year old having that level of consideration, maturity, patience, tolerance or understanding without his ego being damaged? Not me! He helped me by being the way he was with me, to leap over my hurdles. Louise Hayes says that frigidity comes from fear or the belief that it is wrong to enjoy the body. It also comes from self-disgust and it can be intensified with an insensitive partner, for example Wayne, Joshua and Ross (and the list actually goes on). I believe through this experience of mine it can be healed with a sensitive partner and that's exactly how Daniel was with me. He is so gorgeous. If this lasts, if he is real, then I will be the happiest girl I know.

There was one warning bell: something he shared with me, that I promised not to tell a soul, that worries me. I know its fear that keeps him stuck with his problem, he doesn't even want to talk about it. I'll be watching to see how he deals with his problems. He's definitely a thinker and he definitely loves numbers and science, he loves to solve. His intelligence is attractive to me. Wayne and Shaun weren't intelligent and it would rub me the wrong way. He's funny and makes me laugh a lot, another type of intelligence I adore. I told him about being an ex-problem drinker and he's open to discussing it further at another time. I told him about my sexual abuse stuff. That's out now and I feel good about that. Aarh, he is so yummy. My fanny, as Marika would say, is running the show and that's okay with me. My heart was so okay with Daniel. I'm glad I waited until someone felt right for me. I could talk about this forever.

I need to write about Wesley House, I've been asked to work with Angela until she goes back to school. I want to do the art course next year and it doesn't start until February so it actually fits in well. Like Daniel said, give it a day and see how I go. The money would be so good and I'll be doing something

364

I enjoy because I love being with Angela. I still want her to be asked if she wants me to be that role in her life. The working hours are between Monday and Friday, 9:00 am to 3:00 pm, sounds pretty good so far and it sat well with me at the time I was asked. She has settled down enormously. A nine o'clock start is manageable as it allows me to do my morning writings. The book is something I want to write. Maybe I need to be with Angela to help with the book. Who knows? God knows. Liz's Mum says the happiest person is the person who is happiest with their God and she wishes only one thing for people she loves and that is—love itself. She wishes for the people she loves to be loved. She says there is nothing worse than to be with someone you don't love. It is like being held prisoner in jail being with someone you don't love. I agree. Daniel has stepped into my heart and he is welcome to stay.

4/10/00 : Have I told Dad I'm not able to afford rent this week? No. I'll tell him tonight. I will definitely have money next week. I'm feeling good about working with Angela. I'm thinking about introducing her to the program that deals with being affected by alcoholism, a Fellowship of people who would be supporting and understanding. I want her to receive the love that was given to me in those rooms from the women who were there. Wesley House can't take her in forever. Sooner or later Angela will grow too old for the government organisation and she knows it. I see the small bedroom in our house and I do think and see her moving in and living with Dad and I. Not now of course, but perhaps next year while she and I are studying. I will hold onto that idea until the time is right. I wonder if she's written her life story today? I wonder if we could put our stories together at the end of it—perhaps that could then be published. Well, first things first let's get the materials for writing our life stories today. We can finish our life-maps we started yesterday and collect some clothes from the op-shop for some of the clothing designs we will attempt to do today.

I feel great with Daniel. We had a blast at rehearsals last night, letting everyone know we are going out together. Yes, some girls got their noses out of joint; that's to be expected. I do think and wonder about his level of faithfulness and then I remind myself it's none of my business. That sounds mad and unjust, but if he's unfaithful and does not let me know then he is the one who will suffer from the secret.

I just thought then that Angela and I could write our books in the next five months before we start school; that feels good.

Anyway I do not wish for him to feel that way. Whatever he does or says to others is none of my business. How I am with him and how I'm affected by him is my business. If the worst does happen for whatever reason, well that's another story. I have thoughts about him using me for sex. I simply say to myself that if he is using me for sex then the main thing is that I'm enjoying it and condoning it and so it's okay with me. I chose to do what I do because I want to do it because it feels right for me. I thoroughly like him and I want to be intimate with him. If he is using me (it doesn't feel that way) then he'll be the one who will feel bad about being unfaithful. It's been my experience that it is the unhealthy, selfish, hurtful, secretive motives with others that will damage the one doing it the most. Yes, it affects the other person involved, but the person doing it has the mixed thoughts and bankrupted spirit, which only leads to internal disaster. That is what I understand as a form of suffering. I do not wish that upon Daniel or myself to suffer in that way.

Dad, hmm, it feels a little awkward. I wonder how he's coping. It feels naughty that Daniel comes into my bedroom while Dad is here. Well I'm twenty-seven years of age and my Dad is fifty-four. Daniel is special to me and I'm entitled to do as I wish in my own room and to spend as much time as I choose in my bedroom. I pay rent because this is my home so I'll treat it as I would normally if I were living with a friend. If Dad has a problem, he can always come and talk to me about it. I'm going for a walk with Dad today about 4:30 pm. I have netball to go to as well as having dinner with Debbie. I'll see how I go. I failed to call Ruby yesterday, so it's something I'd like to follow up today. Perhaps Ruby and I can do drawing on Friday night. I will let Tamika know I'm not available to work Friday because that's the only twelve-step meeting I can get to that deals with being affected by alcoholism in others. I wonder if Angela would like to come with me? It's okay with me if she comes along because I have nothing to hide.

Daniel is sleepy as I write. He is so tired. It's 7:20 am and I can hear Dad shaving in the bathroom. I must do my writing. When Daniel stayed over last time I forgot to write.

Angela and I went to the library and she signed up for a library card and she borrowed 'The Artist's Way' and she is to start it on Monday. She's excited about doing it.

Dad's leaving earlier than normal. I wonder why? I hope he didn't hear Daniel and I being intimate last night. Probably did, oh well, that's life. Daniel is still sleeping so soundly. I'm happy to work 9:30 am to 3:30 pm each day with Angela. It's six hours per day and that suits me to a tea. I get to continue rehearsals, netball games, and I'll speak to management about Angela coming with me to have singing lessons with Carmen. Angela's other carer says it's a fantastic idea. I thoroughly agree. That way I can keep my singing appointments and work at the same time. I don't know about therapy though. I think that is this Monday coming. I must check. Also, I've sent my overdue tax from three years ago to my old accountant in Brisbane whom I trust. I needed to ring the Brisbane office to redirect my mail to where I'm living now as they were going to receive mail from the Taxation office. While I was on the phone I asked if they could do my tax and they said yes they could. So it's now set that I'm sending all my tax information to them and I'm stoked that it's finally getting done.

I dreamt of having the responsibility of looking after a baby until it slipped out of my hands in front of a group of people including Jezza. I felt a little embarrassed and laughed it off saying, "I'm only human." Jezza was giving a talk to a quiet group of people while Daniel was holding me around my waist standing behind me. I knew I loved Jezza and I knew being with Daniel was right for me. It was okay and comfortable with me to be with Daniel knowing that I chose not to be with Jezza. I say Jezza has his own stuff to mulch through and I'm powerless over that and I don't want to change it either. I dreamt about guitars and stuff but that's another story.

Ruby came over last night and she has landed in the lap of a beautiful man. We were both ecstatic and overjoyed by the fact that both of us met gorgeous men who gel with us. I remember distinctly the conversation we both had last week about accepting that we wait for the right guy to be with us. We didn't expect it to happen that quickly considering we agreed we'd rather stay single for a long time, rather than to be with someone whom we don't love, or to be with someone who is 'close enough' to being the right man for us. Amazing.

6/10/00 : I felt a bit uncomfortable last night while Daniel and I were watching a movie and I still feel it now. My thinking is that he doesn't really like me that much; he's in it for the sex. I'm telling myself I'm not sexy enough, I'm not that great, it'll probably end soon, give it time something will go wrong. So I'm pulling away because I want to protect myself from being hurt. Let it begin with me. It is what I do and say that matters. Everything changes all the time. Nothing is forever. I'm powerless over someone else and their way of being. I'm powerless over the way I am. Just right now, Daniel is holding me while he sleeps. Dad is walking around in the kitchen making himself a cup of tea.

I need to ring Dr Wilmot to let him know I can't make it to therapy this Monday and apologise for not letting him know sooner. I need to call Louise and let her know it will be this Thursday when I have the sixty dollars and ask if it's okay to come and collect the canvas she's preparing for me. I want to ring Portia, Louise, Mac and Simone. I especially want to call Portia. I need a twelve-step meeting today, there's one at 11:00 am I can get to. I would like to get to the Monday night meeting but I'm committed to be at rehearsals for the time, umm. I look forward to painting my guitar teacher's painting and picking up the wardrobe from the Salvation Army Op-shop. I wonder if I could pick up a couch from there if I keep my eyes open?

What else can I say? Angela described what we in the twelve-step program call 'a spiritual awakening'. She had a profound understanding that lifted her crazy self-defeating thoughts and yucky feelings. Her carer was glowing in amazement at Angela's experience. Angela and I went to the river for a walk and talked for a long time. We shared secrets with one another and that was great for both of us, especially for her. It was getting honest and being free from shameful secrets that make us ill inside. I talked about the Fellowship to her to give her some idea what it is about; she may need it one day. I feel we all need it; I believe we all need each other. I need to call Triple J about the women's group who help one another to stay safe from predators. I can do that today. What to do now? I'm open to great joy and love.

ANOTHER DAY : Pippa says I have a gift and I should use it, follow it and develop it, because she believes I was born to paint, draw, sketch and dig my hands in sculpture. At this moment I have a mummy cat sitting on my lap digging her head into me. She is so sweet but it makes it very hard to write. Now she's rubbing her face past my feet. She's very in need of love and attention.

My neck is not in good shape because I slept wrong. I can't turn my head to the left because I have a nerve that pinches when I do. I'm not excited about my art. I really don't believe I'm that good, not as good as the adored Mr Brett Whitley. My head wonders. 'Are there any good art courses here in the country?' I'm struggling without one. I suppose I'm lacking drive and confidence. Pauline developed her confidence in the art course here at TAFE. She now owns a large art studio for her own works and workshops for others. I do want to be on stage, TV and radio. It all takes little steps first. I have grave insecurities I'm embracing. I guess this is why I need to take one step at a time. I only hurt myself when I compare myself to others, like Pippa who's been singing since the age of two and Daniel who's been performing and singing for many years. Pippa has an eating disorder and she hates herself and her body. How I do not wish to be like that again. How fortunate I am to have been relieved from the obsession of food. Another God job. How magical is it that Pippa is going to record music of her own, how fabulous. Just because I have a gift with art doesn't mean it's the only gift I have and the only one I need to follow, although that's what I got from Pippa. She says I'm not unemployed; I'm an artist. I'd love to be great at art without the hosh-posh courses. Why can't my art be accepted the way it is without a degree? I'm going to have a look at Pauline's exhibition at the Mitchelton Winery before it ends. I'd like to take Pippa with me. She says she's been thinking lots about me lately, like I have of her. We are both encouraging each other through difficulties that we endure. We acknowledge we are spiritual friends. She sees the best in me as I do in her. I don't like it when she says I'm better than her because it invalidates who she is. I must tell her that next time I see her.

Jesus, my neck is sore. I thought of putting a small book together that has a collection of insights. I could begin with that. I have lots of helpful understandings that could be tools for others to use. It could be put into a book for each day of the year.

I've been enjoying Daniel and the time with him so much. I've relaxed with him and myself where I allow myself to joke around and I'm now better at 'going with the flow'. He bought me a seventies blue velvet bed head, it looks so sleazy but I love it! I allowed him to buy it for me just because I liked the look of it. It wasn't easy for me to receive it because it's so 'out there'. He gets involved in my life. I'm to take note of the beautiful things he says and does. I've experienced a shift in me and I'm grateful to feel free to love and be loved. Just for today all is okay and God knows what he is doing.

ANOTHER DAY : I'm amazed how relaxed I've become within myself with Daniel and being on stage. Last night I did the monkey routine for the first time to fill in the absence of Elle and I kicked arse. I didn't get a chance to rehearse, only by myself at home, not even to the music. I loved it. I didn't panic and I danced beautifully. No one was the wiser whether I had done it before or not. I feel growth and my confidence is building, this is very exciting.

I dropped Daniel at the local pub and it was the first time I wanted to go out disco-dancing before he was ready. I was too excited about dancing with Vicky, Tamika and Debbie. I danced with such joy and freedom. I got my groove back. I was delicious. Daniel came and went throughout the night and I was okay with that. It felt good to let go and continue on with what I wanted to do. He asked me for a lift home and I prompted him to travel with other theatre members so that I didn't have to stop dancing. I felt it was my night out for once and I didn't want to run on his schedule. I even told him it wasn't my fault he wasn't having any fun in town. Go girl! I did have the thought of him wanting to be with other women, but it did not overpower me. I had an absolute ball. I'm enjoying the little things, for example; climbing into bed with him and laying my leg over his is so pleasurable for me. To smell him near me is yummy to me. To wake up and know he's there is comforting for me. To feel good inside and that is a miracle. It's taken three months for me to relax with Daniel, to be able to share with him my silly thoughts. To allow him to be upset with me and not go in and attempt to change him is a delight. It is a delight to see him decide to come and see me after a misunderstanding. I feel God working with us. I feel I hear God saying, "Trust me and all will be okay."

I've only had six hours sleep. I had to get up to see if Dad was home. I wanted to find out more about Carolyn, the love of his life. How wonderful to see my Dad at the back of the show talking with Tamika during act two when I returned from ducking into town to grab some goodies with Daniel. He visited a mutual friend to pick up a letter sent by Carolyn to my Dad. She wanted to talk to Dad and in the letter she told him she loved him and that she's still single. Dad was chain smoking. Dad doesn't smoke. He doesn't know how to handle the exciting feelings he is experiencing. There's a clear distinction between the love he has for Carolyn and his affections toward Joyce. Joyce doesn't come close to Dad's heart, as does Carolyn. I bet you he's thanking his lucky stars now that he returned to my Hometown and broke off his relationship with Joyce. Before the letter he'd been blaming me for his lack of trust in moving here. When I read that card, I jumped up and down a thousand times. Dad's already got his rules and regulations set down in his mind trying to control the situation. He's afraid of being hurt and humiliated. It's unavoidable. He has jumped on the rollercoaster ride of love, as Linus would say. Yippee! He's alive again! Go Dad!

Pippa's read the two diaries I gave to her to read. I thought it would be helpful in some way for her to read the first diary I wrote showing my worst state with food and the craziest thoughts so that she would know where I've come from. I gave her the second diary (the last diary I have made entries in) to show her my growth; that food obsession and eating disorders can pass, to show her hope. She read them within twenty-four hours of having them in her care.

When she first passed them to me I said to her, "I understand that you didn't read them because they are very full on and obviously not very useful to you." She said she had read them both because she couldn't put them down! Her Mum kept peeping her head through the door to see if she sleeping telling her to put the books down. She said that she would shove them under her pillow to hide them so she could continue reading until the early hours in the morning. I was very surprised. I didn't know they would be so interesting. She said straight to my face that if she were me she would write them into a book and get a publisher to publish it. I repeated the words to her, "Really! Are you sure? Really!"

I've come home and pulled out my collection of my writings and realised that I've been sitting on my book the whole time, but I had no idea until Pippa pointed it out. I remember reading from 'In The Meantime' about how we are all God's creations and, being God's creations, we all have gifts and we are all individually sitting on gold mines and it's a matter of trusting they are there and letting God present them to us. I really got what the book was saying because in that moment as I looked through my pile of writings, I knew these journals had to be typed and turned into a book to give hope to others. It felt right and I trust what feels right within my heart, for within my heart is where my God resides.

God has shown me my gold mine, my treasure. "God, I will type out the words and do what's in front of me one step at time. If You want this to be a book for people to read then You'll need to create it. In 'The Artist's Way' it says, "God, I will take care of the quantity. Can You please take care of the quality?" If the book is not meant to be published and it is only a process for me, then so be it, remove it out of my life when You are ready. For now I will trust this is a calling for me today. Please put the people in my path to help me through this process if this is a book You do want, and need, to be published.

Twelve years later…
Going within I am willing to be carried along on an unimaginable
journey by allowing my life to be filled with faith and belief, to
begin letting life unfold its wonders and its destiny for me one
step and one day at a time

OLD THOUGHT: Others are more important than I am
NEW THOUGHT: There's a me in my relationships I am important

I thought I was wrong and bad if I felt upset with others. I would let others deny the validity of my experience because I believed their feelings were more important than mine. I forgot along the way that I was also part of the relationship. I thought that as long as they were heard, understood, and happy, I would be happy. As long as they were good, I was good. I skipped over my experience and fell into the delusion that I could make people happy so long as I never told them how I felt! That was a decision that took me to a guaranteed destination—the true pathway to misery, isolation, futility and unhappiness.

When Linus said he felt I "dumped on him", he had a right to feel that way. However, this did not mean he could discount or dismiss my hurt feelings about his behaviour. I accepted that he had feelings but I couldn't allow him to be inconsiderate of mine. When others react with anger, retaliation, or argument, I am free to remind them that I am only speaking about how I feel about their behaviour and how I would prefer to be treated. I don't make this about them. When others feel angry or hurt by this, they fail to recognise, or even acknowledge, that I am also in the relationship and quite capable of having hurt feelings as well. Until we each develop mutual respect for our right to have our own feelings, then compassion and understanding for each other will never be part of our experience.

Am I expected to always be happy in my relationships—am I never to be upset? If so, is it really possible for others to never to be upset by me? I don't think so! In the past, when others expressed how they felt hurt or upset with me, I would cry. This was a perfect response because it prevented them from telling me exactly why they were upset with me. Because of this, they felt afraid to come and talk to me. Today I'm much more prepared to hear another's upset with me (...sometimes I react with tears; I accept I do that sometimes, I am human). Today, to the best of my ability, I encourage others to let me know if they are upset with me. It's the only way I will truly know them and to see if we can work things out. As some things can't be.

It's inconsiderate and unloving of me to skip over my responsibility to demonstrate love, understanding and compassion for their pain. It is not appropriate for me to retaliate, argue, or tell them what I feel about their treatment of me. I like to practice the principle, 'First Things First.' The person who first approaches about their feelings is the one who needs to be heard first. However I have found that this is much easier in theory than it is in practice which I think is a skill which I'll continue to develop throughout my life because trying to talk with someone who does not see it that way will not let me talk and/or be heard.

Often, when I share my feelings with someone, they can react defensively and angrily, and launch forth with a list of their hurt feelings toward me—before acknowledging what I first shared with them. Others often find it hard to hear what it is I am saying. They can find it hard to listen to me first, as they insist I listen to them. Others can quickly justify their actions and make negative judgements about me and the argument takes off on a wild goose chase. The conversation gets right off track and becomes all about the other person, how they feel and think. I have supported others to avoid acknowledging that there is a 'Me' in our relationship by being distracted by their barrage of words and criticism about me. I don't need to be distracted by this behaviour now that I know what it is. It's OK to be heard and to be acknowledged when I am sharing my thoughts and feelings with someone. It is important that I value myself by respecting and validating my thoughts, feelings, and experiences, and I can demonstrate that by acknowledging them and expressing them if and when the time is right. The main thing for is, I am aware there is a 'ME' in my relationships with others and that I do count, equally to the other and it might take a few goes over a period of time to establish this. And if there is no progression toward being a 'ME' in the relationship where I am considered I just might find myself not investing as much time or energy as I once did if our relationship is going to be ALL about them. I find myself being more mindful about giving my time and energy to nurture those relationships where there is a 'ME' that both are treated as important and treated with consideration and kindness.

OLD THOUGHT: I have to work everything out right now
NEW THOUGHT: Follow what I know & make it up as I go

I thought I had to make sure I did all the right things to make things happen. I think I gathered this idea from others. The most influential were the teachers at secondary school who told me if I didn't work it out before I left school I'd be doomed forever. I had to plan for my future and leave no room for errors. I thought being on unemployment benefits was the worst thing that could ever happen to a person and so I decided it would never happen to me. I surely didn't know about the effects that alcohol would have on me. It is a socially acceptable drug after all. Nor did I know about the effects of another's sexual behaviour would have on me. I had no idea about how eating disorders, mental disturbance, depression and anxiety can negatively impact upon a person's life and affect my choices and direct my future. Naturally, they weren't considerations for me at secondary school because I was not aware of them to start off with. I just had to work everything out myself and make sure I got it right, somehow.

Well, I tried. I tried really, really hard to make the right decisions so as I wouldn't stuff up my future. It never stopped me from making decisions, which caused pain. It was a lot of pressure trying to control tomorrow and what it would bring, or whom it would bring, or which way I would need to go. It caused me great anxiety and stress. I certainly didn't live in the present moment – how boring anyway, right! I didn't know the power of living in the moment back then.

Along the way I learnt to follow what I knew and made it up as I went. This allowed room for error. This allowed room to explore all possibilities. This allowed room for Life to guide me instead of me guiding it. My ideas were much too small for what Life had in store for me. Always, Life had plans that were more fantastic than I ever could imagine.

This new way of thinking allowed me to trust my feelings and thoughts, my own ideas, and myself. It allowed me to have some fun also, to let Life 'show off' and invite me to do things I normally wouldn't do. It allowed me to give things a go and to challenge others' ideas, which at times, sounded convincing, but they just didn't sit right with me. Like my girlfriend Marika often said "By 'making it up as we go' makes life feel more like an adventure". 'Follow what I know and make it up as I go' worked for me and this is what happened when I believed in it.

In 2000 I had a strong feeling to write a book. I had no idea what it was going to be about, I just had a feeling—that is all. I wrote 20,000 words about some topic I cannot remember now, however I felt I wasn't on the right track, so I trashed it and asked the Higher Power I understood at that time to show me if I was meant to write about something else, and if so, what was I to write about.

It was a Thursday afternoon and I was on my way to pick up the children. I was a nanny at the time, when it dawned on me I could choose to go back to my Hometown to live with my father. I didn't have any children or a partner to consider. I become aware of the fact that I thought I could never live with my father again. When I was a kid I thought it would be offensive to Mum if I asked to live with Dad. I was seven when Mum and Dad divorced and it made me cry to think perhaps I had not left it too late. I felt this was important and it scared me to think I would return to a country town - my Hometown. I feared that I would be a step backward and not forward.

I called up a very dear friend of mine and shared this experience with her. Courtney suggested I hand it over to the Universe and see what happens. So, I said to my higher power, 'If you want me to move to the country, you will have to give me a really good sign that you want me to go there, otherwise I won't go.'

The next day I went to a twelve-step meeting and I had a strong urge to rock up to the café first before anyone else arrived from the meeting. I was usually the last one to get there as I loved to chat to the members straight after the meeting. I sat down by myself in anticipation for the arrival of other members. A young guy I hadn't seen in months came up and greeted me with a warm smile and said hello. He asked me "So, when are you moving back to the country?" Baffled as to why he'd asked me that question out of the blue I replied, "Is it because I'm wearing country looking clothing that you ask if I'm moving to the country?" "No" he says. "I started this course in visual meditation and in Thursday's class I envisioned you in my mind packing up your bags and moving to the country". 'Oh my God', I thought, 'That's unbelievable!'. I told him I'd have to be pretty stupid not to get that message and told him about the idea of moving back to my Hometown, which was on the same day he visualised me moving to the country. I didn't tell him I quietly asked my higher power - again, 'Look that was a really good sign, can you please give me another one just to make sure?'

I called my Mum on the Monday and shared with her the idea of moving back home. Mum sounded surprised, "Oh, that's funny." "What's funny?" I said curiously. Mum proceeded, "A voice told me yesterday to clean out the spare room, as one of my children were coming home". Shocked and horrified I thought, 'You're kidding me, aren't you?' My Mum hadn't really done a lot to the spare room since I left home at eighteen. That was another really good sign but because I felt my higher power was asking too much of me I asked for ONE MORE SIGN just to make sure! I know I am painful! LOL.

The next day I went to my singing lesson and told my teacher about what had been happening and she looked me straight in the eye and said, "You need to go back home and sought things out with regard to your relationship with your parents. Once you've done that, your creativity will take off. You need to go back home and heal the past." Something in me knew what she said was right. I accepted the strong feeling to go back home and the following day I gave work notice I was leaving.

When I moved in with my father I began my sabbatical (a rest from work) by beginning a creative course in the book 'The Artist's Way'. I also took up guitar lessons, continued painting and drawing, got back into netball, joined a touch football team, continued singing lessons, continued to write in my journals, wrote poetry and songs, started a love for vintage/op-shopping and joined a theatre arts group. I got in touch with who I really was and started living my dreams by doing the things I loved or excited me.

I thought I could relate to Pippa whom I met in the theatre group about the insanity I had with food and having to have the perfect body. I wanted to talk with her about it. But I believed at the time she wouldn't believe me so I thought perhaps if I gave her the first journal I wrote at the age of twenty-three and my last journal at twenty-seven, she would find it easier to relate and believe I found a way out by reading how I did it.

She gladly took my two journals and the next performing night she handed them back to me. I felt like such a fool to think she'd find my journals interesting or helpful. Before she got a word out of her mouth I apologised for giving them to her. "No" she replied, "don't apologise. I really enjoyed them. I had to hide them from my Mum. She kept ducking her head through the door to see what I was up to. I shoved them under my pillow whenever she came in. I stayed up all night to read them. You must turn your journals into a book as they would help so many people!" There it was—the book I felt I needed to write, was right under my nose!

That night when I went home, I opened up the cupboard in the laundry and there I saw, stacked on top of one another, my journals. My friend made the suggestion; she could see what I could not. She saw the value of my experiences written in my journals. The thought of it made my heart feel excited.

I typed my journals into my computer but I had no idea that they would become what is now this unique creative self-discovery book based on sharing, writing, creativity, meditation and community connection. It's like Life knew all along what it was I needed to be working toward and It guided me each day through my sharing, my writings, my drawings, my meditations and my interactions with others in my community. Over time, through connecting with myself, others, my community, and with Life I moved away from only focussing on myself and self hate and moved toward developing a way of living which required me to keep an open mind in order to be guided along the path which became uniquely mine. A new life awaited me and arrived once I rose above self-reliance into a living faith in the generosity of Life always providing guidance and blessings for me. I came to believe great happiness and a fulfilling and healthier life could be available for others by showing others how 'follow what I know and make it up as I go' created that for me. It was and still is my hope that this book, which Life and I created together, would do just that - to demonstrate the power of embracing new thoughts of love and acceptance really has.

OLD THOUGHT: I'll work out how to live my dreams on my own
NEW THOUGHT: Encouraging others to live their dreams helps me to live mine

Yes, I can try to work out how to live my dreams on my own if I want to, however I've found it's far more fun and exciting when I've shared my journey with others. The fact is, I don't know everything. Others can share things with me I haven't thought of and inspire me in ways I never dreamed of.

My Mum saw my talent and gift with creativity very early on and took me along to an art course to see what I thought. Even though it looked interesting enough, I didn't feel at the time I could really take creativity that seriously as I believed I wasn't genius enough to do that. Yet, my Mum could see something in me I could not and encouraged me anyway. Thank you Mum!

Marco spotted my joy and ability with art straight away. I rejected his support at the time. I felt so annoyed and embarrassed when he'd talk to me about my art or about taking my art seriously. I felt mixed emotions, mainly pissed off and inadequate. However he could see in me what I could not. He could do what I could not. I remember one day rocking up to his studio apartment and he was so excited to show me what he had done. On his curved white walls he splattered red paint, some abstract image, one spot beside his bed and it looked incredibly cool. I had no idea how he had the courage just to do it. He was someone who I thought didn't have a creative bone in his body and yet he could fly like a bird when he was creative. Go figure! The idea, if he can be so creative then perhaps I can too and that has always stayed with me. Thank you Marco!

Liz encouraged me to design linen. Again I felt I wasn't good enough to do that either. She took the kids and I to a large art show I had entered into. We found my artwork sitting out the back, not hung up in the exhibition. I felt humiliated and bad that Liz drove all that way to see my work rejected. The art show had rejected my all time favourite piece of art...on page 77. Liz didn't let that stop her from encouraging me to be creative. Thank you Liz!

Pippa could also see what I could not and she told me I should follow my creativity after she had seen my artwork hanging on my walls in every room. It started to begin to become easier to hear what others had been encouraging me to do over time...lots of time. Thank you Pippa!

A year later I sold my first piece of work to one of my bosses. She loved the painting I showed her and she gave me $200 for it. Wow - someone actually bought my work! She was another person who encouraged me to go back to study, to study something which involved creativity. My ears this time, were really listening. I heard her. I quit my job and got into a graphic design course in my Hometown. That course opened up my heart and mind. For the first few weeks I couldn't sleep. My mind exploded with creative ideas as soon as I put my head onto the pillow and as soon as the morning came my mind was creating more ideas. I discovered I had been bored in many of the jobs I had. My soul and spirit just loved being creative.

While I was studying I supported a friend in her adventures with baby fashion. It was a creative avenue I loved, but just not enough to keep going. One day I stood in my bathroom and the voice in my head asked me, 'what would you rather? Would you rather see your baby designs in a shop or would you rather see your book on a shelf?' Reflecting upon how far I had come since I first started to write in my journals, I felt I had won a million dollars having found so many freedoms from the old thoughts, which crippled me, however it didn't feel right not to share this jackpot with anyone. I felt it was a greedy thing to do to keep how I found my way through and out the other side of these painful experiences. With this realisation I let my friends dream go and decided to follow my own dream knowing that after all the work I would put into the book it may never reach a bookstore shelf. Perhaps the only person it may have reached was myself and even that was better than not living my own life's purpose.

Life has helped me to create this book with ALL the help from ALL the people who encouraged me to keep going along the way. This also includes all the people in my life who have known me one way or another, I believe, have contributed to making and creating this book.

A few years ago I found myself not working again. I had an undiagnosed physical illness and a toddler to love and look after while my partner worked to keep up with our bills. I envisioned running a group for young women, where we sat in a circle sharing stories with one another, eating food together, creating, meditating together and inspiring one another to reconnect with our community. I ignored this vision because I didn't have any funding to support it. I thought of offering my help for free but feared I would look non-professional if I did that. Over a period of a few months impending doom awaited me in the mornings and night. I asked myself, why was this? What's going on within in that perhaps needs attention? This quiet voice inside my head said, 'what would you rather? Would you rather keep your vision about sharing your journey and experiences to yourself or would you rather trust the vision you have been given and offer to run groups for young women, even if it's for free? After all, don't you feel really excited about getting together with women and sharing and caring for one another?' Well the answer was quite simple - YES! I want to be sharing with others to carry the message that there is a way to live happier, healthier and more fulfilling lives if we support and inspire one another. The next step was clear. I spoke to someone, at a local youth service provider, about the vision and ideas I had. They were as excited as I was and they found funding to run 12-week self-recovery groups through sharing, writing, creativity, meditation and community connection for young women! How amazing is that! It wasn't long before I realised I needed to put the 12 week program together with the book (my journals). See, another example of how sharing my dreams, ideas and visions with others supports and inspires me to keep going and growing.

And then there's the real gift, encouraging others to live their dreams is the key ingredient to help me to live my own. It is by watching others change, grow and begin to be who they really are that inspires me to continue to do the same. Thank you!

To all those who have encouraged me to keep going - Thank you!

And a special thank you to Life for guiding to put all of this together in a book. I feel this is the first book of many more to come. I have continued to journal my journey and the journals are – you guessed it – all stacked on top of one another in my cupboard ready for me to type up. I said to my Dad, "I hope it doesn't take me as long to get the next book published as it has with this book!" Dad responds with a smile, "It will be every 40 years we'll see a book written by you if that's the case". I just laughed. But quietly I thought 'I hope not!" Hahahahahahahaha. All I need to do is to do my part and let everything else unfold - sometimes quickly and sometimes really, really, really slowly!!! The book would have been incomplete had it been picked up by at least one of the many publishers this book has been presented to. Thank goodness for slow and steady, at least we'll get it right. Or perhaps not, but better luck next time right. I wouldn't let failure get in the way of having a good time at trying to succeed! And as one young friend likes to remind me, 'We only fail when we fail to try'. I've loved the ride so far and encouraging others to live their dreams has brought me so much joy.

What a gift!

SACRED CREATIVE FOCUS
LIVING MY DREAMS AND HELPING OTHERS LIVE THEIRS

It's healthy to have dreams and it's healthy to find out what they are. My dreams gave me something to look forward to and more importantly, gave direction toward creating joy, excitement and fulfilment in my day. The trickiest thing for me has been to continuously believe that I can explore things I'm excited or curious about. Staying determined to do the things, which brought me joy, took a lot of courage and still does. When I could not or cannot see where to turn I ask Life for direction.

I spend time with people who believe in me; people who saw treasures in me that I could not see for myself, people who believed great things could happen for me, people who were supportive, people who were positive, and people who could see opportunities for me, people who were not intimidated by any difficulties I was facing. Although I could not see it at the time, these people were the answers I received from Life over and over again.

One of the quickest ways to believe in myself is to believe in others. It was often a suggestion given to me by someone who changed the direction of my life. I was encouraged by others to move forward to remembering who I really am. 'Someone' saw 'something' in me, which I did not and this is what I hope to do for others. What I give away comes back to me, and that's the beauty and power of helping others live their dreams—they help me live mine.

Has someone made a suggestion to me recently that made me feel excited about it? Did I follow through with the suggestion? If not, what stopped me? Are there things I would like to have done or would like to do, but something happens and I'm unable to give it a go?

SACRED CREATIVE ACTIVITY

It's time to live my life by living my dreams. May I go out from here to follow my joy and experience the excitement, which comes as the result of thinking I can do what I love and be who I love! May I have great and glorious visions of who I really am and where I really desire to be and centre all my decisions great and small to experience this. May I 'Follow what I know and make it up as I go'. Today I can make something that represents that I am moving forward toward being who I really am. Maybe I'll create a sketch or a painting, a sculpture or paint something on a rock I found on the side of the road. I'm choosing to let my sacred creative voice guide me to create something symbolic so when I look at it I will remember I am moving into the greatest vision of who I see - ME! May I let time and experiences, the good, the bad and the ugly be my friend to do just that.

SACRED MEDITATIVE ACTIVITY

Today I shall think of doing something kind and unexpected for someone, without hesitation or resistance—I'm just going to do it. It could be a sticky note with words of appreciation stuck on someone's car window of someone I know, or perhaps I'll send a CD to someone without saying who it is from, or bake a cake for your neighbour, or if I know someone who is stepping out of their comfort zones I shall be willing to either go with them or write a letter of encouragement or pick a flower for a stranger who passes me by. Whatever or wherever my imagination takes me—I shall follow it. It's fun and rewarding to have my attention focussed on the joy of giving to others. Creative thinking and spontaneity can create unimaginable and joyful outcomes for others and myself.

COMMITMENT STATEMENT

I .... am willing to put aside everything I think I know about myself, my life, my past, my future, in order to have an open mind to having a new experience with living my dreams and helping others live theirs. I am open to the possibility of living my dreams and helping others' live theirs, receiving new thoughts, and living a new life. I shall now go within, listen to myself and go out and live life being who I really am with a grateful heart and an open creative mind shining the way for others and myself.

Signed: ....

never	some- times	mostly	always
☐	☐	☐	☐

I know who I am
I am happy with who I am
I look after my own needs and myself
I sleep well
I enjoy exercising my body and mind
I wear clothes I really like to wear
I am comfortable in my skin
I really love and accept my body
I enjoy eating food
I am not on a diet
I feel good when I spend time with myself
I can ask for help when I need it
I find my mind is filled with kind and loving thoughts
I can think clearly
I embrace and accept my feelings with ease
I am myself in my relationships with others
I feel good around my friends
I'm at peace with my relationships with my family
I'm open and honest with others
I spend time with people who share similar interests
I'm able to trust others
I'm really good at making decisions for myself
I believe I have talents and abilities
I really enjoy how I live each day
I believe I'm a loving and caring person
I know my thoughts well
I know my feelings well
I have good relationships with professionals
I respect myself
I can easily say 'no' to others
I can say 'yes' to those things I feel joyful about
I forgive others easily
I find it easy to give new things a go
I complete those things I start
I'm doing most of the things I desire to do
I look forward to my future
I dream about and look forward to having a wonderful life
I believe I am a person who has a lot to offer others

never   some-   mostly   always
        times

DO I LOOK AFTER MYSELF PHYSICALLY?
Take regular, daily showers
Eat when I am hungry
Stop eating when I am full
Rest when I am tired
Go for walks, a run, or do some physical exercise?
Drink water daily

DO I TAKE CARE OF MY THINGS?
Keep where I live clean and tidy on regular basis
Wash my clothes on a regular basis
Sew up holes in my clothes or missing buttons
Only lend my things to others I trust
Spend my money on those things I need before those things I want

DO SOCIALISE WITH OTHERS?
A member of a group
Play sports with others
Watch entertaining things with others
Attend family get togethers
Go along to local workshops, concerts, events and activities
Catch up with friends
Say 'yes' to invitations that make me feel excited

DO I TAKE CARE OF MY MIND?
Read books which interest me
Go exploring; eg. check out the a secondhand bookshop
Aware when I've watched too much TV
Aware when I've been on the phone too long
Aware when I've been on the computer too long
Spend time with someone who I find fascinating

DO I TAKE CARE OF MY EMOTIONS?
Write about my thoughts and feelings
Take time to know what I am feeling
Take time to know what I am thinking
Take time to know what I believe and value
Take time to know what I need
.... continue over the page

never   some-   mostly   always
         times

DO I LET OTHERS KNOW WHAT I NEED?
Do I dance when I feel like dancing
Draw or create when I feel like being creative
Sing or hum when I want to
Cook or play for fun

DO I TAKE CARE OF MY SPIRITUAL BEING?
Take time out from others
Read spiritual books
Being kind to others and myself
Stop, pause and relax when I am indecisive, confused or brain fried
Be present in the moment: what I can taste, touch, smell, hear and see
Do things that make me laugh
Weed the garden
Give something to someone without wanting anything in return
Turn my phone on silent or off from time to time

DO I TAKE CARE OF MYSELF IN RELATIONSHIPS WITH OTHERS?
Share stories that make me laugh
Say 'no' to things that make me feel uncomfortable
Inform others what I need to be ok
Talk about the things that matter to me
Talk about my feelings; happy, sad or mad
Ask questions when I feel confused
Know when to walk away when I need to
Express angry or hurt feelings without put down or threats
Share my time with different people
Talk to others if I feel unsafe in a relationship

DO I TAKE CARE OF MYSELF IN THE WORK PLACE?
Take regular breaks
Ask questions when I am unsure about a particular duty
Find out what is expected of me
I am paid for all the work I do, even my over time
Ask for help when I need it
When I feel upset I talk to the person who I feel upset by
I support and encourage others as much as possible
I encourage others who gossip to talk to the person they're upset by
Have food and drink on my breaks

understanding	playful	inquisitive	paralysed	lost
confident	courageous	inspired	insulting	pathetic
reliable	energetic	attracted	ashamed	unbelieving
easy	liberated	intrigued	indecisive	despair
fortunate	optimistic	attracted	fatigued	aggressive
delighted	provocative	nosy	sore	despicable
overjoyed	peaceful	admiration	powerless	skeptical
gleeful	at ease	engrossed	perplexed	frustrated
thankful	comfortable	enthusiastic	useless	resentful
important	pleased	hardy	annoyed	disgusting
amazed	encouraged	warm	diminished	distrustful
sympathetic	clever	curious	embarrassed	distressed
interested	surprised	bold	inferior	incensed
receptive	content	secure	upset	dispairing
accepting	quiet	touched	guilty	unsure
kind	certain	brave	vulnerable	tragic
impulsive	relaxed	sympathy	hateful	tense
free	serene	daring	dissatisfied	boiling
frisky	bright	close	shy	fuming
animated	blessed	challenged	empty	indignant
spirited	reassured	loved	unpleasant	insensitive
thrilled	loving	optimistic	miserable	victimised
wonderful	concerned	comforted	stupefied	mournful
calm	eager	unique	forced	restless
great	impulsive	hopeful	offensive	heartbroken
gay	considerate	irritated	detestable	dismayed
joyous	affected	lousy	disillusioned	doubtful
lucky	keen	upset	hesitant	agonized
festive	affectionate	incapable	bitter	threatened
ecstatic	fascinated	enraged	numb	appalled
satisfied	sensitive	disappointed	misgiving	cowardly
glad	intent	doubtful	woeful	humiliated
cheerful	certain	hostile	provoked	fearful
sunny	tender	determined	terrible	crushed
merry	absorbed	dynamic	lost	tearful
elated	anxious	passionate	thrilled	dull
rebellious	alone	snoopy	aroused	terrified
happy	excited	excited	discouraged	tormented

Please note that any combination of these symptoms can be present in an eating disorder, because no one eating disorder is exactly the same as another. It is also possible for a person to demonstrate several of these signs and yet not have an eating disorder. It is always best to seek a professional opinion.

BEHAVIOURAL WARNING SIGNS

Constant or repetitive dieting (eg. counting calories/kilojoules, skipping meals, fasting, avoidance of certain food groups or types such as meat or dairy, replacing meals with fluids)

Evidence of binge eating (eg. disappearance of large amounts of food from the cupboard or fridge, lolly wrappers appearing in bin, hoarding of food in preparation for bingeing)

Evidence of vomiting or laxative abuse (eg. frequent trips to the bathroom during or shortly after meals)

Excessive or compulsive exercise patterns (eg. exercising even when injured, or in badweather, refusal to interrupt exercise for any reason; insistence on performing a certain number of repetitions of exercises, exhibiting distress if unable to exercise)

Making lists of 'good' and 'bad' foods

Changes in food preferences (e.g. refusing to eat certain foods, claiming to dislike foods previously enjoyed, sudden interest in 'healthy eating')

Development of patterns or obsessive rituals around food preparation and eating (eg insisting meals must always be at a certain time; only using a certain knife; only drinking out of a certain cup)

Avoidance of all social situations involving food

Frequent avoidance of eating meals by giving excuses (eg. claiming they have already eaten or have an intolerance/allergy to particular foods)

Behaviours focused around food preparation and planning (e.g. shopping for food, planning, preparing and cooking meals for others but not consuming meals themselves; taking control of the family meals; reading cookbooks, recipes, nutritional guides)

Strong focus on body shape and weight (e.g. interest in weight-loss websites, dieting tips in books and magazines, images of thin people)

Development of repetitive or obsessive body checking behaviours (eg pinching waist or wrists, repeated weighing of self, excessive time spent looking in mirrors)

Social withdrawal or isolation from friends, including avoidance of previously enjoyed activities

Change in clothing style, such as wearing baggy clothes

Deceptive behaviour around food, such as secretly throwing food out, eating in secret (often only noticed due to many wrappers or food containers found in the bin) or lying about amount or type of food consumed

Eating very slowly (eg eating with teaspoons, cutting food into small pieces and eating one at a time, rearranging food on plate)

Continual denial of hunger

Warning Signs, Eating Disorders Victoria, Last Updated: 7.5.2012
www.eatingdisorders.org.au/eating-disorders/warning-signs.html

no yes

☐ ☐ At times I decided to stop drinking for a week or so, but I only lasted for a couple of days

☐ ☐ I wished people would mind their own business about my drinking

☐ ☐ I switched from one kind of drink to another in the hope that this would stop me from getting drunk and the things I did when I was drunk

☐ ☐ I thought because I didn't have to start the day with alcohol that this meant it was a sign I didn't really have a problem with it

☐ ☐ I thought because I didn't need to have a drink of alcohol to stop my hands from shaking that I didn't have a problem

☐ ☐ It baffled me how some people I knew could drink without getting into trouble

☐ ☐ I had many problems connected with my drinking

☐ ☐ My drinking had caused trouble with the people I live with

☐ ☐ I looked out for abandoned drinks or tried to scab off others supply of alcohol at parties when I felt I didn't have enough or had ran out

☐ ☐ I told myself I could stop drinking any time I wanted to, even though I kept getting drunk when I don't mean to

☐ ☐ I missed days of work and study because of drinking and at times rocked up hungover

☐ ☐ I had "blackouts". I couldn't remember the things I had said and done when I was drinking

☐ ☐ I felt my life could be better if I did not drink

☐ ☐ Did you relate to four or more of the above statements regarding the problems I had with alcohol? If so, like me, you too might be in trouble with alcohol. Alcoholics Anonymous may be able to help?

no   yes

☐ ☐ Do you worry about how much someone else drinks?
☐ ☐ Do you have money problems because of someone else's drinking?
☐ ☐ Do you tell lies to cover up for someone else's drinking?
☐ ☐ Do you feel that if the drinker cared about you, he or she would stop drinking to please you?
☐ ☐ Do you blame the drinker's behavior on his or her companions?
☐ ☐ Are plans frequently upset or canceled or meals delayed because of the drinker?
☐ ☐ Do you make threats, such as, "If you don't stop drinking, I'll leave you"?
☐ ☐ Do you secretly try to smell the drinker's breath?
☐ ☐ Are you afraid to upset someone for fear it will set off a drinking bout?
☐ ☐ Have you been hurt or embarrassed by a drinker's behavior?
☐ ☐ Are holidays and gatherings spoiled because of drinking?
☐ ☐ Have you considered calling the police for help in fear of abuse?
☐ ☐ Do you search for hidden alcohol?
☐ ☐ Do you ever ride in a car with a driver who has been drinking?
☐ ☐ Have you refused social invitations out of fear or anxiety?
☐ ☐ Do you feel like a failure because you can't control the drinking?
☐ ☐ Do you think that if the drinker stopped drinking, your other problems would be solved?
☐ ☐ Do you ever threaten to hurt yourself to scare the drinker?
☐ ☐ Do you feel angry, confused, or depressed most of the time?
☐ ☐ Do you feel there is no one who understands your problems?

☐ ☐ If you have answered "Yes" to any of these questions, Al-Anon or Alateen may help you.

no	yes	

FOR ADULTS

I felt hurt and embarrassed by someone's sexual conduct?

I searched for clues about someone's sexual behaviour?

I lied about or covered up another person's sexual conduct?

I had money problems because of someone's sexual behaviour?

I felt betrayed or abandoned by those I loved and trusted?

I felt afraid to upset the sexaholic for fear that they might leave?

I tried to many ways to control somebody's sexual thoughts and behaviour by dressing suggestively, trying to stop them from watching pornography and being sexual in order to keep them from being sexual with others?

I used sex to try to prevent argu ments in the relationship?

I thought there was something wrong with me when I thought someone else's sexual thoughts and behaviour shouldn't bother me?

Sex played an all-consuming role in relationship?

I believed I was ugly and constantly questioned my emotions and my sanity?

I have felt responsible for others sexual behaviour?

I felt angry and stupid for not knowing about someone's sexual acting out behaviour?

I have engaged in unwanted and physically dangerous sexual behaviour?

I have experienced being suicidal as the result of another's sexual behaviour?

I was preoccupied with anothers sexual thoughts that it affected my relationships with my children, my co-workers, friends and family members?

I neglected my emotional and physical health while in a relationship?

I didn't know it at the time that I prevented someone going to jail and other legal trouble.

I blamed others for someone's sexual behaviour?

I felt confused about what is true or what was right when talking with someone about their sexual thoughts or behaviour?

I avoided painful emotions by using drugs, alcohol and food and by being too busy?

I have felt ill at ease that someone has been inappropriately attracted to my child and I

I felt alone or too ashamed to ask for help?

Did you relate to four or more of the above statements regarding the problems I had with other people's sexual behaviour? If so, like me, you too might be in trouble. S-Anon may be of help?

GOING WITHIN TO GET OUT

no   yes

FOR TEENAGERS

☐ ☐ I often felt hurt, ashamed or embarrassed by the sexual behaviour of a family member or friend.

☐ ☐ I felt afraid to upset the sexaholic for fear of his or her reaction.

☐ ☐ I felt afraid to tell my parents or another adult about the problems I was having.

☐ ☐ I found myself searching for clues about another's sexual behaviour.

☐ ☐ I had family members, friends and teachers ask me to spy on another to tell them what I knew about the sexaholic's behaviour.

☐ ☐ I felt responsible for the sexual behaviour of a parent, family member, friend, teacher and boss at my work.

☐ ☐ Adults shared information with me that made me feel uncomfortable.

☐ ☐ I have lied to others or made excuses about someone's sexual behaviour.

☐ ☐ I have found it hard to work out what is true from what is not true when talking with the sexaholic.

☐ ☐ I've been suicidal because of another's sexual behaviour.

☐ ☐ I had been sexually abused and I was afraid to be alone with the sexaholic.

☐ ☐ I prevented someone going to jail and other legal trouble as a result of their sexual behaviour and I feared that this kind of thing would happen again.

☐ ☐ I found it difficult to keep up with my schoolwork or other responsibilities.

☐ ☐ I felt it was my job to keep my family happy.

☐ ☐ I have felt uncomfortable and embarrased by the sexaholics comments toward my friends and I.

☐ ☐ I felt a lot of hate a lot of the time.

☐ ☐ I learnt how to cover up my real feelings by pretending I was okay when I wasn't.

☐ ☐ I feel weak and like a failure if I felt I needed to ask for help.

☐ ☐ I felt terribly alone most of the time, even when I was with family and friends.

☐ ☐ Did you relate to four or more of the above statments regarding the problems I had with other peoples sexual behaviour? If so, like me, you too might be in trouble. S-Anon may be able to help?

If you have any questions or wish to make a donation, please feel free to contact us through the following means.

Website: www.goingwithintogetout.com
Email: goingwithintogetout@gmail.com
Facebook: GoingWithinToGetOut
Twitter: WrittenByAGirl